FEATHERS IN A HIGH WIND

FEATHERS

IN A HIGH WIND

*In this chancy game of life
Laughing lips shout, Finders Keepers,
But for every finder born
There's a loser clipped and shorn,
Left to weep and left to mourn –
       Losers Weepers:*

BY:
FLOSSIE DEANE CRAIG

Copyright © 2015 by Flossie Deane Craig.

Library of Congress Control Number:		2015914918
ISBN:	Hardcover	978-1-5144-0656-4
	Softcover	978-1-5144-0655-7
	eBook	978-1-5144-0654-0

All rights reserved. No part of this book may be reproduced or transmitted in any form or by any means, electronic or mechanical, including photocopying, recording, or by any information storage and retrieval system, without permission in writing from the copyright owner.

Any people depicted in stock imagery provided by Thinkstock are models, and such images are being used for illustrative purposes only.
Certain stock imagery © Thinkstock.

Print information available on the last page.

Rev. date: 11/07/2015

To order additional copies of this book, contact:
Xlibris
1-888-795-4274
www.Xlibris.com
Orders@Xlibris.com
721652

We dedicate this printing to the memory of Flossie. She was indeed a most interesting woman. Among the library of wonderful and fascinating works she left behind was this true story of her life in Northeast Arkansas in the early 1900's. We celebrate with her the intimate knowledge this book brings us of our own family history and the lifestyle in which she lived and to which she adapted. What a treasure she has given us. Thank you Pana (Pawnee).

Prologue

The little mill town of Paragould, dependent on its timberlands and agriculture for its economic independence, lay snuggled in the northeast corner of Arkansas. Paragould was a church and school town, and the leavening influence extended social status to all corners. All persons were invited and encouraged to participate in church and school activities and to allow the gifts and talents of the individual child to come to full bloom.

It was to Paragould in 1891 that Albert Oscar Mounce brought his wife, Martha, and firstborn son, Marion, to live a few short months before the second child, Flossie, was born. He had "blazed the trail" by going ahead and learning the cooper's trade, leaving Martha to lonely months of waiting and hoping on the little forty-acre farm that had been his inheritance. He had made the move because of a feeling of responsibility for the family he had started. His children must have a chance to attend good schools. Also they must live where they could take advantage of such cultural opportunities as the county seat afforded.

Albert and Martha had moved their church letters from Old Macedonia, where both had been baptized as children "into the fold." Martha Jane Haddock was twelve at the time; Albert, fifteen—but already Albert thought of Martha as his girl and had every intention of marrying her as soon as age and circumstance allowed.

Settling himself into his own berth in the cooper shop at last, he sold his farm and bought a small house on a corner lot. Two lots, in fact, so that he could make a garden and his growing children would have room to romp and play.

The third child was a son, Earl, and in due time another girl, Lola, was born, and at last a baby girl, Jannyce. In Paragould, the children grew up in "the nurture and admonition of the Lord," knowing no social life outside church and school all through their formative years.

Within the limits set by Albert and Martha, their children were free, but early in life they learned their limits. As, for instance, no child was allowed in the kitchen before Albert and Martha had their morning hour alone.

Mama dressed her reddish gold hair high on her head in the daytime, but at night it was brushed and hung in long braids to her waist. She was fair, with soft brown eyes and a heavenly fragrance of Black Locust perfume, her one extravagance, or the smell of fresh baked bread or of vanilla used in her baking, but always the smells of Mama were sweet and unmistakable—and somehow very comforting.

Papa's hair was black as coal—and as shiny—parted on the side and the ends brushed back over his hand, to form a long curl that sometimes drooped low on his broad forehead. The Papa smells were exciting and endearing: bay rum shaving lotion, for he shaved every evening when he came in from work, and the good wood smell that lingered in his hair. That smell came from the hot staves, where he had stood over the cresses to char them before fitting the barrels into the windlass, fitted the cable around the big end, and slowly pulled the hot staves into shape to take the hoop.

I am Flossie, and my earliest memories are of the low conversations and sudden bursts of laughter that emanated from that forbidden kitchen area while it was yet dark outside. I would steal from my bed and creep into their room and snuggle under their covers just to be near them. I tested their pillows, sometimes choosing to lay my head on Mama's scented pillow, then again choosing the heady man smell of Papa's pillow.

It was an early habit of mine to keep a daily journal—not that I wrote in it daily, but I would always pick it up at some point and enter the accounts of my life . . . or my thoughts . . . or questions about life. I would also keep mementoes and letters in my treasured keepsake box.

Now, if you have time, I would like to tell you a story. It is compiled from my journals and treasures that I carried with me as I was whisked about on life's journey . . . .

Chapter 1

May 19, 1912

My heart lifted on a glad beat for the first time in months, and I turned my face to the window that the other passengers might not see and wonder at the joy I could not hide. I was going home to marry Alex Walker at last. Then the rhythm of the wheels took up the song, the whistle ahead screamed the good news, the engine's bell clanged in joyous abandon—or so it seemed, until I saw a range cow clear the ditch beside the track, her tail high in the air in wild alarm. Only then did I realize that the whistle and the bell had been to warn her to get off that track if she wanted to go on living. Might be significant, might be meant as a warning for me to jump the track I was on again if I expected to escape with my ornery hide intact. It was a sobering thought, and the zest for this new development and the gladness died.

I forced myself to face a few salient facts, and immediately old resentments came flaring, the more fiercely perhaps in that they had just been formed by the breath of a quickened happiness. What a fool I'd been to think of marrying Alex Walker. What a fool I'd be to do it. How could I have let myself be drawn into such an idea? Yet why else was I hurrying home this fine May morning?

Nothing short of a letter from Papa could have brought about this sudden turn of events. "Greetings and Salutations," it began—Papa was always being funny, "and I hope I bring you glad tidings of great joy. Alex Walker is home. He stopped by yesterday. Said to tell you to come home Sunday. I've not the first word of advice to offer. Your heart must tell you what's best. I trust you don't decide something in haste that you will later regret."

I'd met Alex first at Parrish Business College. He'd attended State Normal College and had his teacher's certificate but could not bring himself to teach school, so he was cramming a business course. As cub reporter on the Soliphone, I was filling a lack in my requirements by using the last two hours in the afternoons for a quick course in shorthand and typing.

Nobody introduced us, and I had always been a stickler for the social amenities. We were both seated at opposite ends of the long row of typewriters, and as we leaned forward, our eyes met and we "recognized" each other instantly. At the end of a long stare, both of us grinned. In fact, he laughed out loud, and when the session ended, I was not surprised to find him waiting at the foot of the stairs. He walked me home. A lot more might have been said, or inferred, by two people in the same length of time, but I don't see how. Not until he started to leave did I think to ask his name, and even then, it didn't seem very important.

I don't recall just how we became engaged. Both of us just seemed to take it for granted that we would someday get married. He mentioned it from time to time, as though there was no question. On my part, I set about filling a hope chest. I had my cherished dream of a little white house where I would someday reign as Mrs. Alexander Walker—and where Alex would come home to me and to our children at the end of the day.

A surge of hot anger rose and burst in my throat. Alex was to blame for my marriage to Will Wilson—and the subsequent humiliation of divorce. How confidently I had waited his coming that long-ago Sunday afternoon. Even until well in the afternoon, it had not dawned on me that he might not come. Then, of course, I supposed that he would call me on the phone or, perhaps, drop me a note of explanation.

Next day, as reporter, I stumbled onto the news item that one Alexander Walker, of Main Shore, had spent Sunday as the guest of Miss Mag Hawley, on Vine Street. With vicious jabs at the typewriter keys, I included that tasty tidbit into the local news under my own by-line, well knowing that it would give Alex a bad moment when he read it. He'd be hard put to decide what attitude to take when next we met.

As it turned out, the attitude Alex took had nothing to do with it, seeing that by the time he got to me, I'd worked up an attitude of my own—and held it. Nothing he could say or do had any bearing on the case. "I am glad," I told him airily, "that I learned in good time that you are a liar and a cheat. It's much better to know it now rather than later, when I might find it hard to explain such behavior to our children."

It had been at this crucial point that Will Wilson came home for a few weeks before starting a big advertising campaign for Cudahey's Whisky. Will was twenty-six and nicely established in the field of advertising. Naturally I was flattered when he concentrated on a whirlwind courtship. That my heart still yearned for Alex had so filled me with consternation that I turned to Will as a means of forgetting. The night Will got around to saying, "Darling, I love you," made a quick change in my feeling. The words had a magic.

I couldn't recall that Alex had ever said he loved me. I got out his letters and reread them, one by one. He hadn't said it a single time in his letters! This fact so angered me that I snatched them up and ran to the cow barn. There I tore every last one into small bits and dug a hole in the corner of the barn and buried them. Once the letters were covered, I stomped upon them, packing the earth down well. It was then I dried my tears and promised myself they were the last I would ever shed for Alex Walker.

We were heading into a hard winter. The bitter winds, ice, snow, and slush were in store. Will's next trip would take him to South Florida. He reminded me of this as he told me how much I would enjoy the big hotels, the sun-warmed golden sands, and the gentle variable winds.

"I wouldn't rush you like this, baby, but my time is running out. Marry me. My work leaves me plenty of leisure time to have a wonderful honeymoon while we get to know each other better."

I don't know what I'd thought would be expected of me as a wife. But when I found out, with it came the knowledge that I could not fill the requirements—not with Will Wilson. The intense urgency of his passion, once we were alone, frightened me almost into insensibility. He claimed my body, as was his right, but none knew better than him that I was as truly a virgin at heart on the day my divorce was granted as I had been in body on the day he married me.

Being a divorcee was not funny, not in the little town of Paragould, Arkansas, in the year 1911. Divorce in that day was seldom heard of. It made me a stranger. People who had been lifelong friends now peered furtively from behind lace-paneled windows, curious to see how a divorcee would conduct herself. My lawyer had suggested that I retain my married name. "No matter where you go," he said kindly, "the fact that you've been married will follow you. If you take your maiden name, which would be the natural thing to do since there are no children, the word would follow that you had been married, and there would be the added stigma that you were trying to palm yourself off as an unmarried girl." But this change in old friends was more than I could bear and was the cause of my flight from my old hometown.

Not that I found things any different in Campbell, Missouri, being the only divorcee in that little town. But at least those people were strangers, their curiosity somehow more bearable. But I was still a "grass widder" and might as well have been living in a glass cage. I immediately identified myself with a church and its activities and tried to avoid even "the appearance of evil." Even so, there wasn't a man, married or single, who wasn't acutely aware of my presence—not a sweetheart or wife that didn't stiffen and draw possessively nearer to her man when I entered a room. For all this, I told myself furiously, I could thank Alexander Walker.

The train slowed for Paragould, and I spied Alex at once. I was getting angrier by the minute. Hurrying home on the dot just because Alex had *told* Papa to tell me to get there! His eyes were painfully uncertain as they searched each window for the sight of me. My wayward heart leaped into my throat, but my injured pride yanked it back inside the cage of my protective ribs. Alex's face cleared as if by magic as the conductor helped me down. Alex stepped forward with his well-remembered air of insolent amusement and took my bag.

"What are you doing here?" I asked in a low voice. It was as though two years and a marriage had not happened since our last meeting. We were taking up exactly where we'd left off.

"I came to meet you," he said.

He touched my arm to guide me through the crowd, and I drew away from him instantly. "I'd prefer you not to touch me," I said coldly. "You were quite positive I'd be here, judging by 'the cat that ate the canary' smirk on your face."

"Didn't your papa write and tell you I said to come home?" he asked, in all innocence.

"He did. And it would seem that all you have to do is to say, 'Hop, little toady,' and I will hop. Well, let me tell you one thing, Alex Walker . . . ."

"No, you listen to me first, Flossie. Nobody knows better than me that you didn't have to come just because I said so. If it will help your feelings any, I'll admit that I wasn't at all sure that you would, not until I actually saw you in the flesh."

I remembered the strained, uncertain look as he searched for me on the train.

"But the fact that you did come surely indicates that you decided to come, for whatever reason, so why are you so all-fired mad?"

I hurried on before him in silence.

"The honey locusts are in bloom," he ventured, catching up and trying to peer into my averted face.

No response.

"They was in bloom the first time I walked home with you from business college, or can you remember when there was a time like that with us?"

Silence.

"They was in bloom when I walked by your house last Wednesday afternoon late."

I sighed.

"I hadn't meant to go in. I just thought I'd stroll by kinda for old times' sake, but my feet turned in, in spite of me. Once inside, everything seemed the same. Old folks just as friendly. Lola—say, have you seen Lola lately? And I didn't feel any different toward any of them. So's I got to thinking that things might not be any different with you and me either . . . if we could ever get together again. I heard you'd got a divorce."

"Yes," I answered finally. "I guess that's about the first thing anybody hears about me these days."

He touched my arm to cross the street, this time I noted, with not quite so much confidence. As we turned onto Main Street, he continued, "I knew you wouldn't pay any attention to any letter I'd write. That's why I got your pa to do it. A feller can do a lot of crazy things trying to forget a girl, and still not forget her."

My heart turned over. For the first time I felt a touchstone with Alex, a bit of common ground to stand on. A girl could do a lot of crazy things trying to forget a boy too—even marrying the wrong fellow— and still not forget him.

Suddenly I stopped rushing. It was as Alex had said—the honey locusts were in bloom. It was enough to soften a heart of stone the way the fresh morning breeze came washing over us, laden with the heady fragrance it had picked up in passing from the heavy panicle of cream-colored blossoms that hung like great clusters of dusky white grapes in the feathery foliage overhead.

Almost immediately I was enveloped in the bosom of my family, finding solace in Mama's close sweet-smelling embrace; a robust welcome in Papa's merry black eyes and hearty kiss; Jan's welcoming embrace; and how my eyes popped at the sight of Lola, just turned sixteen. "Whatever in the world is happening to you?" I screeched, pushing her from me for a better look.

"Nothing's happened to me. Nothing ever does," she assured me, with all the impatience of sixteen, "except that I'm growing up at last."

"Well, a nice fine job you're making of it." I gasped. Her coloring was exquisite. Such a clear warm skin she had, with the same snapping black eyes that Papa had, and black brows and lashes, coal black. What made her beauty so arresting was, I decided, the fact that her hair remained the color that had caused Papa often to murmur as he tumbled her curls about, "Such riches you have, Little Rags, so much fine gold."

She had caught the babyish curls back with a huge bow of blue satin ribbon. Beside this radiant one, so full of laughter and high spirits, I felt my own fine skin and brown eyes and auburn hair fade to insignificance, and my twenty years lay heavily upon me.

We sat long at the table after the noon meal, all except Lola. Her best friend, Clara Kinsey, came by for her, and they left to join a group on a kodaking party, a popular Sunday afternoon pastime.

Papa was wound up. Organizers for a new Socialist Party had been creating quite a stir in Paragould. Papa was much interested and was making an intensive study of their literature. "Neither of the old parties is doing much for the workingman, Alex. We just have to face it. This may be the one way of calling the attention of the powers that be to our sad plight."

Presently Mama and I sent the men to the front porch while we put the dishes away and had our own visit. With the kitchen spotless, Mama said, "I think I'll lie down for a little while, Flossie. Papa will come in when you go out and give you and Alex a chance to talk things over."

But I didn't go out. I went to my own room and threw myself across the bed, filled with a sense of futility and frustration. So dejected was I that I wept—and about Alexander Walker, of all people! And having wept, I slept.

I was awakened a long while later by Mama, bustling about in her usual energetic manner.

". . . and I'm not trying to make any decisions for you, Flossie."

She was opening my suitcase and shaking out the dress and laying out the hat that I'd brought along with the full intention of bowling Alex completely over.

". . . but the day is slipping away in a hurry. Your dress is so pretty—well, you get a quick sponge off while I press it. Then you either send Alex about his business or come to some understanding with him. He keeps watching that door for all the world like a hungry pup that hopes somebody will relent and toss him a bone."

Alex was satisfyingly impressed when I walked nonchalantly out onto the porch. He stopped what he was saying and stared with his mouth hanging open. But almost at once he recovered his poise and said, "Gosh, am I glad you showed up! Another ten minutes and I'd have been a dyed-in-the-wool Socialist. They need to put your Pa out in the field to organize the party. That man's a natural-born persuader."

Then his face sobered, and he said peremptorily, "Get your hat and mine, Flossie. We'll walk down to the bridge."

As of old, I turned to do his bidding. I stared thoughtfully at my reflection in the mirror as I adjusted the floppy leghorn, fluffed up the purple silk violets that decked it, and shook out the heavy purple velvet streamers of ribbon at the base. Unless I took time to think and deliberately set myself against him, I always did Alex's bidding. And on the instant, my heart had no desire but to please him. Well, listening to my pride had got me nowhere. But listening to my heart—would that be good for Alex, and where would it lead me? Absently I picked up the ruffled net parasol, scarcely larger than the hat it so ineffectually shaded, and lost in thought, I took Alex's stiff white hat from the rack in the living-dining room. I walked beside Alex down the front steps and out the front gate, conscious of Mama's and Papa's eyes following us in parental blessing.

Conscious, too, that all of my small world knew that Alex and I were back together again. Where we belonged, their glances seemed to say, as they nodded and waved or called a greeting to us all along our block. I was glad when we neared the east end of the street and the houses became fewer and fewer, and their occupants less well-known to me.

As we walked, my mind had been busy. From the exalted eminence of my injured pride, I took my stand . . . and held it. This was no time for light chatter. Alex had sent for me. I had come, but he would have to find the words to say whatever it was in his heart to say to me, and without any prompting from me.

A soft wind ran laughing through the blossoms overhead, and a few of them set sail and showered about us. The folds of my pale yellow voile, with its clusters of purple wood violets, billowed about me as the wind tugged playfully at my skirts. Alex walked beside me with solemn tread. Had he been acting as pallbearer at the funeral of one well-loved, he could not have looked more mournful. Well, good. Let him feel serious for once in his carefree life. I was finding this no laughing matter. Why should he find it easy sailing?

Ten blocks we walked in this fraught silence before we reached the wooden bridge that spanned Rushing Creek at the edge of town. Alex lowered the parasol as we stepped onto the bridge. We stopped midway, and Alex took off his hat and laid it and the parasol upon the wide wooden banister. We leaned far over and gazed into each other's eyes, only this time we gazed at our reflections in the limpid waters below us. I saw what I'd known was true. Alex's reflected face smiled hopefully up at me. Watching him intently, I smiled pensively back at him. He stripped a splinter from the banister and dropped it into the water below. Instantly our reflections merged, then sprang apart, and merged and sprang apart, just as our hearts were doing at this moment. Alex's left hand, palm upward, was inching toward me along the railing, his long supple fingers flexing. With no words spoken, both my hands were suddenly lost in his, myself at sea in the depths of his wide gray eyes.

"Flossie . . . Flossie, honey, I . . . I thought this time would never come."

He caught me to him, and I suffered his embrace because it comforted me somewhat to feel this trembling uncertainty in him—to know, in being thus close to his pounding heart, that his heart had cried out for me in the same way that mine had cried for him. The knowledge I had long coveted I now had, and I gloried in it. But when he whispered, "Flossie, tell me you love me as you used to do."

I pulled away from him. "And what if I did?" I all but sobbed, clinging desperately to the vanishing remnants of my pride.

"Would you marry me if I was to ask you to?" he spoke doubtfully, feeling his way back to me as one walking without sufficient light to guide him.

"I . . . I reckon I would," I said, and Alex's manner changed before the words were cold on my lips.

He became at once his debonair self as he laughed and said teasingly, "Well, I just might ask you that little question one of these days and set my mind at rest once and for all."

He looked at his watch and frowned. "But right now, if you're to catch your train back to Campbell on schedule, we'd better be making little tracks."

He picked his hat up and put it on in the old familiar way, so far forward that he had to tilt his head back to see me. He caught his lush lower lip between sharp white teeth and lifted my chin with the tips of his fingers. For all his laughter, his eyes still pled his case with tender eloquence, and as of old, my heart lifted to his, and we laughed together in the sheer joy of having found each other again.

On the leisurely stroll back to the house, I pondered many things. How was it that Alex needed no words? I was sure that he would be content to start anew, his mistake with Mag Hawley and my mistake with Will Wilson all water under the bridge. I was equally sure that, sooner or later, every detail would have to be discussed, tagged, and labeled, before I could dismiss it from my consciousness. Finally it came out. I couldn't hold it. "We've got a lot to talk over, Sun."

He shook his head ruefully. Inadvertently I'd used an old term of endearment. How free and innocent our first love had been. I'd felt not the slightest hesitancy in telling him that I felt I'd lived my whole life in darkness until he, my sun, appeared. I had not known what it meant to be alive until I met him; I told him this myself because I wanted him to know it. And I could call him Sun, in any crowd, and no one but ourselves the wiser. I was reminding him that he was the *sun of my life*. This was part and parcel of our love. Could we ever recover lost ground in our relationship? Whether he realized it or not, we were a far cry from it at this moment.

He hugged my arm to his side with entreaty. "Not now, Flossie. We have such little time left together. Please forget all the bad. I'd be glad to forget it forever."

In a moment alone before he took me to the train, he gathered me close and let his lips come to rest on mine, waiting. I longed to respond to his kiss and could not. "Shame on you for a stingy," he said, shaking his head reproachfully. Then turning suddenly brisk, he added, "I'll see my lawyer tomorrow and have a paper drawn up that I think may be a safeguard for our future. It will read something like this: 'I do solemnly swear that I will not get mad when we start a rehash of what's over and done with and would be much better forgotten.' Next time I see you, we'll go before a notary and sign it." Then he added gravely, "I wish with all my heart that we could forgive and forget . . . without words. Why can't you do what your heart tells you to do anymore?" He ended on a note of impatience.

On the way to Campbell, I sifted all the evidence and came up with one irrefutable fact: whatever it was between Alex and me could be resolved only in marriage, and our attraction for each other was not purely physical. I was sure, or else seeing each other in the flesh again would have wiped all else out, as though it had never been. No, our need for each other lay deeper than that. I determined to give a two-week notice in the morning and return to Paragould and Alex.

But this time I would take nothing for granted. I would not marry him until he explained the Mag Hawley incident, though I placed great restraint on myself by resolving never to force that issue with him. Nor would we be married until Alex himself urged it—and that without any prompting from me.

Chapter 2

September 27, 1912

The summer was pleasant enough, as summers come and go. I'd got out the Star of the Magi quilt I'd been working on prior to the Mag Hawley incident. From the darkest corner of my closet, I had resurrected the twin sofa pillows and finished embroidering them. Also the half-dozen pairs of pillowcases I'd stamped in the long ago and had not cared to look upon again until now.

Alex, still unwilling to teach, had made a share crop with his father, he told me. Now that the harvest was ending, he was hauling logs in to the lumber mill. For this he used a team of oxen and a log wagon, coupled to an unbelievable length to accommodate the huge logs that were being cut from his father's timberlands. He stopped by the house frequently on his way to and from the mill, but I seldom saw him for any length of time, except an occasional Saturday afternoon—and Sunday, of course.

I'd grown a bit restless of late. We still had not had the talk I knew we must have before I could be at peace. He had still said nothing about a specific date for our marriage, though he talked casually of it as a thing eventually to take place.

So it was that when the Socialist Party, locally organized at last, set up shop and launched a weekly newspaper called the Call, I offered my services, which were immediately accepted. I served arduously in every capacity—from reporter to printer's devil. I even did a bit of editing now and again when Mr. Clampitt was out lining up advertising. Or I would solicit advertising, write the copy, and later collect for it.

Papa sometimes contributed well-thought-out articles having to do with the problems of the laboring man, which were legion. Socialism was an entirely new *-ism* in our section, and the little sheet was creating considerable attention and comment, not all of it favorable, which I found quite stimulating.

I couldn't even guess why Alex and I were still unmarried. I began to feel as though I were to stand marking time forever, and to no purpose, when he stopped by one Saturday afternoon late and told me to pack a bag, something to sleep in and something to wear to church with him the next day, and ride home with him on his wagon.

Mama was scandalized at the gossip sure to arise from the incident. Besides, she told me in an aside, it wasn't decent or right for me to ride out of town, even with Alex, on that contraption. But I had my own reasons for wanting to go. Alex probably thought I was too proud to ride out of town in this manner. Besides which, it seemed a move in the right direction that he was ready at last to present me to his people. I wondered if it had taken him all this time to condition them to receiving a "grass widder" in their midst.

"Are you sure that your mother's expecting her, Alex?" Mama asked anxiously. Seeing that I was determined to go, she was rushing around at a great rate. Alex took a rope and fastened my bag to the frame of the wagon, shook up the bag of straw, and helped me to my seat.

"Well, maybe not at this partic'lar time, Miz Mounce," he drawled, "but she and the girls been pesterin' me all summer to bring Flossie out, so's I this evenin' decided so to do." He leaped to his seat on my right, catching up the lead line in his left hand. With his right, he lifted the long black snake whip from its holder, then coiled and snapped it back with a terrific crack. The sleepy oxen stirred, shoved their shoulders against the wooden yokes, and we got slowly under way. I turned to call a goodbye to Mama and saw her nervously plaiting the hem of her apron as she gazed after us.

The sun was at our backs, casting the shadows of the oxen before them. Those shadows looked like strange long-legged prehistoric monsters as they plowed unhurriedly along. Alex had said it was four miles out to the farm. Well, I knew we'd be until well after dark getting there at this rate. It was late September. Frost had touched the leaves to a riot of gay colors. The days were still summer days, but the mornings and evenings were chill. There had been no rain lately, and the dust kicked up by the oxen struck my nose with a malodorous pungency.

I was strongly aware of the presence of the man at my side. For Alex was a man now. His shoulders had broadened since we first met, and he seemed to have gained an even stronger assurance. His crisp brown hair still glinted to gold in the sun, and though I protested mightily, he persisted in wearing the small sideburns.

"But why?" I had asked.

"Because, that's my trademark."

As far as he was concerned, that settled the matter, and he did not shave them off.

Alex's cheeks and lips had the fresh coloring of a healthy four-year-old, and an artless, though not always completely innocent, expression on his cherubic countenance. Then there was that quizzical little quirk to his eyebrows. He used his eyebrows, I thought, as a beetle uses its antenna, feeling and sensing a change in my mood, adroitly turning a bad moment aside with a laugh and a few bantering words on his way out. For Alex didn't remain long if a bad moment was in the making, especially if he'd been the cause of it. He just didn't want to hear about it, either then or later. If he continued as he had been all summer, what chance was there that we would ever arrive at an understanding?

He still gave those peremptory commands too. This, I had to admit, I didn't mind too much. If his commands coincided with my own wishes, it was easy to obey him, letting the blame for the outcome rest on his shoulders. If it were something I had no intention of doing anyway, his command afforded me a solid foundation on which to stand and do battle.

"Alex, what if your people shouldn't like me?" I sat up very straight as the idea occurred to me.

"What if you don't like them?" he countered. "That's one thing that I know works both ways. In any case it's time we found out. They got nothin' against you that I know of, except that you once married Will Wilson. I can't blame 'em for that. It sticks in my craw sometimes till I about gag on it."

So for all his seeming indifference, his thoughts were running in the same vein as mine.

"And do they know why I married Will Wilson?" I inquired sweetly.

As his glance shifted from mine, my voice rose. "Alexander Walker, I can tell by looking at you that you just let them think that there I was practically in the act of getting married to you when along comes this Will Wilson that I'd never seen before in my life, and I took off after him with my tongue hanging out and gave him no rest until he married me, leaving their darling little Alexander in the lurch! You . . . you pig . . . how I hate you this living minute for that!"

"Keep your little shirt on, will you? I had to go on livin' with them, didn't I? Besides, nobody had to tell them that I'd spent the day with Mag Hawley . . . They can read, can't they?" And there it was in plain black and white. They must have figured out for themselves that that was what caused the bust-up. "Now, will you tell me why you published the good news to the wide world? You knew dang well I didn't want that in the paper."

"I'm nothing if not a conscientious reporter," I said complacently. "That was given to me as a news item. It wouldn't have been fair to my paper to withhold it." How I loved each hurting word as it rolled from my tongue. I'd been waiting a long time for a chance to say these things to Alex. I knew he would hurt me too, and I winced at the thought; yet I welcomed the long ride with him through the quiet evening. He couldn't run from me now with some flippant remark. He would have to stand up to me, and I'd get the first real glimpse I'd had of Alex, the man.

He'd hung the whip back in its holder and held the lead line in his right hand. His left hand lay on his knee, and he seemed totally absorbed in watching the coordination of mind and muscle as he flexed his fingers. My eyes rested on the soft luster of the big pearl in its heavy gold setting. This, he told me, he had bought from a man in his crew when he was traveling with the Chicago Portrait and View Company. The man had got into trouble and needed a hundred dollars. Alex went with him to a jeweler to have the ring appraised. It was worth four hundred, the jeweler said, in spite of the slight flaw underneath. I occupied myself with the ring to keep from rushing things. Let Alex come to it in his own good time, now that he himself had opened the subject between us at last. Finally the question came. "Tell me one thing: who told you I spent the day with Mag? I accused her of it."

My voice rose in spite of me. "It doesn't matter who told me. The fact that you did it is the only thing that matters to me." I paused long enough to bring it back down to conversational level. "While we're on this subject," I said when I felt safe to continue, "I want you to get one thing straight. Throughout our lives together I'll be able to stand up under hardships and disappointments. I've lived long enough to realize that life is no bed of roses. But I've got to be able to believe that when you tell me a thing, it's true, and that you will be as faithful to me in body as in heart, as I will ever be to you."

Alex's eyes met mine for a fleeting moment, then shifted uneasily. Slowly he closed and unclosed the fingers of his left hand. His face clouded with an old anger, and I was surprised to find that he could scowl like that. "I was so blasted mad, I could have shaken your teeth out the day I rode hell for leather into town to have it out with you, and you clammed up on me."

"Since I had no intention of going on with you, Alex, I saw no point in going into a discussion of a matter so repugnant to me."

He blew an angry breath and glared at me. "I just decided I'd give you the cure, then and there, and stay away until you sent for me. But no, dang my hide, you have to take the bit in your teeth and up and get married on me."

It was my time to ask a question. "Who told you I was married?"

"Just try to imagine this," he raged. "There I was at work on the timber job, when into the woods ride Ma and Belle. Without a word they laid the Soliphone in my hand. Spread all over the front page was this sweet little story. I read the heading, then stuffed the paper in my hip pocket and told Ma I might be a little late for supper as I wanted to mark some trees for tomorrow's cuttin'. When the men had gone I sat down on a log and read every blasted word of it. Then I tore that paper to little pieces, kicked a hole in the ground, and buried 'em a foot deep."

A thing that had long gnawed at my vitals lay quietly down never to rise again. Alex had torn the paper to bits as I had torn his letters when I realized he'd never told me he loved me. What sweet solace to my aching heart.

"Then what did you do?" I asked, wanting now to know all.

He gave a short sour laugh. "I kicked every stump and chip for twenty feet around. I've never been that mad, before nor since, and I laid my head down on a log and prayed to God that Wilson would be so mean to you, that you couldn't live with 'im."

He'd cried too. I knew he had cried without him saying so, and I was glad. My own wounds were beginning to heal, and I was drawing nearer to Alex, the love of my life, by the minute.

"Will had asked me to marry him, but I hadn't given my answer— the night you brought Old Mag to the oyster supper at the North End Chapel. Tell me why you did that, knowing I'd be there?"

"Shame on you, calling her Old Mag. She's no older than you are— and a Sunday school teacher besides."

"I well remember one Sunday she didn't teach," I snapped.

"Oh, but she did. I happen to know a feller that she taught quite a lot that Sunday." I looked at him in utter exasperation. Need he be so insolent about it?

Then he sobered. "It was like this: I'd ridden into town on my wheel and was pretty danged hot when I got to her house. I stopped by for a cool drink, with no intention of stayin' longer than to get my breath before comin' on to your house. But her sister and family, she lives with them, had gone to Brookland for the day. She made a pitcher of lemonade, and we sat around laughin' and talkin'. Things seemed too interestin' to leave when she went over and drew the shades. She said to keep the hot sun out."

"I decided you were truly in love with her when you brought her to the oyster supper to show her off to me," I needled him purposely.

"I didn't take her to show her off at all. She'd been pretty free with her favors, but that night she laid the law down. Unless I took her to the oyster supper, no more lay-around."

He broke off to call attention to my ringless hands. "Hey, where's your weddin' ring? I been meanin' to ask when I got round to it. The paper said a double-ring ceremony in the church parlor.

"I lost the engagement ring once when I was turning the ice cream freezer. When I poured out the ice, the ring was twisted beyond repair, the opals scratched and shattered. The wedding band is too wide and heavy for comfort, so it's in my junk box."

"Besides, you just don't like to wear Will Wilson's ring. Lola told me," he gloated. "Now tell me why you came floatin' over to take mine and Mag's order?"

"Because everybody was gawking at me, wondering what I'd do, and I wanted them, and you and Mag as well, to note that you meant no more to me than any other fellow and his girl that had come to eat supper with us."

He turned and stared thoughtfully at me. "Ever' time I shut my eyes for weeks, I could see you as you looked that night—a foot taller than you are in that slim black dress and little ruffle apron."

I was laughing and shouting with glee down deep inside of me.

He continued, "When you leaned over to take my order, I'd have sworn I smelled honey locust."

I giggled happily. "You did, Sun. You know it's Mama's favorite perfume and I'd been pilfering. I hoped you'd notice it."

"Hmmm," he said, staring thoughtfully back at what must have been a very bad moment for him. "Anyway, I got to lookin' at Old Mag after you'd served us and floated around on your rounds. I'd never really noticed before how fat and sort of blowsy lookin' she was. The longer I looked, the less I liked what I saw, and once we were outside, I jumped into my buggy and rode off and left her standin' there. I didn't want to play lay-round with her . . . never again . . . as long as I lived."

I gasped. "You mean you just rode off and left her to walk all that way home alone in the dark?"

He made a funny sound in his throat. "Nobody had to worry about Mag in little things like that. She knew her way round, even in the dark."

An early frost had touched the leaves with a gorgeous color. Though it had been a warm day, there was a subtle chill in the air as the sun sank in the west. I pulled on the sweater Mama had handed to me at the last minute and tied the green silk scarf over my ears. Alex tugged a blue denim jumper from beneath the sack we sat on and slipped into it.

"I was just thinking: what if you don't like livin' in the country?" he asked.

"Why, that's ridiculous. I adore being in the country . . . and I do know what it's like," I hurried on, seeing the skeptical way he looked at me. "I've spent two to six weeks with Grandmother and Aunt Lydia in the country nearly every summer of my life."

"Yes, but it still could well be that you don't know what *livin'* in the country is like. I've often noticed what a wonderful time people visitin' on a farm seem to have. Livin' on a farm is not the same thing for the ones that live there. There's an endless stream of chores. It keeps comin' to me that you've never worked any in your life."

"*Alexander Walker,* what are you talking about? All of us work. We have to if we want to keep on living."

A silence fell between us, and a great golden moon peeped over the treetops, hesitated, then headed steadily up the sky. It was the witching hour. Alex felt it too, for he moved closer and slipped his arm about my waist. I turned half from him, the better to relax against him, my head coming naturally to rest in the hollow of his shoulder.

"My, but you smell good." He drew a slow rapturous breath against my cheek. "And that's another thing. You always smell as fresh as a clover patch in bloom. No other girl I've ever been with ever smelled half so good."

"Well, hurrah for my side!" I laughed and turned to give him the kiss I knew he was fishing for. I felt exceedingly warm and giving toward Alex at that moment.

"Being together like this makes everything right." He sighed contentedly, making his chin stubble scratch my cheek gently. "Things have just reached that point with me. When we're together things are right, even when they're wrong, but I'm one po' mizzable wretch when we're apart."

This reminded me of a love story I'd read in a magazine the day before. This young black boy was so in love with his gal, Lizzy Belle. He made a poem about it as he hurried to her one evening. I laughed and quoted it:

*Oh, Lizzy Belle, Lizzy Belle,
You makes me quite mizzibel.
I nevah is happy
Unless you is vizzibel.*

The words produced a strange effect on Alex. Something like an electric shock passed through him, and his arm was immediately withdrawn. I bent forward to see his face in the gathering dusk, but he had shoved his hat low over his eyes and was safe in its shadow. "Why did you take your arm away?" I faltered.

"Why did you say what you just said?" he asked in a choked voice.

"Why did I say what I said about what?" I asked wonderingly.

"What you just said about Lizzy Bell?"

I relaxed at once and told him the black boy's love story. When I'd finished, he took the long black whip from its holder, drew it back expertly, and snapped it with a loud crack overhead. "Get a move on, Ned! Hi ya, Jim!" and his voice sounded boisterous and happy.

Lights were now beginning to appear in the farmhouses along the way. Alex had a clear tenor voice, and he began to yodel cowboy songs, calling a greeting from time to time to silhouettes in windows and doorways.

"*Hi-lee o-ladee, oh, my ladee, hi-lee o-ladee, oh, my ladee, hi-lee o-ladee-o, oh, my ladee, o-ladee-o,*" he sang sweetly and hugged me in a sudden rapture. "Hey, Jake, you better draw them shades, boy. I got a lady with me on this old rattletrap tonight!" and he laughed in high glee when the shadow moved forward, breeches in hand, and hastily drew the shade.

It had been a long ride, but at last we came to a halt beside a mailbox under a huge spreading oak. Alex jumped lightly to the ground and reached his arms for me. "We're here, O Lady, crawl down," he commanded, and I crawled down.

His lips brushed my cheek lightly as he set me on my feet. He guided me toward a light that shone dimly in the doorway of a big rambling white house almost hidden away in the trees. The light was the only sign of life.

"We'll be a little quiet," Alex said. "They've gone to bed and left a light burning in the hall for me."

"Oh, they couldn't have," I protested. "It can't be more than eight o'clock."

"Then they've just settled. Pa goes to bed at eight."

"But what about the others?"

"When Pa lies down, the rest lie down. It makes it easier on everbody that way. He wants to hear no chirp out of chick nor child once he's in bed. This time of year he's there at eight. A bit later on and he'll move the family bedtime up to seven."

The light was moving into the porch now, held aloft by a small woman who was buttoning a blue wrapper at the neck with her other hand.

Alex raised his voice only slightly. "Company, Ma!" He pulled the latch on a wrought iron gate and guided me along a flower-bordered brick walk to broad steps leading to a wide verandah.

Ma crept noiselessly forward, shielding the light with one hand and peering anxiously toward me. There was something downright hostile in her manner. "Which one is it, Alex?" she asked sharply. Her voice had the sound of a veiled menace.

"Why, it's Flossie, Ma. You been wanting me to bring her out long enough . . . Well, here she is. Take her, now, and make her feel at home while I turn out the team and feed. Did you save me any supper?"

Alex turned abruptly and left us. Ma advanced, her manner suddenly affable and friendly. "Sakes alive, Flossie, I'm glad to see you, child." She caught my hand and said softly to Alex's retreating back, "Don't I always save you some supper, gumpy?"

My breath eased a bit as I followed her through a long hall and a still-longer back porch and into the kitchen. "Jist wash yore hands there at the kitchen shelf, honey. Pore yore slops in the bucket underneath, and I'll set out a bite to eat." As she laid places for two and assembled the food from the safe and icebox, she chattered. "The girls is goin' to be tickled to death, Flossie." Then she turned to me, her face troubled. "I hope you don't feel too bad about the way I acted when I saw Alex had a girl with him." Then she blurted, "I thought it might be Lizzy Bell. If it had been, he couldn't have brought her into this house, and

I do mean it! Do you want sweet milk or buttermilk to drink, honey? I got plenty of both."

"Buttermilk," I stammered, my mind busy with Lizzy Bell. Now who in the world was she? Mag Hawley's successor? Beyond a shadow of a doubt. Well, Ma wouldn't have welcomed her. That was plain enough. She had welcomed me. I'd take up the little matter of Lizzy Bell with Alex at a later date. Just now I was as anxious to establish amicable relations with Ma, as she apparently was bent on doing with me, calling me "honey," doing her best to make me feel at home. Alex joined us, and halfway through the meal our voices and laughter must have risen a little for there was suddenly the sound of a raucous exasperated cough from the front of the house.

The eyes of mother and son met in a look of half-guilty, half-amused understanding.

"Pa didn't get off to sleep yet, it seems," drawled Alex.

Ma giggled nervously and began hastily gathering up the dishes as we finished with them. She was small and compactly built and beautifully proportioned—and quite surprisingly young. Her eyes, the deep blue of spring violets, were widely spaced; her hair, scarcely more than shoulder length, was jet-black and curly. It had been braided in a thick loose braid for the night, but tendrils escaped and rolled themselves into ringlets at the temple and neck. Her hands were small and well-shaped, but I noted that the skin on the forefingers seemed somewhat rough and discolored "from an endless stream of chores," Alex had said.

As Ma ushered me into the girls' room, I turned in time to see Alex blow me a kiss before ascending the stairs to his own room. Ma set the lamp on a bureau, and I glanced around the room. Two girls sat bolt upright in one of the big beds, their eyes all but popping from their heads, the covers held tightly beneath their chins.

"Now, girls, Alex has brought Flossie out to spend the night with you. Stop lookin' like a couple of goggle-eyed perch and light right in and make her welcome—and no gigglin' and loud talk, mind you. Flossie, the biggest girl is Mattie and the little un is Belle. Belle's ma died when she was a tiny mite and we adopted her. Mattie's ma died when she was five, she was my sister, and we took Mattie to raise as our own. Goodnight . . . and all of you settle as soon as may be. You know how Henry is when his rest is disturbed."

"We listened and figgered who had come and would've come out but Pa hadn't had time to get to sleep," offered Belle apologetically.

"Not much rantin' and rushin' about goes on round here, once Uncle Henry takes his bed," said Mattie in deep disgust, "an' I want you to know that when I get a home of my own I'm goin' to set up ever' night of the world till at least nine o'clock." She had merry brown eyes, and her pale brown hair was done in curl papers. Her skin was fair, with a light sprinkling of freckles, and she had a high round bosom.

"I should apologize for coming in on you like this at such an hour, but Alex invited me and it didn't seem late when we left town. The oxen walk so slowly," I said.

"What did he mean, makin' you bump all the way out here on that loggin' rig? He could as wells to of gone in after you in the mornin'. Though I'm truly glad yore already here. I could fix that other bed fer you, but we couldn't talk a bit if I did, without Uncle Henry hearin'. Belle and me been sleepin' together fer two years now, so's we could talk a while after we lay down at night. Keep so busy all day, and loud talk at night always sets Uncle Henry in a rage. You'll find everthing you need fer gettin' off ta bed on the washstand in the corner . . . if we got it, that is."

On the washstand stood a bowl, pitcher, and soap dish, flaunting crudely fashioned red roses and green leaves. "Belle painted the flowers on our bowl and pitcher. It was as plain as an old shoe. She done it to match the roses in the wallpaper." On a newspaper beside the washstand stood the inevitable slop jar, which completed the bedroom ensemble.

I tossed the dress I was wearing over the back of a chair to use as a sort of screen and was soon inside the heavy orange silk pajamas, noting the quaint tucked yokes and ruffled embroidery at the necks and sleeves of the nightgowns the girls were wearing. But the girls were enraptured as I emerged from my dressing room, their eyes not missing a trick as I unpacked my best blue taffeta, shook the wrinkles from it, and slipped it on a rack for church tomorrow.

"Blow out the light and come on," breathed Belle, turning the cover back to make room for me.

"You sleep in the middle," Mattie instructed, "so's we can both be next to you." Eager hands seized me in the semidarkness and guided me into the place made ready for me.

I'd never enjoyed sleeping on a featherbed. At Grandmother's or Aunt Lydia's, my first act always was to pull the bed apart and stick that featherbed underneath the mattress. As I settled down now, I felt those smothering feathers squashing up around me and two ardent warm bodies pressing close on each side of me, and when Mattie, in her anxiety to make me cozy and comfortable, tucked the cover tight beneath my chin, I came up fighting for air.

"I can't stand it!" I gasped. "I never could stand it. Let's don't have the cover so close, or so much of it. It's much warmer sleeping in the middle than on the side."

Mattie threw the spread and the top quilt back at once, then caught the hand next to her firmly in her own and said, "Jist don't turn either way, Flossie. Flat of yore back you can visit with both of us at the same time. Belle, feel how soft her little hands are."

Belle took my other hand timidly in hers. "Ohhh, Mattie, just like a baby's, ain't it?"

I thought for a moment that I could not bear it. Then I berated myself for being a selfish beast in the face of such wholehearted admiration.

"Won't we have fun talking about everything tomorrow?" I suggested desperately. "Don't you think we should settle down and go to sleep now? I'm awfully tired from that long ride."

That settled it. They commiserated with me on that score, but neither relinquished my hands. I loved the moonlight, now flooding all outdoors, and lay watching the pattern of leaves on the cream-colored blind as the wind stirred the branches of a tree on the south side of the house. A turkey gobbled halfheartedly, and I smiled remembering how, as a child at Grandmother's, I had crawled on my belly along the fence where a great gobbler had gone to roost, reached up, and gave his beard a sudden twitch. It had been just such a night as this, and the gobbler had gobbled in a way that made my heart stand still. He often chased me on the yard in the daytime, and I wanted terribly to give him an anxious moment in return. I waited breathlessly until he had settled and yanked his beard one more time before I felt he'd been sufficiently upset. I was nine that summer, and his excited gobbling delighted my childish heart, though I remained grave and unsmiling throughout the escapade.

An owl hooted in the grove across the road. A dog barked on a neighboring farm. Mattie and Belle began to breathe deeply, regularly, and a silence brooded over all.

So these were Alex's people. Married to him, they then would be my people. From Ma and the girls, I had nothing to fear, I thought. But I stirred uneasily when I thought about Pa.

I went to sleep at last, picturing in my mind what I would say to Henry Emerson Walker when first we met. To my surprise, no words came to me that might fit the occasion, and I fell asleep with a feeling of dread. I would have to meet Alex's father, heaven help me, but nothing I'd seen or heard of him gave me any reason to look forward to that fateful hour.

Chapter 3

September 28, 1912

The girls slipped out and left me sleeping. I woke to the harsh cry of a flock of guineas and sat up in time to see them rise as one body and sail out over the black iron fence and land far out in the pasture beyond. Here they set to potter-racking with power and unison.

Alex's people must think me lazy. I scrambled out of bed and made a hasty toilet. As I stooped to sweep the covers from the bed, I saw Mattie and Belle coming in through the yard gate with great pails of foaming new milk.

I tackled the featherbed as I'd seen my grandmother do. I turned one end down even with the other and beat it thoroughly, then reversed the procedure. I straightened it and grasped the edge nearest me to give it a quick turn, but my feet slipped, and I took a nosedive into the middle of it. After turning it, I could not pat it smooth enough for covers and spread, so I left it till the girls had time to finish it.

As I walked onto the back porch, I felt like running back to hide, for Alex and his father were coming through the gate from their morning chores. Alex cleared his throat nervously.

"Pa, this is Flossie. Flossie, this is my father . . . ."

His voice sort of died out, for Henry Emerson Walker had not paused in his stride but passed on by without looking at me, only nodding slightly in my general direction.

"Good morning, Mr. Walker," I faltered.

I was almost never conscious of a feeling of timidity when meeting people, but I was at a loss now, and I didn't like it. Alex reached the step below me, took me by the arm, and drew me firmly toward him.

"Want to walk on the yard till breakfast is ready?" He tried to make his voice casual. We followed the brick walk around to the front gate. "Ma's fall pinks," said Alex miserably, nodding at the flowers that bordered the walk. "The buds will soon start poppin' now—pink, yellow, bronze, and red. It'll be real pretty a little later on."

Ordinarily, I would have told him that those were chrysanthemums, but now it didn't seem to matter. We leaned sadly against the front gate. The leaves of the maples across the road had been retouched to rose and gold. Fingers of light from a newly risen sun etched the symmetrical outlines of the trees against a pale morning sky. I tried to concentrate on this beauty, knowing that Alex was avoiding my eyes.

Was this Pa's usual manner when meeting a guest? Was he displeased with Alex for bringing me out? I swallowed at the lump in my throat and was considering how I would ask Alex about it, when I was startled by the clanging of the bell that hung from a scaffold at the back door.

"We'd best go right in. Ma won't like to be kept waiting."

Panic seized me. I wanted to beg Alex to tell them that I never ate breakfast, but the smell of good country ham and steaming coffee was too much. We took our seats hurriedly, for Pa already sat at the head of the table, waiting for us to bow our heads.

"Dear Lord, we thank thee fer thy keep throughout another night. We ask thy guidance through the comin' day. Give us thankful hearts fer this ire food, and all other blessin's, Amen."

When I raised my head, I glanced instinctively at that stern, unsmiling face and caught my breath in frightened surprise to find him deliberately appraising me. Having met his gaze, my pride sustained me, and we regarded each other unfalteringly for one long fraught moment. Then Henry Emerson Walker gave me his rare and charming smile.

His smile warmed me, and I smiled in return, noting the oddly rounded temples and the way his hair sprang from his scalp, giving him an air of arrogance and distinction. But the minute I smiled, all semblance of warmth left his face, and his eyes took on a keen, listening look. A shiver ran down my spine.

Ma was setting dishes of hot oatmeal at each place, and the family went into action. "How many eggs this mornin', Henry?" she asked, as

Pa helped himself to the sugar and cream and passed it to me. We were eating on the long table in the kitchen.

"Three, I reckon," he spoke laconically, opened a fluffy biscuit, and dropped a sizable hunk of butter into its smoking center. Ma broke three eggs into the hot skillet, watched Pa, and just as he finished his oatmeal, she lifted the eggs onto a small heated platter and put them beside his plate. Then she brought him fresh hot biscuits right from the oven.

"How many fer you, Flossie?"

"One, thank you."

Ma fried it, then took her seat at the table, spread butter on an open biscuit, reached for a blue crock, and ladled golden honey over all. She was not frying eggs for herself nor even asking the others if they wanted eggs. Pa must have divined my unspoken question.

"The rest of 'em don't eat eggs. Not at this time of the year when the price is up. Somehow, or somehow else, they jist don't seem ta keer fer 'em." He laughed softly.

My eyes traveled round the table. No one looked up except Ma. Suddenly she sat forward on her chair, her eyes riveted on Pa, now eating ham and red bottom gravy, and spoke with startling intensity. "I wouldn't eat a egg if I was starvin' plum to death."

A hush fell over all. Alex coughed nervously.

"Pa, how about me hitching old Fanny up to the buggy and taking Flossie for a ride round the country? Would you like to go, Flossie?"

Before I could answer, Pa cleared his throat with a terrific rasp. "You know what I told you, young man! Though it's come to a pass where you pay mighty slight attention to anythin' I say. But you two be back in good time fer Sunday school. And I also want you should stay fer church."

By the look on Alex's face, I knew that Pa had given his consent.

"Yes, sir," said Alex meekly.

"Which don't mean that I in no ways approve of the ride!" barked Pa.

"You'll have plenty of time to get ready. It takes me a good while to curry Fanny and get her hooked up and get myself dressed." Alex winked slyly at me as he rose to leave the table.

"You girls get right into these dishes, now, whilst I churn," urged Ma, and she scalded the dasher and set to work. I started stacking dishes.

"I got the room straight all except smoothing the featherbed," I offered, thankful that Pa had taken himself elsewhere. Ma held the dasher suspended.

"You mean you can't make a featherbed? What kind of beds you all got, fer pity's sake?" Then a light broke over her face, and her lip curled disdainfully. "I know, more'n likely you got them scan'lous things like Rhea's got all over her house. I'd as lief sleep on a board mysef!"

When we started dressing, Mattie and Belle could hardly get themselves assembled for fear of missing something that I was doing. They watched spellbound while I brushed out my braids and arranged my hair in a series of swirls and puffs. They gloried in the rustle of my taffeta petticoat and dress. They reveled in my perfume, touching their hair and skin with it at my invitation. Mattie set the mouth of the tin flacon against her upper lip and left a wet spot, inhaling rapturously. They placed their sun-browned arms against mine, the better to gloat over my white skin. They fingered lovingly the diaphanous net collar and cuffs of my dress and stood scarcely breathing while I adjusted a small blue toque at the proper angle.

"We wore our new white shoes all summer and they don't have to be cleaned yet," boasted Belle, tying hers on.

"I reckon they don't!" exclaimed Mattie indignantly. "Put 'em on, step out to the surrey and ride to church. Get out and go in and play the organ and sing. Say the lesson. Listen to the sermon. Go out and get back in the surrey and ride home. And take 'em off again! Uncle Henry don't want us to wear them shoes out. He don't want us to catch us no feller, neither!"

"Sssssh!" Belle gave her a meaningful glance.

"Well, that's the truth if ever I tole it, Belle Walker!"

"You better not let Pa hear you say that. He wouldn't like it and you know it."

"Well, I don't like it neither, my own sef." Mattie's eyes were flashing fire as she turned to me and added in a grieved tone, "I do believe I'd spunk up to him once't in a while if it weren't fer Belle."

"And not get took anywheres fer a month?" prodded the younger.

"Well, but, Belle, Sherman Drew's been trying to get to me all summer and I ain't got to talk to him yet, 'cept about thirty minutes at last month's all-day singin'."

"What about me and Silas?" Belle softly sighed, carefully crimping the lace at the neck of her blue and white tissue gingham. "Ever since Pa found that note he left fer me in the sugar barrel, I don't get a chance to so much as step outside my class . . . or the choir."

There was a light rap at the door.

It was Alex, resplendent in blue serge and black low quarters with gray spats and tie. He was wearing a black derby hat. I wanted to tell him how handsome he looked, but it was an awkward moment for both of us. Ma was at his heels, and the girls were all eyes. So we marched stiffly down the hall and out to the buggy, conscious that Pa had taken his seat on the veranda so as not to miss anything.

Alex helped me into the buggy, jumped in beside me, and spread the buff-colored dust robe, with its enormous pink roses and wide fringe, across our knees. He reached for the lines and the whip and gave Fanny's rump a flick or two, and we were off at a smart trot.

Alex glanced at his watch. "Two hours and a half," he calculated, his eyes narrowed. "I think we can make it round."

"I'm going to love this," I exulted. "Why don't you come for me oftener?"

He shifted uncomfortably. Depends on Pa's mood whether I can ever have the buggy or not. You can see how his moods run."

I thought about it, and I could see.

ENGLEWOOD GROCERY. I read the sign swinging above a sprawling white building on our right. A mate to the bell at the back door of the house swung from a scaffold at the corner. "If it so happened no one was 'tending store' when a customer came, he had but to ring the bell and someone would come," explained Alex.

A small cottage set well back in a deep yard next to the store. "Silas Campbell and his mother and sister live there. His womenfolks came to keep house for him. He teaches at Spilling Brook. Silas has been making a try for Belle, but it sure gets Pa hot under the collar. Nice fella, far as I can see, but he don't own a farm, so's he's no good in Pa's eyes."

Fanny trotted steadily on, her black mane flowing in the wind. He pulled her to a halt as she drew the buggy up on a high wooden bridge.

"This is some more of Rushing Creek." Alex pointed with his whip. "Meanders a long way round, but finally manages to empty into Big Lake."

"The bridge seems too big for such a small stream," I said.

Alex laughed. "She gets to be a man when Little Toll's Run gets a gorge and belches her full after a spring freshet! Toll's Run empties into Rushing about three miles back, bringin' us all the water from the hills west of town. To the right there lies the Englewood Church and Eight Mile School building and grounds. Pa donated the land and timber for the buildings. The little house back of the school building is a spare. No cropland goes with it. It's just for labor in seasonal rushes, fruit and cotton pickers and such."

I was astonished. That Alex lived on a farm I knew, but that the estate embraced an entire village I had not known. Perhaps that was why Pa had not wanted Alex to drive me over the countryside. I thanked my lucky stars that Alex and I knew that I'd fallen in love with him without having knowledge of his father's holdings.

To the left was a four-room cottage. Crisp white curtains were at the windows. In each end of the front porch was a swinging pot of ground ivy.

"Behold the cherished domicile of Onnie Emerson Walker, known far and wide as Little Onnie. Big Onnie is my granpap. He's Ma's pa. He's visiting in the hills right now, but he makes his home with us and you'll get to know him later."

I was looking back at Onnie's little gray cottage. "How clean everything looks."

"Ann keeps it so. Reckon you can keep one as well?"

"If I can't, you can help me with it." I laughed easily.

A quick shadow crossed Alex's face. "I'll never do it, and you might as well know that first as last, O Lady!" He turned and looked at me unwaveringly in the eyes, and I knew that he was telling me how things would be with us.

"Feller can't rightly tend his business tied to his wife's apron strings. With Onnie, it's different. He likes having Ann in the field with him and she likes being there. So it's no trick at all for him to help her so's she can go right on out and help him. But I wouldn't want it. I'll never expect you to go to the field, but I will expect you to run the house in decency and order. Ever' feller to his own trade is what I say."

We approached an unpainted box house on the left.

"Hank Scogging and his orphan brood live there. He married an Indian squaw, and last year she died and left him with two girls about grown and a houseful of little uns."

A lane cut through between this house and Onnie's and on down in front of the "spare" house and disappeared in a forest. Another house, a corncrib, and a henhouse could be seen setting back in what appeared to be a limitless field. Just above the first trees back on the lane could be seen another roof and chimney.

"The Dinglers farm this field and a shiftless lot they are. Woody lives in the house back down that lane."

On and on we drove, still viewing Walker farm and timberlands. We turned east, and Alex showed me the piece of timber he'd been cutting on the day Ma and Belle had brought him news of my marriage.

We came to a crossroad and turned back north. SPILLING BROOK SCHOOL was in tall black letters above the wide double doors of a white building. "This is where Silas teaches."

"For pity's sake, how much land does your father own?"

"Oh, somewhere in the neighborhood of two thousand acres. This piece of timber here on your left cuts clear back in behind Onnie's place. Never had an axe in it and you'd think it was Pa's eyeball the way he guards it."

The road wound round, and we soon turned back west again. But we no longer had the road to ourselves. People on every kind of horse and mule and in every kind of horse-drawn vehicle were on their way to church. Their faces were shining with the good soapy scrubbing they'd just had and with anticipation of a big day, and they greeted Alex with a hearty goodwill.

"Good grief! Look at the humanity swarming in that dooryard. Don't tell me all of them belong to the same family?"

"Yeah, they sure do. That's the surest crop Bill Nolly grows. Make us a fine bunch of cotton pickers one of these days if we can just bear through it till they're big enough. Jennie and Tennie's the oldest. They're twins and nine years old now. They picked around a hundred pounds a day last year—day in, day out. That soon counts up, you know."

"But . . ." I had started to ask, *What does the mother of all this brood think about it?* But I didn't have to ask. A frail little washed-out woman appeared in the doorway, dangling a dirty dishrag in one hand. She looked at me unseeingly, pushed her straggling hair back with one forearm, raised a skinny bare foot and scratched the other shin with it, and faded from view again. Suddenly I wanted to cry. Perhaps it was because I could see that another little predestined cotton picker was well on the way.

"That's Reller Nolly," Alex said.

We entered church just as Mattie took her seat at the organ and began to play "O Come All Ye Faithful." Alex led me to a seat beside him in the choir, found the number, and we joined the singing. I could scarcely restrain a smile, for Alex buckled into the tenor with the same wild abandon with which he yodeled cowboy songs.

Sunday school over, Alex introduced me to a number of people, none of whom I would have been able to recognize if I met them on the street the next day. Then we were singing again, loudly and joyously. Most of the congregation fell to their knees for the long ardent prayers. And Brother Sherrill, gentle and mild, became another man once his text was taken.

"Brethren and sisters, I take as my text today, the entire 117th Psalm:"

> *Oh, praise the Lord, all ye nations.*
> *Praise Him, all ye people.*
> *For great is His love toward us, and the faithfulness of the*
> *Lord endureth forever. Praise the Lord!*

Thirty minutes sped by on wings as Brother Sherrill helped the good people of Main Shore to count their many blessings. As he warmed to his subject, the veins stood out on his face and neck. He swung himself upward and outward with the force of his motions until he seemed to cling to the rostrum by the tips of his toes.

"We have just experienced one of the finest growing seasons in years. We now approach the harvest. No longer do we have to worry as to whether or not the cotton bolls will stick on till it's made—it's white in the fields! No longer do we have to wonder whether or not we're going to make corn—it's made! The sorghum, the sweet pertaters, the canned and dried fruits, vegetables, the bins in the smokehouses is running over. There's beef to be butchered and hogs to be fattened and there's milk and there's butter and there's chickens and eggs. God bless you, and nobody has to go hungry. Praise His Holy Name!"

"Ah, this is indeed and in truth a time to worship and to praise Almighty God. He has showered us with loving care. He has blessed our humble efforts. He has been mindful of our needs. He has smiled on us all, the just and the unjust, and I want all of us to join in singing hymn number 164. 'Praise Him, Praise Him, Jesus our Blessed Redeemer.' Everybody, sing it!"

Mattie played it with spirit, and the congregation sang it gladly, like a joyful hymn of praise.

After the preaching, Ma called to Brother and Sister Sherrill to follow on when they'd a mind to, caught Belle and Mattie into her protective care with a single swoop, and ushered them on before her, making sure that there should be no loitering behind. Pa was already seated in the surrey, and Alex and I soon followed in the buggy.

I offered my services in the kitchen. Ma brought me a shepherd-checked gingham apron with a row of stately trees done in white cross-stitch above the hem. Then she ushered me into the dining room, which I had not yet seen.

The floor had been scrubbed with white sand until it was satin smooth and as white as no floor I had ever seen before. There was a long narrow table, handmade of fine timbers, and arranged round the table were ten rush-bottomed chairs, four to the sides and one at each end.

A massive old safe, scrubbed to the same smooth whiteness as the floor, stood against one wall. Opposite stood a serving table where an array of quaint old-fashioned pieces of glass and china reflected the light. Ma opened the safe with a proud flourish.

"We'll use the cloverleaf dishes today," she said simply. "You can set the table, Flossie. Knives and forks are in the lower drawer, spoons in the stand on the second shelf."

There were maroon-colored cloverleaves on gold-banded dishes and gold-banded crystal goblets. The knives and forks were old, their white bone handles yellowed with time, the steel blades and tines polished till they gleamed softly like old silver.

Ma didn't believe in cooking on Sunday, except in emergencies. This had not been an emergency, and plenty of time had been given to preparations. The safe, the ice chest, the smokehouse—all yielded up their treasures, and the table filled as if by miracle with roast chicken and dressing, baked ham, green beans, potato salad, sliced tomatoes, spiced apples, grape marmalade, cucumber pickles, butter, milk, cottage cheese, big pale biscuits, and crisp brown corn sticks. Ma had set the kettle to boil on the little oil stove, and she brought a pot of steaming coffee and set it beside her plate. Not knowing who would take coffee, I placed half a dozen saucers and cups beside the pot.

Pa was doing the honors in the back porch, offering fresh towels to the guests. Ma hurriedly ladled halved peaches from a jar as Mattie made her last trip in from the kitchen, proudly bearing a huge coconut cake, which she placed in the middle of the table.

"Baked it my own sef." She bobbed her head with quick satisfaction as she passed me.

Pa ushered the others in, and Alex came through from the kitchen just as Pa said, and oh how casually he said it: "Was Mounce, but she's been married, you know. Fellow by the name of Wilson, so they say." There was an audible gasp from Sister Sherrill. I steeled myself for a scene.

"Flossie Mounce, that's a mighty familiar name to me." Brother Sherrill was smiling blandly into my stricken face and offering his hand as though we had not just shaken hands at church. "And by the looks of you, I'd say you must certainly be the daughter of Albert Mounce, though I haven't seen that lad since before your time."

I gave his hand a grateful squeeze. "Yes, Albert Mounce is my father." I smiled proudly.

"Well, now, I want to know!" He held my hand a moment, searching my face. "Yes, I can even see the favor of Martha Haddock round the mouth and chin, now that I know to look for it. But you got the Mounce eyes. I baptized your ma and pa, child, about a month before they was married. Both of 'em converted under my preachin' at Old Macedonia."

"I've heard them tell it." I was happy to remember it.

Brother Sherrill turned to Pa. "This young lady comes of mighty fine stock, Brother Walker. Her granny on her pa's side was the daughter of Betty Lee Naval, who was a cousin to old Robert E. Lee, so the story goes."

For some reason, best known only to him, Brother Sherrill was enjoying himself. He seemed to find special pleasure in explaining my family background to Pa. But the twinkle died out of Pa's eyes. He urged us all, in a churlish voice, to be seated and called on my newfound friend for the blessing.

Why had Pa wanted to embarrass me by alluding to my marriage?

The old folks were settled under the trees at last. Belle and Mattie had gone to see Ann, who was "sick to her stummick" and expecting in March. Alex and I sat in rockers on the shaded front veranda.

"Ma, I'm going to take Flossie over to the orchard and fields," called Alex.

"Well, but, Flossie, you change into yore other dress and shoes. And, Alex, you fetch my yellow sunbonnet out of the back gallery for Flossie."

We went through a woodlot where slim turkey hens made plaintive small cries. Huge turkey gobblers strutted, spread their tails, raked the ground with the tips of their wings, gobbled fiercely, and shook empurpled wattles.

When we came to the orchard, Alex said, "How about some apples? You can have my hat to gather 'em in." He handed me the enormous straw katie he'd been wearing and stopped under the first tree and selected a beautiful Arkansas black and passed it to me. I wiped off a place and bit through the black-red skin and deep into the orange-colored meat and made a wry face. Alex laughed heartily. "They're no good till the frost touches 'em and they've been packed away long enough to mellow. We save our Christmas apples from these. Take some home with you. Wrap 'em in newspaper and put 'em away. Long about Christmas you can have some of the smoothest apple eatin' you've ever done."

"But I don't like mellow apples. I like them spicy and juicy and tart."

"Why didn't you say so? Come on and we'll get some russets. They're about as beautiful as an Irish potato with the scale, but they got everything else you mentioned."

There was a crisp popping sound as I bit into one, and the juice ran down my hand. Alex took out his handkerchief and wiped it off. Beyond the trees, there were three long rows of grapevines. Purple, red, and white, the clusters hung among the leaves, and the "bloom" had a warm silvery frost over them. Alex selected a few choice ones and piled them on the apples.

When he opened the mule lot gate, I stood rooted in my tracks as Alex stood back for me to enter. "They won't hurt you, silly!"

But I wouldn't go. "Well, they're coming at me with their necks stretched out."

"That's because their trough's dry and they want me to pump 'em some water." He primed the pump with water from a can beneath the trough. The mules began nudging at each other for a place at the long trough.

To the right of the mule lot, a new apple orchard had been set. Beyond it, reaching to the road, stretched the pasture where Fanny, Bess, and Sadie—all brood mares—grazed, their mule colts frisking beside them.

"Why do you keep so many mules?" I asked idly.

"Pa likes to raise 'em. We need a lot of work mules. A team brings a nice hunk of cash in a lump sum. Feller makes a down payment on a team and Pa takes his note for the rest. If he has a good year and no sickness, he pays it off. If a bad year or a new baby, Pa takes the team back and sells it all over again to somebody else. I always say it's the easiest money made on this farm."

We made the rounds of cotton and cornfields and back through the chicken yard.

"You might as well begin to learn now." Alex laughed as he reached for an egg basket and hung it on my arm. "Start gathering them eggs,

O Lady!" From a pump inside the laying pen, he filled the waterers and measured mixed grain into the hoppers.

What Ma called the "back gallery" joined together the back porch with the smokehouse and extended clear across the back of the house. Alex opened the smokehouse, and together we counted the eggs, one hundred thirteen of them, into a big wooden tub. How cool it felt in there and what a multitude of smells it had. Hams and sides of bacon wrapped and sewed tight in paper and sacking hung in the corner; onions, their tops braided, were suspended from the rafters; strings of pepper and bunches of mustard seed were drying on the wall; potatoes of both russet and sweet were stored; canned and dried fruits, cans of lard, and crocks of honey filled the shelves. A long trough filled with fresh water, which was connected by a pipe through the wall with the pump in the back gallery, held crocks of cream and butter and churns of milk.

In the corner I saw something I had never seen before. "What in the world is that?"

"That?" Alex asked absently, marking up the number of eggs on a chart that hung over the tub. "Oh, why that's Pa's newfangled incubator and brooder." He laughed. "One round with that son of a gun and he give up quick-like! You know, we might just give that old crate a tryout ourselves, one of these days. Pa will always buy his own ready-hatched from now on."

He reached behind the mirror outside the door, took down the key, and locked the smokehouse. "Feeling discouraged?" he asked, lifting my thoughtful face with his fingertips.

"No."

"Think you could stand it to live here on this farm with my folks?" My throat tightened spasmodically.

"Ann and Onnie don't live with your folks."

"Pa wants us to live here, and there's plenty of room."

"I like your people all right, Alex. But I don't want to live with them. And I don't want to live with my people. I just want my own home and my own things."

"Even right at the start?"

"Especially, right at the start."

"Pa thought it would be a good idea for us to stay here till I could sort of get on my feet."

"What Pa thinks and what I think is two different things, I bet cha," I said, trying to be funny and trying not to get mad. But Alex wouldn't smile, and my temper flared.

"All right then, let's face it! Do you still want to live with your folks? Then let's call our little deal off and you stay right here with them. If you're not old enough to be weaned, then you're not old enough to get married!"

My voice had risen, as it had an old way of doing when I got excited. Alex frowned, and I yelled at him, "You might as well know it now as later, Alexander Walker. I have no intention of moving into a house with anyone, your people or anybody else's!"

"Sssssh!" Laughing, he put out his hand to cover my mouth, and I slapped it away furiously. "Calm down, O Lady, they'll hear you," he said and began stroking my shoulder and arm as one would gentle a rearing colt. "Don't bust your backing strap." His jaw set resolutely. "It's just me and Pa for it, but I promise you I'll make some sort of arrangements so's you can have your own bailiwick. Though it will be a mighty poor-do and not like what either of us is used to." He mopped imaginary sweat from his brow. "Wheeew! What a temper, and over nothing too. Shame on you."

Standing thus close to me, his hands on my shoulders, his eyes were suddenly suffused with desire.

"Pa don't know what he's doin', makin' us wait till Christmas to be married. I reckon I love you too much, Flossie, even when you've got a mad on." The words came tumbling out on uneven breaths as he caught me closely to him. "I wonder if you've got a notion of what you do to me. I . . . you . . . Oh, sweetheart . . . I need you . . . now."

Never before had Alex kissed me so roughly. I stared at him in astonishment. And then suddenly I realized. So it was Pa who had set our wedding date. How I loved knowing that!

Chapter 4

November 18, 1912

Haven't you had days when everything wrong that could happen did happen? This had been such a day with me.

It actually began when I awoke yesterday morning with a periodic migraine headache. It shoved and kicked me around all day, until it tried beyond my strength to bear. I dampened my pillow with frustrated tears as soon as I found myself alone that night.

In the morning I waited until I heard Papa leave for work. The girls were off to school, and Mama had settled down to write a letter to Aunt Lydia before starting her day. When she looked up and saw me, she said, "Sister, you look like you got up on the wrong side of the bed this morning. Let me fix you a cup of coffee."

She suggested that I go back to bed and let her call Mr. Clampitt and tell him I wouldn't be in to work that day. We were shorthanded as it was, and I knew a hard day lay ahead, so I pulled myself together and went to the office as usual.

Would-be poets, God sustain me, had become the bane of my existence. If only I didn't care. I don't know what it is about the Socialist movement that inspires the muse, but not a week passed that one or more poems had not been submitted for publication. Usually these were patterned after "Take My Life and Let It Be" or "A Psalm of Life." Unfortunately, I'd been born with a natural ear for cadence and rhythm, and it was like an excruciating physical pain to read these cries from overburdened hearts as they limped, halted, staggered, and broke down completely at the end of the line.

Aldine Reynolds, new to the work, was the biggest thorn in my flesh. His last had been designed to fit the tune of "Onward Christian Soldiers." But as I read his lines and hummed the air, it was like trying to fit a beautifully cut garment on a sloppy old gal that bulged in all the wrong places. However, at that moment, confronted by the irate Reynolds, I wished with all my heart that I had let 'er bulge.

"Will you kindly tell me, Mrs. Wilson, who it is that keeps tampering with the poems I write and send in to this paper?" He was speaking with considerable restraint, and I had not the least doubt that he well knew who had done the tampering.

Pressing fingertips to my throbbing temples, I tried to look innocent as well as pained. "Please explain exactly what it is that has you so upset," I said carefully.

"I made two longhand copies of the last poem I sent in. I hold in my hand the duplicate copy. All I ask is that you check it against the version that was published, and you'll have your answer to what has upset me." He was still holding down hard on a wrath that was threatening to get the best of both of us.

I took the copy he extended with trembling fingers and said regretfully that Mr. Clampitt was the editor and he was out at the moment, but if he would leave the copy with me, I would call it to Mr. Clampitt's attention when he came back. My tone and manner let him know this was how it was going to be.

He glared at me, snatched a handkerchief from his hip pocket, and blew a blast with his nose that might well have given the Call its name, then departed, pulling the door shut behind him with a bang that shot through my aching head like a red-hot needle.

I turned wearily to the window and saw Frank Carpenter, his head low against the chill north wind, crossing the street. He was met midway by old Dick Finnesy, and they stood a moment in earnest conversation. Then Joe Martin, Sam Wiggins, and Joe Shelton rounded the corner together, and I was stumped. What were so many coopers doing away from their berths at one time? A funeral in their ranks would be the only thing I could think of that might account for it, yet I'd not heard Papa say anything about a death.

I took a couple of aspirin tablets and comforted myself with the fact that Aldine Reynolds's lines, as published, at least fit the tune they were meant to be sung to. I had settled down to read proofs when the door burst open and Alfred Jamison blew in with the wind. Al was Will's best friend, and the sight of him set up a flutter in my heart. He looked unusually grim as he hurried to me and said, "Will's in town for a few hours, Flossie. He told me to see you and tell you to forget that crazy divorce and meet him at the courthouse within the hour. He said it might embarrass you to have to tell your folks and pack your trunk, and anyway he hasn't got time to wait for that. He said to come on and get married. He'll take tomorrow off in Memphis and buy you some clothes and some luggage, but he's got to have you with him."

How in the world could Will Wilson ever stand the sight of me again? I'd given him nothing but anxiety and embarrassment in the months I'd been married to him. The next minutes I spent explaining to Al that I had divorced Will because our lives together were fantastically unreal and impossible. I was about to be married to someone else. Those minutes passed like hours and were mercifully ended by Mr. Clampitt's return.

But late in the afternoon, I caught a glimpse of Will Wilson himself, half hidden in a doorway across the street, and knew he meant to walk home with me. I put on my outdoor things and hurriedly made a back exit and kept to the alley for three blocks.

I reached home very low in my mind. When I opened the door, there sat Papa, another cooper out of place, dressed in his Sunday best and leisurely reading his paper. Across from him sat Mama, being sweet and pretty for Papa, as was her habit, calmly embroidering. In the kitchen I could hear Lola and Jan preparing supper, probably for the first time in their lives, I think. The air was heavy with a tense strangeness.

Deliberately I raised a grin and began. "Good evening, fellow citizens. We are now here assembled . . . ."

But I was not long in learning why coopers were at leisure on this bluest of Mondays. They had gone out on strike, an unheard of movement, and they were organizing themselves into a trade union, just as the carpenters had done, and the painters, in recent months. The plan was that come next Labor Day, the coopers, organized to a man, would also be marching in the parade to the music played by the town's brass band, its musicians also organized. Things were moving fast.

Papa was still talking. "Pekin Cooperage was paying below scale and Mr. Herget got downright stubborn about it. He was paying top scale for wine cask, but everything else was below. A committee met with him some weeks ago and had waited on his reply but nothing happened. In a closed meeting we decided to go out on strike." He was smiling, and his black eyes snapped.

"How long will it last?" I asked, remembering that our bank balance was weak and wavering and was never to be depended on in long stretches.

"Not long, we think, with the stores stocked to the roofs with Christmas merchandise. In a factory, mill, and shop town, who is to buy all that Santa Claus if not the factory, mill, and shop men it was stocked for? It's not just the coopers." Papa laughed now. "The men in the heading shop and planing mill walked out too. How long do you think the merchants of the town can keep going without all those payrolls? They get practically everything all of us make every week. We are their living, honey. No, I can't think the strike will last long."

Halfway through supper, Alex came in. He left his overshoes on the porch, tossed his fur-lined cap with the earflaps on the rack, hung up his overcoat, and flung himself on the couch. "Don't fix a plate for me, Miz Mounce. I just had supper at Aunt Rhea's and come by to have a session with Flossie. Uncle John tells me you coopers walked out on Pekin today, Mr. Mounce."

"The pay hike is long past due, so I expect we'll be hooping them off again in no time, Alex," Papa said.

"Uncle John seemed to think Mr. Herget might take himself a European holiday and leave you fellows with it."

"The price of everything's going up"—Papa sounded stubborn—"and wages just have to rise with it. Mr. Herget had his chance to do the right thing. Ours is all piecework, you know, and wine casks were the only things he was paying regulation scale on."

"What do you think, Miz Mounce?" asked Alex.

"The men will be back to work in time for their wives to do Christmas shopping." Mama laughed.

"God bless you for saying that, Martha. I needed it," said Papa, and he reached over and patted her hand.

Alex said, "I've come to get a furniture list Flossie's been working on. We will furnish only two rooms at first, but they are sixteen-by-twenty-foot rooms, one for cooking and one for living and sleeping. Pa says we'd better buy it now and haul it out to Big Lake before those gumbo roads get too slick to travel."

This was Alex's way of telling me that his application to teach school at Big Lake had been honored. He added, "Seventeen miles is a long haul for a team anytime, but with a load like we have, we'd better start before a snow works that goo to a loblolly three feet deep."

I almost forgot my headache as I got out the furniture list and started checking it with him. When I mentioned the floor coverings, Alex frowned. "Hold on a minute, O Lady. I don't know about that."

"Well, I'm just telling you." I laughed. "Put it down, Sun. One nine-by-twelve green and ivory linoleum for the kitchen. One heavy buff colored matting for the bedroom."

"Pa and Ma been keeping house quite some time now without a rug on the kitchen floor and he'll tell me that right quick."

"Maybe they don't want linoleum on their kitchen floor, and that's all right with me, but I happen to want it on mine, and that will have to be all right with them." I was trying to keep my voice down, but it was rising in spite of me.

"But you see, honey . . . ."

"No, I don't see myself hauling in buckets of white sand and drawing tubs of water to scour my kitchen as clean as theirs, not when I can have a linoleum and wipe it off with a wet mop."

"Flossie, Pa won't . . . ."

"Listen to me, Alexander Walker! Did you come here tonight, as you said, to find out what I want in my house, or did you come to tell me what Pa said I could have?"

"How about a couple of bedside throw rugs to get out of bed on and let it go at that," he persisted.

"I want my floors covered, Alex, and they're going to be covered or I won't be keeping house for you," I said stubbornly. I glared hotly at him and had the satisfaction of seeing him swallow his Adam's apple a couple of times before the next words would come.

"Are you sitting there telling me that you'll keep house with the floors covered, or you won't keep house?" He gulped.

"That's just what I'm saying," I said it steadily, but my heart misgave me. What if Alex didn't have enough money to buy even the inexpensive coverings I'd asked for? "That is, if you have enough money to buy them. Is there enough money, Alex?"

"Oh, I can manage the money part of it. It's Pa I'm thinking about."

"Well, don't be silly. Is it Pa's money you're spending? And think of it this way. Is it you and Pa buying the furniture, or you and me?"

"That's just it, Flossie," he said miserably. "It's me and Pa that's buying the furniture."

At the stricken look on my face, he hurried on.

"You see, it's like this, on account of him being in the retail business, he can get everything I buy at wholesale. It will make quite a nice little saving for us on such a bill of goods as we're going to need."

I choked on that one. "You mean that I can't even come along when you go to buy my things? That it won't be for me to decide which of two things I may want? Of all the . . . Oh Alex, I just don't see how I can stand it!"

All the pent-up emotions of that long miserable day rose to plague me, and I burst into tears. He sighed resignedly and drew my head to his shoulder. I doubled my hand into a fist and beat a tattoo on his chest. "How can I ever love and live with my things, knowing I had nothing to do with the choosing of them? I've just been living for the time when we could go together."

I straightened up and glared at him, the tears streaming. "But I'm telling you this for the last time: Pa or no Pa, I want my floors covered and nothing can change that."

He handed me his handkerchief. "Well, blow that nose and shut up squalling. It's just me and Pa for it, but you'll get your rugs . . . that I promise you."

He sat looking at me for a long moment, and it came to me that there was something different about Alex tonight. There was a look of strain about his mouth and eyes, and I became suddenly contrite, now that the rug question was settled.

"Something has happened," I said with conviction. "It's something that I don't know about. Alex, what is it?"

He caught me to him, and the strength and passion of his embrace frightened me. His kisses rained on my hair, my face, my throat. I had never seen Alex like this. "What's the matter with you?" I asked, straightening my hair.

"There's nothing the matter with me that being married to you wouldn't cure," he said. "We should have been married when you first came back from Campbell. But Pa wouldn't hear to it. He said wait till Christmas. He thought you wouldn't wait . . . that you'd be married to somebody else by then. Well, all right . . . I've waited like he wanted me to, and now a pretty mess things are in."

"Alex, what are you talking about?" I asked, trying hard to follow him. He shrugged wearily.

"Oh, it's nothing, forget it, and don't worry about tomorrow. I'll get everything as near like you said as I can find."

"Even my princess dresser?"

"Especially your princess dresser." He grinned.

But my heart refused to find happiness to comfort it when he was gone. As I prepared for bed, I kept wondering in just what way Alex thought things were messed up. The harvest was over, and such money as he had made was safely banked. He was still earning by hauling timber for Pa. He was certain of a school to teach for the winter, and in another community so that there would be no strain because of the fact that I would not consent to live with his folks. But, remembering the haunted look in Alex's eyes, I felt instinctively that something had gone wrong, something I probably couldn't do anything about if I did know, so why couldn't I be content to let sleeping dogs lie?

Why did there always have to be a fly in the ointment? Alex and I would be getting married at last, and soon. My furniture would be bought and hauled to my new home by this time tomorrow night. Sure it will be bought, my heart sneered, for Pa will buy it. Pa. If Alex ever showed the first sign of turning into that kind of . . . if Alex ever . . . if Alex . . . .

I could get no further with my thinking than to imagine myself married to Alex and Alex stomping up and down before me, acting like Pa. This was too much. I buried my face in my pillow to smother the sobs and let the tears roll.

December 7, 1912

During the past two weeks, Papa met with the coopers in Union Hall every day. He wrote pieces for the Call and read Socialist literature. Mama, making no to-do about it, quietly arranged to take over Paragould as her territory for Maddox Products. After her sample case arrived, she would wait until Papa left the house each morning, then set out upon her rounds of house-to-house canvassing. She was a born saleswoman. She sold coffee, tea, spices, extracts, home remedies, and toiletries. No woman tried to keep house without the things Mama was selling. Each week she delivered a consignment to some section of town, collecting enough to pay off the company and buy groceries for that week. Never having done anything to earn money before made her a bit timid at the start, but as her sales increased, her confidence grew, and it seemed to me that Mama bloomed happily through what was, to most shop wives, a frugal and crucial time.

Another change had come about in the Mounce household, and that was Philip Allen. The Allens were the newcomers from St. Louis. They had bought the Jansen property out on King's Highway. Now the father and two sons were engaged in putting in a huge brick building near the railroad, the place that was to house their wholesale business. They had also put in a general store at the corner of Locust and Main. We had to pass that store on our way to and from town. Phil, the man left in charge, was not long in discovering Lola, passing as she did each day on her way to and from Paragould High School.

From the first, Mama was worried about Phil's attentions to Lola, and not just because he was so much older. "What does a man of his background mean by coming east of the tracks for a sweetheart? He's a college man and could have his choice of any girl in town."

Papa looked up from his paper and grinned. "Have you taken a good look at Lola lately, Martha?"

His question brought to mind a remark I was beginning to hear often: "Lola Mounce is the prettiest girl that ever grew up in this town." But more than her beauty drew others to her. She had the gift of happiness. It didn't take anything to make Lola happy—she *was* happy.

"Besides," Papa added as an afterthought, seeing that Mama's face still wore a troubled expression, "a young man that spends hours each week coaching a girl in trigonometry so that she won't fail her midterm exams, has honorable intentions, take my word for it."

December 12, 1912

"Whoooopeeee!"

I quickly came awake with a delightful shiver at the sound of Papa's snow cry. As far back as I could remember, he had awakened the neighborhood with that peculiar whoop and holler when he got up and found the earth covered with snow. I listened to the muted silence that came with a heavy snow and burrowed deeper into my pillow.

Papa was back at work. The strikers had won, just as he predicted. Life had resumed its old flavorsome goodness. I heard him when he softly called to Mama that the rooms were warm and the oven hot. When I heard her scamper to the warm room to dress, I sneaked quietly into her room and crept into her warm place. A childish habit, yes, but I still liked to do it on occasion. No place else did I experience the same feeling of peace and security as in a bed recently occupied by Mama and Papa.

Hearing Mama laughing merrily was the usual accompaniment to the indistinguishable murmur of Papa's voice in the early mornings. It was their one uninterrupted hour together. No child was allowed to stick a nose in the door of that kitchen till Papa had gone to work. This was a rule that it now occurred to none of us to break, so long had it held.

The sound of Mama's merry laugh was doubly reassuring this morning. It helped to wipe out the memory of the nightmare she'd had in the night, an experience that recurred at intervals with a puzzling sameness.

Marion and Earl were my two brothers. Earl was two years younger than me; Marion was two years older and the firstborn of the family. The boys were as different in taste and ambition as it is possible for two boys to be, but neither of them was willing to become a cooper by trade.

Earl was restless in school and a little wild. He yearned for adventure and could hardly wait to get started. The memory of some of his escapades had reconciled us all to his absence when he suddenly decided to join the navy. Papa chuckled. "Uncle Sam will now administer the discipline that young sprout needs and teach him a trade as well. He's always wanted to be an engineer, and it's my guess that Uncle Sam will make one out of him. He's good material."

But Marion had craved knowledge. Papa had given him two years in college and then a business course before his savings ran out. But the little mill town of Paragould irked Marion terribly. It cramped him at every turn. But when he talked of going out into the world to seek his fortune, Papa had grown suddenly very stern.

"When you go, Marion, you will be taking my name with you, and I ask you to remember that. It's an honorable name. See to it that you don't drag it in the dust."

Marion had been hurt. "I'll change my name, Papa. If I shame it, then it will be my own name that I've shamed. If I add a bit of luster to it, I can always change it back."

Marion was twenty-one at the time, and a week later he had told us all goodbye. He was leaving town to play the guitar and sing in a medicine show that was headed west, the direction he had decided to take. This, he said, was a pleasant way to pay expenses on his way to California.

More than two years passed with no word from Marion. Three times Mama had had this strange nightmare. Her dream was to see him once more, and she spoke of it often. In sleep this dream seemed about to be realized. Marion was coming home, and her heart was singing with the good news. She was busy with preparations for his homecoming when something happened. When at last he arrived, she saw him through a mist of pain. He was there, but she could never quite reach him. Each time she woke crying with pain in her shoulder, and each time the whole household roused and gathered round in helpless concern until Papa could fully waken her and assure her that all was well. "Of course he's all right," Mama would say at last, drying her eyes. "I never lie down at night but that I leave him in God's care, nor wake in the mornings but that I ask God to be with him and guide and sustain him through the day." Then she would add, "I don't know why I have that same silly dream. I can't tell you how real it is."

But my mind was soon busy with other matters. Alex and I were to be married on Christmas Eve. The day had been set at last. My heart rejoiced.

December 24, 1912

Christmas Eve dawned bright and clear, though fourteen inches of snow had fallen in twenty-four hours preceding that sunrise. All day Mama, Lola, Jan, and I were busy with last-minute preparations. I'd chosen a brown suit and an eggshell satin blouse to be married in. The blouse had a boned lace collar and a frill of rich ecru lace held in place by bands and buttons of brown satin. My hat was of brown velvet and satin, a pert brown bird with black beady eyes perched on the left front of the crown.

By midafternoon Mama had gone to her room for a brief rest before dressing for the evening. Lola and Jan had rushed to town for some last-minute purchases—and for a word with Phil, no doubt. I had just finished dressing when Alex appeared, looking very spruce in a new navy blue suit, with gunmetal spats and a tie.

All day I had counseled with myself. I would hold my peace on this one day, going along with Alex if he came up with some quaint suggestion not in keeping with my plans. I wanted no contentious word of mine to cast a shadow on this day. But I had made this high resolve without reckoning on Pa.

"You might as well come out with it and get it over," I said to Alex, seeing that his mind was in a fidget about something.

"Well, it's going to throw the fat in the fire when I tell you, but Pa has made arrangements for Brother Sherrill to marry us at five o'clock."

"But Brother Sherrill lives in Brookland," I said. "Besides, you've told Pastor Hartley that we'll be in the church parlor at seven, so he can go right on to the Christmas pageant at the church."

"Yes, but it's only ten miles to Brookland and the local runs at 4:10. We can be married there and catch the regular train back at 5:45. Pa knows this, as well as we know it. He and Ma both took a stand on it, and Brother Sherrill's expecting us."

I took a deep breath. "Wait till I tell Mama I'm going to town with you to buy my Christmas present," I said quietly. There was no need to upset Mama at this stage of the game. I knew Lola would throw a fit, but we'd handle that when we came to it.

Alex bought a pair of beige kid gloves for my Christmas present. I slipped them on and put my brown ones into my bag. We stopped by Latkin's to pick up the gold cuff links I was having monogrammed for him. I'd thought that once inside the jewelry store, Alex would weaken and buy a wedding band for me. But he would not. "Having a wedding ring didn't keep you married to Will Wilson," he lowered his voice to say when I looked longingly at the display of wedding rings while waiting for my package. "We'll wait and see if your wedding to me takes before we buy a ring."

I had hated the ride on the filthy little local, holding my pretty new gloves tight in my lap for fear I might soil them by touching something. I'd hated, too, the breathless trudging through deep snow the three blocks to their home.

We found a warm welcome awaiting us at the Sherrills' cottage. Brother and Sister Sherrill and their daughter Lily received us with open arms. We left our overshoes on the porch and went inside. "Let me take your things, Flossie," urged Lily. Mrs. Sherrill threw the dining room door wide to show us that she had spread a wedding feast in our honor.

"We must catch the 5:45 back," I said, "so I will just keep my things on. And you shouldn't have fixed for us. Mama is expecting us, you know, and we couldn't possibly eat both places."

Sister Sherrill was disappointed. "Well, you must at least eat a piece of my fruitcake and have a cup of coffee with us," she insisted, and she and Lily left the room and reappeared almost immediately with the cake and a pot of the steaming brew.

The brisk walk and the hot coffee made the small room seem unbearably stuffy. I had removed my gloves, and now I unbuttoned my coat as Brother Sherrill asked us to stand for the ceremony, stationing Sister Sherrill and Lily behind us. He himself advanced slowly to the small center table, picked up his book, and opened it with ostentatious solemnity.

Looking calmly over the scene, Brother Sherrill cleared his throat and began. "We are gathered together this evening for the purpose of joining in holy wedlock these two precious young people." He paused and examined the license.

When I saw him wince, I knew that his eye had fallen on the name Flossie Wilson, and I wondered if he had qualms, fearing that he might be aiding and abetting adultery.

If so, he must have overcome his momentary doubt, for he continued in deep, sonorous periods. "Because of the love these two have long borne each other, they now present themselves before me for the purpose of becoming man and wife, both in the sight of God and man. Out of the fullness of my love for all young things, dear children, I feel impelled to sound for you a word of warning: the road that lies ahead of you is long and rough. You will find it necessary to bow your heads humbly beneath the yoke you are about to take upon yourselves, lest that yoke bite in too deep. The way of life has long barren stretches. Pull with and for each other when you come to these wastelands, else you may be wrenched apart in the stresses and strains of daily living. We will now proceed." He picked up his little book again and began reading the marriage ceremony.

I was too warm. Nevertheless a shiver ran over me. This, the time that had to come—this the inevitable moment. The room reeled, and I held my breath with the fateful portent of it all. But Alex and I both would have it. Neither of us had seemed to be capable of taking up our lives and living them apart from each other. I stole a look at Alex and was sure he shared my feelings, so pale and intense was his face. Brother Sherrill's voice droned on, now near, now far, and we made our responses.

"I forgot to ask. Is there a ring?" he finally asked.

"No ring," said Alex defiantly.

"Then join hands," came the command.

To my surprise, Alex turned and took both my hands in his.

"This is a moment weighted with meaning for both of you," said Brother Sherrill. "May you never, in all the years to come, forget the solemn vows you are about to repeat after me:"

"I, Alexander, take thee, Flossie . . . ."

As my eyes met Alex's, an uprush of wonderment at the beautiful simplicity of this small ritual brought a sudden surge of joy to my heart. At the same instant, a light broke in Alex's eyes, and his color returned. We seemed suspended in time as we pledged, "Till death us do part," and a moment later heard the fated words:

"I now pronounce you man and wife."

Brother Sherrill asked us to kneel before him, and he raised his hands above our heads in benediction as he prayed, "Dear God, we pray thy richest blessings on the lives we have just joined together in thy presence. Bless the home they are about to establish, and the children of this union, that they may be raised up in the nurture and admonition of the Lord, even as both of them have enjoyed the blessings and privileges of Christian homes. Go with them all the way, Father, giving them strength according as they have need, and in the end bring them safely into thy fold at last. We ask it all in the Savior's name. Amen."

As we passed the little church on our way out, a group was practicing for the Christmas pageant to be given later in the evening:

Silent night! Holy night!

Alex and I joined in singing the next line:

All is calm, all is bright!

All was indeed calm and bright. The dusk had deepened while we were in the parsonage, and now the heavens, thickly studded with stars, were brightened by a big round moon just climbing up the eastern sky. The people were in their homes at this hour, preparing for the evening's festivities, and Alex stopped under the corner streetlight and swung me toward him.

"Just wanted to take a look at my wife." He grinned. "What do you think of the present situation, Mrs. Walker?" he asked politely. "I never had such strange feelings as while I was standing there taking unto myself a wife."

"I think we both got scared at the same time, and both of us got glad in the same moment." This ceremony seemed to be the one thing neither of us cared to go on without, so we should now be able to go on our way rejoicing. I lifted my face to my husband's first kiss.

"Till death us do part, O Lady. May neither of us ever forget that." He caught my hand in his, and we hurried along toward the grimy little station.

Back in Paragould the streets were filling with the evening crowd. There was the sound of sleigh bells, sudden bursts of laughter, snatches of Christmas carols, and the smell of good coffee and fruit and evergreens. The myriad lights on the town's Christmas tree had been turned on, and small trees gleamed and sparkled in most of the houses. The shades had been left up and curtains tied back so that passersby might see the glory within.

"Hot tamales! Red hot tamales! Get 'em while they're hot!"

Mr. Stafford's cry rang out on the crisp wintry air, doors flew open, and happy children ran out with bowls and coins to buy his delectable morsels. Stafford and his hot tamales had been as much a part of my childhood as had been the mill whistles and the sound of Papa's five-pound hammer as he walked round and round a barrel, beating a rapid tattoo on the hoops as he made it ready for the cradle.

When we arrived home, almost at once we were seated at the table, everyone dressed and ready to go immediately to the church parlor for the ceremony. Phil had come to escort Lola to the wedding, then on to the Christmas tree and the elaborate program that had always been a part of our Christmas Eve.

"I believe I'll cut the cake now," I threatened, brandishing the knife.

Lola squealed. "Not till after you're married, silly. We'll have cake and coffee when we get back."

I glanced at Alex, but he refused to meet my eyes. Papa said, "I think we have time for a carol or two before we go. We have two boys and three girls at the table with us this evening, Martha. He started singing "O Little Town of Bethlehem." Mama joined right in, then the rest of us. Alex stole a look at his watch. When the song was finished, he rose with his glass.

"I want some more water," he said.

And I said, "Oh . . . let me get it for you," as we had arranged, and we made our escape into the back porch and into the outdoor garments we had hidden there. Then we went tearing around the house like mad. As we passed the dining room window, Alex yelled, "Come on, everybody, let's go get married!"

When we reached the end of the block, we paused and looked back. Phil and Lola were coming out of the gate, frantically pulling on wraps as they came. "This might turn out not to be so funny. Alex, tell them," I panted.

But Alex shouted, "No, let's go!" and snatched me by the hand and dragged me along with him. The moon touched the frosted snow, and the world sparkled and gleamed around us. The air quivered with the joyous expectancies of the season. As we ran and the blood started racing through my body, my spirits rose. At the moment this did seem to be great fun.

"Wait! Wait for us." Again and again the faint pleading cry reached us, and still we rushed on. At the corner of the parsonage, we leaned against the fence to catch our breaths, and soon Phil and Lola were upon us.

"You mean old things," gasped Lola. She was badly winded and mad as a wet hen, as I knew she would be. "If you'd got married without me, you could have buried me tomorrow! For heaven's sake, we can't go in like this. Here, Phil, hold my hat and lend me your pocket comb."

I looked at Alex, but he clearly had left me to face this one alone. "We meant it all for a joke, Lola, but for the life of me I can't see what's funny about it," I said.

"It'll be something to laugh about afterward," said Lola. "I'll get over my mad as soon as I've had time to get my breath."

"Alex, you tell her," I said miserably. He opened his mouth, but no sound came.

"Tell me what?" Lola asked, her glance flitting from one to the other suspiciously.

When Alex still said nothing, I glared hotly at him and blurted, "Whose idea was this anyhow?" Then I turned to Lola. "Honey, don't be mad. We . . . that is . . . well . . . we are already married. Brother Sherrill performed the ceremony at five o'clock."

Her black eyes flashed fire for a moment. Then with a little cry, she collapsed in Phil's arms. Alex made a feeble effort to placate her, and I was glad when he got soundly smacked for his pains. Phil gave her a little time to weep, then drew an immaculate handkerchief and began mopping up the damage. Over her shaken figure he regarded us both coldly. "I want you both to know that I think it was a pretty scurvy trick," he said.

"I'll think of something to do to make you sorry," sobbed Lola. "If it takes me a year. I swear I will."

"Don't mind too much, baby," soothed Phil. "We'll get married one of these days and we won't let them know a thing about it till it's all over."

As the significance of his words penetrated the gloom, Lola lifted a face grown radiant through her tears. "Oh Phil, my love, I thought you'd never say it!" she gasped.

"Well," drawled Phil, winking at us, "men have to wait for little girls to grow up and get through school, don't they?"

Alex grew suddenly cocky and strutted forth like a bantam rooster. "What do you think of our little joke now, sister? What else could have brought you a proposal . . . with witnesses?"

"What a wide, wonderful, beautiful world." Lola laughed. "Nobody has ever done anything to make me mad. There's nothing to forgive. I love everybody and everything's just perfect." She ran happily from one to the other, giving each of us a hearty kiss and hug. "I only hope that you two are half as happy as I am this minute," she gurgled.

Our first night together, Mama had insisted on giving up her room to us, but in spite of the safety I always felt in her bed, I regarded it with some misgiving when at last Alex stood thoughtfully winding his watch for the night.

"Would you mind taking a ten-minute walk?" I asked nervously, hating myself for the silly trembling that had taken me.

"Why not?" asked Alex, greatly surprised. "It's a nice night for it, snow halfway to my knees and a wind coming at me right off of an iceberg." But as he looked at me, his resentment cooled. He put his top coat on, settled his hat firmly on his head, and let himself out the front door without another word.

No sooner had the door closed behind him than I heard the dining room door open, followed by a murmur of words. Papa had joined him for that little walk. When Alex returned, I was completely under cover, shivering like a leaf.

Presently he said, "Mind lending me a hand, O Lady?" He stood at the bedside, his back to me, dangling the drawstrings of his pajamas in one hand. "Not used to tying these danged things in the back," he said casually, "but tonight that's the way I'm gonna wear 'em." He glanced briefly at me, his eyes twinkling, but it was no laughing matter with me. When I'd finished tying the strings, he turned and threw the covers back to make room for himself, before turning out the light.

"Jehoshaphat!" he yelled. "Get out of that bed and open up that double blanket. I could get pneumonia. Takin' me out of my woolen blankets and outin' flannel quilts and layin' me out on a coolin' board like this between two sheets. Well, I'm not aimin' to be treated in such a fashion, not even on my weddin' night."

Alex meant every word he was saying. I rolled out of bed, and together we arranged the cover to his liking. I raised the east window six inches and crept back into bed, my teeth chattering like mad.

Alex lay quietly on his back for several minutes, as though turning some weighty matter over in his mind. What had Papa said to him? Whatever it was, it shamed me, though I was grateful to Papa for anything he might have said that would win consideration for me at this hour. Then suddenly Alex's arms were around me, my head pillowed on his shoulder. "Do I smell honey locust?" he asked casually.

"Yes, Mama must have squeezed the atomizer over the bed when she made it. If it's too strong, you can turn your pillow."

"No, I just got a hint of it. I like the smell. It always brings back such a heap of things I like to remember."

"Like when we first met?"

"Yeah, like that. Pa will drive in after us tomorrow, in person. I guess we both ought to feel honored. Never knew him to volunteer such a thing before in my life. We'll spend one night there before going on to Big Lake. We were sure lucky to get most of our stuff out there before this last mess of weather. Mules will be doing good to drag an empty load over those gumbo roads after this begins to thaw."

"I'm sorry the Logans didn't get moved, Alex. I hate the thought of moving into the house with other people."

"Well, that's the way with sharecroppers. They're not obliged to move till the first of the year, you know, though they would've moved as a special favor to us if they could've got possession of the place they're moving to. But that old lady is down with pneumonia. I guess we can make out. Pa says, be good for us to find out what it means to live in one room, which is how him and Ma started housekeeping."

"How old was he when they married?" I asked idly.

"He was twenty-six, but Ma was only sixteen." I was born before she was seventeen. I just weighed three pounds. They carried me around on a pillow till I was six months old, and bathed me in sweet oil and wrapped me in an outing flannel diaper."

"And did you live?" I giggled. He took the cue and finished the old joke.

"They say I lived and done well." I was so relieved at the casual turn things had taken that I laughed happily.

"How much land did your pa inherit?" I asked.

"None, Pa was a poor little boy at ten. He lived with Grandma Martha and his brother and sisters in St. Francis. Aunt Safronia and Grandma still live there. Grandpa died before they moved here from Tennessee. Aunt Roena's farm is down the road from Pa's. Uncle Joseph died when I was about ten.

"Anyway, Pa did the chores till he was old enough to hunt and trap. When he'd saved a hundred dollars he bought a hundred acres of that river bottomland from the government for a dollar an acre. After he made a clearing near what he figured would someday be a main road, he built a big room with a big fireplace in it and moved in. He began adding to his land along and along, and finally put in a little country store. Only kind of work I ever saw him do. Never saw him walk behind a plow or wear a pair of overalls in my whole life!"

But I wasn't thinking about Pa. My thoughts were with a little sixteen-year-old girl and a three-pound baby in that tiny cabin by the roadside. "Was there a doctor there when you were born?"

"No, they had an old midwife. They say Ma didn't have proper care when I was born. She got childbed fever and sort of went out of her mind for a while. She finally come to herself though and when I was two years old Onnie was born. Only two they ever had of their own."

I didn't know when the trembling stopped, but I was lying close and warm in Alex's arms at last. This was where I had so longed to be, and it was heavenly to lie side by side with him, our conversation punctuated with occasional light kisses. "Sleepy yet?" he asked.

I sighed contentedly. "I think I'm getting sleepy. It seems so wonderful, Alex, that we're together at last."

"You don't feel like there's a strange man in bed with you?"

Papa had talked to him! That was what I'd said about Will Wilson. That each time I went to bed with him it was like lying down with a strange man—someone I had never known before. "No," I said, feeling shamed.

"Did you at first?" He seemed to hold his breath for my reply.

"I did act silly, Alex. I just can't tell you why I acted like that."

"Well, maybe I know already, and it's all right, honey. I've got a secret I want to tell you when I get to know you a little better." He chuckled against my ear. "But I guess there's no partic'lar rush. It's like your Papa told me, we've got our whole lives before us."

This was as I'd dreamed it would be with Alex. He would wait for time to work her magic; he would ask nothing until I was ready to give. I must have fallen to sleep feeling thus tenderly cherished, for the next thing I knew it was morning.

Chapter 5

December 25, 1912

Pa stood with his back to our stove, fur-lined cap in hand. "You'd better ferget style fer once, Flossie, and think some of yore comfort. Four miles in an open sleigh in this kind of weather calls fer a heap of wroppin' up. I noticed some skifts of cloud blowin' up in the southwest as I come in. Like as not, it's brewin' a rain and a turn to warmer, but the wind's keen 'nough to be bothesome right now. Annie put yore Christmas present in ta keep yore laigs warm, but you'll need head and shoulders well kivered too."

Papa and Alex struggled out with endless boxes—and at last the big black brass-bound trunk that Will Wilson had bought me when he planned for me to go traveling with him. Pa was wearing a narrow expensive brown wale corduroy hunting suit. His fine brown leather boots, laced nearly to his knees, had the four-inch cuffs of heavy woolen socks turned down over them. A heavy brown overcoat with a brown beaver collar was now unbuttoned and thrown slightly back.

"Did you have a nice Christmas, Mr. Walker?" Ma asked politely.

"Eh? Oh yes, if plenty of good vittles and a warm far to sit by is nice, we had it, and the family all well and at home. Them's the main things, I always say. Alex, of course, was out a pocket, but he'll be there fer a good part of the day."

Alex got into his overcoat and slipped on earmuffs for the ride. I put on a white and green wool sweater under my green coat, packed my hat and veil, and wore instead a white and green toboggan, a wide knitted white scarf, and my white knitted gloves with the green lacings. Papa and Mama followed us out, helping to wrap me up. I'd never feel the cold. The bottom of the sleigh was filled with fresh hay, and Alex had reheated and wrapped hot bricks for our feet to rest on. Our Christmas present from Ma was a crazy quilt of wool, the pieces fitting in however they would and all seams covered with fancy feather stitching in bright silk thread. After Pa had watched us admire it and cover our laps with it, he mounted the front seat and pulled a heavy black velour lap robe over his own knees, and whether by accident or design, the corner that flaunted two full-blown red roses was left fluttering in plain view. We turned to wave and throw kisses to Mama, Papa, and the girls and were on our way.

The restless mares, sporting huge red tassels on their bridles, hit a lively pace, and I loved the merry jingle of the sleigh bells. It was my first ride in a real sleigh, and a joy welled up in me. Joy was in Alex's heart too, and he had to sing. Out of respect for Pa and the good day, he left off his cowboy yodeling and kept to hymns and carols, and presently I overcame my timidity in Pa's austere presence and joined in. When I took up the soprano, Alex's voice soared into a sweet clear tenor. Pa, as though too warm, unbuttoned his earflaps and turned one back, cocking his head slightly to one side, the better to hear. Alex winked at me, and joyously we let ourselves go.

The sun touched the shimmering landscape with a magic beauty, even though Pa's "skifts of clouds" were definitely in evidence. Smoke spiraled from huge chimneys and small chimney pots all along the way, marking the spots where families gathered in the blessed reunion that was part and parcel of this day. Next Christmas, God grant it, a light would be shining through a wreath of holly in our own front door.

As we neared Englewood it was apparent that all had been on the lookout for the Walker sleigh's return. Doors began to fly open, and boisterous cries were borne to us on the wind. "Did ja get 'er, old boy?" and "Hold 'er tight, young feller!" and "Wait till we get there, old man. You got it comin' to you!"

I was surprised when the family received us in the parlor. This, then, was a state occasion with them. Ma greeted me warmly, though she did not kiss or embrace me. It was the girls who took my wrap and showered me with affection.

Ma was claiming my attention again. "I made Alex give me the big picture you had made for him, Flossie. I told him that could be his Christmas present to me, that he would have you now. I want to be able to show the people that come in how my daughter-in-law looks, you know. And this is Granpap, Flossie," she added, as an old man slowly rose from his seat before the blazing logs and came toward me, peering sharply at me with his one good eye.

Granpap subjected me to an intense scrutiny. I took the hand he offered me, but a wave of timidity washed over me when he drew me resolutely toward a window for closer inspection. I lifted my chin and smiled as bravely as I could into the glare of that bright blue eye. Presently he grunted and released my hand he had held so tightly. "A leetle mite proud and high-strung, son," he said, turning to Alex. "You'll need to handle her with a light rein."

The others laughed, and Ma quickly interposed. "Don't you mind Pap fer a minute, Flossie, he's bound to have his little joke."

"Joke?" snapped Granpap. "Did you say joke? Well, ferget and lay a heavy hand on the reins one day and watch 'er take the bit in 'er teeth and bolt on you, son. You'll find out quick enough how much of a joke it is."

The table was a picture to appreciate. Ma brought a huge turkey, delicately browned at the last minute. While we were washing the dishes afterward, Onnie and Alex went out to stretch the new wagon sheet over the hoops and to load my trunk and boxes for the journey the next day. When Alex came in, Mattie handed him a list and asked him to check it.

"Them's yore supplies," Pa said, "and you'll find 'em all packed in boxes to the left of the door as you go in the store. And don't ferget to add a 10 percent carrying charge, young man. Yore no better than the rest, but yore weights is honest weights. I put them things up my own sef. And one more thing: you'll be having a chivaree tonight. What you gonna use fer refreshments?"

Alex stood considering for a moment. "How much sugar you got in the house?"

"Maybe not more than a pound or two," said Belle.

"Hey, Flossie, make out a list of whatever you'll need for it. I want you to make up a lot of that divinity candy and a mountain of popcorn balls. We'll give all comers a real treat for once."

We spent the afternoon making candy and popcorn balls and getting acquainted. It was fun. Onnie and Ann seemed to enjoy it more than any of us and, at the height of the fun, decided to spend the night. Onnie slipped home when it was nearing night to do the chores but was back with us in a little while.

We settled down in the front bedroom after supper, this being the family living room. A square table stood between the two front windows. It held a gramophone, its huge red horn, shaped like a morning glory blossom, swinging from a metal arm by a delicate chain. Boxes of cylinder records lined the wall, and a ladder-back chair stood beside the table. I was invited to occupy the chair and choose the entertainment for the evening. I was glad to be thus occupied, conscious as I was that every eye was upon me.

Alex, I noticed, was very much like Ma: neat and compact in body, the same childlike beauty of feature, the same artless expression.

Onnie was like Pa, except Pa was of leisurely habits and Onnie moved as though operated by tightly wound springs. If he stooped to put a log on the fire or went to the kitchen to get Ann a drink, every move was one of speed and purpose. His hair was a shade darker than blonde, and his voice deep toned and pleasant. But I was beginning to see that Onnie had Granpap's wry sense of humor.

Ann, obviously pregnant, had her thick sandy hair piled in a loose coil on top of her head. Her hands and feet might have been those of a twelve-year-old child. She was tired of herself and everyone else tonight, plainly evident in the restlessness she seemed unable to control. Presently she said, "Let's go home, Onnie."

Onnie heaved a sigh, and his lips tightened stubbornly. "I'll be glad when this thing's over and we can light someplace . . . anyplace. If we're home she wants to be somewheres else. If we're somewheres else, she wants to be home. Well, you had yore chance to say if you'd go home tonight, or stay fer the chivaree, and you said you wanted to stay, so we're staying."

"It's cloudy all over now and a light mist falling. Maybe they won't come after all," I said.

"Take more than that to stop 'em." Mattie grinned. "They'll be here."

Just as I began to feel relaxed and thought we'd settled down for the evening, Pa rose and as though he were alone let down his suspenders, unbuttoned the fly of his trousers, and stepped out of them. He had already taken off his shoes to toast his toes. Now he gave his pants a quick shake and hung them over the bedpost by the suspenders. Standing there in his drawers, he turned the covers back, adjusted the pillows to his liking, and tucked himself in. I gave Alex a startled look, and he nodded at the clock. It pointed to seven. Pa had moved his bedtime up an hour in deference to the season.

The girls had stolen from the room some minutes before. Onnie and Ann said goodnight and left us. Alex rose with an elaborate yawn and told me he thought we best had go on up to bed. Ma lighted an extra lamp on the mantel and handed it to Alex. "You and Flossie can sleep in your bed, Alexander," she said cheerfully. "Goodnight, Flossie, I hope you sleep well."

We met Mattie and Belle coming down the stairs. "We fixed yore bed and laid out yore things," whispered Mattie, squeezing my hand.

"We wanted to fix the room across the hall, fer me and Mattie to sleep, and let you and Alex have our room, but Ma wouldn't hear to it," said Belle, as though apologizing. "She said fer you to sleep in Alex's own bed and that was the end of it."

"I'm sure everything's going to be all right," I said. Seeing that she still looked doubtful, I said warmly, "Thank you both, you've been so kind to me."

Alex marched ahead like a torchbearer lighting my way. We passed along the upper hallway and entered the door at the left. Surely we had made a mistake. There stood Granpap, stripped to his red flannel underwear, calmly hanging his britches by the suspenders to the post at the head of his bed. My eyes swept the room. No, there were our own things spread on a bed in another corner of the room. Besides Alex was setting the lamp on the bureau and winding his watch for the night.

"Blow out that light," I whispered, remembering Granpap's keen blue eye, and we prepared for bed in the dark. Alex was in bed first, and I found his arms held out to receive me. I sat on the bed next to him, lowering my head carefully to the pillow. Not for my good right arm would I have made the springs beneath me give out one tiny squeak. I was as conscious of Granpap as though he stood beside the bed with a light, peering at us with interest with his one good eye. To my relief Alex was of the same mind. I was exhausted by the long day and fell asleep bursting with desire: the desire to scream at the top of my lungs. Why in Sam Hill do we have to sleep in the room with Granpap?

Suddenly bedlam was in full cry. Guns blazed away beneath our windows. Cowbells jangled. Kettles and tubs were being beaten enthusiastically with iron spoons and spikes in relentless hands. Somebody had manned both farm bells, chickens began to cackle and the turkeys to gobble, and the guineas to potter-rack. Even the mules brayed, and the mares whinnied. There was singing and shouting and now and then a wild screech of laughter. It was pandemonium.

Alex bounded out of bed and lit the lamp. Granpap was scrambling into his clothes. "You'd better take time to tie them shoelaces, Granpap. You'll step on 'em and fall all the way downstairs and we'll have to stay over for a funeral."

"Let's lock the door and not go down," I suggested.

Alex looked at me like he thought I was crazy. "You don't know much about these chivarees, do you? They've come for me and they'll get me if they have to bust every door on the place down. It's happened to others before me."

I sat up and ran my feet into felt slippers and slipped on the red corduroy robe. I tied the long red satin sash in a small bow at the waist, letting the ends trail to the hem. I straightened my hair the best I could and ran a powder puff over my face. As we descended the stairway, Ma was unlocking the front door.

"I had to let 'em in," she screeched above the din. "They had a rail and swore they'd ram the door through if I didn't!"

"Let's ride 'em on a rail, boys!"

"I'm not stopping till I duck 'im in the hoss trough. That's what he done to me, dang his hide!"

"Nothin' but tar and feathers will settle my score with that lad!"

"Make it easy on me, fellers, and I'll feed you good!" cried Alex.

"Come out from behind yore wife's skirts and take yore trimmin' like a man," yelled a big brutish man, who caught Alex by the foot and threw him sprawling. In an instant he was borne through the long hall, kicking and fighting like a wild thing.

"Well, come on, girls, let's go to the kitchen," said Ma. "I don't know of a thing else we can do." She sounded about ready to burst into tears.

Granpap had gone before us and put a roaring fire in the big range. There were only a few girls and women in the crowd. They looked merry and rosy in the lamplight, the fine mist sparkling like jewels on their gay fascinators and woolen mittens. All were talking to each other at once, though not one of them took eyes off of me, and presently Ma was taking me around the circle, introducing me to them, one by one.

"This is the daughter-in-law I been telling you about, and you wouldn't believe me, would you? Well, here she is to speak fer herself now." There was defiance in Ma's attitude that I could not understand. But at this point there was a quick rush of feet, and Alex burst in through the back door and grabbed a towel from the rack and began to dry his dripping head. The men and boys crowded in behind him. Alex bound the towel turban style about his head and bowed deeply to the ladies.

"They did it anyway," I said indignantly. "Alex, let's not feed them." This was only a gesture on my part, and they were quick to respond.

"What we done ain't a smidgen ta what we will do if we're left to starve!" shouted one, and another took up the cry for food.

Alex joined me in passing heaped platters of divinity and popcorn balls. When he bragged that I made the divinity, they said that was why he married me.

It was no trouble to locate Sherman Drew and Silas Campbell. Sherman was the huge dark fellow that had thrown Alex to the floor. He made for Mattie now and maneuvered her a little apart from the others. I noticed that she didn't withdraw the hand he grabbed. The fun-loving Mattie listened to his whispered words, and then they both laughed till they had to lean against the wall for support. No wonder. When Sherman laughed, everybody turned to laugh with him, whether they knew the joke or not. He laughed all over, and the black curls tumbled in his eyes and had to be brushed back.

But Silas and Belle were oblivious to it all. Silas, tall and slim, stood looking down at Belle, talking earnestly. His hair was brushed sleekly back, his clothes of better cut and material than the garments worn by the other men. Belle was giving her undivided attention to every word he uttered, her heart in her eyes.

Presently a circle formed, and Granpap took the center. This seemed to be the accepted procedure. He began cutting didoes, and someone started clapping hands. Pa cleared his throat with a loud rasp. He hadn't bothered to leave his bed, and I gathered by the sudden cessation in the racket that all took it for granted Pa thought things had been carried far enough. There was a hasty and subdued leave-taking. Twenty minutes later the fire in the range, slowly dying of inattention, was the only evidence that there had been a chivaree. The house was quiet as a tomb.

December 26, 1912

When I awoke next morning, both Alex and Granpap were gone. I dressed hastily and met Ann coming out of the room across the hall.

"My, how slim and nice you look," she said, "but you just wait. The first thing you know you'll be looking like me. What will you do when you find yourself like this?" and she made a wide circle with her arms, even beyond the considerable circumference of her own body.

"I guess I'll just grin and bear it like the millions before me have done, and the millions yet to come."

"Well, maybe. But being pregnant ain't funny. I puked my socks up for three solid months. Time I began to feel like a human again, I started to bulge. I want you to know I hold tight to this bannister when I start up the steps. I'm that clumsy, and if I was to fall . . . my God, what a splatterment!"

A stack of quilts halfway to the low ceiling had caught my eye. "For heaven's sake, what do they do with all those quilts?" I gasped.

"Makin' quilts is a winter pastime at Englewood, Flossie. Some of them, of course, belonged to Mattie's ma and she'll take 'em when she marries. Some Granpap brought with him when he come to make his home here. But most of 'em Ma made along through the years. She gave me and Onnie one like she give you and Alex, and she's making one of 'em for each of the girls."

I moved over and looked into the room. There were two beds there. The one that hadn't been slept in looked like it held three featherbeds. There were huge feather pillows with stiffly starched ruffled shams. *Good Morning* and *Good Night* had been embroidered on them in turkey red. A sudden resentment surged in me. "Can you tell me why with all these beds in the house it was necessary for us to sleep with Granpap?" I blurted.

"Sssssh!" warned Ann, as though the very walls had ears. "I'll leave that one for you to puzzle over. I got plenty of things of my own I haven't got figgered out yet. Right now, if we know what's good for us, we'll get ourselves down to breakfast." She added this hastily as the bell at the back door clanged peremptorily.

Alex was in high spirits at breakfast. "Well, O Lady, we'll get to try out our new wagon sheet today," he said.

"Among other things," said Granpap drily, spearing a biscuit with his fork.

"She won't sag nor come loose anywhere. Onnie and me got her as snug as four walls," Alex continued as though he hadn't been interrupted. "A bad mizzly mornin' out there, and the snow's beginnin' to slush a little. I'm glad we haven't got much of a load. And you'd better wear your toboggan again, Flossie."

"I have a brown toboggan and scarf if you'd rather wear them than your hat and earmuffs," I suggested.

"By all means, yes," Pa spoke up, sliding three eggs from the platter to his plate. "He takes a plum dee-light in all that gal stuff. You might try sprinklin' a mite a puffume on him too. He'd like that somethin' tremenjous."

But later Alex tossed his hat and earmuffs into a box and put on the brown toboggan and scarf. "This just might be nobody's business but ours, you reckon?" he said. It struck me how very daring he thought he was being to walk out right under Pa's nose so attired. To reward him for his bravery, I turned impulsively and gave him my first spontaneous wifely kiss. I was immediately caught into a bear hug and smothered.

"Two nights of pure unadulterated hell," Alex muttered roughly. "It's one thing to feel bighearted and hold a tight rein on your wedding night, for reasons, but by the eternal . . . ."

There was the sound of a heavy footfall in the hall, and a firm hand grasped the doorknob. I broke from Alex and busied myself with the straps of my suitcase. It was Pa. "Did you think ta pack that alarm clock? You got nobody to get you up mornin's now, and you shore can't hold yore school unless yore there to open up on time ever' mornin'."

"I got the clock," Alex said sourly, then laughed. "Not that I'll need it. I'm aimin' to be a smart early-to-riser like my Pa before me."

Pa threw him a suspicious glance, as though not quite certain that his leg wasn't being pulled by his eldest.

The family stood, humped and shivering against the cold, as we settled snugly in the covered wagon for the long ride. But it was Pa, who trudged through the softening snow to open the big gate for us to drive through. I peeked out, and for a wonder, his really charming smile broke through the stern mask of his face as he took off his cap and waved me a parting salute.

When we reached the store, Alex hopped down and quickly unlocked the door, loaded the boxes in the wagon, locked the door, hopped back in the wagon, and we were once again on our way. We were cozy inside the wagon. I hugged myself joyously. I had won out on the most important of the many controversial matters that had come up to plague Alex and me. We would not be living in the house with his folks. My mind flew ahead in anticipation of our arrival at our own future place of abode. What would it be like?

That was not the only unanswered question in my mind. Why had we had to sleep with Granpap? Was it Ma's idea of a joke, or was there some other reason behind it all? Besides that, who was Lizzy Bell? But my mind shied away from that one. I felt I'd be happier never to know and resolved never to ask. What was on Alex's mind when he, at this moment, sat lost to me in thought? Well, these nagging little matters would have to wait their turn. Had I not just been marking time until this precious day so that I could begin living? I was concerned with an upsurge of newness now that seemed to be rising in me like a tide. Alex adjusted drawstring and reins to his liking and then turned to take my lips in a hungry kiss. I gloried in the quickening pulse as the hot blood rushed through my body and beat like a hammer in my throat and sang in my ears. I opened my eyes to find Alex regarding me with a surprised and misty-eyed tenderness.

The road was terrible, but the mules jogged steadily along. We rocked and jolted by turns and, long before noon, had started filching good things from the basket the girls had fixed for us. When Alex saw I was sleepy, he propped his feet on the front of the wagon and made a cradle for me of his lap and arms. I pillowed my head on his chest, and the wagon creaked and rocked and rolled, and I slept in utter contentment. I woke with Alex kissing a muted circle round my face, pausing each time in passing to let his lips rest lightly on mine.

When we reached Stinson's Mill, Alex became very animated. "Goin' into the homestretch now, O Lady. Three more miles of stress and strain and the trip's over. I'll turn at this corner to walk down that lane to the school buildin' when I come 'round by the road. You see that square white buildin' back at the edge of the woods? That's where I'll suffer. Sixty-odd heathens: from chart class to eighth grade, from eight till four, five days a week, for $65 a month. I must have been in love when I sold myself into bondage. I doubt not that'll be the hardest money I'll ever earn."

"You don't like children?" I asked wonderingly.

"Children have nothin' to do with it. It's being cooped up inside four walls, day in and day out, that goes against my grain."

"Well, for my own part, I'm glad you're qualified to teach. It seems a nice way to get hold of the money to hire some of the heavier work to be done."

"Except my plowin'," Alex said quickly. "Plowin' is one job I ask no man to do for me. Come spring, that's the most satisfyin' thing I ever done in my life, but no hoein' or weedin' or pickin' cotton for me."

"How will you get it done?"

"Pa always manages. A few transients come through in the rushes. Then there's always some wantin' to pick up a day's work where they can to help out on rations while the crops growin'. What Pa can do, I figure I can do, and more. He's made it without schoolin'. He gave us boys as much schoolin' as we'd take. Someday I'll own more land and stock than Pa ever thought of ownin'."

"Looks to me like you would have married a country girl," I said.

"Ain't it the truth? Me gettin' my heart set on you like I did just don't make sense. Pa was against us gettin' married before you ever married Will Wilson. He said your people lived from hand to mouth and you wouldn't bring a dowry with you. He wanted me to marry Stella Norse. Old Man Norse give all three of his girls a farm to start 'em off when they got married. But, like I told Pa, it was you or nobody for me, so's he finally come to it."

He leaned forward, spread the canvas opening, and pointed to the right. "Rowlands live just there. Pay attention, for these are your new neighbors I'm showin' you. Turners live in that shanty back in the field. Sharecroppers they are, and a sad case—all got consumption. The old lady died last year. The old man has took his bed for the end. Got a skinny little girl about fourteen, and she does the cookin', washin', and ironin' for the two boys and keeps care of the old man. The boys hunt and fish a lot, so's they may have enough to eat, but that's no fit house for people with lung trouble to be livin' in. Low and damp there, and comes a big rain and they're swamped in."

As the dusk deepened, lights appeared in the houses, and smoke spiraled up from chimneys as supper got under way. "Colbys live just ahead. She's a widow woman with two grown children. They own their own farm and get through pretty well till chill and fever time. Then first one and then another comes down with malaria."

I stirred uneasily. "Is this an unhealthy place to live?"

"Could be called that, I reckon. People keep goin', but most of them have a swarthy look. Whites of their eyes turn yellow and not much life in some of 'em."

"Listen here, you didn't tell me that! I don't want to live where there's a lot of malaria, Alex."

"Keep your shirt on, O Lady. Malaria seldom shows up till fall. Some never get it. Maybe we'll be among the lucky few. Besides, Pa keeps stocked with plenty of chill tonic. It's one of his best sellers." He nodded toward a small decline in the road ahead. "We're coming to Biddy-Boo Bajou. Never has an overflow unless the lake gets up and backs into it."

A wide low bridge, without bannisters, looked as if it might have stood tall and thrown itself across a wide stream that gurgled and sighed sluggishly through the center, where the ice was beginning to melt. Bare willows lined its banks.

"That's Big Lake." Alex nodded to the left. A cypress brake loomed over us. The trees swayed and groaned mournfully in the wind, and hundreds of the bare knees jutted up through the icy waters.

"And on your right you now behold the future dwelling place of Mr. and Mrs. Lester Alexander Walker." I strained forward in an effort to see. A wide board fence enclosed a generous yard. An unpainted frame house stood on a slight knoll. Lights shone in the tiny, little windows, and smoke belched from the biggest chimney I had ever seen, and it rose and was whipped about by the wind. A wide veranda adorned the front of the structure. Alex let out a war whoop and pulled the smoking team to a halt. The front door was flung wide, and the smell of frying sausage and strong coffee rushed out to cheer us.

"Get out and rest yore mules," called the shadow from the doorway, detaching itself and coming toward us, quieting the barking dogs as it came and yelling at the kids to get back in the house and stay there. "I tole 'em you'd get here," he said, extending a hand to Alex, who had reached the ground and gone to meet him.

The bricks were long since cold, and I was beginning to feel the chill. Besides, I was cramped with the long sitting. My feet tingled unpleasantly when Alex lifted me to the ground. The dogs and the children followed us in, the dogs sniffing inquiringly at our legs and the children crowding close in round-eyed wonder.

Carrie Logan came in from the kitchen, wiping her hands on her apron as she came. "What's yore name, honey? Flossie? Well, I knowed I couldn't start in calling no wife of Alex's only by her married name. Flossie, this is Flo Ella Lancey. Looks like I dreaded having this last baby the worst of any. Flo Ella got bighearted and come to see me through it." Flo Ella grinned at me and backed into the kitchen.

Alex and Tom Logan went to feed and bed down the mules and then to unload my things. I directed them where to set them.

Then Carrie Logan became impatient. "Listen here you all, I cooked that supper to be et, not to set there and sob itself cold. Ever last one of you pile into that kitchen and light into them vittles. Takes but one time to eat, and all this can wait till later."

We crowded into the lean-to kitchen. We pulled split-bottom chairs from beneath a lone shelf at the back of the room and seated ourselves at the places set for us. Carrie stood at the stove in the right-hand end of the ten-by-sixteen-foot room and began passing the hot tasty food.

"When we found we couldn't get possession and was going to have to make room fer you all," Carrie said, "we stowed everthin' we could spare in back of the smokehouse to leave yore room empty. I then got Tom to put me up this here shelf, and I don't know but that I'll do the same when we get moved. Ain't never had it so handy 'bout cookin' and dishin' up. Flo Ella, pass that bowl of fresh butter to Flossie to go on her hot baked tater. I churned last thing this evenin' and I know that butter's good."

"Help yoresef to that rice and gravy, Alex, and pass it along," said Tom. "Carrie opened these pickled peaches special fer you, remembrin' how you love 'em. Give this young man some milk, Carrie. Coffee might keep him awake tonight."

"If keepin' awake is only reason he won't drink coffee, I say he might as wellst to have it. He prob'ly won't be doin' much of a job of sleepin' noways."

I felt the blood rush to my face. How could they think such talk was funny?

"Never thought I'd live to see the day I'd haf to live under the same roof with Alex," mourned Flo Ella. "Always high-tailin' it 'round these bottoms, tryin' ta beat ever' feller's time with a gal, then droppin' 'er like a hot tater the minute he done so."

"Now, Flo Ella, whose time did I ever try to beat with you?" Alex teased.

"Maybe that's what's eatin' on 'er," said Tom, but Flo Ella joined as merrily as any in the laugh that followed.

"I hope you don't think I'd be caught at a dogfight with sich as him, not when I can have my pick and choice of any feller in the county. Boys fom fu'ther away than Main Shore comes to see me, though God knows I could a had Alex Walker any day I took mysef the notion."

I leaned far over to take a look at Flo Ella. Her eyes twinkled impishly, and she continued, "I anyways deserve better treatment at yore hands than I'm gettin', Alex. Who do you think slaved fer you like a field hand on Christmas day, scrubbin' yore floor and layin' yore manolia so's you could tear round the country havin' a high old time? Who you think swep' down them cobwebs and toted out all them ashes? Fool with me much more and I'll cart all that filth back in and leave it where I found it."

At last the bantering meal was over, and we found ourselves alone. I had Alex put a fire in the stove and fill the copper-bottomed wash boiler with water for baths. Then I set to work unpacking linens and bedding and making the little bare room more homelike. Alex followed me anxiously about, and it dawned on me that I needed to set his mind to rest on a certain little matter. "I like my things, Alex. They are probably the very ones I'd have chosen if I'd been along." He relaxed visibly.

I spread my robe across the two reed rockers before the fire to screen off a dressing spot for Alex. "You get your bath while I finish setting things to rights," I said. "But first, get the hammer and put up these curtain rods. I want to hang the curtains."

"Can't that go till mornin'?" he pleaded.

"No, I can't stand the sight of this bare room, and I don't want to wake up to it like this in the morning. You can put up those fixtures while you're waiting for your bathwater to heat." I turned back to unpacking the box of bedding.

"That's a mighty pretty embroidered sheet you've got in your hands, but it's just as cold as a plain one, and you needn't think I'm going to sleep on it," Alex paused to say.

"Don't worry. I'll wrap you in wool, my precious." I laughed and reached for the blue and yellow plaid wool blanket Mama and Papa had given us for Christmas.

I put a good damask cloth on the cheap walnut table. A snowy lace-trimmed scarf on my princess dresser, then arranged my toilet articles with care. I rummaged in my trunk for a box of artificial apple blossoms and a vase and arranged a centerpiece for the table. I was dimly conscious through it all of Alex bathing: of Alex emptying his water, of Alex fixing a fresh tub for me. And then he was beside me, where I stood in rapt contemplation of my handiwork.

"I'm glad you did it," he said generously. "It makes everythin' a heap more right." The smell of clean flesh and shaving cream was pleasant. He looked so like a cherub standing there in his nightie that I threw my arms about him in sudden tenderness and kissed him rapturously.

"We're home, Alex," I said.

"Well then, how about me washin' your back for you? I don't mind waitin' up . . . ."

"Into that bed with you, and I won't be long," I said, then hurried with preparations for my bath.

I'd pinned my braids snugly to my head that morning, and wearing the wool cap all day had made my head feel itchy. After I was ready for bed, I smoothed a scented healing lotion on my skin, which felt drawn and tender. I unpinned my hair and went to the dresser for comb and brush. Alex gave a low whistle and bounded across the floor.

"Gosh, honey, let me brush it . . . will you? I always wanted to see it down. Gee, it's below your waist and thick, gosh almighty!" He took the brush and made a few careful strokes though my hair. I tried to stand it but could not.

"I hate to be so touchy, Alex, but I never could stand to have anybody fooling with my hair but Mama." He looked a little hurt, pulled one of the rockers around, and seated me on his lap.

"All right, hurry and get through with it then. I want to rock you to sleep this first night."

I was frightfully tired, though I hadn't realized it until now. When I finished my hair, I sank gratefully against him, and he began humming and rocking gently to and fro. "*Bye, o baby, bye o bye!*" he crooned.

It was lovely, sitting there at last before our own fire. It was wonderful to feel myself thus tenderly loved and cherished. Now relaxed, I gave myself over to the increasing warmth of Alex's kisses. A languor crept through me, and my body went suddenly limp, a dead weight in his arms. Alex chuckled deep in his throat, rose with me in his arms, and bore me triumphantly to bed. My surrender was complete.

Was this what Will Wilson thought had happened to me the night I hung limp in his arms, frightened out of my senses when his arms closed around me and his strong muscular lips closed over mine with frenzied insistence? Was this why he had . . . was this . . . Oh, for heaven's sake!

Chapter 6

January 17, 1913

It was Monday almost a month later that the Logan's received a card in the mail, a rare thing with them, saying that they could move Friday. Alex brought the card to them from the corner beside the school, which was as far as the mail route ran. But today, after they were all packed, a boy rode up to say two of the children in the family had come down with the measles. But since they were the only two that hadn't had the measles, the moving could get under way as soon as they recovered. With a groan, Carrie set about unpacking the things she couldn't do without.

Living in the house with the Logans, temporarily, was not so bad in itself. Carrie respected our privacy and kept the door between our rooms locked so that the little ones wouldn't annoy me. But it was proving irksome to live under the same roof with Flo Ella, because of Alex.

He seemed conscious of her from the time he came in until he left next morning. They went at the same time to fill their buckets at the pump, and Flo Ella put off her milking until Alex was ready to feed the mules so he could "mind off" the calf for her.

Both of them liked to sing. Here in the bottomlands a singing school was held winter and summer, and any grown person thought shame on themselves not to be able to read notes. We gathered often in the evenings for song fests around the Logan fireplace, always at Alex's or Flo Ella's suggestion. The rest of us usually sat and joined in the singing. But Alex and Flo Ella stood, sharing a book, and singing against each other till veins stood out on their neck and temples.

By the time the song ended, (and they never skipped a verse,) they were panting as though they'd run a mile, and often collapsed against each other for support through prolonged paroxysms of laughter.

Resentment was born in me when Alex, at the sound of the creaking pump, would drop whatever he might be doing, empty the bucket into kettle or dishpan and sail out for a fresh bucket of water. They were both out there now, after Alex had jumped up from grading his school papers. I set resolutely about my dishwashing, determined not to mind, when there was the sound of scuffling feet and smothered laughter on the front porch. The front door burst open and Alex catapulted inside, spilling half the bucket of water on the floor. Almost in the same instant the Logan front door opened and I heard Flo Ella make some laughing remark as she went on to the kitchen with her bucket.

I washed dishes with elaborate unconcern, stealing a glance at Alex as he set what was left of the bucket of water on the side table. He was breathless and animated. He hurried into the back porch for the mop and cleaned up the mess he'd made. Then he returned to the end of the dining table and the interrupted task of grading papers.

Apparently much preoccupied, he presently glanced up to say, "I forgot to tell you, Flo Ella wants to have a dance in the other side when the Logans move out. I told her she could.

"But I don't want her to," I said quickly.

"Neither do you want the whole country side down on you by breaking up one of their long established customs. Here in the bottomlands nobody has a house big enough to give a dance in. Ever' time a renter moves out, a dance is given in that house before the next tenant moves in. I told her she could have the dance. I still say she can have it."

He was busy with his papers once more and I knew that, as far as he was concerned, the incident was closed.

"Do we have to go?' I asked.

"Unless you want to impress on them that you think you're too good to mix with their like . . . yes. In any case, Im goin'."

Right that minute I didn't care what he or any of the rest thought of me, but I refrained from saying so.

January 20, 1913

That afternoon, when my first monthly cycle had rolled round, I was stricken with the usual headache and Alex was at a loss. He learned fast though not to address me unnecessarily and not to expect me to laugh at anything. I had always gone to my job, headache or no headache, and I kept up my small household duties as usual, but found no joy in them. The relief on Alex face when he came in from school and found me freshly clothed and in my right mind was funny to see.

"Gosh, that was bad, O Lady. Do you have it like that ever' month?" he asked.

"I'm sorry Alex, but I usually have two or three days of it."

He regarded me speculatively. "I wonder how it would do to take you out of your habits for a while."

"Do you mean have a baby?" I gulped.

"Sure. What's wrong with havin' a baby?" He sounded stubborn.

"Well, I just think it's too soon. Just one thing at the time, please. I'm not even used to living with you, and Ann says the first sick that goes with being pregnant is terrible. It doesn't just last three days, it lasts three months. Hers did.

Alex turned and left the room and my heart sank to my heels. His expression struck me as being that of a man with a purpose.

January 21, 1913

This afternoon I sang as I cooked supper. I ran to the window at the sound of a gruff, "Hallooooo!" and saw a ramshackle old buggy, drawn by two sweating horses wobble to a standstill at the gate. The dogs started barking and Tom Logan went out to greet the visitors, a man and what appeared to be his son. Presently all returned to the house. A few moments later the Logan kitchen door opened and somebody knocked on mine. It was Carrie and she was in something of a state. "Can you possibly feed those two men their suppers?" she implored.

"Who are they?" I asked, as though it mattered.

"If God don't know 'em no better'n I do they're a couple of lost souls," she said impatiently. "They're drivin' through and Tom asked 'em to have supper with us, could do no different, seein' as how they stopped at suppertime. But the baby's had colic all day long, what with all the runnin' in and out, and Flo Ella's warshed and scoured the kitchen and is as cross as two sticks, she's that tard."

"I'll take them," I nodded, and her face cleared at once. She thanked me, and patting the back of the snuffling little thing on her shoulder, she pushed the two older children ahead of her back into her own kitchen.

When Alex came in I told him about the visitors. "Have them come on through and wash up while I put supper on the table."

Alex outdid Pa at his best. As I went forward to greet our guests, Alex said, "Flossie, this is Dr. Haskell and his son, Adolph. My wife, gentlemen."

I stifled a giggle.

"I hope you didn't put yourself out too much for us," said the doctor, with a gallant bow, as his eye quickly appraised prospects.

"Not too much really. My husband eats a cold lunch at school every day, so I always see that he has a hot meal in the evenings."

My wife. My husband. The taste of the words was like a sweet morsel on my tongue.

Not having Mama at the helm made me a little nervous, but just as he had copied Pa, I copied Mama. Standing proudly beside my chair, I said, "Alex, you take your usual place. Dr. Haskell, you sit here on my right, Adolph, on my left."

When we were seated there was a slight pause. Alex was about to ask the doctor to say grace, but seeing that his eye was riveted on the plate of hot biscuits, he passed the biscuits instead. "Just help yourself to the croquets, Alex, and start the dish around," I said, and the meal was under way.

"Ah, hot coffee," said the doctor, and downed the scalding brew in a few loud gulps, passing the empty cup back to me. "I was badly in need of that."

When his hunger was partly appeased he began to talk. We found him highly entertaining. "I can live anywhere I'm a mind to," he said, ladling gravy over a fresh mound of creamed potatoes.

"He can live anywhere he wants because he knows so many things most folks don't bother to learn," said Adolph. This was the first word we'd heard from him. I watched, fascinated, while he wiped his greasy thick lips on the back of his hand, leaving his napkin neatly folded beside his plate.

Dr. Haskell used his napkin with quite a flourish. "And a lot of things people just don't bother to remember, even when they've learned 'em. I'm a veterinary by profession, but I prescribe for all the awdinary human ailments: biliousness, malaria, dysentery. People are always coming to me with this sickness and that. I give 'em their dosage, telling 'em exactly what it is. After a few weeks and they're back . . . same thing the matter with 'em, but they don't bother to think back about what it was I done for 'em, so I prescribe all over again and collect another fee."

"He's got a barber chair too," boasted Adolph, "uses it to cut hair or pull teeth in, whichever one a feller wants done."

"Oh yes," said the doctor grandly, "I guess I'm what you might call a jack of all trades and a master of none. But it comes in handy in my way of living. I build houses and swap hosses too, but my reason for doing all this is so I can hunt and fish. That's what's put me on the road now, looking for new fishing streams and hunting grounds. How is it around here?"

"There's some pretty good fishing in the St. Francis River, and its fair here in Big Lake. I've been hunting these bottomlands since I was knee high to a grasshopper. Turkeys and ducks and wild geese gets scarcer ever' year. Mostly squirrels, rabbits, coons and possums now, unless you got a fondness for wildcats. There's plenty of them. Oh yes, there is a crane roost over on Newton Island, thousands of them. Been their breeding grounds as far back as I can remember, and the island smells like something you wouldn't have if they'd give it to you. But the cranes are there, though I never heard of anybody shootin' one."

"Well, one thing, son: if you never ate a crane breast steak, you got a treat coming up. My wife cooks 'em to a turn. When she comes, we'll make a raid on the island and have a crane breast steak breakfast to celebrate our settling in. I think I'll buy a few acres around somewhere and build right here."

Alex flashed me a look and the doctor hastily continued, "You don't need to be afraid to have me settle in your community, son. I carry my own weight and am beholdin' to no man, livin' or dead."

There was something distinguished looking about the doctor, dirty though he was. His black suit was shabby and wrinkled, and his once white shirt collar almost gray. But he had a noble brow, a heavy shock of black hair, handsome features, and he wore a flowing black tie of finest silk.

"I don't think I like having a doctor for our first visitor," I said, after they were gone. And they had to go, seeing that neither we nor the Logans had room for them to sleep.

"You mean you think it might be a bad omen?" Alex teased. My small superstitions were always amusing to him.

"Maybe," I said shortly.

"Well, it's easy to get around that one. Just decide which of his other trades you think might bring good luck to our house, and say that our first visitor was a dentist, or a barber, or a carpenter, or a hoss trader. All of that wrapped in one hide strikes me as being a sizable asset to any swamp."

January 25, 1913

Saturday morning was cold and bleak. I had finished my work and set a Dutch oven of beans to bake on the hearth. Alex had spread a newspaper before the fire and settled down to clean and polish his shoes and boots. I was whipping lace on the white voile curtains for the tiny windows in the other room.

The huge chimney occupied the center of the dwelling and the double fireplace supplied heat to both large rooms. Ancient black andirons held the four and a half foot logs in place. Alex and Tom usually assisted each other in setting back logs in the fireplaces each morning, and this usually lasted through the day. The firebox was finished with wide shoulders that turned across the front and served as a mantel. There was a kitchen shelf on the left, and medicine shelf on the right, and the chimney proper ascended and disappeared through the roof.

"Alex, we've got to do something about that room," I said suddenly.

"What now?" he frowned.

"It's those walls. That's the gloomiest room I ever saw in my life. It's just those two tiny windows at the front, and no other light coming in. I know I can't stand it."

"You're out of your mind if you think I'm going to spend money on a rented shack that I won't live in but one year."

"I'm not out of my mind yet, but I will be if you go off every morning at daybreak and don't come back till night, leaving me shut up in this dark little hut alone," I said impatiently. "We could tack canvas on the rough walls and paper over it. If only the walls were smooth, I could paint it, but it's so rough."

Alex scowled. "I'm putting out no money and no work on this house," he said stubbornly.

But my will in this one thing was stronger than his power to combat me. Arguing hotly the pros and cons, we finally came to an agreement. Alex would get some rolls of slick blue builder's paper on his first trip to Paragould, and we would fasten it to the wall with tacks and bright tin washers.

I frowned when I saw Flo Ella pass our window and knock at the door. But when Alex rose to let her in I had to laugh. She was wearing one of Carrie's long dresses, three sizes too large. Her hair stringing down her cheeks, was topped by a rusty colored old velvet hat trimmed with three bedraggled ostrich tips. She carried a disreputable old black satchel over one arm and hobbled with a cane. She walked all humped over and spoke in a quavering voice, her lips tucked in as though she hadn't a tooth in her head.

"I come to tell you-enses fertune," she quavered.

"Mine's made." I grinned and stitched on.

Nothing daunted, she turned to Alex. He had set a chair for her and resumed work on his shoes. She ran on and on with her chatter until finally Alex gave her his palm to read. She took his open hand in hers, and with the fingers of the other hand she traced the lines in his palm, then played a quick creepy-mousey up his sleeve as she talked. Alex's face flushed and he jerked his hand away.

"Here, you give me back that hand," she said, still in the quavering voice, "thar's somethin' you need to know, young man, and I come here a purpose to tell you." Alex held out his hand again and she resumed. "Yore an ornery cuss, and jist like all ornery cusses you've already lived too long. But be warned, young mister, fer it's like the preacher's always a sayin', be shor yore sins will find you out. Yore bein' accused already. A little gal with big black eyes . . . ."

Alex leaped to his feet, overturning his chair, and suddenly they were both on the floor, locked in what was apparently deadly combat. They kicked and struggled, but Alex finally succeeded in turning her flat on her back and pinning her to the floor by sitting astride her middle and holding her arms spread eagled. Flo Ella arched her back and bucked like a bay steer in her effort to dislodge him. This added up to one too many for me. I got up and kicked Alex in the butt with all my might.

"You get up from there this minute and get out of here before I do something we'll all regret," I snarled into his startled face.

"Listen, Flossie, Flo Ella . . . ."

"The show is over," I interrupted, "You get out of here and I'll take care of Flo Ella."

He sprang to his feet, snatched his hat and jacket, and left the room. Released from his weight, Flo Ella sat up and began dazedly collecting her things for a quick getaway. I firmly insisted that she "sit down."

"You're older than I am Flo Ella, and you should know better than to carry on in such a manner with another woman's husband. It becomes more evident each day that it doesn't matter to you that Alex is married now, but being his wife, it matters a lot to me."

"Flossie, I swear to God I didn't mean no harm, honey. I knowed Alex since he were a little feller, him always comin' ta these bottoms when his Pa come a huntin' and fishin', and later to do his courtin', and . . . ."

"I'd feel the same if you'd known him since the day he was born. This sort of horseplay hits me wrong and I want it stopped. You can go now, but there's one thing you'd better remember . . . no more such games with Alex."

"Well, but honey, I want you to know that I'm plum heartsick you took it the way you did."

Flo Ella's face was so earnest and contrite that for that moment I felt myself the culprit.

I knew that enough had been said and done about it, and that I would never mention this to Alex again, so long as I lived.

February 1, 1913

Saturday morning I felt wonderful. Flo Ella had taken herself elsewhere for the weekend. In spite of the bitter cold, Alex and I had wrapped up and taken a long ramble though the woods. "Just the same, O Lady, the leaf buds are swelling," Alex pointed out to me, and my heart rejoiced. The winter would soon be over.

February 17, 1913

Monday after my chores were finished I put a fire in the stove, set a pan of sweet potatoes in to bake and put on a pot of black eyed peas. Seeing that the oven was hot, I mixed oatmeal cookies and set some in to bake.

I had no house dresses, so I had planned to first wear out the skirts, sweaters and office blouses that I had in such bountiful supply. Slim as I was, I put on a well boned long corset. I dressed as for the office and smiled to see that the calves of my legs bulged more than usual above my high laced kid boots. A gingham apron was too prosy, so I chose one of white organdy, with a lace-trimmed ruffle and wide ties.

Then I heard Pa's voice saying, "Whoa, Fanny," and ran outside to greet him. "Never saw the cold hold on so," he grumbled, as though we'd been talking for hours, "though of course we need a hard cold fer the butcherin'. Alex paid fer half a hog, so I just decided I'd fetch it on to you while it's fresh. Got to feed the starvin' heathen, you know." He was tying Fanny to the fence.

"Yes, heathen or not, we still get hungry," I nodded. "Alex was wondering if you'd butchered yet. Is there anything I can do to help?"

"Yes, you can take this deeshpan of sausage meat and head and feet, and keep out of me way and don't let it drip on you. You got no business with an apun on like that on a week-a-day no how. Now don't try to help with them boxes, they're heavy, and either get to the side or stay behind me. When I start with a load, I don't want to find you underfoot."

He set the first box in our end of the front porch. I tucked the fresh flour sack that covered the contents down tight, threw Alex's raincoat over it all, and weighted it down with heavy sticks of firewood to keep the Logan dogs from pilfering.

"Unpack that deeshpan fust off, Flossie. Last thing Annie said was fer me not to get back home without that deeshpan."

"Why didn't Ma come with you?"

"That's a silly question to ask, child, and her with a butcherin' on her hands. All that sausage to be ground and seasoned and stored, pig feet to be pickled, head cheese to be made and lard to be rendered. A fine time fer a housewife to go visitin'."

He was disgusted with me. It struck me that, of the two evils, he preferred riding into the bottoms to bring our meat to us, to helping with the necessary at this time. We'd be going to Paragould in a few days and could have brought the meat back with us.

He chuckled. "She can hardly wait till she gets things back out the way, so's she can cook her up a mess of fresh pork and cabbage and pone bread. With it she eats a passel of cucumber pickles and onions. It always makes her sick, but she does it anyhow. We had walked into the kitchen as he talked and he now began to back out. "Hey, look what I done. Left muddy tracks all over yore clean kitchen. Thought I wouldn't take me overshoes off till I'd fed and watered Fanny. What a mess . . . ."

"Don't give it a thought, Pa," I said, and hurried to the back porch for the wet string mop and ran it over the tracks.

"Well, what do you know?" he exclaimed. "That one was sure quick over with. No, I won't set till I've tended Fanny. You better fix me a bite to eat whilst I'm out."

When he came back in he hung his overshoes in the porch where the dogs couldn't reach them and went to stand at the fireplace, his back to the fire. He drew a big silver watch by its heavy gold chain from his pocket and said, "Eleven forty-five. I made putty good time, but I started early. I'll have to eat and start right back, and I'll then be till bedtime. The road is that bad."

He had been teetering back and forth on heels and toes as he talked, watching me take another sheet of cookies from the oven and spread them to cool on a fresh tea towel. "I think these have cooled enough for you to eat some, if they won't spoil your dinner," I said.

There was a ruddy glow in his cheeks, and his eyes sparkled with interest as he bent to sniff appreciatively and select a cookie.

"What's in them besides raisins?" he asked, listening with his eyes to the flavor.

"Pecans. The Logans had gathered the black walnuts and pecans before we came. That's what's in the big packing boxes in the front porch. She told me to take all I wanted, they'd be a burden to move, so on sunny days I sit out there and crack and pick them out and store them in pint jars as I empty them. They're nice to have for my baking."

"These taste fine," Pa allowed. "But I'm thinkin' 'bout all that white sugar. I insist on my womenfolks makin' ginger bread and molasses cookies fer their weekday bakin'. A woman can pitch more out the back door with a teaspoon than a man can bring in at the front with a shovel."

Was he reprimanding me in my own house, or was he just making conversation? "I have to have something extra for Alex's lunches, and for him to munch on when he comes in every evening. He's always starving."

"But these raisins, now," Pa persisted. "The pecans maybe, seein' that they didn't cost you anythin', but how 'bout the raisins?"

Surely Pa was only trying to help me in my inexperience. No offence was intended, I decided, looking at him, so I would take none. "A package of raisins costs ten cents. It'll make about four batches of cookies. To me that doesn't seem like an extravagance."

Pa helped himself to another. "Well, I expect you got mighty leetle idee yet what it takes to run a house, though you lived in one all yore life." He stooped over to watch as I began to roll out biscuit dough. "Roll yours, eh? And use a cutter. Annie makes hers out by hand and no woman can turn out better biscuits, always a plenty of crumb in hers."

This touched a sore spot. Scarcely a meal did we sit down to that Alex did not speak of his Ma's biscuits, so full of crumb, and make disparaging remarks about mine. I spoke up in my defense. "I suppose we all cook as our mothers before us. Papa once suffered a very bad stomach trouble, and the doctor said it was because he ate too much soft hot bread. He told Mama to roll the dough thin and bake the biscuits brown. That way they're hardly more than two crusts, and after a while Papa's stomach trouble cleared up."

As Pa reached for his fourth biscuit he asked, "Does Alex like 'em so?"

"He fusses some," I admitted, "but I think they're better for him, and he'll get used to them in time."

Pa listened with his eyes as he ate: the fresh white tablecloth, the bouquet of artificial flowers, the lace-trimmed curtains, the sparkling green glassware. "You'll learn to go a leetle mite slow on white tablecloths fer everday, surely. A waste of soap to keep 'em fresh, besides makin' a shorter life fer the cloth. What you need is to get you some oil cloth. It can be wiped right off with a damp cloth and save all the bother of keeping clean changes."

This was a chance I'd been waiting for and I laughed. "You have just caught yourself in your own trap Pa. I insisted on the linoleum for the kitchen floor for the same reason you're urging the oil cloth on me. It needs only a going over with a damp mop to make it look as fresh as new. Saves soap, or sand, and water, and time, and labor, and looks better. Besides, I don't have to leave the door open on a cold day till the room dries out, taking twice as much wood to warm things up again."

Pa glared at me for a moment, then reached for another cookie and finished it and his dish of peaches in high good humor, pushing his chair back. At last he said, "Well, I don't know, Flossie. I truly don't know. You and the boy may make it together, and I hope you do, but you sure been raised different. You been raised not to do without anythin' you can get the money to buy. He's been raised not to buy anythin' he can do without. Where you'll find common ground to stand on is beyond me."

I wondered what Pa would say when he found out about the rolls of builder's paper to be tacked up and left in a house we would occupy for so short a time. "Our love for each other is the plot of 'common ground' we stand on, Pa," I said quietly.

"Well, I've knowed that little plot to become a battle ground, once the couple come down to earth and really started livin'," he snorted.

I followed him to the buggy when he started to leave. "Well, bless my soul, I was about to take Alex's little trunk back home with me. Bought that fer him when he was six," he chuckled. "Annie mended up all his old underwear and oddments of work clothes. She said he'd need 'em fer changes when he starts makin' a crop." He carried the trunk inside for me.

After I had finished the dishes I went to sort the clothing in the little trunk and put it away. In the tray was a jumble of old letters, among them the ones I'd written him years ago, these tied with a soiled piece of pink ribbon. The ones Alex had written me were long since dust.

I picked up a fat letter at random, drew it from the envelope and looked at the signature. Yours anytime, Mag, I read, and winced. I folded it quickly and stuffed it back. I picked up one with a different handwriting and looked for the signature. Yours forever and beyond, Minnie. Who, for pity's sake, was Minnie? I peeked into another. It was signed, Don't keep me waiting too long, Susie.

In our family, one iron clad rule was observed. Nobody read another's mail except by invitation. Well, I hadn't read these letters and of course I wouldn't read any of them. Not for anything in this world, I thought, idly picking up another in Mag's bold handwriting. I squirmed miserably and my hands shook with the shame of it, but I took those pages out and read them.

My eyes all but popped from my head. This was not a letter, really, but a ribald filthy poem. I was fascinated, even while a faint nausea grew in me. I'd never read a thing of this nature before and some of the lines etched themselves in my mind, there to remain to the end of my life. I put it back in its envelope and tossed it in with the rest. Let Alex unpack his own trunk, doing whatever he liked with such as this. But, I added to the things I'd like to know one more question: Why had Ma sent all those letters out, knowing I would be left alone with them long before Alex came home? Did she hope that I would read them, as I'd read the one, to my sorrow, and start a big fight with him the minute he got in? Well? Mag Hawley had separated us once. Should I let her come between us again? I hastily labeled a corner of my mind, *The Things We Don't Talk About*, and tossed Mag in. I took up the copy of St. Elmo that Mama had sent me to while away an idle hour, and sat down to read.

After supper I told Alex about the trunk. Keeping very busy I watched him furtively as he opened it. He was squatting on his heels, whistling, when he raised the lid. The whistle died out and a thoughtful look came over his face. He picked up the packet of letters tied with the soiled pink ribbon and tossed them into his dresser drawer, then lifted the tray and dumped the remaining contents into the flames.

"Why didn't you cut up that box of fat and get the lard on to cook, Flossie? And get the head and feet on to cook? It's turning a little warmer and that stuff ought not to set too long."

Panic rose in me. I knew nothing about rendering lard and pickling pig feet and making head cheese. But I had no intention of Alex finding this out . . . if I could help it.

"I decided to wait until morning," I said easily. "I spent quite a lot of time with Pa, and made cookies and cooked a full meal in the middle of the day."

"I salted everything down and stored it in the smokehouse, except what you're to take care of. But be sure to get at it first thing in the mornin'." He stood looking at me a long moment, then added, "You look a little funny to me. Feel all right."

"I'm all right," I said firmly.

"Time for your headache?"

"I'm due for it, but I don't have a headache," I said shortly, and added, "I didn't want a baby the first thing, Alex."

"Now don't start frettin'. You may not have one started. But if you do, I want to hear no bellyachin'. You knew that could happen anytime, didn't you? Well, see it through like a man," he said stoutly.

A long peal of hysterical laughter burst from me.

"What's funny?" Alex said to me suspiciously.

"I was just thinking how bravely a man could carry a baby through a long pregnancy," I said.

Alex had the grace to look sheepish. "You know good and well what I meant," he said.

February 18, 1913

When I started to get up Tuesday morning a wave of nausea took me and I fell back on my pillow. It crept up from the soles of my feet, turned every muscle to water, gathered in a sickening slime in the pit of my stomach and washed up into my mouth. I heaved and swallowed. I gasped and lay limp. I was completely undone.

Alex had made the fires and gone out to feed. "No bellyachin'," he had said. Pride rose strongly in me and I forced myself to get up and dress. I washed my face and wrists in cold water and felt somewhat revived. The mirror had never shown me a face more wan, even with a headache, and I hastily applied a bit of rouge and powder.

Halfway through breakfast, Alex noticed I wasn't eating and spoke of it. I told him I wasn't hungry.

"Drink your coffee then," he said.

I couldn't bear the thought of coffee. "I'll finish packing your lunch first," I said, and left the table. When I handed him his lunch he looked at his watch, sprang up for his coat and hat, and ran out to jump on the saddled mule he had left hitched to the front gate. For the first time since we married, Alex had forgotten to kiss me goodbye.

I bundled myself against the cold and walked to Newsom's for milk and eggs. "Alex's father brought us half a hog yesterday," I said chattily when I paid her. "I want to render my lard today. How do you render your lard?" I asked.

"As others render theirs, I reckon." The old lady looked over her spectacles at me in puzzled surprise.

I might as well be honest with her. "Please, Mrs. Newsom, I never rendered any lard in my life, and I don't want Alex to find out." I laughed nervously.

"Ohhh," she nodded wisely. "Well, it's simple 'nough. Cut the fat in strips, then in short pieces. Pile it into a pot and start a far under it."

"I'll have to cook mine in a preserving kettle inside," I said.

"Good as any . . . if the pot's big 'nough to hold it. Better add half a cup of water to start it off and keep it from stickin'. The water'll 'vaporate . . . as it cooks."

When I reached home I soon had the lard on and started searching through my cook books for a recipe for pickled pigs feet and making head cheese. I could find neither and knocked on Carrie's door resolutely. "Do you have a good cook book?" I asked.

"The world's best," she said with pride. From an old trunk she took a book and unwrapped it from an old tablecloth. It was a fine thick white book, lettered in gold. There was no indication that it had ever been used. I thanked her and took it to my room.

I sat down with pen and paper and copied many of the recipes. When I returned it, I said casually, "I found some grand recipes, but not what I was looking for. How do you get a hog's head ready to cook? You know, the eyes and ears and snout . . . and the feet. How do you cook those?"

Carrie looked at me appraisingly. "Get plenty of warm water ready, honey, I'll be in and show you directly."

When she came in she brought her own sharp knives with her.

"Well, here's how it's done," she said. She grasped the head firmly by an ear and with one clean swipe severed it from the head. She quickly reamed the dirt from the inner ear, then with much turning and scraping and washing, held up the member with every blemish removed. "Now the eye," she said, and slipped a finger inside the shrunken lid and, with the sharp point, ran around inside the socket and lifted ball and lid out.

"All right," I said through tight lips. "I'll try it now." I tried valiantly to do as Carrie had done and managed to finish the other ear. But when I started gouging my way into the eye socket, I retched, all went black, and I sank senseless to the floor.

When I came to I was on the bed. Carrie turned and sent Flo Ella back to the other room with the children, then told me to lie still. "I'm steeping you a cup of tea. I'm also taking this mess to my own kitchen to finish. You drink your tea and take a little nap and you'll feel better. We'll let the fire die out under the lard till you wake."

"Oh Carrie, you're so good to me, but please don't tell Alex," I begged.

"I'll never tell him, Flossie, and I'll beat Flo Ella black and blue if she dares open her trap about it."

"If I knew the Walkers wouldn't find out about it, I'd take that old hog's head out in the field and bury it so deep nobody could ever find it," I sobbed.

The nap helped, and when Alex came home the pigs feet were pickled, the head cheese was made, the lard was rendered and the kitchen in order.

If anybody ever told him of that bad day, I never heard of it.

February 21, 1913

Logans were moving at last. During the morning I went down the road to see Mrs. Colby. I found her peacefully dipping snuff before the fire.

"Do you know where I can find somebody to wash for me?" I asked. Her eyes flickered and her face stiffened. She spat deliberately into the fire, then turned and looked me up and down.

"Be ye sick?" she asked.

"No. That is . . . not really. But, it being so crowded, I've just washed out the things we had to have and a big wash has stacked up. I thought if I could find somebody to help me this once, I could manage from here on out."

"Well, if'n yore not sick, yore no better ta warsh yore own filth then the rest of us. Was you sick, I'd warsh you up and there'd be no churge, that being as one neighbor to another, but I fearsomely misdoubt you bein' able to find anybody ta warsh yore dirt fer you . . . long as yore well."

I thought things over on my way home and decided to put in the rest of the day cooking something ahead. I'd get Alex to go to the little store down by the bridge and buy me some tubs and a wash board. I'd never managed a big washing alone, but I'd often helped.

"No use to touch that other room yet. I'll be back fer the dance," Flo Ella had shouted, as she kept a precarious balance on the last load.

Having nothing to divert my attention, I attempted a cake. It turned out rather well, so I baked a pie. I baked half a shoulder and an oven full of sweet potatoes and a big pot of beans.

I was looking for Alex any minute when a man rode up to the gate and yelled, "Hello the house!"

When I went to the door he touched his hat and said, "My name's Carter, ma'am. I'm buying up cattle. Do you have any to sell?"

"No, we haven't."

"Is the man of the house at home?" Suddenly I took fright. Not only was Alex not at home, the Logans were not here either, and it was growing late. Just then I heard Alex yodeling and laughed in my relief.

"He's on his way," I said. "Won't you get down?"

"I'll just wait, thanks," he said. I returned to the kitchen.

Alex invited Carter in and as we sat round the table talking, I heard a wagon pause out front and then drive on. The sound of hurrying feet announced Flo Ella's return for the party. I could hear her making a fire in the other room and saw Alex grow restive and inattentive. Presently he asked Carter to excuse him while he filled the wife's water bucket. He emptied the bucket into the kettle and dish pan and sallied forth.

I talked on for a moment, then on an impulse, stepped over and opened the door to the other room. Alex stood in the middle of the vacant room, bent double in silent laughter. Flo Ella was standing in the open door of the lean-to hooking her corset on over her long underwear, her skinny body contorted by a variation of comical convulsions. She didn't mind Alex seeing her thus, was doing all in her power to make it worth his while, but the moment she saw me she dodged out of sight. Alex reached the front door without even moving, apparently, and closed it firmly behind him.

"I think the revelers are beginning to arrive," Alex said to Mr. Carter as he returned.

"Yes, the fun will soon start," I said, politely covering my strange behavior. "If you'll sit here by the fire, I'll clear the table and set things to rights while we're waiting."

Less than an hour later thirty or forty people were in the other room. The string band was getting tuned up, and a set for square dancing was in the making.

It was at this point that Alex and I entered the room. A big hulking man in high laced boots, blue denims and a red plaid shirt came straight for me. "Have this dance with me, Miz Walker?" he asked politely.

Alex thrust his chest out like a bantam rooster and said, "No, Craven, she's not dancing!"

I'd never had anything anger me so. I placed my hand on the stranger's arm as if Alex didn't exist and said, "I was just hoping someone would ask me. I'll be a lot of bother to you because I've never been through the figures, but this seems a good time to learn."

As my partner hustled me to my place, I stole a glance at Alex. He stepped into our room for a chair, leaned it against the wall and sat in it, his eyes closed. I felt wildly exhilarated at the evidence of his discomfiture . . . enough bad moments he had given me!

Young Craven, obviously quite set up by his conquest, seized my hand in his huge paw and prepared for action, as two fiddlers accompanied by a guitar, swung into the stirring strains of "The Irish Washerwoman." I had a fleeting glimpse of Old Man Stone leaning nonchalantly against the doorway as he shifted his cud of tobacco to the other jaw and sang out:

"Honor your partner, lady on the left, all join hands and circle left!"

A wiry lad of about fifteen was beating a steady tattoo on the fiddle strings with a pair of knitting needles. The dance was now under way and still more people crowding in.

"First couple lead right, four hands across."

The music warmed up, the calls came through and the stamping feet beat a steady rhythm, which was presently punctuated by joyful yelps when the tempo increased.

I was snatched up and tossed from one pair of strong rough hands to another in right succession. Through the mad frenzy of that dance, my feet seemed never quite to touch the floor. Dust began to rise from the floor in a stifling fog, augmented by clouds of smoke from the rancid pipes of bystanders, and the steam from countless streams of amber juice being loosed on the fire. I caught the stinging smell of raw whisky as a man I'd never seen before breathed heavily upon me, but the next moment a high-stepping young giant had caught me on the rebound, jiggled me madly, and then flung me to the next man around. The world spun round at a terrific rate, and I began to feel that I could not long survive without a breath of fresh air. I blamed Alex for letting me in for this and hated him with a passion at that moment.

"Lady on your left and circle right and a do-ci-do!" yelled that hateful old man, and I was seized by a monster on my right that saw to it that I did a do-ci-do with speed and dispatch.

"All break hands and commence home!"

"Thank you, dear God!" I breathed under my breath.

Craven bowed awkwardly before me and thanked me for the dance. It had ended only just in time, for Craven appeared to swing like a pendulum in midair as I tried to smile at him.

I was near my own door and I ducked through it and out to the back porch just in the nick of time. I had never been so wholeheartedly and enthusiastically sick in my life. Alex was beside me instantly, one arm encircling my waist, the other holding my throbbing head while I let go everything that was in me.

Much chastened, I permitted myself to be led to my bed. Alex drew our blinds, closed and locked our doors. He took my washcloth from the little line behind the stove, fixed a basin of water, and bathed my face and hands. He brought the slop jar, a glass of water, my toothbrush and paste. When I had finished he removed the things, then methodically undressed me and slipped my nightgown over my head.

Not a word had been spoken. Tears of shame and gratitude seeped from beneath my lowered lids. When Alex removed my stockings he pressed his lips for an instant against my instep . . . this, his apology. I laid a hand tenderly on his bowed head in acknowledgement of the sorry part I'd played in the mess.

When he lay down beside me, he leaned on an elbow and kissed a muted circle round my face, at last letting his lips rest pleadingly on mine. My full surrender was in my response, and the matter was never mentioned again between us.

We heard later that liquor flowed free at Flo Ella's dance and there were altercations, but no casualties. But we slept like babes in each other's arms. We knew nor cared when the frolic ended.

Chapter 7

February 26, 1913

The weather had moderated considerably, and my first wash day dawned clear and bright. Alex had worked all evening after school the day before getting things ready for me. He built a bench, stretched the line from the big cottonwood tree to the corner of the smokehouse. He even filled the tubs for me. He looked the situation over with complacency. "I put four nails in top of the green sapling I cut for your clothes prop and bent them over the line, so I know it won't be slipping on you. There's nothing to stop you now, and I'll be glad to have some clean shirts for a change."

There hadn't been a day Alex hadn't had a fresh shirt. I flared, "Since when have you had to go to school in a dirty shirt? Answer me that, Alexander Walker?"

"One at the time . . . nothin' to choose from . . . one clean shirt. I'm used to havin' my drawer full of 'em, and more hangin' in my wardrobe, not just one at the time, washed out, and wear that or nothin'."

With nothing to hinder, I knew I'd be finished by noon. I went blithely to work, even sparing enough breath for an occasional burst of song. But the sheets were like circus tents in my unaccustomed hands. Alex slept inside the double wool blanket. I couldn't stand it next to me and folded two sheets, one to lie on and one to cover me, and spread them on my side of the bed inside the blanket. I had put the last clean pair on the bed that morning when I changed it, and had six dirty pairs to battle with this morning. When at last they were on the line I stood frowning discontentedly at them. Puddles were forming on the ground beneath them. I sighed and returned to the tubs.

At twelve I stopped for lunch, the dirtiest of the washing yet to be done. To keep from dissolving in a welter of tears, I took up a seed catalog and sat down to make out a list of flower seeds to order along with the garden seed. In a perverse mood I decided to list everything I saw that I wanted and present the list to Alex without blinking an eye. The list totaled more than eight dollars and the little game left me feeling refreshed. I tackled the washing with renewed zeal.

In the sun and wind the sheets had somehow gotten dry, so I took them down and started hanging the other white things. Halfway through the first dish pan of white things I came across the white crepe kimono with the big purple chrysanthemums. Not only had the purple flowers faded into the snowy background of the garment itself, but into Alex's best white shirt beneath it, and my tucked white linen blouse above it. Why hadn't I soaked that thing in a salt solution, as Mama always did to set the color, and then washed it by hand the first time? I was too tired now to care about anything. Maybe the sun would draw the faded streaks out. I hung the things up, all of them dripping dismally. At last the colored things were finished and I strung them along the back fence, having run out of line.

I sat limply on the back steps with a sigh of relief. But before the sigh was completed I saw the knot around the big oak begin to slip. I sat in wide eyed horror while the line sagged, then whipped loose with a loud swish, carrying its dripping burden down along the ground.

"Oh merciful God!" I wailed. I rose and threw myself prone on the back porch and gave way to the flood of tears that had been threatening me for hours. I wept until I couldn't squeeze out another drop.

Then I heard Alex coming and ran to meet him. "The line came down," I shouted. "You didn't have it tied right. It slipped and dragged all my white clothes through the dirt while they were still wet."

"You had too many clothes pinned to it then," he glared at me.

"I thought you were supposed to pin wet clothes to a line. I thought that was what a line was for." I glared back at him.

"Besides, there's no sense in any two people having any such stack of wash as I saw piled up there this morning."

"With nothing but little things washed out by hand for weeks? You don't even know what you're talking about. You're trying to blame me with the line slipping, but I want you to know that I know that if it had been put up there right I could have hung featherbeds and quilts and pillows from end to end of it, as I've seen Mama do all my life, and it wouldn't have slipped its moorings. It is everything that I washed and will have to be boiled and washed and . . . oh my gosh . . . my kimono!"

I hurried to the back yard, snatched Alex's white shirt and my white blouse from the line and took them in to boil as I cooked supper. I didn't want Alex to see that mess, not with him acting the way he was.

"Get back out here and unpin these danged things if you want me to fix your line," yelled Alex.

I unpinned them in a wild rage. Alex didn't even care that I had all that work to do over! "While you're at it you can just empty the tubs and fill them with clean water. I've got to wash in the morning," I snorted.

If only I could have had a hot bath and crept into my clean bed.

But Alex had to have a hot meal, and I had to make something for the next day's lunch. Feeling very like a martyr, I put a good supper on the table. Then I couldn't eat any of it. As Alex reached for his seventh biscuit he growled, "Why won't you make your biscuits out by hand as Ma does and bake 'em with plenty of crumb in 'em?"

A cold fury swept through me but I kept my voice cool as I said, "Let me have the plate and I'll take up some hot ones," and I gathered the last one onto the plate and carried them out the back door and emptied them into the swill pail.

"Hey, what do you think you're doin' with them biscuits?" yelled Alex.

"I stirred them in with the slops, something I should have done long ago. You'll whistle a different tune lad, before I bake you another. After the day I've had I only wanted a bath and my bed, but I put a fire in the stove and cooked the best meal I could for you and your thanks is to sit and growl about the biscuits . . . ."

"I only said . . . ."

"What you've said practically every meal I've cooked for you and now I'm telling you that if you'd wanted Ma to cook for you all your life why didn't you stay with her and leave me in Campbell! Besides . . . ."

"Flossie!" He called out to me like I'd been in the next county, "for God's sake hush. Why do you keep on and on . . . ?"

"Why do you keep on and on? Who started this fight anyhow?" I asked the ceiling and shrieked with derisive laughter. Then I went for him. "While I wash the dishes you take that boiler of water and scrub that floor in yonder." Saying that to him lifted my spirits for the moment.

Alex wiped his moist red lips with his napkin and blinked at me. "You mean you expect me to go in there and scrub that filthy floor?" he gasped.

"You'd never give it a thought if I went ahead and did it. What's wrong with it as a job for you?"

"I told you before we married that I'd do no housework. You might as well know now as later that I mean for that one to stick." He set his jaw stubbornly and drew his lips to a thin line.

"A lot of things that we both meant to stick will likely slip a notch before this thing is over with. The clothesline did, and I don't doubt but that you meant it to stick too. Besides, who told Flo Ella she could have the dance, and that without consulting me in the matter. Well, they carried through on their 'old established custom' and that room and the fireplace both are spattered with dried tobacco and snuff spit and vomit, and you are the fine strong young fellow that's going to scrub it up . . . my back hurts."

Without another word Alex tossed his napkin on the table and took off his sweater and hung it up. He rolled up the sleeves of his shirt and undershirt, every move deliberate, and got his gum waders and buckled them on. He took the water bucket, the extra lamp, and left the room in great dignity.

"Put me on some bathwater before you get started in there," I called after him, and then I was surprised when he did.

My anger had given me a spurt of energy that permitted me to finish my tasks in record time. I could hear Alex scrubbing and muttering in the other room and knew that he was emptying one of my washtubs to finish the hated job. By the time I was ready for my bath I was limp with fatigue. I filled the foot tub with hot water and sank into one of the rockers for a quick sponge. Halfway through I sat staring mournfully into the fire, all the fight gone. Alex came in from the other room and stood beside me. I passed the wash cloth to him. "Will you dip this cloth in hot water and rub my back with it?"

"Gosh, O Lady, you look thin as a razor tonight," he said, rubbing my back gently.

"Morning sickness," I mumbled against my knees. "I lose my breakfast every morning of the world. I might as well not eat."

He picked up the hand next to him and examined it. "You must not know how to wash," he said. "I've seen a lot of women at their washing in my time, but I never saw them with their knuckles blistered like this. Don't they hurt?"

Because of his kindly tone the hot tears formed and seeped from beneath my lids. Dear Alex. He wasn't mad at me because of the hateful things I'd said. And he was sorry about the blisters.

The next morning as I stood making out biscuits by hand, Alex paused beside me. "Go ahead and roll and cut the biscuits, O Lady, you're the cook. Besides, I honestly like them better so. Don't know why I pestered you like I did about them."

"I don't know why I held out against you as I did. As long as you're the one I'm cooking for, I'd as soon make the biscuits as you like them." But I rolled and baked a few for myself. Alex ate the thin ones first. Alex. How was I ever to get used to Alex's funny little ways?

March 7, 1913

The next time Alex got paid we went to town. We had decided to buy another bed and other things we'd forgotten in spite of all the lists I'd made. We'd buy a three quarter size springs and mattress and Alex could make a wooden frame and slats. I wanted green and white plaid gingham to make a flounced cover for it, and I could use the pretty embroidered sofa pillows on it. This would serve as a bed when we had company, as a couch in the corner of the kitchen for daytime lounging, leaving our bedroom fresh and dainty.

We started right after school on Friday evening. It was midnight when we neared Englewood. At the sight of a light in Ann's bedroom window I begged Alex to stop. "I just know the baby's here," I said.

It was. Ma sat before the open fire, the little one across her lap, stretching its bare pink toes to the open fire. Onnie, wearing an outing flannel nightshirt, sprang from his bed and struck a pose. "Ladies and Gentlemen," he announced. "We have with us tonight, Mr. Lester Emerson Walker, now two days old. At birth he tipped the scales at twelve and one half pounds. Is there any one present that wants to question this?"

"Gosh dang, watch 'im strut!" scoffed Alex. "You'd think he born it by his lone self. Didn't you have anythin' at all to do with this Ann?" he turned toward the bed.

Alex hadn't even greeted his mother, though he hadn't seen her for two months. I stepped over and kissed her forehead. "How are you, Granma?" I asked.

Her eyes danced. "Just an old Granma now, sittin' by the fire and nussin' young'ns . . . don't I look like a Granma?"

At thirty-six Ma looked no more than twenty-five. It would not have seemed strange to find her lying in bed with one of her own. I told her so, and she shook her soft ringlets in pleased agreement.

"How was it?" I asked Ann, leaning above her. She turned her head wearily on her pillow. "It's too soon for any of it to be funny to me yet," she whispered.

March 8, 1913

At breakfast next morning Pa was all smiles. "A mighty fine boy," he said complacently, "and named fer two mighty fine illustrious gentlemen."

But his good humor didn't last when he found we were going on to Paragould. A misty rain was fast turning to sleet. "You should a went whilst the weather felt good," said Pa.

"Well, seeing that we didn't, we're going on, now that we've started," said Alex.

"Money's burnin' a hole in yore pocket, no doubt. Besides, yore team don't matter none."

Much as I had looked forward to choosing a few things for myself, Alex had to do the shopping alone. I was exhausted when I got to Mama's and lay on the couch in the dining room, while Lola told me that Grace and Claude Bonifield had bought the house on the corner and were expecting a baby.

"We've been having the most fun," said Lola. "Grace is using the satin and net of her old evening gowns to make the prettiest bassinet I ever saw in my life and she bought a whole bolt of nainsook, and we're making the tiniest little clothes, you can't believe."

"I saved all my papers and magazines for you to take back with you," said Mama. "I think Papa has a book he wants you to read."

Papa and I had our little talk while Mama and Lola were preparing supper. He said that Mr. Herget had been plenty mad about the strike, and had been resentful ever since it was settled. The blame had come to rest on Papa. Perhaps because he'd been chairman of the committee that waited on Mr. Herget, even though all that was done had been decided on in open meeting.

"Funny thing," Papa lowered his voice, with a hasty glance toward the kitchen, "but it seems there must always be a scapegoat, and it looks like I'm elected." He shook his head, "I'd get in there and battle through it with Mr. Herget, but this is no time to be losing my job . . . which is probably all it would come to.

March 14, 1913

For a week I could hardly take time to eat. Alex was caught up in the wave of enthusiasm that enveloped me. Two bluebirds building a nest in the first blush of spring couldn't have been happier or busier. When at last the paper was up and the matting down, I had Alex nail some blocks of wood beside the window facings on which to place the curtain rods. I made narrow valances and let the curtains come barely inside the facings, giving as much light as possible and an appearance of width. It helped a lot. I had enough of the checked gingham left from the couch cover to make side drapes for the windows in the other room, and when it was all finished as I'd planned, I began to feel at home at last.

Friday was the first evening at home, when all was done as planned. I prepared everything for Alex to arrive home. I filled the new reading lamp with oil and set it on the small center table between the two big rockers before the fireplace. I placed the magazines and books that Mama had given me, which we hadn't had time to read, on the lower shelf, and made a plate of fudge as a surprise.

We had just settled cozily down when a wagon pulled to a stop. There was a loud "Hallooo, the house!" Alex got up and opened the door and Granpap came stumbling onto the porch, almost tripping himself on trailing quilts and blankets.

"Wanted to come a visitin' son," he grunted," seein' you got a extry bed now, but dinged if I wanted ta take a chance on freezin' plum ta death, so I brung me plenty of kivers."

For a joke I put a hot water bottle in Granpap's bed. He raged about it considerably, but he let it stay there. "I got right chilled on the way out, in spite of me kiver," he said. "I've got two featherbeds there at Annie's and I want you and Alex to have one of 'em. He was raised on feathers and he'll be missin' 'em. Annie keeps harpin' that you didn't even bring a featherbed to the family, Flossie. Yore more than welcome ta one of mine."

I didn't even want a featherbed to battle with as I'd seen other women do, and to lug in and out for sunning and airing. But I refrained from saying so.

March 21, 1913

To my surprise I found it very pleasant having Granpap in the house with us. I felt that he liked me. He praised the meals when I put them on the table and ate with evident enjoyment. He protested mightily when I fussed over his comfort, but he was glad of every little attention I showered on him. I could hear him boasting to Alex later.

At breakfast one morning Alex told me that Mama had sent the medicine like the doctor had given Grace for morning sickness, but he had forgotten to bring it home. I decided to go to school with him and get it. For no reason at all I put on my wedding suit. Time was going by and it would go out of fashion without having been worn.

Waiting for me to dress threw Alex late. He unsaddled the mule and said, "We can make it on time if we take a brisk walk. It's only a mile and a half, straight shot, through the woods. You can come back around by the road."

"No, I want to walk back through the woods. I love to walk in the woods, Alex."

"But you might get lost by yourself."

"Ridiculous. A straight shot through the woods and get lost?"

Then I found my first violet and that worried look on Alex's face grew. "You're not payin' any attention to which way you're goin'. Why don't you pick you out some landmarks or somethin' if you're determined to come back through here alone?"

"Will you stop worrying about me and let me enjoy this walk?" I was getting impatient. Alex said no more, but he took some papers from his pocket and began to tear them to bits and drop them along the way. Then tore strips from his handkerchief and tied them to twigs from time to time and finally reached for my handkerchief. I wouldn't let him have it.

When it was time to begin school, I stood back and watched the children marching in, each with a smiling greeting for Alex. He had tried to get me to go around by the road to the last. Even as he waved goodbye he jerked a thumb toward the road and I shook my head and ran laughing into the woods. Not for anything would I miss that woodland ramble without Alex to hurry me. Taking my own good time I should be home by nine thirty.

Shoulders back and chin up, I strode along. Granpap said he was going to start clearing the garden for the plow this morning. I'd get him to dig some flower beds for me too. Life in me always responded to the weather and this was a gay and somewhat boisterous day. Spring was surely the season to be joyous. I thought about the little being coming into life within me, though there was nothing to remind me of this as yet but the morning sickness. Dear God, let the little body be perfect, and bless it with a zest for living. I felt resolute and strong with purpose this morning, blissful and brave in my approaching motherhood.

Redbuds were out. Dogwood buds were swelling. I broke a twig and found that it was sassafras. Mama used to buy sassafras roots from an old man who brought them around in little bundles in the spring. We drank that as a blood purifier and the smell of it brought back the flavor to me. Suddenly I wanted a cup of hot sassafras tea more than anything. I got down on my knees and started digging with a stick for the roots. I must have worked for twenty minutes before I broke loose a piece and rose in triumph.

A little farther along I came upon a huge blackgum tree. The snuff sticks commonly used in these parts were taken from the blackgum tree. Carrie told me a smooth twig was cut in lengths and peeled, then one end of the little stick could be chewed into a soft mop for dipping up the snuff. I chose a nice smooth twig. Why wouldn't it make a nice brush for cleaning teeth? I had a notion to try it.

I didn't feel rushed about getting home. Granpap would be busy in the garden, and I was sure to get back in time to fix his lunch. Then everything suddenly looked strange to me. Woods . . . everywhere . . . nothing but woods! And I was beginning to feel hot, and tired. Besides, I didn't remember all these briars as we came through. Why in the world had I worn my new suit? There were some pulled threads at the hem already. I took off my coat and laid it beside me, the medicine in the pocket. I unwrapped the paper Mama had mailed and sat reading the news, the warm rays of the sun falling across my shoulders.

When I started out again I looked for those silly little markers Alex had tied and dropped along the way. Not a marker did I see. Oh well, just a straight shot through the woods, he had said. So I faced straight toward where I knew home to be and started walking. No use getting in a panic, just keep walking. I was bound to come out somewhere. No woods ran on forever.

For hours I walked, keeping an eye out for markers. Now and then I rested, but not for long. It was while resting that the feeling of panic threatened me—better to keep moving. Alex had insisted that I wear my gum waders because of the cold damp ground. They were getting heavy and weighted me down like gunboats.

My throat hurt from breathing through my mouth. I was weak too, not having eaten any breakfast, to save myself the trouble of losing it. There was no noise except what I made myself, the sighing of the wind and the call of birds. I jumped and screamed when a huge owl, disturbed when I caught at a limb near where he sat, made a quick swoop past me and settled almost without sound on a more distant limb.

The sun was now directly overhead. Maybe I was going in a circle, as I'd heard people did when they got lost, and would presently end up back at the schoolhouse. I had been sloshing through occasional puddles of water. But suddenly I was in almost to my wader tops and could see no ground around me where water was not. How had that happened? I decided I had veered too much to the right all the way, turned left and began walking as rapidly as my failing strength would permit. The moments of terror passed when the water again became puddles and I found my way back to higher ground.

Safe out of the dismal swamp at last, I stopped to listen. I could hear a faint sound all right, as of someone chopping wood. I was perhaps an hour, drawing nearer, and then losing the sound, retracing my steps, hoping and fearing, before at last I came to the edge of a clearing, in the midst of which perched a small unpainted cabin. Between the house and the swamp great trees had been felled and the limbs trimmed and piled. The logs would be hauled to the mill as soon as wagons could be brought in over the boggy roads. A young man was chopping wood by the little house, the sound of the blow reaching me each time the axe was in midair. All those logs! How was I ever to find my way over or through them to the house?

Taking the boy as my objective, I started clambering over trees. He spied me at last and, axe suspended, stood looking at me, mouth gaping. When I came near enough for him to hear, I asked if I might have a drink of water. Speechless at the sight of me coming in out of the swamp like an apparition, he nodded. Finally he turned and yelled, "Ma!" and wheeled and split a huge block of wood with a single blow.

I struggled to open the gate, held shut by heavy weights strung on a chain. I got it opened, but the heavy weights wrenched it from my hands and it came back with cruel force against my heels. A little old woman came hurrying through the house. I had stumbled to a seat on the front doorstep.

"May I have a drink of water and rest a little while?" I asked, unbuckling the heavy waders.

She stood looking suspiciously at me, and then said, "Come inside, then. I reckon I can't refuse a body a drink a water."

As she turned back to the kitchen, I fell exhausted across the bed. I was almost too far gone to raise my head for the water when she brought it, but was somewhat revived when the glass was empty.

"If yer that tuckered, put yer feet on this paper and yer head on that piller!" That strange little woman spread a newspaper for my feet and pulled up a split bottomed chair and sat in it, hanging her heels on one of the rungs. She ran her hand into the pocket of her voluminous skirt and drew out a snuffbox and stick. Chewing the mop end to the desired softness, she dipped it full of the strong brown snuff and popped it into her toothless jaws.

"Think I don't know who ye air, don't ye?" she asked, squinting wickedly at me.

"I don't know whether you know me or not. I'm Alexander Walker's wife. He's the new school teacher. I don't remember seeing you before."

"Ye never saw me, missy. I was hid 'hind them bushes. I hid when I heard hosses on the road, and I saw ye and yer fine young feller drive by in a livery rig fom town . . . ."

"Oh no . . . you're mistaken. I've been having morning sickness and went through the woods to school with him this morning to get some medicine my mother sent me. I got lost in the woods and . . . ."

"A likely tale, missy. But if'n it's true, whar's yer medersin," she ended triumphantly.

I turned sicker than ever. Not only did I not have my medicine. Somewhere in that dismal swamp, I had left the coat to my wedding suit and I knew that I would never see it again.

"Guilty look on yer face is answer 'nough. Yer caught in yer own trap. Why don't ye jist shell down the corn and say that yer young feller got tard of takin' yer sass. Ye was blessin' 'im out good fashion when ye passed me, and he dumped ye in the swarmp, and rode back without ye. Ye been wanderin' all night in the swarmp. Anybody can jist look at ye and seed that."

"It was cool this morning when we started out, and I put on my coat. I've lost it somewhere."

"Tell on, sister. Tie yersef up in knots. But I ain't believin' a word of it." Her lower jaw shot forward and her venomous little eyes darted over me like flames.

I had to get out of there. I rose weakly and fell back, her watching me avidly. Finally I struggled to a sitting position, steadied myself and said, "I'd better be going." But when I stood, I felt like I'd been stretched on a torture rack.

"I gest maybe ye had," she said sarcastically. "Thar's nothin' heer fer sich as ye, ye can mark that down."

I buckled on my waders. The pink silk scarf hung in tatters when I tied it round my straggling hair. As I was leaving, the chopping ceased and I knew the boy was watching me, axe suspended.

"Wait thar," shrilled the old woman. She came running after me. "I want to give ye a chanct to prove the tale ye tole." She reached my side and pointed a skinny finger toward a small chimney pot just visible above the tree tops. "If yer the new school teacher's wife, ye surely ta God recognize a old landmark. Whose house is that showin' jist above them trees?"

It looked like any other chimney in that section to me. "I don't know," I faltered.

"Jist as I thought!" she nodded with satisfaction. "That, my fine missy, is Newsom's."

"I buy milk and eggs from Mrs. Newsom," I said, hazily. "If I can get there, I know my way home."

"What's a keepin' ye?"

"I don't see how I can get there through all those logs and mud and water," I stammered.

"Walk the logs ta the corner of yon field, foller that fence fer a mile and a quarter and yer at Newsom's." She wheeled without another word and flapped her wide coat tail back to the house.

I started bravely out, walking logs, and looked up directly to find myself heading straight into the swamp again. I turned and called to the boy and asked him to guide me across to the corner of the field fence. He dropped his axe and started toward me.

There was a piercing shriek and the little old woman came tearing like mad from the house. "Ye leave my boy alone, ye good fer nothin' strollop!" she screeched, waving an old slat bonnet at me as she came.

"Ma, be still," the boy stepped threateningly toward her. "She jist axed me to show her how ta git 'crost them logs, and I'm a aimin' ta do it!"

"Ye shet yer tater trap, Marcus. If she's got to be showed, I'll do the showin'. Foller me," she snapped at me, and set off across the logs. When she reached the corner post she gave it a smart smack with her hand and said, "This, my fine young missy, is the corner post! In full sight the whole time, yet ye have it fer a 'cuse ta tote my boy off right under my nose."

I had no energy left with which to generate one spark of anger. The whole thing was too ridiculous. "Thank you," I said weakly, and passed on, leaving her working herself up to a fine lather in her fury.

Smoke was rising in great swirls from the burning piles of weeds in the garden as I came in sight of the house. Smoke rose from the big chimney too. In its setting of grand old trees, I thought I had never seen a house so beautiful. Even the creaking and groaning of the cypress trees across in the lake's edge had a dear familiar sound. I felt that I'd been gone for weeks.

"I fixed me something to eat," Granpap called out cheerfully, then dropped his hoe and came to meet me, peering anxiously at the strange bedraggled creature that was me.

"I've been lost since eight o'clock," I told him, and burst into tears.

It was Granpap concerned for my comfort now. He brought a foot tub of hot water to soak my feet, and made me a cup of tea and brought me a piece of sausage in a biscuit. I slipped off my skirt and blouse and got into bed, sleeping the sleep of exhaustion for the next two hours.

I woke up hungry and opened a can of peaches and got out a plate of cookies. I was warm in robe and slippers and called Granpap in to celebrate.

"I can't figger out how Alex ever let you start back through the woods by yer lone sef. Folks with a real sense of direction could get lost in them bottoms."

I told him Alex was in no way to blame. He seemed to hold his breath for a long minute, his bright blue eye piercing through me, then decided not to say it after all. "I found a row of parsnips in the garden, Flossie. Finest I ever saw, and I'm right fond of 'em. I want you to put on a big pot full fer supper. I even sawed you off a ham hock ta cook with 'em."

I couldn't stay in the house while the parsnips cooked. I never had anything make me as sick in my life as the smell of them cooking. I told Granpap I thought the sun would do me good, and sat on the back doorstep and read, running in and out with my breath held only long enough to put more wood in the stove. When they were tender at last, I opened the house and let it air out before I could stand to go in and finish supper.

When Alex came in he stood still while I told my sad story. His eyes were stormy and he took a step toward me and opened his mouth, then decided not to say it. His expression softened a little.

"Looks like what you need is a keeper," he said, and turned to help Granpap plan the garden.

March 22, 1913

I was in a state of rapture over the gardening. I'd had my fun with Alex about my order for flower seeds and plants and came out altogether better than I had expected. I now had two red running roses, one for each side of the front doorstep, and Alex had promised to build trellises for them. I had giant pansy and nasturtium seed, also giant zinnias, petunias and the quaint old-fashioned spice pinks that Aunt Laura grew along her garden walk. Granpap looked a bit querulous, then turning to wink at Alex, yielded to my plea for a walkway down the center of my garden, and threw up the beds accordingly.

March 24, 1913

    Monday morning while the men were having breakfast and I was packing Alex's lunch, a man rode up and called out. "Hello the house!" Alex went to look through the window and hastily ducked outside. Granpap, coffee cup in hand, went to the window and stood peering anxiously out.

    "Who is it?" I asked, running the mop over the splash of coffee he had just spilled.

    "Ain't jist sure I rightly know," he said.

    I stepped over and looked out. "It's the man that's been here twice to see Alex," I nodded. "Alex was squirrel hunting once and hadn't got in from school the next time. Guess he thought the best time to see Alex would be before he left the house after breakfast."

    As we stood watching, the man reined his horse around and rode quickly away. When Alex turned toward the house I noticed that his face was white and his step had lost its buoyancy.

    "Aaron Bell?" asked Granpap.

    "Yes," said Alex, and their glances caught and held. Then Alex turned to me. "Hand me my lunch, Flossie, I'm running late." Seeing that I was about to question him, he added hastily, "You and Granpap take good care of each other." He brushed my cheek lightly with his lips and was out the door.

    I couldn't stand it. I ran in front of him. "Who is Aaron Bell and what did he want?" I demanded. Granpap had followed me to the porch.

    Alex licked his lips and answered. "Why, he's just Aaron Bell, is all I know, and he wants to lease me a piece of land for the timber that's on it."

    "How much is he asking?" Granpap's voice fairly crackled.

    "Two hundred dollars," said Alex, and his voice could have been no more full of awe if he had said, "A million and one dollars."

    "A costly piece of timber, I'd say, son," he said softly, and returned to the kitchen.

    "Well, so long," Alex said, as he pulled away from me and ran to the gate.

    "For heaven's sake, it's no life and death matter that I can see," I blurted to Granpap. "If Alex wants the timber, why can't he say so, and if he doesn't, then why can't he tell the man in plain words and save him the trouble of coming back again?"

It was a lovely day and Granpap took me along the bayou to show me the best fishing places, under a cottonwood tree, in the bend beside a clump of willows. "But how can I bear to stick a hook into those little wiggle worms?" I asked.

Granpap laughed shortly. "Ya only got ta git hungry 'nough fer a mess a goggle eyed perch ta 'member that fish er to eat and worms er to catch 'em wit. You'll come to it . . . in time."

March 29, 1913

We followed Granpap home at the end of the week and found things in a state of turmoil at Englewood. Ma and Mattie, their eyes red with weeping, were up to their elbows in the preparation of a feast. Pa was stomping up and down the kitchen in a fine rage.

"Whatever is the matter?" I asked. Pa glared at me and left the room by the other door.

"Belle Walker gets married tomorrow," Ma intoned the words in a singsong voice that sounded like a funeral dirge. She sighed, and added with a shake of her head, "Pore little thing."

"Pore little thing sure 'nough," snapped Mattie, her eyes flashing. "If she didn't have her sef one more time wit Uncle Henry last night! When she tole 'im she was plannin' it, he cut his suspenders and went straight up." Then her eyes sparkled delightedly. "But Belle was eighteen last week, so's what could he honestly do? Worth livin' a lifetime ta git to see the way she spunked up to 'im one time. When he reared back and laid the law down, she took a runnin' go and landed on it with both her little feets and stomped the eternal far out of it. She'd kicked her shoes off ta warm her feet before goin' ta bed. When she sassed him, he made a grab fer her and she ducked under his arm and made a run fer it. He caught 'er out in the hall . . . ."

"And I have never heard such words come out of a little thing's mouth in my whole life," said Ma in holy horror, "and where the child could have learnt sich is beyond me . . . and she fought 'im like a wildcat besides."

"Yessir, she fought 'im," Mattie nodded with satisfaction. "Broke loose from 'im before he could hurt 'er, and she took off down the road lickety split. Been rainin' and there was plenty a cold mud out there, but it didn't stop her. She made it to Onnie's and tole them that she only tole 'im that she was gettin' married 'cause Uncle Henry once tole her that his girls would be married from their own home, and by a preacher. But if he didn't want her married at home, then she'd run away with Silas and be married by a Justice of the Peace in Paragould."

"It's a mercy Henry didn't bust a blood vessel when Onnie told 'im," mourned Ma.

Mattie giggled hysterically. "Didn't leave Uncle Henry no choice but to tell them to come on here to be married. You know he ain't gonna have a girl he raised runnin' off to be married like a common strollop, with none ta keer how things come off. So now we're havin' a weddin' after church tamorree," she ended triumphantly.

"I knowed she was plannin' it when she took her cotton pickin' money and bought that length of white satin and that pearl bead trimmin'. Mattie and me even helped cut and fit the dress . . . never lettin' on."

"Just wait till you see that dress," gasped Mattie. "Satin feels like it's haf a inch thick. She paid three dollars a yard fer it."

"It's Silas not havin' so much as an acre a ground that's settin' so hard on Henry's stummick," said Ma.

"I'm gonna get myself sick and tard of foolin' around here one of these days, and there'll be more shenanigans in the Walker household," said Mattie, with a fleeting glance at Ma. "Sherman's got his mind made up and he's workin' on mine, and I got a feelin' he's gonna have a big success one of these days."

"How's the baby?" I asked belatedly. "We waved to Ann as we came by. She was sitting in the window with a roll of blankets on her lap, but we didn't see the baby."

Ma smiled approval. "She keeps him wropped up good. Most young people now days fan their little young'ns round with their bare heels to the breeze, then wonder why they have colic fer six months. That's one that's not been cold, nor hungry."

"Gits a mite older, I'm going to teach him to smoke," said Granpap, speaking for the first time.

"Jist let me hear of it," snapped Ma. "You all get yoreselves ready to eat. I got other things to do besides puttin' in hours on a extry meal here."

Halfway through the meal Alex rocked his chair back on its back legs and said, "Ma, Granpap didn't like our store-bought bed. He said for us to take one of his featherbeds home with us, so that next time he comes he'll find a comfortable place to sleep."

"You'll take one of them featherbeds over my dead body." Ma bit off the words sharply.

"But Ma," protested Alex, "look at all these featherbeds in this house. I can count nine, two on three different beds, and I can't see what it would hurt for me to have one."

"Where's Flossie's featherbed, pray tell? Ann brought one with her. Both of my girls will take one with them when they go, and pillows, and quilts, and sheets, and blankets, and bedspreads. No girl of mine gits married without bed and beddin'."

"But Annie, looks like I could give these chilren one of my beds if I wanted," pleaded Granpap.

"Maybe you could, if you had one to give," Ma spoke with painful emphasis, "but when I give you a home, Pap, I took sich as you had fer yore keep and them beds now belong to me, and they're stayin' right here, so make up yore mind to that!"

March 30, 1913

My heart ached for Belle. They had prevailed on her to come home to dress that morning. When she sat down to breakfast Ma had said mournfully: "This is the last time Belle Walker will ever eat her breakfast!"

When Belle had been pouring her bath, Ma had said in sepulchral tones: "This is the last time Belle Walker will ever bathe her body," and Belle's tears seeped from beneath her lids and dropped into the steaming bath. Ma continued: "And so it is that Belle Walker took her last bath in her own tears."

"Stop it, Aunt Annie!" Mattie stomped a foot and stood with blazing eyes. With a secret smile Ma turned and left the room, as though satisfied with the work she had done. I followed her.

"Why did you do Belle like that?" I asked.

"Because I want her to look sweet and modest at the ceremony," said Ma, preening herself. "No girl I raised is goin' to stand there simperin' like a fool while she gets married, flouncin' her skirts and gigglin' like Rady Sardis did the day she got married. Should a girl a mine act like that, all I'd ask fer her would be a decent burial. I could kill her with my own hands."

After church the members of both families and Brother and Sister Sherrill gathered in the parlor. It had been aired and swept and garnished and Ma's treasured lamberquin brought forth from its tissue wrappings and elegantly draped over the center table. The brass base of the parlor lamp had been polished until I could see myself in it from where I sat.

Mattie had taken her place at the organ when Ma stepped to the door and nodded, she began to play "Hearts and Flowers," the dulcimer stop pulled out. As Ma seated herself, Brother Sherrill rose and took his stand at the center table. We listened to the footsteps in the hall, and knew that Pa had shortened his heavy tread to accommodate the lighter tapping of Belle's heels. They marched sedately in, Pa flushed and ill-pleased in his Sunday black, Belle shy and resentful in white satin. How tiny she looked.

Mattie missed a note as she turned to watch Belle take her place before the minister, but played steadily on as Pa took his seat and Silas and Sherman entered the room. She hurried through the last bar and hastily took her place beside Sherman. Only once did Belle's eyelids flutter upward, then she fixed her gaze on the floor and held it there throughout the ceremony.

It was like being at a funeral. The wedding, with Pa's consent, was without his approval. He let this be known by clearing his throat with a loud rasp at the outset. Nobody looked happy except the irrepressible Mattie and Sherman. This day, they too, could be openly together, and who didn't like it could lump it.

When the excitement had all died down and we were well on our way home, a thought came to disturb me. I was a big disappointment to Ma as a bride for Alex, in that I had brought with me no featherbed. Well, I wished her much joy of the nine she had, even if she could sleep on only one at the time.

Chapter 8

April 5, 1913

Today as we planted my flowers, and Alex and I had a few sharp words. As I happily patted the dirt down over the last of the seeds, Alex said, "Well, there's two dollars I spent for somethin' we can't eat!"

It sounded so like Pa that it sickened me. I could see Alex, the easy, the happy-go-lucky Alex, becoming arrogant and overbearing. I couldn't love him if he got to be like that, and I made up my mind not to let him.

"I made up my list for over eight dollars' worth, Alex, and compromised for two, so just figure you saved six dollars on that deal. Life figures up to a few things besides working and eating and sleeping for me, and the sooner you find that out . . . ."

"Stop it," yelled Alex.

"I will not stop it," I yelled back. "I've as much right to say what I want as you have, and I intend to go right on saying it, so make the best of it."

"You've had plenty to say up until now, but I've decided to do a little of the talking," he growled ominously.

"Well, I'll talk right along with you, and while I'm at it, I want to tell you that I don't like you slogging it through the woods till all hours, leaving me alone after dark to wonder what in the world could have happened to you."

"Well, stay out here and talk it over with yourself. I'm tired of listening to it," Alex said. He went to the house, got his gun and left.

April 25, 1913

Days were getting longer and school was almost out. We'd have days of high wild wind, then warmer days and showers. Alex waded around so much he'd taken cold. It had been raining all night and the clouds were scudding, dark and full of purpose overhead. I said when he started to school. "You'd better take your inhaler, and your rain coat."

He ignored me and started off without either. "Well, be stubborn and catch yourself a flock of pneumonia. Who cares?" I flared. But I relented and ran after him, walking with him as far as the field fence, as he was walking that "straight shot" through the woods.

I had never been so restless. I washed out a few things by hand and hung them to dry in the high wind. I took them in and ironed them. By ten o'clock the rain was falling in a heavy downpour. By one o'clock the whole world, so far as I could tell, was a sea of water and it was still falling. I liked walking in the rain, so I rolled Alex's raincoat into a tight bundle, his rain helmet inside, and put on my gum waders, raincoat and hat. I would take his things to him, going around by the road, and then I could walk the short way back through the woods with him. I could surely walk three miles by the time he dismissed school at four, even in this weather.

I didn't know when my sick stomach settled, but for days I'd been feeling wonderful. I sang now as I plodded along, enjoying the slogging of my waders in the mud and water. I still had enough breath to hum snatches of a tune now and then, and as I rounded the turn in the lane that led to the schoolhouse, I could see the school door fly open and the children come pouring out. As they began to meet me I called out to them and asked if it was time for school to be out. "No, ma'am, but Mr. Alex said while it was slacked off for all of us to hit the dirt for home and not to stop nowhere for nuttin'," and they kept passing me by in a big hurry.

"I'll give one of you boys a quarter to run back and tell Mr. Alex to wait for me." I kept calling to them as I hurried along, but there were no takers.

Then my heart stopped beating for a long moment. Alex had come outside and was locking the door. I screamed for him to wait for me.

The last of the children had passed me. I watched Alex drop the key into his pocket and, without a backward glance, set briskly off toward home.

I hurried forward, knowing that I could never catch him if I had to go all the way around the lane. I had a chance if I'd take a shortcut across the field. I dropped my bundle over and climbed to the top of the rail fence. I cupped my hands and called "Yoo-hoooo! Alex!" at the top of my lungs, but Alex didn't pause or look back.

I picked up my bundle and started jumping the cotton rows. The bare stalks were tough and strong and whipped my legs with cruel stripes at every jump. With my eyes set on Alex, I'd plunged into a bog of thick wet gumbo and couldn't pull my foot out. In desperation I tried again to call Alex, but a strong gust of wind caught the cry and crammed it back down my throat. At that moment I saw Alex vanish from my sight as he entered the dark wood.

The scream that rose in me finally squeezed itself in a small whimper past the hot lump in my throat. Trying to swallow only made sharp pains run up behind my ears. Alex was gone. I could never catch him now, not with my feet caught and held fast in the sticky gumbo. Alex could take the shortcut home through the woods, but I must take the long road back alone.

That is, if I didn't just stand here for the rest of my life, crying like a ninny. I wiped my eyes, took a deep breath, and started resolutely working my feet free of the clinging bog, slowly backing onto firmer ground.

Much shaken, I started slogging up the long rows to the little shack I spied in the distance. I felt that a drink of water would ease my throat and help steady me for the long walk home. But when a small girl answered my knock and handed me a greasy cup of water, I hesitated at the sound of a hollow racking cough coming from the front of the house. I remembered what Alex had told me: the Turner's live in that house, all of them dying with tuberculosis.

I dared not drink from that cup. "Can you tell me what time it is?" I asked, and when she turned to look I tossed the water to the ground. I thanked her, returned the cup, and hurried away, stopping only long enough to hold that hand under the water falling off the roof and scrub it dry with my handkerchief.

When I got up to the big house on the road, the old man looked at me with suspicion, and none of the grown children dared make a move until he gave them the word. All I asked was for somebody to please hitch up the buggy and take me home. I was by now pretty well exhausted and becoming upset. "I will pay one of the boys fifty cents to take me home," I said desperately. Finally the old man grudgingly told Charlie to hitch up and take me home.

When we got there Alex was coming out of the kitchen, an enormous wedge of chocolate pie on his outstretched palm. He took a big bite and stood waiting as we came to a standstill at the gate.

I jumped down and hurried in. "Alex, pay that boy fifty cents," I said as I passed him. Alex stood talking to Charlie a few moments and I knew he was hearing my story. I sat disconsolately on the side of the bed, waiting for him. When he came in he stuffed the last of the pie in his mouth, reached for a newspaper and spread it under my feet, then settled down to remove the waders.

"I knew what you'd done the minute I got in, both raincoats gone and you nowhere to be found. I was going out to hitch up the mules and come after you. I didn't think you could make it back in all that slosh."

If only he had raged at me, as I expected him to, my pride would have saved me from tears. But seeing no anger in him, I gave way to the pent up storm within me. He was on one knee unlacing my shoe when my gorge against that autocratic old man rose and burst.

"Not a child dared to speak until he did!" I stormed. "His wife, either. Who do the heads of these country families think they are, God's Anointed?" My voice rose in spite of me and I beat my fist on Alex's shoulder. Alex lost his balance, but regained it with full composure and started untying the other shoe.

"Well, he's the head of the family . . . ain't he? Who else would be the head of the family, if not the father?" I don't see nothin' strange in it. You're just overwrought."

"Alex, please, don't say *"don't see nothin' strange."* For heaven's sake, try to remember that you're a school teacher. These slovenly habits of speech are sure to count against you."

"Don't bring that up again, will you?" His smooth brow broke at last into a heavy scowl. "I don't talk no worse than I ever did, and who's out here but you to call my hand on it? Besides, I can pass tests in English that you wouldn't dare to tackle . . . ."

"Then more shame on you that you don't care enough . . . ."

"But I talk as I learned to talk at my mother's knee, and I'll probably continue to do so to the end of our lives together, so's it might be a good idea for you to save yourself some breath." He stood glaring down at me for a moment, then added hotly, "And quit acting like a blinger, it don't become you."

I covered my face with my hands and hoped I wasn't going to cry. How I wished I hadn't goaded him. What made me do it?

"I guess I just want to see you perfect in all things, Alex," I said humbly. "Knowing that you have the knowledge makes it hard for me not to urge you to use it. A man in your position . . . ."

"If you call teaching school my *position*, then stop worryin' 'bout that. I don't aim to make a career of it. The kind of money I'm interested in can't be made teachin' country schools, and I mean to make a lot of money before I die."

May 5, 1913

Things went much better when school was out. I felt wonderful. While Alex waited for the ground to dry out enough to plow, he hired Adolph and cut, hauled and racked the summer's supply of stove wood. The Haskell's were our neighbors now. Doc had bought twenty acres down by the bridge and built a new house.

The first time I saw Burma Haskell was when we went at last for the crane breast steak supper. She must have weighed nearly two hundred, though she wasn't fat. The house was clean as a pin, with new scrim curtains at the windows, and she had baked a big chocolate cake. It was still warm. And the steaks were delicious. She prepared them with a flavor that reminded me of wild duck.

After supper the men went frog gigging, leaving Burma and me alone. She was no time at all in finding out that I was pregnant, though I was not as yet showing. When we settled for the evening she got out her mending and started telling old wives' tales.

I had not as yet faced the hour of my delivery, and suddenly I was afraid. "Be careful not to do no work that'll stretch your arms above your head, Flossie," she said solemnly. "Don't even sleep with your arms above your head. There's danger of wrapping the cord around the little things neck and choking it plum to death. I've knowed it to happen, time and again. And it'll help a lot when your labor comes on to fold a pair of your husband's old britches and hide them under your pillow. And be sure to have a black bottle ready and when the pain comes on, fit your lips over that bottle and blow with all your might . . . that's so you won't waste your pains by screaming."

I couldn't stand it. I looked around desperately seeking something as a distraction and saw the big gramophone and a box of cylinder records. "Do you mind if I play some records?" I asked.

She looked as if she'd been cheated for a moment, and then grudgingly gave her consent. I put on the first record my hand touched and had never heard so mournful a ballad:

> *Soon beyond the harbor bar,*
> *Shall my bark be sailing far,*
> *O'er the world I wander lone,*
> *Sweet Belle Mahone.*
> *O'er thy grave I weep goodbye,*
> *Hear, oh hear my lonely cry,*
> *Oh, without thee what am I,*
> *Sweet Belle Mahone?*
> *Sweet Belle Mahone! Sweet Belle Mahone!*
> *Wait for me at Heaven's gate. Sweet Belle Mahone!*
>
> *McNaughton, John Hugh,*
> *"Belle Mahone" (1867)*

It was my one evening of entertainment since I'd been living at Big Lake, and I was truly glad when Alex came to take me and his frog legs home.

I had a horror of the big green frogs at first, but Alex pulled the tendons in the legs, so they wouldn't jump around in the skillet as though still alive, and the meat was so succulent, so sweet and deliciously tender that I was soon frying frog legs and eating them as happily as though it had been chicken.

May 6, 1913

Alex built a chicken yard against the side of the smokehouse and fixed nests high under the eaves, buying fifteen hens and a rooster. It was fun to have my own eggs, and to set the hens when they went broody. In fact, I found the days flying by on wings, with so many new and interesting things to do. My heart seemed to dance along on the sunbeams in the bright spring mornings and I was forever bursting into what I came to know as my happiness song:

> *Come, thou Fount of every blessing,*
> *Tune my heart to sing Thy grace.*
> *Streams of mercy, never ceasing,*
> *Call for songs of loudest praise.*

Digging in the garden on that morning I had found a bed of red worms. I found a can and crumbled dirt in it, as Granpap had shown me, and put a lot of the squirming things in it. They burrowed at once beneath the damp earth. In the afternoon I took the can of worms from beneath the front doorstep where I'd hidden it, sneaked one of Alex's fishing poles and went down on the bayou beneath the cottonwood tree. I had never known such peace as came to me, sitting there in the warm afternoon sun, now and then hooking a nice perch.

I was soon handling the worms without qualms, and nothing could have equaled the nonchalance with which I placed a platter of fish and corncakes before Alex at supper. His surprise added to my enjoyment. Altogether it had been a perfect day.

May 10, 1913

Alex loved to plow and was cheerful and happy through the time of planting. "Been expecting you to holler about going home," he teased me one day. "Guess if you're not going to get homesick, I'll have to. I feel the need of a change."

How different it felt, riding along in the soft spring air. Brush piles were burning everywhere, and fields newly planted. At Englewood we learned that Silas had been given the summer school at Spilling Brook again. Moreover, Pa had rented him one of the small farms there. Mattie was really "queening it" around the place, as Alex called it, being the only chick left under the home roof.

"I've still got to find a man to take over the home farm," Pa grumbled. "I helt it back fer Alex, but no, he has to go traipsin' off to the ends of nowhere, and it's hard to find somebody I can trust that close to the store and the smokehouse. Ever' young'n on the place breaks and runs like the dogs was after 'em the minute they get old 'nough to be any mortal help to me and Annie."

Granpap came sidling into the room, a scowl on his face. "Anybody gonna tie this goddam string round my neck?" he growled.

Pa turned on him with a snarl. "How many times I got ta tell you that such language ain't ta be spoke in this house?"

"You two stop it this minute," snapped Ma. "Turn around here, Pap, and let me tie that tie, and you stop yelpin' like a kicked hound dog 'cause yore asked to dress right one more time in yore life and look pleasant long 'nough to get yore picture took. We got four generations in this family right now, and we sure aimin' ta git a picture of it."

Ma was wearing her best gray poplin, with a crisp hemstitched white lawn turnover at the neck. She pinned the gold hoop brooch in place, the gold hoop earrings that matched it dangling coquettishly in her pierced ears. She settled a shiny black sailor in place, tilting it slightly over the right eye. She turned her girlish figure about to see if all was right behind, then turned to fuss at Mattie. "Onnie and Ann passed in the buggy fifteen minutes ago," she scolded.

"Well, go get in the surrey yore own sef, Aunt Annie, and leave me be, I'll be there now before you are."

The surrey had been newly painted for spring, and the fringe brushed out. I watched wistfully as they took their seats and pulled the dust robes over their laps. I stood by as they pulled away in the surrey, then I climbed wearily onto the big spring seat in the wagon behind the mules.

When we drew up in front of Mama's my heart melted. The locust trees were in full bloom. As Lola ran to help me down from the wagon seat, she sang, "You've got new dresses! You've got new dresses!"

And I did have new dresses. Mama had started selling what she called her "Magic Formula." It was a skin preparation, and with a skin like hers she could have sold mud packs. "I can't carry the heavy sample case anymore, but I can take a sample of this in my purse, and I've had wonderful success with it. I thought you would need maternity dresses soon, so I had a couple made up for you. All I ask is that you have your picture made for me in this new dress before you begin to show." The dress she was fastening on me was beautiful. It was made of pink crepe de chine, with heavy lace yoke and collar, and a draped skirt.

"You can wear my new spring coat and hat to the studio," said Lola. "Grace is going to give you all her maternity things. She says she never wants to see one of them again."

I wouldn't look at Alex. What if he balked? But when the time came he brushed his clothes and walked to the studio with me. Once inside he became suddenly self-conscious and dropped weakly into a chair while the photographer was jockeying for position. I walked over and rested the tips of my fingers on the arm of his chair. The photographer said, "Hold it," and that was all there was to it.

After we left the studio I was feeling very relaxed while walking along with Alex. "It seems hard to believe this is the first time I've been on this street since we married," I said. Alex was as surprised as I to realize that this was true. There was a sudden rush of feet and I turned just as Mattie grabbed me in her arms. Sherman was with her.

"Flossie, we're already married," she gurgled.

"Oh oh!" said Alex, thinking of Pa. "Now you have stepped your foot in a mess."

"Well, one good thing: from now on it's my own mess my foot's in, and that's something." She laughed happily. We shook hands with Sherman and wished them both much joy.

"I only hope I'm safe buried back in the bottoms before you break the news to Pa," Alex said, as we left them.

That night Papa and I had a chance for a quiet word together. "Is Mr. Herget feeling any better toward you?" I asked.

"Everything's fine, now that we know what the trouble was. Dutch Shultz was making wines. Everybody got a raise but Dutch. He wasn't due a raise, because Pekin Cooperage was paying regulation scale on wines. But we couldn't get it through his thick head, and he thought he was being discriminated against. So he worked against me to Mr. Herget. But he was mad at Herget as well, and when Herget's son drove out to pick spring violets with his sweetheart and her mother and tied his fine rig up to a tree on the creek bank, Dutch slipped out and cut his harness all to pieces, just to relieve his feelings. He was caught red-handed. But by that time he was so mad he told why he had done such a thing, so Mr. Herget sent for me and apologized. I laughed with him about it, but when I started to leave the office I told him not to forget that the fellow who painted me so black still carried the brush."

May 11, 1913

Chaos reigned when we reached Walker's next afternoon. Pa was having his sweat without much notice being taken of it, for Ma and Mattie were lost in plans for furnishing the little house beside the store.

But Pa was bound to have his say, even though Mattie interrupted right in the middle of it to say, "Go ahead and get yore mad over with, Uncle Henry. I'd ruther take what follers than go through what pore Belle went through beforehand. That would have took all the joy out of it fer me. You know good and well you got to have somebody you can trust ta tend this home place. Onnie got it planted with what help you could stir up fer 'im, but he can't keep both places goin'. So I've elected me and Sherman fer the job. I can tend that store as good as you can any day, and Sherman's a good farmer, so I can't see what yore yellin' about."

"Alex and I had pictures made yesterday," I put in, trying to turn the tide.

"Mattie tells me you was downtown with a lot of new duds on. Must be nice to have rich kinfolks ta dress you up and have yore picture took," sneered Pa.

"Besides," said Mattie," Sherman and me would like to have a little honeymoon, if you don't mind, Uncle Henry. The only thing I want you to give me fer a weddin' present is to hitch Fanny to the buggy and you and Aunt Annie go visit Alex and Flossie fer a week."

Pa's face turned red and he gasped audibly.

"I mean it," said Mattie, pressing her advantage. "You been talkin' about goin' down there fer a few days of fishin'. Ta my way of thinkin' there couldn't be a better time. Go now, before the weather gets so hot, and before the summer rush is on."

"Fishin' is fine now, Pa," Alex put in.

"And we'd be so glad to have you," I lied heartily, anxious to give Mattie a chance for a few days of happiness unhampered by Ma and Pa. "Alex and I can take the three quarter bed, and you all can have our room. I want to show you my garden . . . and my chickens."

"Why, now, I ain't been a pleasurin' in ten years," said Pa. "Can you imagine me and Annie off on a pleasure trip?"

"We got as much right to a pleasure trip as the next one," snapped Ma. "Go get hitched up. I can be packed by the time yore ready!"

May 13, 1913

"That old rowboat of yores shoulda been named the Drudge," said Pa, wiping the sweat from his brow as he and Alex came up on the bank where Ma and I waited Tuesday evening. They had a long string of fish.

"It's the feller that rows it is the drudge." Alex grinned. "You women might as well get the skillets ready," Alex said. "We're fixin' to have a fish fry. We invited the Haskell's to join us."

"That Doc's quite a feller," Pa chuckled.

To my surprise I was enjoying Ma and Pa. In their own home, trying to keep everything straight and everybody under control, they were people with heavy responsibilities and big ideas, or "notions," as Mattie called them. But here on the lake, with no responsibility but to enjoy themselves, they were people on vacation, without a care in the world.

Ma told me about the time she was "off" when Alex was born. "Had an old midwife, and no doctor," said Ma, "and she let me get childbed fever. I don't think a thing causes that but filth. She wouldn't let me have a drop of water on me fer nine days, except a damp rag to wipe my face and hands, and I lay there in that mess and took the fever. I was a while getting over the effects of it. After I was up and around, I knew I wasn't acting right, and when any one would ride up to the gate and holler, I'd hide behind the door, or get in bed and cover up till they'd gone." She laughed a little sadly. "I remember that I'd sit flat on the floor to wash my dishes too, with the dishpan between my knees, the rinse pan on one side, the drain pan on the other. Now what could make a body do things like that?"

I felt like telling her that I thought one thing that might make it would be a sixteen year old child having a baby in the middle of a clearing, with nobody but an ignorant midwife in attendance. I felt like I could never seriously hold against Ma any of the little things she did, like making Belle cry so she'd look modest at her wedding.

Pa and Doc Haskell got to vying with each other on hunting and trapping stories as they sat around the table after supper. Ma was tripping about the kitchen like a girl. "I haven't seen Henry like this in years," Ma exulted in an aside to me, and I could well believe it.

May 17, 1913

Not one thing happened to mar the pleasure of their visit, and it was with real regret we stood to see them go. "You must do this again soon," I insisted, and Pa gave me his charming smile and a courtly bow.

"I'll say this fer you, Flossie, you make a pow'ful nice place to visit at. I never been treated nicer anywhere I been, and I want to thank you fer the fust vacation I've had in too long."

Ma gave me a hearty hug, though she didn't kiss me, and both were smiling and waving as they drove away, a big bucket of dressed fish for the others under a shade of pine boughs in the back of the buggy.

I turned to Alex and laughed. "Pa didn't look sick to me. He just needed a chance to get a good laugh one more time. Ma says she knows he's ailing. Keeps complaining, she says, and he's taken to reading the advertisements and buying every new patent medicine that comes out. She says he reads the symptoms that brand's supposed to cure, says that must be what's the matter with him, and lays in half a dozen bottles. She said she knows he's taken a number three washtub of patent medicine in the past year. Why doesn't he go to a doctor and find out what ails him?"

Alex grinned. "Pa thinks doctors are humbugs, and that they keep you comin' to get your money. Time and again I've heard him say that he may die a pauper, but it won't be because a doctor humbugged him out of what he's made."

May 19, 1913

When the corn was big enough to be plowed, my spirit was exalted. Growing corn had filled me with wonder as a child. I could remember stealing into Papa's garden in the early morning and falling on my knees, and with the tip of an eager tongue, filching the drop of dew from the bright green chalice of each stalk, all the way down the row. My knees would be worn to the bone if I started on such a foray down through Alex's big field of corn. But I liked taking a jug of cool water and some pie or cookies to share with him under the big pin oak tree at midmorning. The rich earth smelled heavenly as it rolled from the shining plow, and Alex was always full of a sweet contentment when turning the soil.

He had made a backrest for me in the row boat. We had named it the Night Owl, and he had enjoyed painting the name on the side, with a crude free hand drawing of an owl, a big brown owl on a yellow boat.

Sometimes I would take a magazine and pillows and make myself comfortable under an umbrella while he fished. Sometimes I fished too. Sometimes I took the small hand net and caught minnows for him to use as bait. He gathered water lilies for me, their red brown stems feeling like India rubber in my hands, their wax like petals cool and lovely.

One day Alex shoved the boat up under a cypress tree to rest in the cool shade a moment. I raised my eyes and stared straight into the beady eyes of a huge snake, coiled on a limb directly before my face. For a moment I was paralyzed with fear, then managed to gasp, "Alex, you've got me under a snake!"

Alex had his head bowed as he mopped the sweat from his neck with a bandanna. He looked up, his mouth hanging foolishly open for a moment. He looked at me and burst into boisterous laughter. I had a wild impulse to grab that snake by the tail and slap him right across the mouth with it. Livid with rage and fright, I clung to the sides of the boat, helpless. There was then a powerful backward stroke of the oars and with a swoosh, we were safely out in the open again. "That was a water moccasin," gasped Alex, "you would have died if it had bit you."

"Is that why you laughed?" I wailed.

His face was ashen. "I don't know why I laughed . . . don't know why . . . it sure wasn't funny." He was visibly shaken.

I said, "Well, I'm sick to death of this lake, anyhow. Are we to spend every waking idle hour on it? Take me to the house this minute."

May 24, 1913

It was Saturday morning that Onnie, Ann and Lester came riding up to the gate. It was a complete and joyful surprise to us. "Ann's brother, Jack, has been at the farm a few days"—Onnie laughed—"and I nailed him to it to look after things till I could come a fishin' one time. Ann's been wantin' to come down too."

The boys, of course, started rigging up fishing tackle and getting bait. Ann had brought a couple of fryers, dressed for the skillet, and we soon had the noon meal ready. In the afternoon, having nothing better to do, I decided to bake a cake for Sunday. I'd wanted to bake a Lady Baltimore cake, a favorite with Mama, but had not had the courage. With many misgivings and a fine show of nonchalance, I undertook it now. To my vast pride and surprise it turned out well, and I set it in the middle of the table, a monument to my skill as a cook. I could see that Ann was impressed.

The boys were even more impressed when they came in, hot and tired and hungry, dragging a string of fish between them. "Throw the dag-blamed fish back in the lake," gloated Onnie. "I been honin' fer some honest-to-God cake fer a week . . . and don't try ta put me off with one piece, either, Flossie. I want to eat my fill."

Thoughts of my Sunday dinner went glimmering as Ann laughed and set the coffee pot on and added more wood to the fire. "Gee whiz, how you all stand it in here?" gasped Alex. "It's hot as a brick kiln. Set that little table out under the walnut tree, Flossie, like you do sometimes, and let's have it outside where we can catch a breeze now and then."

The cake was eaten to the last crumb. Ann took the baby and settled in the hammock, the boys on the front steps. Alex had taken down a bar of carborundum from overhead and was putting a fine edge on his Big Daddy Barlow as he talked. "Ain't that a frog sticker though?" he exulted, pulling a hair from his head and whacking it expertly in two with the razor like edge of the blade. At the sound of horse's hooves beating on the bayou bridge he looked up, dropped the knife and rock, ran to the corner of the yard, vaulted the fence and went to meet the rider.

"That's Aaron Bell again!" I said in exasperation. "Him and his everlasting timber deals. I wish he'd let Alex alone." Ann sat straight up in the hammock and she and Onnie looked long at each other. Neither said a word, so I started clearing the table. I carried a tray of cups and saucers to the kitchen. When I returned Aaron was riding back the way he had come, and Alex was coming back to the house, trying to grin, his face white and set.

"What did Uncle Aaron have on his mind?" Onnie said, in an expressionless voice. Alex stood looking at him, but said nothing.

"Well, Alex, has it got you down?" I said. "Do you have to look like half your family just died?" I turned to the others. "Aaron Bell has been trying to lease Alex a tract of timberland ever since we came out here. Will you tell me why he can't give the man a definite answer? Bell can't force him to take it if he doesn't want it, surely...."

"Can he, Alex?" asked Onnie. "Can he force you?"

"He hasn't done it yet," said Alex grimly.

"What's his askin' price?"

"Two hundred dollars! Where would I get two hundred dollars at this stage of the game?"

"He'd probably settle for half that, cash on the barrel head," said Onnie.

"Begins to look like I'm elected to pay it," said Alex, and my mouth hung open in astonishment.

"Heh! Heh! Uncle Aaron, puttin' over a big timber deal. I didn't think he had it in 'im." Onnie laughed mirthlessly.

"Aaron Bell any kin to Lizzy Bell?" I asked idly. Alex's eyes flashed a startled look at me as he started to close the heavy knife and put it in his pocket. The sharp blade closed pitilessly down on his right forefinger, cutting it to the bone. "Look what you're doing Alex. I never saw you so careless. Now you're in for it. You will carry that scar to your grave."

Ann ran for a basin of water, while I got ointments and bandages. I had nothing to sterilize the wound with but a bottle of cologne. Alex writhed in pain when I dripped cologne into the cut, then I wrapped the wound, holding it together the best I could, and saturated the wrapping with Mama's special brand of healing oil.

Ann called for unbleached muslin and needle and thread and sat down to make up a supply of finger stalls. "Looks like he'll be needing them for some time," she said.

Onnie said, "Well, that leaves me to dress the fish by myself, looks like. All right, Alex, you can feed and water the stock and do the other chores."

I had gone to put some things in the dirty clothes barrel in the little shed room when the boys stepped up on the back porch, their arms full of stove wood. They were talking earnestly and something in their voices made me stop to listen. "So you better come right on home with me, first thing in the mornin', and get it over with. Save trouble in the long run. Pa's going to be sore as a vaccinate, but who else is there to see you through it?"

I stepped out and confronted them, expecting I don't know what. "Who else is going to see him through what?" I demanded.

Both boys stood looking at me a moment, silent and big eyed. Onnie blustered, "See him through this crop, of course. I guess you got but little idea what it takes to make a crop, but Alex just ain't got it. I heard Pa tell him mysef that he's got to save 'nough from his teachin' to see him through his crop, and he ain't done it. If you think Pa's goin' to like hearin' about it, you got another think comin'! Alex is in fer hell with Pa and he might as well face it. He still owes him a hundred dollars on the team and wagon . . . now this. I sure don't envy Alex from here on in."

I relaxed, I had not put into words the thing I feared, but certainly asking Pa for a little money to see us through six weeks was nothing. Alex would be teaching again, the summer school beginning the first of July. We hadn't been around Pa since we married that he hadn't warned us he meant us to "tote our own weight" through the summer. Well, for heaven's sake, we had to live, didn't we? I couldn't see where we'd wasted anything.

June 30, 1913

The last of June burst upon us in a heat wave. Even the nights were hot, "Cotton weather," gloated Alex. "Hot nights and you can't sleep for the sweat runnin' down your neck. You can know your cotton is growin' by leaps and bounds."

But the cotton wasn't all that was growing. The baby was. I'd almost forgotten I was pregnant in the past happy healthful weeks. It had quickened at the turn, and the bounding new life within gave me many startled sleepless hours.

Mama's last letter had told of Lola's attachment for Grace's baby, "She could love him no more if he were her own," Mama wrote.

"She'll be havin' one of her own the first year she's married," predicted Alex, "never saw a girl so crazy over babies. "Anybody's baby! Ann said she nearly ate Lester alive the day they stopped by there with him."

"Well, who wouldn't? I only hope our baby is half as sweet as Lester, and half as happy. He's always ready for a play."

"Well, Phil Allen sure is going about things in the right way. Buyin' his lot and buildin' his house before he gets married."

I looked up in hurt surprise. "That's a nice thing to do, if it's possible," I agreed, "but, for heaven's sake, Alex, when would we have gotten married if we'd waited until you were able to buy a farm and build a house. Most people live out their allotted time without a foot of ground to call their own, except the little lot they have set for their final resting place in a cemetery." Alex said nothing. "Why, if we had to have our home paid out before we married, we never could have married."

"Which might have been just as well," Alex said, deliberately.

"Yes, of course, unless they felt about it as you and I did," I faltered. I couldn't bear to look at him for a moment, and when I did, the front screen was closing softly and he was bounding across the front yard, where he vaulted the fence and was gone.

For days my heart was troubled. I strove in vain to understand Alex's changed attitude toward me. I thought back to our conversations trying to find what I had said that could keep him in this strange mood. Not that Alex was unkind to me. It was more as if he were not even present. His eyes seldom met mine, and were quickly averted when they did. And the only time his arms were around me now was when, in desperation, I would go to him and place them there. As the child grew in me and my pressure symptoms increased, I longed for Alex to massage my back, to rub my aching sides, to relax me when I lay down to rest. But his move to comply with my request, on the few occasions I'd brought myself to ask, was so disinterested that I found no comfort in his touch.

July 7, 1913

Summer school opened on schedule. I'd fallen into the way of dividing the washing so as not to get overtired, and the consequence was that there was hardly a day that I didn't have some washing or ironing to do. I'd asked Alex to draw the water for me again.

"There's just no sense in two people having so much wash anyway," he stormed. "Most of the stuff you pile out here's not even soiled. Look at those sheets . . . slept on only one night."

"Please, Alex, let's don't go over all this again," I said wearily, "I have to wash, so just draw the water."

"But I know I'm right this time," he insisted, "I'm asking you one more time why you are washing sheets that have been slept on only one night?"

"Well, I'll tell you, if you insist on it!" I flared, my voice rising in spite of me. "You mess around at that stinking lake every spare minute. Then you come crawl into bed with me without taking a bath, after I draw the water myself and heat it for you all day long in the sun. You may not know it, but that old fish smell is all through you. You're saturated with it. You smell like an old dead turtle this living minute!"

If he had to go around acting like an insulted monarch, it might as well be with reason. He was astonished at my outburst and I was glad to see his discomfiture. He glared at me for a moment, opened his mouth as if to speak, then turned abruptly away and filled the washtubs for me.

But I was instantly ashamed, and so lonely that I could have cried with the pain in my heart. What had happened to the joy we once found in each other? It was the only thing that made all the rest of it bearable. I had to consider every word I spoke for fear it might not please Alex. My little jokes fell flat. We seldom found anything to laugh about. Alex was so preoccupied that I felt less lonely when he was away than when he was beside me. The night before I had laid a hand on his shoulder as I passed him, and a flicker of aversion had flashed across his face. He'd rather I didn't touch him. And this was no "mood." He'd had moods before and they'd worn off.

Next morning I dressed carefully, as always. The band of my skirt wouldn't fasten, so I hooked it together with a large safety pin. But my hair was rich and glossy, my skin clear, my eyes bright. I felt better than I ever remembered feeling before, except for the pressure symptoms. I enjoyed my food, and my awareness of all things seemed heightened. The food I ate nourished the new life under my heart. The very air I breathed was bearing life to that little body. But the baby was something I couldn't talk about with Alex. He scowled at the mention of it, and the time was fast approaching when I would have to assemble a layette. In fact, if I had some materials to be working on now, it might help me to be less aware of Alex's indifference. But when I mentioned the things I would need, he said, "You haven't got any baby yet. We'll cross that bridge when we come to it."

"Nobody waits till a baby's here to get ready for it Alex," I said patiently. "Most women are half through with their sewing by this time."

"You don't say," he said, and his tone enraged me.

"I do say!" I flared, but before I could say more he broke in.

"Give me a little time, can't you? You'll get something by the time you need it, and not before."

That night a cool wind sprang up following a shower and I drew closer to Alex for warmth. The baby plunged and stretched luxuriously, kicking out vigorously against Alex's back, which, as usual, was toward me. He sprang up at once, sitting on the side of the bed. "For God's sake, do you have to get against me with it?" He snarled, and I was surprised by the note of hysteria in his voice. "Are you just trying to torture me with it? Isn't there room enough in this bed for both of us? Even when I get clear over on the railin'? If there's not, I can take the other bed."

A sob broke in my throat but was instantly stifled. My pride would not let me give one whimper. I lay still to gain control and Alex continued. "There's just nothing that gives me a feelin' like that does. I don't see how you stand it. If I was in your place and it started rearin' like that around inside me, I'd run till I lost it, or I'd run till I died!" he ended desperately. Was he apologizing for his behavior, in his way, or was he suggesting that I do something that would cause me to lose the baby?

"Will you put that in the form of a suggestion?" I asked quietly.

"Well, I just mean that I couldn't stand it," he stammered.

"Lie back down, Alex. If somebody moves to the other bed it will be me. I want you to have all the room you need to be comfortable."

I went to the lean-to for a quilt and took the other bed. Soon I heard Alex breathing heavily and knew that he slept, but I had many things to think about, things that I had put off as long as I could.

Sooner or later I was going to come to the fullness of my time. Who was going to attend me? Doc Haskell? He had attended Liddie Slatten, and now she and her little baby lay in the same grave. Of course, they said the baby was born breeched, tearing her all to pieces. She had hemorrhaged and died, and the baby had lived less than twenty-four hours. I had heard that Mrs. Newsom was a good midwife, but when I asked her she shook her head, "Laud, child, I ain't tended a case in almost two year now. I'm gettin' too old fer sich lively parties, For one thing, I can't haif see what I'm doin' by lamplight any more. No, honey, I wouldn't promise to take yore case at all."

I went to sleep without having consciously come to any decision, knowing I must decide how I was to be cared for when my time came and feeling that I could not trust Alex to make proper arrangements. Alex was like a stranger to me. I laid a pillow over my head so that I could not hear him breathing. Alex, who was once my lover, whose child I was bearing, with whom I must spend the rest of my life. There was something there that I didn't understand.

I had no thought of leaving Alex or of him leaving me. But I would take up our personal differences and iron them out with him later. Just now I must figure on where to go and what to do about having the baby. I needed peace of mind, and a chance to build up my morale for the ordeal that lay before me. After that . . . .

Chapter 9

July 19, 1913

Two weeks brought changes I had not anticipated. Alex was moving my furniture to town. Funny, how things had worked out. Funny as a crutch!

That miserable day I'd left Big Lake, we had stopped by Walker's for dinner. When Alex announced that I was going to stay in town till after the baby was born, he might as well have exploded a bomb beneath the dinner table. A chance remark of Pa's precipitated a climax.

"I see by the Soliphone this morning where Mary Leash's husband that had come back to town Saturday, went on a toot and let a load of lead through Mary's leg because she wouldn't go back to him."

Alex frowned thoughtfully. "I told her somethin' like that was bound to happen. Last time I saw her she said she had a threatenin' letter from him and that he had started drinkin'. A feller that's drinkin' to drown his troubles is just as like to do one thing as another."

"I didn't know you knew Mary Leash," I remarked idly.

Pa cleared his throat and a look of sly cunning overspread his face, although he kept his eyes carefully on his plate. "Oh yes," he drawled deliberately, softly. "Alex always seemed to make quite a point of knowin' all the *grass widders!*"

The glass of cold buttermilk which I was raising to my mouth seemed to veer of its own accord. With all my power of control I managed to catch it and get it safely on the table before it spilled its contents into Pa's now startled countenance. Quickly I pushed my chair back and ran from the room. I climbed into the wagon, raised my umbrella to protect me from the sun and there I sat, stiff and proud, until Alex finished his dinner and joined me.

When we reached the house on Main Street, things were not going well. Mama was nervous and distraught because of the goiter she had developed. The doctor had said it was from carrying the sample case. Lola was covered up in the household duties and fretful because of delays in her marriage plans.

"Mama is so easily upset," she told me. "The doctor says she's going through the change and that it's necessary for her to be kept as quiet and free from worry as possible."

My heart sank. I should not have come home without a word of warning. Should I go back out with Alex? One look at his lowering countenance decided me against that. I had said I was coming to town to have my baby. He had sneered at me for it, but on the whole, had seemed relieved. He had seemed also to take a fiendish delight in telling the Walkers of my desertion, for in their eyes it amounted to that. No, I could not bring myself to eat such a big hunk of humble pie and go crawling back out there. Something could be worked out.

The next morning Mama called me in to talk with her. "You must go out and find yourself rooms somewhere, Flossie," she said. "It isn't that there isn't room for you here. It's just that I don't like this shifting of responsibility. If you are here with us, Alex will cease to worry about you. This is his baby that you are carrying. It's coming and provision for it is his concern and yours, not ours. We're having all we can do to keep afloat and try to get Lola ready to get married. You have two months or more to go yet, and you and I wouldn't be very good for each other just now." She smiled regretfully.

"Of course, Mama . . . I'll find rooms. And I'll have Alex to pack the things I need and move them in. He's arranged for a tenant for the house and needs it empty for the widow and orphans and their things anyway."

I tried to make my voice cheerful and light, but I felt like an outcast, even while I could see the good sense in all that she was saying. What a good daughter I was to come dump my troubles in my sick mother's lap.

July 21, 1913

I rented two rooms with Alma and Lucius Thompson. Lucius was one of the six Thompson boys and a cousin of Alex's. Alma let me have the rooms for five dollars a month.

Alex wasn't in a good mood when he brought the furniture, but then he never was anymore. Doggedly he did the things he hated doing, putting down the floor coverings, hanging shades and curtains, arranging furniture. The rooms presented a pleasant aspect when we had finished but I felt like my back would break. After we had gone to bed I was so miserable I could find no comfort. Finally I woke Alex.

"Do you think I could be going into my labor?" I whimpered.

"God forbid!" groaned Alex fervently.

"And why not?" I bridled. "Heaven knows I'm tired to death and would rather carry the baby round on a pillow the first two months of its life than where it is for two months longer!"

Alex switched on the light and stood looking bleakly at me.

"I wouldn't have you go into your confinement now for anythin' this world's got to offer me!" he blurted, "You stay in this bed for days and don't even draw a long breath if you can help it."

"Why, Alex, you're all upset," I said wonderingly.

"Why wouldn't I be upset," he gritted. "That baby could be born without hair, toenails, or fingernails, but nobody could ever convince Ma that you hadn't carried it the full time. She said as I drove by today that she guessed you wasn't gettin' moved any too soon, that you looked like you was ready to be down to her. Don't have it now. I mean . . . well . . . just don't have it now, Flossie!"

"Did Ma say that about me?" I asked furiously.

"Well, just keep your shirt on! Yes, she said it. You ought to know by now what she and almost everyone else thinks about grass widders!"

He had seated himself on the side of the bed, so I gathered my knees swiftly up under my chin and let go with every ounce of strength in me. Alex had no chance to save himself and landed sprawling on the floor.

"What do you think you're doing?" he yelped, picking himself up with an injured air. I drew a deep breath, counted ten, and expelled.

Then I sat up, deliberately rearranged pillows and covers, turned off the bed light, and lay down.

July 22, 1913

When Alex started to leave, I asked, "When will you be in again?"
"When do I have to come again?" he asked.
"You don't have to come at all!" I flared, "seeing that it seems to be such a dread on your mind."
"Well, I guess I didn't mean it the way it sounded," he said lamely. "I'll try to get in every two weeks or so. If you need anythin' you can call me, but try to call early mornin', at noon, or late at night. Through the day all hands will be in the fields."
He kissed me absently at the doorway. I followed to the steps, watched him drive away and stood waiting till he turned the corner, waiting to wave him a last farewell, but he gave no backward glance. I thought of how eagerly he used to rush in to see me, no matter how much work he'd had to do that day. He had come so eagerly when I had not needed him. Now that I did, he seemed anxious to make his visits as few as possible.
I sighed and went back indoors, put the kitchen to rights, eased off my robe and got into bed.
I got up only when necessary for the next three days until all signs of the immediate distress had passed.

August 23, 1913

Alex had left me ten dollars to buy the material for baby clothes. "You can make that do," he had said flatly, "for it's all you'll get. No need in makin' up a lot of stuff. Not till you see how the baby gets along,"
Lola went shopping for me and we cut out the layette. With this to occupy my time, the days passed much better than I had hoped for.
I would not call Alex sometimes for days. But no matter how long I waited, he still did not call me. I hated having the people on the party line know that it was always I who made the calls to a reluctant

husband. But this morning I felt better. Alex had called the day before . . . he would be coming for dinner. He had been in on Thursday, he said, but had gone to the fair. By the time he thought about it, it was too late to come by so he had just gone on out without calling me!

But he was coming for dinner today, so I made the house fresh and baked a big chocolate cake. As I worked, my heart felt lighter than it had for some time. At least Alex had called me this once. When he came, I would show him the baby things I'd been working on, perhaps this would make things seem more real to him. I hoped it might make us feel a little more as if we belonged to each other again. Deliberately, I pushed unpleasant things out of my mind and toyed with imaginary conversations that I would hold with him when he came at last.

But at three o'clock Alma called to me. "Flossie, Alex is on the phone. He's calling from the fair grounds."

When I picked up the phone I said, "Yes."

"This is Alex. Last day of the fair, you know, so I came on out here with Pa. He's ready to go now, so I won't have time to come by. I paid your grocery bill today. Just tell Cal anytime you want anythin'. He can bring it home to you, and I'll settle along and along."

"All right, Alex." The receiver clicked and there was no goodbye.

August 30, 1913

About twice a week Mama and Papa came strolling in at dusk, bringing a portion of something special for me to eat. Jan would stop in on her way home from school every now and then. Lola occasionally spent a night with me, but she was living with her head in the clouds and was full to the overflow with her own plans.

The workmen were putting in the floors, doing the woodwork, and painting the outside of the new house. Now she was shopping for her furnishings. Together she and Phil went from store to store and they made up lists of their findings and prices, and studied them as a general pores over his war maps. Together they decided on which pieces they would buy.

The Walker clan came and went, but none of them came to see me. I was in utter disgrace.

I found much joy in sewing quietly by the hour. In the evenings I took my exercise by walking around a block or two. I read good books and magazines.

I, without end, let the problems of life slide away, like water off a duck's back. Later I would take up the threads and start weaving again. Just now I had enough materials to carry through on what I had started.

October 4, 1913

The early frost had touched the leaves and left the trees decked in splendor. I had now but to wrap myself in a blanket when I lay on the deck chair at night and watch the neighborhood as it scurried to and fro, and finally settled down. This was the most contact I had with my fellow beings, watching other women's children come in from school, their husbands come in from work, hearing them call back and forth about matters of seeming importance.

And so I passed the days of my waiting.

October 18, 1913

I got up this morning feeling much better. Many of my aggravating pressure symptoms had vanished, and I hummed as I went about my little routine. About the middle of the morning Alex burst in upon me unannounced. He surprised me by throwing his arms around me and giving me a kiss and a whirl around the room. He was in high spirits.

"Get on your best bib and tucker, Mrs. Walker . . . we're dining out!"

"Dining out?" I gasped weakly, conscious at once of my own appearance. "But where?"

"Secret."

"Well, I don't believe it's safe for me to go anywhere." How many times I had longed for him to suggest that we go somewhere, anywhere, and now that he had done it at last, I was afraid to go.

"I'm not supposed to let the cat out of the bag, so I'm not going to tell you that Phil and Lola went with a bunch of friends to the fair at Little Rock yesterday, got married, and sent a wire back to your mother.

They'll be in on the evening train, and she has really been in a swivet all day, putting the big pot in the little one. They're fixin' to have the fatted calf."

Suddenly Alex laughed. "Your Mama's got a chair and an extra blanket at the foot of the brass bed. She said she knew no bed was long enough to hold Philip Allen and his feet too, so's she set the chair to catch the overflow."

"How am I going?"

"Why, I've brought Cal's delivery wagon. Get a rush on, now, so's I can get it back to him in time to get me back over to the house for supper. I don't want to get in late on what I saw and smelled as I came by."

"Alex, you're going to have to drive slowly," I admonished, as he set a chair and helped me climb to the seat of the light wagon. "And do drive through the alleys all the way!"

"I'll make as few bobbles as I can and you just make sure you hold everything until I get you safe back home again."

Phil was one joyous bridegroom. Lola seemed a little pale, a little nervous, but her face shone with an unearthly light.

When Lola slipped the knife into the great white mound of cake, it struck something. We watched Lola as she carefully cut a huge wedge of the cake from the third layer and put it on a plate for Phil to share with her. From a cutout made to receive it, she lifted a small white china doll, and she squealed and held it high. Phil burst out in a great laugh, for the doll's little backside was covered with a glob of the chocolate goo. He seized his napkin, took the doll from Lola, and carefully wiped it clean. "I might as well start practicing up," he said.

It was the first hearty laugh I'd had for ages and at its height things began to happen. A pain shot into my back and quickly cut a burning streak around my hips. "Get me home, Alex . . . Now!" I gasped, through clenched teeth.

October 19, 1913

It was eleven o'clock the next morning when I heard the baby's first cry. Alex brought the Bible to my bed and made the entry: born October

19, 1913, Cerece Monique Walker, weight 10 1/2 pounds. Then he rushed to the phone and called all hands at Englewood and told them he was now the proud father of a 10 1/2 pound *boy*.

My heart sank to my heels. Alex had his heart set on a boy. Would he feel pride in his little girl and love her?

"Gosh, Flossie, I'm willing to swear you're about the strongest woman on the face of this earth!" He groaned, rubbing his arms, his face contorted with pain. "You all but pulled my arms out of their sockets, by gosh!"

"You men!" scoffed Mrs. Nettles. "How you do suffer at childbirth. I'd like to live to see the day when every man had to take his turn at havin' a young'n, and then hear him tell about it afterward. I'll be bound and determined that the world has never yet heard such a tale of woe!"

I was weak and weary unto death, but before I drifted into sleep, I smiled to think that the period of waiting was over. The comings and goings of the rest of them grew fainter and fainter. Now only an occasional word registered in my mind and hung there, meaningless and inconsequential. Thankfully, I relaxed my hold on things and slept.

November 14, 1913

"But you'll have to go," fretted Pa.

Cerece was nearly a month old and this was the first time I had seen him since the day I ran from his table.

"Annie's been sick a week now and she's took ta naggin' at us continual about she ain't seen Alex's baby yet. I fetched the plush lap robe and a plenty of bricks ta heat and warm you against the cold."

"I want to go." I hastened to assure him. "It's just that I haven't been right in my hips since the baby came and the doctor said I was to keep quiet for three months. Getting in and out of the surrey might throw me back in bed."

"Well, I must say you look the picture of health," assured Pa, "and if gettin' in and out of that surrey is what's a troublin' yore mind, Alex and me can sure make a packsaddle and get you to and from the carriage without touchin' a foot ta ground."

"There's such a thing as pampering yourself too much, Flossie." Alex would not sit down but kept stalking impatiently about. "Besides, it's not cold out there. It's a fine day for riding. Pa and me had plenty we could a been doin' without takin' a day off to come in here for you. Seein' that we're here, the least you can do is to get ready and go!"

To dress and go someplace again seemed a tremendous undertaking. Moreover, after being so long alone, the thought of being with so many people at one time, some of them likely to be hostile, filled me with apprehension. But as preparations got under way, I grew excited and happy, and an hour later when Pa and Alex stood at the edge of the porch and made a packsaddle with their hands and arms, I laughed gaily, as I rode to the carriage with an arm around each of their necks. There they settled me in the back seat beside the baby's basket. Pa drove the mares with a fine air of pride, perhaps because Bess had a new mule colt trotting by her side. Alex sat beside Pa, relaxed and smiling at last, and tossed a remark over his shoulder at me from time to time.

I wasn't glad that Ma was sick, but I was glad of anything that would bring me back into the family in good standing. Ma looked all washed out, but pretty as a picture. She greeted me cheerfully, though her eyes flashed beyond me to the basket bearers and she motioned them to set the baby on the floor beside her bed. We watched her as she appraised the baby with critical eyes, toyed with the tiny hands, and raised the clothing to feel how the feet and legs were set on. Then she untied the white woolen cap and slipped it off, that she might feel the formation of the little head. "Why, it's all right!" she breathed, with a sigh of relief. "I dreamt last night that it had a frog's head and feet and that was the reason nobody said anythin' to me about going in to see it, or bringing it out here to see me. What did you name it?"

"Cerece."

Her brow puckered as if trying to understand. "Sounds like a girl's name," she said faintly.

"It is a girl's name, Ma," I said, looking askance at Alex. "Didn't you know the baby was a girl?"

"No. Alex told us in the beginnin' that it was a boy and that you ain't named him yet, and nobody's told me any different." The light had died out of Ma's face and she dropped wearily back on her pillow.

"Cerece," she murmured, making a mouth. "What a name. Who did you name her for, for pity's sake?"

"I didn't name her for anybody. I chose the name because I liked it and hoped she would. The second name is Monique."

"Mo-neek. Worser and worser, never heard of it!" She sighed. "Onnie and Ann named their first one after Henry and Alexander. I was hoping that if yore baby was a girl, you'd name it after me."

So wistfully she said it. But Rose Annie? God forbid!

Pa was kneeling beside the basket holding forth with a string of baby talk. "Well, it's Granpa's little gurrrl, even if it is named Reecie instead of Annie, and Granpa's plum glad she's so fat and sassy." He slipped a finger inside the little fist and, to his delight, the baby held fast. "Look how she grabs and hangs on." He laughed. "That's a sure sign she won't be an easy one to give up. It'll take a heap of doin' to discourage that gurrrl, yes it will . . . a heap of doin'."

Suddenly Ma raised herself again, her face beaming. "Maybe she wasn't named for me," she said, with satisfaction, "but she's got my twin name. Alex's baby and me is twins . . . Reecie and Annie."

I gave up and turned to meet Mattie's dancing eyes.

"You can take over mine and Belle's old room, Flossie. Save you havin' to climb them stairs. I got to run over to my house and do a few things, but I'll be back in time to serve the dinner. Like as not, we'll have a house full of company before the days over with. Ever'body knows yore comin' out."

"Who told them?"

"I told them!" she said emphatically, and banged the door shut after her.

The months that had dragged by so leadenly seemed like moments now that I was back on the farm, and I wondered how so many changes could come in such a short span. I sat on the side of the bed and stared at the floor disconsolately. The things I had run from! When Alex had played me false, I had run straight into a marriage with Will Wilson. When Will Wilson proved not to be the answer, I had run right back to Alex. When Alex changed as the seasons change, I had run again, this time back to Mama.

I unpacked my things and returned to the others to get away from my own thoughts.

"How long have you been sick, Ma?"

"About a week. They butchered here and you know what that always means to me. I made 'em bring me a big tender cabbage, opened a jar of my favorite cucumber pickles, made me some good egg bread, cooked that cabbage with a haif a pork shoulder, peeled a big onion, and set me down and filled up."

"The last three years she's gone to bed fer a week after gluttin' hersef on that meal. Yet and still, she's done it again!" Pa's tone expressed his disgust.

"Sure, I knew it would make me sick." Ma smiled easily. "But I didn't think it would make me this sick! Time was, here that first night, when I thought I was like to die before mornin'. I always make up my mind that I'm not goin' to mind bein' sick a little if I can jist get one more good fillin' of my favorite dish, but another round or two like this and I may change my mind."

"Another round or two like this and yore mind will be made up permanent." Pa glared at her.

"That's on account of that dead people don't go round changin' their minds, Aunt Annie." Mattie laughed, who had just come in, fresh in a blue checked gingham dress. She smoothed a clean white apron down as she went to a drawer in the bureau and took out fresh linens for Ma's bed. "It did look like that die she would this time, but when we butcher next year she'll be forgot about all this and start puttin' the big pot in the little un again on that pork and cabbage deal she's so fond of."

"You just changed my bed this morning, Mattie," said Ma.

"This is yore best things, Aunt Annie, with the hand-knitted lace yore Ma made fer you the year she died. Yore mor'n likely to have company. If you wouldn't use these things this weekend, I'd like to know whenever!" She began stripping and shaking up pillows and changing them. "And Flossie, I want you to put on that blue striped empire thing yore Ma gave you. I want you to look pretty-fare-nice when company comes."

"I haven't worn that dress since long before the baby came and I imagine it's pretty tight in the bosom."

"We'll find some way to make it do." The way we found was to split the bodice down the front and put in a little vest we made of my best lace edged handkerchief.

Alex phoned Arlien and Selma Thompson. "Get your carcasses over here and take a look at my boy," he told them. "The show will be continuous till tomorrow afternoon."

"I bet ever' receiver on the line went down. Everbody and his granpa will be here before night." Mattie laughed as she bustled about.

After dinner Mattie came to help me dress. She pulled my corset strings a little tighter and watched me do my hair. "I just love the way yore hair curls round and stays where you want it to."

"But it doesn't really curl, Mattie, it just bends easily." My skin had bleached milk white from being so long indoors, and I was much too pale. I felt very self-conscious doing it, but rouge was beginning to be pretty generally used, so I had bought a pot of it and now applied some lightly. Mattie was looking on with wide eyes. Her admiration was so frank and hearty that I returned to Ma's room feeling happier than I had for a long while. My heart lifted as I took the fretting Cerece from her basket and nursed her while all looked on with amusing concern. At last, when the baby lay back panting and satisfied, everybody relaxed because it was evident that I had plenty of "suck" for the child.

Company came, as expected: Arlien and Selma and their sturdy two-year-old, Mary Alice; Jimmy Raines and Willie with their shy three-year-old, Aline. Willie was sister to Arlien and Lucius, one of the numerous Thompson progeny, and a cousin of Alex's. The fun broke out with each fresh arrival, for all had thought the baby was a boy.

"You mean nobody ever told them it was a girl?" Willie said.

"Who was to tell 'em besides me and Lucius? And I told him that as sure as he give it away on me, I'd not pay him the rent nor the grocery bill I owed him. Caught him where the wool was short and the old boy would never dare let out a peep!" Alex laughed.

There was no feeling of strain anywhere now and I was truly glad I had come.

November 15, 1913

The next day was unseasonably warm and when Alex brought the buggy round to take me home. Ma admonished him to put the storm curtains in, so that if the clouds that had been piling up all day brought rain, the baby and I would not get wet.

"I'm not fixin' to rassle them storm curtains," said Alex shortly. "We're aimin' to make it to our own bailiwick before any rain falls."

But we were barely to the edge of town when the wind freshened and the rain came lashing in. Alex urged Fanny up to a vacant house, grabbed the baby basket and ran to the porch. I dreaded the consequences of getting wet and catching a chill, and without thinking I hastily followed suit. I felt the pain as I took the long step down to the ground, but managed to drag myself up the steps. I was limp with pain and apprehension now. When the rain slackened, the wind began to whip around to the north and the air grew cooler by the minute. I began to get cold and then, by the time we reached Mama's, the chill came on. Alex ran in at Mama's to phone Dr. Sewell to meet us at the house. Mama urged me to come in there, but I wanted to get to my own bed.

"She shouldn't have stirred from her routine for another month," snapped the doctor. "The pelvis was sprung when that baby was born, Alex. I told you that. She was getting along just fine, now you've got it all to do over. Get Mrs. Nettles, and keep Flossie in bed flat on her back in T-binders for six weeks!"

Alex was too stricken to move as Dr. Sewell took his leave. When he returned, he went to the phone and called Mama and told her the verdict. We were just beginning to get our finances straightened out. Now we had to go into another prolonged expense. I hid my face and cried, trying not to make a sound.

"What a disappointment I must be to you," I said sadly.

Alex was walking the floor now, running his hands through his hair, and on his face was a look of desperation. "Other women have babies and get up the next week or so and take up right where they left off. I can't understand why the first move you make, you collapse like a punctured balloon!"

"Please get a job in town, Alex. Stay with me until I get on my feet again," I begged, not knowing I was going to say it until the words hung there between us like grinning skeletons.

He turned on me. "I couldn't bear it, living in town!"

"We're poor folks no matter where we live and for my own part I'd rather be poor folks in town than poor folks in the country. At least you know when there's an end to the work day and can look forward to a pleasant evening." As an afterthought I added. "And there's a steady, dependable income . . . however small."

"That's just where we differ. I'd rather be a big frog in my own little pond than a little frog in a big pond."

"But we have to face things as they are Alex. I'm in no shape to be moved out to the country. What could I do if I was out there? And with so much to be done it would drive me distracted. We lived in two rooms at Big Lake. I'll be satisfied to keep living in these two rooms here."

He shook his head stubbornly. "You're barkin' up the wrong tree, O Lady!"

But he had called me O Lady, and his voice sounded less belligerent.

"It wouldn't take a lot for us to live here in town Alex," I said. "You made a good deal of money out there, but what have we got to show for it?"

"Well, we've got a team and wagon and wagon sheet, for a starter! And a baby all paid for, and we had a pretty good living the year we had together."

"Did you come out of debt with Pa?"

"The team and wagon and store account, yes."

"Well, what else do you owe him for, for pity's sake?"

"Pa and me will try to keep the business end of things straight, so you can forget about that part." he said shortly.

"Alex, promise me you'll try to get a job here in town."

"Oh I could get a job, all right." His eyes avoided mine and he took out his watch and deliberately wound it.

"Alex, I feel like I'll just die if you leave me another six weeks flat of my back in here alone!"

"You wouldn't be alone. I'm getting Mrs. Nettles settled here before I leave." My eyes brimmed with tears. I dared not speak, so I turned my face to the wall. I had lost again.

I could hear no move from Alex. I waited until my emotions had subsided and then quietly, steadily, I said, "If you will get a job and give me a year in town to get on my feet again, and you don't like living in town, when that year is up, I'll go back to the country with you and I'll never say town again as long as I live."

"Is that your solemn, sacred promise?" Alex's voice was tense.

"I cross my heart and hope to die." Fervently I went through the old childish ritual.

He sighed like a bellows and plunged. "All right, Flossie, I'll get the job. A year's stretch inside four walls maybe won't kill me. I'm not sure I can stick it, but I promise you, I'll give it a try. But if I live to keep my part of the bargain, you have got to keep yours!"

"Let that be the least of your worries," I said lightly. A year seemed an eternity just then, and it was an immediate reprieve. "Do give me a kiss to seal the bargain." Alex bent above me, and I was surprised to find his eyes suffused with tenderness. His lips met and clung to mine with the first affectionate warmth he'd shown in months.

Chapter 10

November 24, 1913

Alex got the job. Men's ready-to-wear at Pendleton's. Sixty dollars per month: five dollars out each month for rent, ten dollars a month for Mrs. Nettles, six dollars a month for laundry. We could manage on that, for steak was ten and twelve cents a pound, eggs the same a dozen, and all else accordingly.

December 2, 1913

Mama burst in upon me early this morning, just after Alex had gone to the store. Her coat collar was turned high to protect her face from the cold wind, but her skin had been whipped to a rosy freshness just the same, and she smelled like a shower of honey locust blossoms as she stooped to kiss me. Her eyes sparkled, and her whole manner bristled secrets. She inspected the baby, thoughtfully removed her wraps, and stood stretching her fingers to the stove for warmth.

"There's another strike on at the shop," she said, too casually.

"They seem to be getting the habit." I sighed. "Did Papa walk out with them?"

"Oh yes, what else can he do? He's sure that this is the only way and so must do what he must do. The strike was sanctioned by the federation, so there will be a benefit for the strikers. Perhaps we'll be able to earn enough to keep us afloat until things are settled again."

She then said she was planning to do house-to-house canvassing again! She tapped one foot nervously. "How would you like to move back to our house? Lola's gone. Alex has got his job and can bear his own household expenses and he can pay the same rent you pay here. You can put the bed for Mrs. Nettles in the boys' room. She won't be with you much longer. Then when she leaves, Jan and I can help in many little ways until you get your strength back."

"It sounds just wonderful to me and I know Alex won't object to it. Alma and Lucius are getting ready to settle their affairs and move back to the country, and we're going to have to look for another apartment anyway."

December 5, 1913

Papa came in the evening and helped Alex ease me and my blankets onto a cot and into the delivery wagon. How good it seemed to be home again. I listened for familiar voices as people passed up and down the street. It was good to hear the murmur of Mama's and Papa's voices at breakfast each morning and to have them in and out of my room each day.

But I missed the factory whistles, the whine of the saws, and the feel of hurry and bustle that had been such an integral part of my life here. Why, it was almost as quiet in this neighborhood of mill and shop people as it had been in the neighborhood of white-collar workers from which I had just come. Except that this was a sort of ominous quiet.

December 10, 1913

Less than a week later, Papa came bounding up the front steps and into the room where Mama was sitting with me.

"You found a job!" Mama exclaimed joyously.

"Yep, and what a job! You are now looking at the Champion Corn Shucker of Greene County, square in the face . . . ten dollars a week, by grabs. That will buy quite a pile of meat and potatoes for two people, Martha. That and our five a week from the union and we'll skin by."

December 22, 1913

Alex never complained, that I will say for him. But his face lost its happy carefree look and took on an expression of grim endurance. Mrs. Nettles was gone, and I was staggering around trying to get going again, and a sorry job I seemed to make of it. I simply had to learn to walk all over again.

It was Alex's job to fill the wood box in the kitchen and the coal scuttle behind the heater, last thing before he went to work each morning. Mama did endless little services for me and the baby throughout the day. The washing, except for the baby's things, was sent to the laundry.

"Your strength's never coming back until you start walking," Mama said one morning, and by the look on her face I knew I had to start trying.

"You know I can't get out on the street playing creepy-mousey like this," I said impatiently. "I can't even stand up straight yet."

"Everybody knows you've been lying flat and bound tight for five weeks," she contended. "But as far as that goes, you can do your walking after dark. That won't matter, so long as you do it." And that evening I began by walking to the corner and back. I almost didn't make it, but in a week's time I could walk around the block after supper and so finally found my legs again.

December 26, 1913

Is nothing ever settled? For no sooner had I become adjusted to the new order than Papa received a letter from Uncle Ab, who had been foreman for years in the hand shop at J. W. Hamlin & Son, one of the biggest cooperage plants in the nation and located in Little Rock. The letter read:

> Dear Albert,
> There will be an opening here with J. W. Hamlin & Son soon. Tom Shelby, who has been foreman in the machine shop, is being sent to the Argentine. The man they are putting in his place is too light for the job, though they haven't found that out yet.
> This is a good time to pay me a visit, but leave your Socialism and your Unionism behind. Either one would ruin your chances here. Hope to see you within the week.
>
> Regards to all.
> Your brother,
> Ab

January 2, 1914

Papa's thoughts had been long, long thoughts for the last few days. He kept on at the feed mill and while he worked and brooded, Mama slipped out at odd hours with her magic formula. When at last he was ready to go, she proudly added a few more dollars to his small hoard.

January 9, 1914

The house seemed bereft without Papa and his quick light step, his sudden laughter, his bursts of song. In a playful mood, he would get out the old violin to fiddle a few breakdowns, invariably ending up with nostalgic and mournful melodies that left us all in a pensive mood. I missed the long quiet talks I often enjoyed with him and his unfailing sympathy and understanding. In a week's time Mama had received a letter from him.

> Dear Martha,
>
> You are now reading a letter written by the hand of the new machine-shop foreman at J. W. Hamlin & Son. Shelby didn't last till the cressets got hot, though of course I'm just on probation. In a way I feel like a traitor, not making my convictions known, on the other hand, they probably have my case history from Pekin Cooperage. However, after the uncertainties of the past few years, I am willing to be happy in well-doing for a while, and wonder if there is a man who could blame me. They are starting me off at $25 a week. With no one to think and worry about but ourselves, Martha, perhaps we can at last live more as we would like and at the same time lay aside something for the old days.
>
> I will be looking out for a house. I'm missing you more every day and may God hasten the day when we can be together again. I miss you at breakfast more than

any other time. You could always send me off to work feeling like I could lick the world singlehanded.

Love to all, and most of all to your dear self.
Albert.

February 19, 1914

It had been decided that I was to have a suit at last, and I chose one of navy blue serge at the February sale. The hat was a delight to me, a small high-crowned blue felt with the flexible brim caught back at the side by a sweeping blue and gold quill.

I bought a satin blouse, but the pride of my life was the blue and gold taffeta petticoat, with five narrow ruffles that swished and whispered as I walked. The skirt was one of the new models, slit to the knee. Alex really had a qualm when I told him the petticoat had cost five dollars.

"The suit would have fallen flat without it," I contended. "The slit skirt fairly shrieks for a taffeta petticoat!"

"Ye gods, beyond a doubt!" sneered Alex. In spite of which he was just as proud as me when I was once more fully assembled and able to appear in public looking as up-to-date as Lola.

March 19, 1914

I was much stronger. The pain, so long as I kept within my small limitations, had ceased to trouble me. As always, with the first warm days of spring, my mind seemed filled anew with the miracle of growing things. My hyacinths were up, but I longed to see the yard full of gay garden flowers, not just the honeysuckle, the lilacs, snowballs, and roses that had been all Mama ever had time for. I wanted a vegetable garden too. I fidgeted with the idea, but when I finally got up courage to mention it to Alex, he went into a rage.

"Work in that prison all day long, then come home at night and break my back and get my hands all over blisters for a few vegetables. Not if I know myself! Onnie can bring in a little of the surplus that goes to waste on that farm every year, and that'll be more than we can ever use. Try to remember one thing, Flossie. I'm living in town this year!" He pitched a quarter beside my plate at breakfast. "Tomorrow's payday and that's my last coin. I want you to take it and get a couple of pounds of steak for supper."

But when I went to buy the steak, the show window was resplendent with a gay display of flower seed packets, spread like a peacock's tail. The brilliant colors danced tantalizingly before my eyes. I hesitated—and was lost. But even as I paid for the seed, my heart misgave me. This meant that I would have to give Alex fish cakes for supper, and he was so sick of them. I racked my brain for something that I could concoct out of my limited supplies . . . something that would take the curse off my delinquency.

"But it was my last quarter," he glubbed, over a luscious bite of chocolate pie, "and she spends it for flower seeds!" He was addressing the ceiling.

"There was once a poet who spent his last cent for white hyacinths to feed his soul," I offered, feeling a little surer of my footing.

"Well, please to remember next time when it's a toss-up as to which gets fed, my soul or my belly, that I'm not a poet!"

March 20, 1914

The next morning when I went to get breakfast, there was such a little bit of wood in the box that I had to hurry the cooking. Alex just would not keep that wood box filled, and I could not yet go clear to the back of the lot and bring it myself.

Besides, I hated the skimpy way I had to cook, portioning out each thing. Two small slices of bacon each, one egg, stingy little portions of butter, and never was there an adequate supply of sweets. With a nursing baby, I found I had acquired a workingman's appetite and could hardly wait to get to the table at mealtime.

Alex had got into the bad habit of reaching over into my plate while I was up for hot biscuits and helping himself to my egg, my sausage, or preserves.

"I wish you'd try to remember that I have two to feed, Alex," I had protested more than once. "I get just as hungry as you do. I couldn't bear to take a mouthful of food from your plate, knowing you were hungry. How can you take it from me when you know I need it so?"

"Can't tell a bit of difference in the taste of it when you need it and when you don't, honey. I swear it," he had answered lightly.

March 23, 1914

This morning there were only two eggs in the bowl where I kept them. I served the oatmeal and then lifted the two slices of bacon and an egg to each plate. Alex was ravenously hungry and soon made way with his. I was eating mine slowly and with relish and had barely taken two bites.

"Get me some hot biscuits, Flossie," said Alex, and I took the dish to the stove. Like a flash it dawned on me what he had in mind to do, and I turned to prevent it, but I was too late.

My tender, delicious, and personal egg now lay on his plate, and he was in the act of taking the first bite. A quick anger surged up and beat like a hammer in my throat, but I was careful to make no move to excite him. Instead, I moved over behind him, set the plate of biscuits down with my left hand, scooped the soft egg up with my right, caught his head to my bosom, and smeared the gooey mess into his eyes, ears, nose, and mouth. He sputtered and fought and raged, and I stepped back out of reach while he began wiping his face with the handkerchief he snatched from his hip pocket. "What do you mean?" he gasped, mopping at his right ear.

"I mean that I'm hungry, and that was my breakfast. What do you mean?" For a wonder my voice was calm, my eyes level. He glared at me angrily, snatched off his soiled collar and tie, and poured hot water into a basin for washing.

"And don't forget the wood if you want any dinner," I said maliciously.

I could never bear to eat when angry, so I slowly began clearing the table. Presently he dashed through the kitchen and out the back door. I thought, of course, that he had gone for stove wood, but when I glanced out the back window, he was standing with feet wide apart, regarding the woodpile with evident disgust. As I watched, he lightly vaulted the back fence and walked swiftly toward town through the back alley.

I pushed things back on the table, sat down, rested my head on my arms, and found relief in tears. Why was something always wrong? There seemed forever to be some certain thing that he kept doing over and over, something I kept trying to ignore until my resentment toward him reached such a peak that the dam burst and we were both caught in the flood. I didn't know how to handle Alex. I was forever chasing around, pussyfooting, glossing over, pretending nothing was wrong until I reached the end of my patience. Surely I had a mind. I must learn to use it instead of being forever governed by my emotions.

I resumed my work, quiet and thoughtful now. I had learned one thing: Alex would never apologize. Well, I didn't want to go on living like this, so I would apologize at noon.

I bathed the baby and washed out a few things for her. If I kept right up with them, I could do them in an hour each day. Without thinking, I squatted to pick up the soiled collar and tie Alex had left on the floor and screamed and fell on the floor in a cold sweat of agony as searing pains darted through my pelvis like hot needles. Mama came running into the room.

"What in the world, Flossie?" I sat up, trying to laugh.

"Alex left his things on the floor again and I forgot to kneel for them," I gasped. "I just can't squat without that awful tearing pain, Mama. Tell me, what am I going to do about Alex? He left without filling the wood box again." She finished my morning's work, searching all the while for some solution to my problem.

"Suppose you prepare the noon meal, Flossie, all but cooking it. Have it just ready and tell him you will cook it as soon as he brings the wood."

"But he left mad after what I did to him at breakfast, and I had planned to apologize at noon."

"Your apologies can wait this once. Alex doesn't like to miss a meal and he hasn't the money to dash back up town and eat, so he'll get the wood, all right." She thought a moment. "In the meantime, get your bath and put on your red serge skirt and a linen blouse. He always likes that, and put your hair up real pretty. We'll embroider all morning, have a good visit together, and just forget your troubles. You think about them too much!"

By the time I'd finished bathing and dressing, Mama was back. "My, you look ready for the office," she said brightly. "Would you do this scarf in colors or in white . . . if you were deciding?"

"You know me, Mama. If it's something cheap, I let myself go wild with colors. If it's something nice that I will keep and cherish for a long time, I always make it up in white."

"Then it's colors wild. I wouldn't know how to act with a nice piece of linen fancywork in my hands once more."

I got out the lace I was making. It was pleasant to sit rocking thus, stitching and gossiping, as though I hadn't a care in the world. Oh, but I would miss Mama when she moved to Little Rock. Cerece started fretting, and I picked her up to nurse.

"Let me burp her and sing her to sleep one time," coaxed Mama. "I know they don't rock and sing to babies anymore, but I did to mine and I've always wanted to sing her to sleep."

"If you'll sing one of the old ballads, I'll let you," I teased.

"Which one? 'Barbara Allen' . . . or 'Two Little Orphans'?"

"Neither one. I want to hear the one that used to make me hide under the bed and cry . . . 'Little Son Hugh'."

Mama laughed. "I'll never forget when I learned that one. A little girl in the Arkansas River bottomlands taught it to me. It used to make my blood run cold, and I was so afraid at the sight of a gypsy that I ran like a turkey when I saw one till I was half grown." She gathered Cerece up under her chin and began on a high plaintive note:

> *It was on one high holiday*
> *And the drops of dew did fall,*
> *And every scholar in that school*
> *Went out to playing ball, ball, ball!*
> *Went out to playing ball.*
>
> *Then up stepped an old gypsy woman*
> *With apples in her hand,*
> *Saying, "Come with me, my Little Son Hugh,*
> *And you may have one of them, them, them!*
> *And you may have one of them."*

Mama leaned forward and laughed. "The little girl that taught me always said, 'Tham! Tham! And you may have one of tham!'" She leaned back in her chair, evidently enjoying herself, and sang softly on:

> *She took him by his little white hand*
> *And she led him through her hall,*
> *And she locked him in her store chamber*
> *Where none could hear him call, call, call!*
> *Where none could hear him call.*
>
> *She sat him down in a golden chair*
> *And scratched his heart with a pin;*
> *She washed a silver basin clean*
> *To catch his heart's blood in, in, in!*
> *To catch his heart's blood in.*

It was strange that this should be happening to me again, but I felt my heart swell with pity for Little Son Hugh, just as it had done when I was a child.

> *She wrapped him in a winding sheet*
> *Close in her arms to sleep,*
> *She walked with him to yonder's well*
> *Where the water was cold and deep, deep, deep!*
> *Where the water was cold and deep.*
>
> *"Sink, oh sink, my Little Son Hugh,*
> *And never do you swim,*
> *For if you do it will be a disgrace*
> *To me and all of my kin, kin, kin!*
> *To me and all of my kin."*

As the soft voice droned on and on, Cerece could no longer hold her eyes open but drooped like a flower on its stem and slept at last.

The day rolled off and night came on
As night has always done,
And every mother had her son,
But Little Hugh's mother had none, none, none!
But Little Hugh's mother had none.

His mother took a bur rod in her hand
And she walked across the plain,
"If ever I find my Little Son Hugh,
I will whip him home again, gain, gain!
I will whip him home again."

"Here, I'll put her down," I said hastily. "Mama, I'm all over gooseflesh." Mama laughed a little uncertainly.

"I have no doubt that the song was meant to raise goose pimples. My, my, how they did use to sob out those heartbreaking old ballads." With the baby asleep, Mama returned to her room, and I stitched on.

My heart leaped into my mouth, then fell with a dull thud to the pit of my stomach when I heard Alex clear the front steps at a bound.

"Shhhh!" I held up a quieting hand as he burst into the room, then trembling, followed him into the kitchen.

"What in the hang?"

"No wood," I said, making it short. "I went as far as I could without it."

"Gosh it all to the devil." He stamped about. "Like a chicken in a coop I'm penned all mornin' long, after half eatin' my breakfast, and then come home to this. A fine wife you turned out to be!"

"You've heard my side of the story so often. I don't think I'll bother to go into it again," I said coldly. "Besides, there's no time for talk. I'll barely have time to finish up dinner if you get a fire in that stove in five minutes." I resumed my seat, crocheting furiously, well knowing every stitch was wrong and that I'd have it all to rip out later.

I heard no move on his part for a full minute after I sat down. Then he wheeled and dashed out the back door and back in no time with goosenecks and bucker shavings. With this light fuel, the stove was hot and the meal ready in an unbelievably short time.

I had even opened a treasured can of apricots and a box of fancy cookies from the emergency shelf. If this wasn't an emergency, I argued with my conscience, I hoped one never arose.

Alex had seated himself at the table, and all the while I went about preparations. His eyes kept following me, and I got the impression that he was seeing me for the first time in months. Even while he was eating, I still felt his eyes on me, but never once did I raise mine. When at last he had finished, he tilted his chair to the hind legs, a thing that never failed to irritate me, and sat teetering precariously back and forth.

"Kind a dressed up a little for me, didn't you, O Lady?" he said, his voice as wheedling soft as if nothing untoward had ever occurred between us. O Lady! He had said it again, and I had thought he never would.

"A wee mite, maybe," I tried to speak lightly.

"You look just like you used to," he said wonderingly. "I don't know why, but I've always been just a little afraid of you, and I think you know it."

Alex, afraid of me? The idea was entirely new to me.

"I still, by golly, am. I'm always thinkin' I've got you checked and labeled, and then you come out with a new one!"

"Don't expect me to believe that." I tried to make my voice light and careless. "But please don't get the idea that I've enjoyed going around looking like a scarecrow all these months and not being able to do one thing about it!"

In spite of all, my tone was tinged with bitterness, but he seemed not to notice.

"You're sittin' right across from me, Flossie, but you seem so far away," he spoke musingly, as though pondering a thing he found hard to believe.

"Is that the way you like me best?" Oh, why did I say these things?

He caught his lower lip between his teeth and sat staring quizzically at me for an instant, then sprang to his feet and dashed from the room. In no time at all, the wood box was full. He did not forget it again, nor was the incident ever again referred to by either of us.

May 8, 1914

Papa had found a house at last. It was in a good neighborhood and set on a high-terraced yard, but it had only four rooms, and they were small. So he had written the first week in April for Mama to leave some of the heavy pieces with me, knowing she could get nothing for them from the secondhand stores. Many of the pieces had a sentimental value for her. Mama left the mahogany sideboard and serving table with me, running her hand lovingly over the pink marble tops.

"Your Grandmother Mounce gave us this when your grandfather died and she went to live with Aunt Phoebe," she remembered. And there flashed to my mind the pride I had felt at eleven when the massive carved pieces were moved into our dining room. I came into so many other things she left me that I was a week sorting, cleaning, rearranging, and storing odds and ends.

For a long while after Mama left I was at a loss. With her in the house I could always run to the grocery, the dentist, even for short visits with a neighbor. It was now that Mrs. Thomas and Lily became a part of my life. They worked side by side with me, and I paid them with things that were good and usable, but for which I had no immediate need.

Alex took little interest in the baby. As long as Mama was with us, I didn't notice it so much, but now that we were alone, it irked me to see how unwillingly he did the small things needed for her comfort. When I mentioned this to him, he frowned petulantly.

"I just don't like little tinsies, Flossie. I'll probably like her all right when she gets a little older, but I never did like right young babies. Ma can tell you that!"

"Well, when they're your own, you don't let them suffer! The doctor still says I'm not to stoop and lift her from her basket, so hand her to me."

He rose reluctantly and stood glowering down at the little thing. In that instant my anger flared.

"What are you trying to do, figure out some way of getting her to me without having to touch her?"

He gave me a sour grin and lifted her gingerly to my lap.

I had been sitting on the side of the bed folding a pile of clean diapers when she started fretting. I picked her up to nurse. He pulled his chair over and sat facing me. As he watched her, an amused smile hovered round his mouth, and I relaxed.

"Now, you take her and belch her while I finish folding diapers," I said, feeling much encouraged. With an utter lack of enthusiasm, he suffered me to lay the baby in his outstretched arms. She began to turn and twist and pucker her little face into knots.

"Speak to her, Alex. She's a stranger in this big wide world and she'd like to feel that she's among friends! Hold her on your shoulder and as soon as she belches she'll feel better."

The fuzzy little head was pillowed on his arm, but when he went to lift her, she gave a slight belch, and a stream of milk rolled over his sleeve and puddled onto the floor.

"Hey, look what she's done to me now!" he yelled. He lunged forward and dumped her into my lap, his heavy shoe almost crushing my toe that was covered only with a soft felt bedroom slipper.

I doubled my fist and drove with all my might to the middle of his stomach. "Get off my foot!" I howled. He gasped for breath but caught his sleeve delicately between forefinger and thumb and gave it a gentle shake. The scorn I felt leaped in a withering flame from my eyes to his. "Don't get contaminated! That milk is probably poison, being as sweet as it was when she drew it from my breast."

"It doesn't have to be poison for me to hate havin' it on me," he choked. "You'll know when I take up the little Hessian again . . . she puked on me!"

With supreme effort I brought my own voice down to conversational level. "Here, take this diaper and wet a corner of it and wipe your sleeve clean. Then get a rag and wipe up the floor!" He gave me a final glare and got busy. I found the baby wet and changed her. I was beginning to enjoy myself.

"Now, take this diaper and put it with the soiled ones in the box that Mama nailed high for me in the back porch."

"But that's a wet diaper!"

"Sure, it's wet. That's why I want it put with the ones I'm going to wash in the morning."

He rolled his eyes and shied like a skittish horse. The mad came up in me again, and I stood threateningly before him. "Take that diaper, Alex, and put it in the box with the others," I gritted.

Alex looked wildly around, seized a magazine, and held it out like I'd seen him pass the collection plate in church, carefully looking the other way so as not to appear curious about the amount of the other fellow's offering.

He came back in wearing a much abused expression. But I was past caring. At that moment he was no better than a worm in my sight, and I wanted to reach out a foot and squash him flat.

Chapter 11

June 5, 1914

Spring had sped swiftly by and suddenly the first hot days were upon us and the honey locusts in full bloom. Bees busied themselves with the fragrant blossoms all day long. I could hear the whine of the saw mill three blocks way. Long blasts from the big whistle at the stave mill and short toots from the toy whistle at the planing mill marked the periods of the day. By these whistles did the town rise, eat, work, and subside.

The locusts had been in bloom when Alex sent for me. Now that they were in bloom again, he turned to me in the old familiar way. How could there be such a difference in a person? But I closed my mind against the memory of the bitter loneliness I had so lately endured. It was enough to have him come bounding in right on time in the evenings. All day long I lived and worked for but a few daily delights: to have all as it should be for his homecoming, to share with him the small experiences of the day, to revel in the sweet companionship of the long twilight.

For two days we had eaten dried beans, the hated fish cakes, rice and coleslaw, but I had really splurged tonight. I had baked a coconut cream pie. I had two breaded pork chops for Alex and one for me. There was a shredded salad, dressed with bacon drippings, salt, pepper, sugar, and lemon juice; creamed potatoes; and hot biscuits. I timed, I thought, to the minute. I cracked the ice for tea and filled the glasses.

But Alex did not come. I glanced at the clock. Well, it was only five minutes past, he would be in any minute now. I sat on the front steps to wait . . . and waited . . . and waited.

At ten o'clock Alex came in, very loud and boisterous, a thing he never was. Evidently he was striving to appear nonchalant, but I found it extremely irritating.

"Speak a little more quietly, Alex, you'll wake the baby."

"Oh."

I put aside the story I had been trying to read while I lay propped up in bed waiting for him. "Now, begin all over at the start and tell me about it."

"I said, little old Kitty Crandall is back in town."

"And who, pray, is Kitty Crandall?"

"She's an old friend of mine," he said airily. "Somebody you wouldn't know. Her dad was a tenant on one of Pa's places years ago. Funny to remember the little old snot-nosed cotton-topped tag-end she used to be. I just wish you could see her now, Flossie. There's not a gal in Paragould that can touch her for looks!" His face lighted up at the memory of her. "I bet she don't weigh more'n a hundred pounds, but she's round as you please. She never grew tall, neither. She can stand under my arm, and her, a full grown woman, honest she can!"

"Did you measure to see?"

"Yes, we tried it out and it's a fact!"

It was plain to be seen that he still found it hard to credit his senses. "She's cute Flossie, and you wouldn't believe that hair could be so gold! Little old turned-up nose and a dimple in her chin and the smoothest skin . . . ."

Absently my fingers strayed to my own high bridged nose and my heart sank, for I never thought how incongruous a tiny turned-up nose would look with the rest of my face!

But Alex was raving on. "And she does her hair in what she calls a French roll. Starts on top of her head and is smooth as butter to the nape of her neck and stuck there as thick as jam with great big amber-colored hairpins."

I sat up in bed. Alex was so full of his subject he had not seemed to notice my growing exasperation. "What do her people do now?" I asked, setting myself to hear the whole story.

"Her dad's dead. She and her Ma have been runnin' a boardin' house for railroad men in Memphis." His face lighted with a new thought.

"She showed me what she called her lawnjeray: nightgowns, pyjames, tea gowns, satins, silks, and laces, and such silk stockings, boxes of 'em she never has opened, all presents from her men friends, she said."

"Think of that!" I said, beginning to boil. "Why did you stay so long?"

"Just got to talking over old times, you know how it is!" His manner was very offhand.

"I wouldn't think you'd have much in the way of old times to talk over with one you remember only as a little old snot-nosed cotton-topped tag-end in one of your Pa's tenant houses!"

"The talk wasn't all about old times, of course," he said lamely. "Some of it was, well, just jokes and stuff."

"Tell me some of the jokes so I can laugh too."

"They wouldn't be funny to you," he said, his eyes beginning to waver.

"But they were to you?"

"Yes," he answered, honestly. "The way she told them they were. I laughed quite a bit of the time."

"How did you meet her?"

"She was waitin' at the door when I came out from work. Said she was just passin', thought she recognized me and just waited to see. Then she said I must walk home with her and see her Ma. The old lady was proud to see me. She's a lavish good cook, had supper about ready and just made me eat with them. Pork chops, hot creamed potatoes and gravy...."

"Fresh vegetable salad?" I suggested, fearfully.

"What she called a tossed spring salad," he nodded. I drew a deep breath.

"What did you do after supper?"

"We talked a while round the table. Then she took me to her room while her Ma did the dishes. Then's when she showed me all that stuff."

"Did she try any of it on for you?"

"Only a red satin hostess gown, but I couldn't tell much about it on over her street clothes."

"Too bad. Maybe next time she might not be so shy."

"What do you mean?" he asked sharply, seeming to catch the trend of my thoughts for the first time.

"I mean I'm not as dumb as I look and I want you to let Kitty Crandall alone," I choked.

"What do you want to act like that for?" he asked disgustedly. "I haven't said or done one wrong thing, if that's what's eating on you. If I'd been guilty of anythin' wrong, do you think I would have come home and told you? I could as well have said I had to work overtime. You wouldn't have known the difference. Instead, I come home and tell you the honest truth and you jump on me like a mad tarantula!"

"If it's any comfort to you, Alex, I think you are utterly guileless. It's Kitty's maneuvering that I resent, and the fact that you were taken in by it! She took you home and did just enough to rouse your interest, but Kitty's not through with you, don't think that. I just want to be sure that you are through with Kitty!"

He sat staring at the floor, lost in thought. A lump the size of a hen's egg and as hot as hell rose in my throat and needles of pain shot up behind my ears. Surely I wasn't going to cry! I swallowed hard.

"Bring me a glass of water before you lie down," I said hoarsely. "My throat hurts!" And I buried my face against my pillow.

July 10, 1914

Mrs. Thomas had taken over my washing and ironing and mopping in return for sewing. All summer long I had something in the making for her, or for Lilly. Buried under sewing as I was, I dropped everything and ran to the door when I saw Alex enter the gate at midmorning.

"Get ready, quick. They're coming in after us. Granpap died this morning."

"How did it happen?"

"He hasn't seemed right lately, though he's been up and around." Pa said he didn't come down to breakfast. Ma went to look after him and when she found him, he was still dressed, lying unconscious at the head of the stairs. His bed hadn't been slept in, so of course he'd been lying there all night. He never did regain consciousness and died before the doctor got there. Heart, no doubt."

We were ready when Onnie drove up with an extra seat in the spring wagon. Pa and Ma passed in the buggy just ahead of him, with no more than a wave of the hand. They were on the way to buy the necessary things for burial.

How sweet it was to be out again. Alex felt it too, for as we crossed the bridge he leaned over and said, "Breathe deep, Flossie, and let the town stink blow out of your lungs!"

"Granpap loved the growing time more than he did the harvest, Alex."

"Yes, it would have pleasured him to be alive today," he said, sadly.

July 11, 1914

The next morning we set out for Brown's Chapel. Pa didn't go. "This place can't be left unguarded for the day," he said with conviction. "It would only be to invite prowlers."

Ma gave him one long, withering look and flounced out and into the surrey. She sat between her two boys in the front seat. Ann and the babies and I sat in the back seat. It was the first time I had ridden in the surrey and I felt very grand. Ahead of us rolled the spring wagon with its sad burden, Ed and Ray Langley driving slowly along.

Cerece was teething and fretful. Nothing I did seemed to soothe her, so I hung around on the edge of the crowd. The burial service was to be held beneath the trees, since there was scarcely room for all in the tiny church. Alex had brought a chair, seated Ma near the grave and stood by her side. Lester leaned against her lap and Onnie and Ann stood behind her. As I watched, Ma spoke to Alex and they seemed to lock eyes for a few moments. I was trying to get Cerece settled and when I looked back Alex was nowhere to be seen.

Ma was motioning to a tall black haired girl, who came timidly forward through the crowd and placed a sturdy blonde baby in Ma's outstretched arms. Ma bent over it anxiously and I wondered who it could be, then fretfully started trying to locate Alex. He shouldn't leave Ma one minute, with Pa not here!

I turned toward where the horses were tethered and when I reached the surrey, there was Alex lying down in the back seat. "What in the world are you doing here? Alexander Walker, you get up from there and go to Ma this living minute! They're all but ready to start preaching the funeral."

"I can't go back up there!" His eyes were wild and gleamed at me from a pale face.

"Alex, are you sick?" I asked. He stared miserably back at me. "Answer me, Alex. Why can't you go back up there?"

"I tell you, I can't stand it!" His voice rose, hysterically. "Ma hasn't got the sense God gave a flea, and don't you stand there looking like that at me, either!"

The wind was out of my sails. What silly thing had Ma done now that could have upset him like this? Or was it just that he couldn't bear to stand by anybody, through anything?

"Well, if you're not going back, for whatever reason, then you keep the baby and I'll go!" I held her to him but he snatched fiercely at my sleeve.

"You stay here!" he gritted between set teeth, "and keep the baby here with you!" His words angered me beyond endurance and I jerked myself free of his grasp.

"Let go my sleeve, Alexander Walker. It's not decent nor right for neither of us to be present at Granpap's funeral. "But my anger died quickly in my sudden concern for him, for he had fallen back against the cushion, his eyes closed, and the pallor of death on his tortured face. This was awful. Granpap dead, Pa not here, the baby whining on and on and Alex acting like he'd lost his mind. Overcome with it all I hid my face in Cerece's soft little neck and found relief in tears.

October 3, 1914

Paragould was the Greene County seat and this Saturday was given over to the farmers. They began to pass at daylight in the morning, and by midafternoon the tide had turned and they were all heading back home.

Pa stopped by the house, being his best pleasant self, and told me to get myself together, that he wanted us home to visit Sunday.

Then Arlien and Selma came by. "You and Cerece might as well go out to our place with Selma tonight. I can wait here till Alex gets off, then we can go on to Uncle Henry's tomorrow," Arlien offered.

"I've got the beds turned down just ready to crawl into," Selma laughed.

"Let's, have supper here," I said. "Then you won't have to fix when we get to your place. We might as well eat a little bite before we go out."

So it was arranged.

October 4, 1914

"Let me drive, Dubbin," said Alex eagerly. "It'll seem good to have a pair of lines in my hand again."

It was the first time I had heard him call Arlien by his childhood nickname.

"Thought to my soul I'd die when it come time to plow, and there I was grinning like a possum and sayin' to Tom, Dick and Harry, *What can I do for you today?*"

The silly way he said it.

Two spring seats had been set in the wagon and Selma and I were in the back seat, the babies sprawled on a quilt that had been spread over hay in the wagon bed. Alex smacked the rumps of the matched gray mares joyously, and they sprang into a quick trot, glad to find themselves headed for home at last. The sun was just setting, and I felt free as a bird, bouncing along in the sweet summer dusk.

"Except when Granpap died, this is the first time Alex has had any time away from the store since he went to work!"

"I don't see how he stands it," said Selma. "If I wanted to kill Arlien Thompson, I wouldn't know a surer way to go about it than to tie him in town. He can't hardly stand it to stay in there long enough to tend to his business."

October 5, 1914

    Selma was free and outspoken in her manner but friendly and nice to be with. This morning she nonchalantly fried a dozen eggs for breakfast and when I exclaimed over it, she said the cats and dogs could take care of any that was left over.

    Alex rolled his eyes at me and I stared back at him, both of us thinking what eggs had come to mean in our lives.

    Ham and red bottom gravy, biscuits light as a feather. There was thick clotted cream for the coffee, a great bowl of unmolded butter, at least two pounds of it, sorghum, honey in the comb, and blackberry jelly.

    "Alex, don't eat so much!" I laughed, reaching for my fourth biscuit.

    "Why wouldn't I eat? I haven't had a decent meal since I moved to town!"

    "You was always a good liar, Alex," scoffed Selma. "We ate at yore house last night. The kind of meals you have are just as big a treat to us as this is to you."

    "I feel like I'd like to just get out and walk for miles this morning." I yawned, and stretched luxuriously.

    "Well, we don't have to ride," Selma said. "We'll turn the young'ns over to the boys and we'll walk over."

    But Alex urged us to get in and ride with them. He even seemed anxious about it. Selma seemed to think it was because he thought the long walk would be too much for me.

    "I know she looks pale," she nodded vigorously. "She needs the sunshine and fresh air, that's why we're goin' to walk." Which seemed to settle the matter, and scowling, Alex settled Cerece in the seat beside him. I smiled to see how delighted she was and how the new bright hair lay in rings under the tiny blue bonnet.

    I held my face to the morning sun and breathed to my heels. The air was soft and warm and torn to gay ribbons by the clear sweet notes of the singing birds.

    "I hope Pa's pulse is beating steady today." I sighed. "I certainly don't want anything to happen to spoil Alex's one day at home. The whole family seemed to feel it so bad when I persuaded Alex to move into town till I could have time to get on my feet again."

"Yeah, they didn't like that, all right, but never did it rankle them like when you left Alex at Big Lake to get on the best he could, especially when he was beset by a plum nest of his old girls."

"What did his old girls have to do with it?" I asked sharply.

"Seems to of had a right smart to do with it, all in all. Susie Maynard's been crazy 'bout Alex fer years. Neither does she care who knows it. He hadn't any more'n got you moved to town till he stops by on his way to see you one Saturday to hatch up a fishing trip with Clay Prentice. Susie jist happened to be there. I do think that was pure accidental, but when she begged him to stay on the day there with her, he got down and done it. Time after time they met there, till May Prentice tole me she got downright uneasy, fer ever' time her back was turned Alex and Susie was kissin' and huggin'. May finally put a stop to Alex coming there at all, good friends as him and Clay has ever been."

My mind had darted back to the weary months of loneliness that had been mine while waiting for Cerece to be born. The weekends I had prepared meals for Alex, and the over and over again moments of bleak disappointment. Seeing that I had no comment, Selma went on.

"You saw how he didn't want you and me alone together after breakfast, and how he tried to make you get in and ride over? That was because once, when things got rocky, I told him that if ever you got over havin' that baby I was goin' to tell you exactly what he was doin' in the time of it. And now I've done so, thinkin' still that you ought to know it, so's that next time you can manage somehow to keep him with you. A man's got no business being left on his own while his wife carries a baby fer him. He was there when it was started, wut'n he? Then let him learn to ride right 'long with her to pay the fiddler!"

My mind was now stuck on the picture of Alex, kissing and hugging Susie Maynard, while I waited for the baby. How I wished Selma had never told me! The new growth of our love had just now spread sufficiently to cover the old wounds and we had been very happy of late. Suddenly I turned to the ditch beside the road and was disgustingly sick.

"I'd no least idea you'd take it like this!" said Selma, all contrition.

"I'm taking it as most any other woman I know would take it," I said weakly.

I was struggling and fumbling with data in hand. Alex had started to see me the day Mag Hawley had asked him to stay the day with her. He had started to see me the day Susie Maynard had asked him to stay with her instead. He had started home to me when Kitty Crandall had asked him to walk home with her. Was he always and ever thus easily to be diverted from his perfectly good intentions toward me? By the time we reached the big house I was no fit company for anybody.

The men had gone to Sunday school, and Cerece was settled on a pallet at play when I went in. She had a tobacco tin and a teaspoon which she put in and out of a tiny wagon belonging to Lester. A box of other toys set unnoticed beside her.

I offered my services in the kitchen.

After Sunday school, the others came trouping in, and when Lester saw Cerece thus occupying the center of it in Granpa's house, his blue eyes snapped, his lips puffed out, and his breath came out in a wild snort. In one motion he reached her side and snatched the playthings from her. Ann had gone to the smokehouse and the men were settled in the porches.

"I knew that was bound to happen." Ma smiled.

But Selma spoke sharply. "There's a box full of other things, Aunt Annie, why don't you make him let her things alone?"

"He's not big enough to know better," she defended complacently. "Besides, he's used to havin' everthin' to his sef when he comes here."

"I should have brought some of her things for her to play with," I said miserably.

"Well, he would jist've got them too"—Ma laughed softly—"and she wouldn't a had any more to play with than she's got as it is. So I'd not worry about it, if I was you."

"Aunt Annie, how can you make that much difference in 'em . . . and both yore own blood grandchildren?" Selma flared.

"Both grandchildren, all right," she answered, a malicious twinkle in her eyes, "but the one is named Lester Emerson and the other is not named Rose nor Annie!"

Mattie burst into the room, having stopped by home to change into a starched gingham dress and frilled apron. She gave me a rapturous hug and a hearty kiss, "I didn't know you'd got here. My soul and body, Flossie, you look sicker'n a dog. I hope and pray you ain't . . . ."

"Flossie's got a headache," Selma offered.

"And it's time for Cerece's nap," I added gratefully. "I'm going up to get her to sleep, and if you get dinner on the table before I'm down, go right ahead and eat. I ate enough breakfast at Selma's to do me the day. Ask her!"

Upstairs I changed the baby's diaper and lay down across the bed with her. When her pink little tongue cupped the nipple and she tugged so industriously, it seemed to ease my heart a little. She regarded me with a wide unblinking stare and as the milk began to flow faster than she could swallow, her eyebrows turned pink, sweat popped out in beads on her button nose, and her breath came in little short moans. Finally outdone, she released the nipple and a dozen fine streams sprinkled her rosy face while she grinned knowingly at me, panting as though she had run a mile. Suddenly she was very dear to me and I caught her close and covered her with kisses.

When at last she slept, I lay staring at the ceiling. I felt that I ought to do something, now that I knew Alex had been faithless, but I didn't want to. It was in the past and I wanted it to stay there. I hated to be forever dragging some other girl up between Alex and me. If only Alex hadn't . . . .

Well, I would just pretend that he hadn't! I would never let him know that Selma had told me. But what if I should be going to have another baby? Dear God, not that, when I was only just now beginning to feel strength flow back into my loins once more.

Musing thus, I must have dozed, for I was disturbed by hearing Alex taking the steps two at a time on his way up. I knew the moment it dawned on him that the baby might be asleep by the way he softened his tread. The room was dark after the bright sunlight without, and he bent close above me to see if I was sleeping too. He grinned and laid his hand on my bare bosom and gave it a playful shake.

"Come to dinner, O Lady. Fried chicken, fresh peach cobbler . . . ."

"Keep your slimy fingers off me!" I snarled, and could have wept aloud. I had not meant to speak those awful words. I had meant to keep this knowledge to myself, but too late now. Alex's face took on a look of resignation and he drew a deep breath.

"Selma . . . she told you."

"Yes, my husband, Selma told me all about you and dear Susie." The words had the bitterness of gall on my tongue.

"Oh! She told you about Susie." His face actually brightened, "Well, I can explain everythin' about Susie. There wasn't a thing about that that could possibly make you feel bad, Flossie."

"It made me feel so bad that I'm deathly sick. That or something else! I couldn't eat any dinner if my life depended on it. Go eat your own and make whatever excuses you've a mind to make for me. But the minute you're through you get ready to take me home. And don't let anybody call me till you're ready."

Alex stood as though stunned for a moment, then turned and went quietly downstairs.

"It's a danged shame, Flossie," said Onnie, as he settled me and the baby in the back seat of the surrey, "and this is your first time out for so long."

"I wouldn't have had it happen for anything, Onnie, on this of all days," I said mournfully.

"Well, if a body's sick, a body's sick, and that's all there is to it."

He climbed onto the front seat beside Alex, riding in with us to bring the team back. All the way home I hated myself. What good could come of digging into the past? For of course I would just have to forgive it and go on as before. And it would have been so much easier if Alex had not known that I knew I had anything to forgive! We were in for it now, and if I was going to have another baby . . . round and round went my weary thoughts.

"I knew Selma was bound to tell you. That's why I didn't want to leave you alone with her," Alex frankly told me when we were again at home. "I'm not sayin' that it was right for me to spend the night with Susie. I'm only tellin' you that I didn't do Susie no harm. And God's my witness . . . I could have had my way with her, Flossie."

"Are you bragging?" I asked coldly.

"Braggin' my appetite! I'm only tryin' to tell you exactly how it was."

Selma hadn't said anything about him spending the night with Susie, probably didn't even know that he had. But Alex rushed headlong into his explanation.

"Susie's folks was gone to the hills for Saturday night and Sunday. Susie told them she was going to spend the night with May, but she called me and told me she was having a party Saturday night and to come by. When I got there, there wasn't any party. I'd rushed off without any supper and was hungry as a bear, so's we went in and made some fudge and popped corn. By then it was midnight and I was sleepy and started to leave. But she was afraid to stay from then till day alone, and begged me to stay with her. Finally we both got cold and sleepy and decided to go to bed. We kicked off our shoes and went to bed . . . with our clothes on . . . and we kept 'em on!" he added belligerently.

To my surprise his face was brick red at the memory, but his eyes were suffused and soft.

"She just wanted me to hold her in my arms, she said, so's she would always have that to remember, and I done so. Many times as I'd kissed her and sweet as I've always thought she was, you'd think I would at least have tried to go into my act, but I saw she was helpless. There wouldn't have been a thing to stop me, so's I just couldn't. I talked to her same as I would to my own sister, if I'd had one. I guess we both dozed, but I had it on my mind to get up and away from there before sun up, and I made it, at the first crack of dawn. I didn't know anybody knew I'd been there that night till Selma told you."

"But Selma didn't tell me that you spent the night with Susie," I said.

"Then who did tell you?"

"You told me, just now, this is the first I've heard of it."

"You mean to say that you got that wrought up over the few times I saw Susie there at May's with all of them there in the house with us? Why, Flossie, I'm ashamed of you."

"Since you don't seem to think it's anything to meet a girl at a friend's house and hug and kiss her to your heart's content while I'm at home waiting to have your baby, then I pray to God that I'm not getting ready to have another one for you!"

"And I'm telling you that I saw no harm in what I was doing at the time, and I still don't!"

"Well, let's just turn it around then. Let's suppose you had the smallpox, Alex," I said, very earnest, very patient, "and you looked like the very old scratch. And you well know, I might as well of have had the smallpox, the way you shunned me while I was pregnant! Let's say you didn't know whether you'd pull through it or not. Then let's suppose that I left you alone to get through it the best you could and met my old dear friend Harold Perrin. You know him don't you? And just for your information, I'll tell you that he is probably still as much in love with me as Susie Maynard is with you. Let's say I went with him to his house . . . oh wait . . . his bedroom, and lay in his arms while he talked to me like he would to his sister all night, and we didn't do one thing out of the way. Well, except maybe some hugging and kissing. Because there's nothing wrong in that, you know. Now, you tell me . . . would you think that was so harmless?"

"Well, that's different!" he blazed indignantly.

"In what way?" I asked curiously.

"Well, just leave all make-believe out of it. We've got more facts now than we can handle. What I'm trying to make you see is that I wasn't taking anythin' from you at the time. I couldn't make love to you, the shape you was in." His face was the picture of horror at the mere thought of it. "I wouldn't have been kissin' you like that, nor would you've wanted me to. But Susie wanted me to. And, anyway, what's a few kisses?"

"Don't you sit there and tell me that I didn't want you to hold me and kiss me. That was all you. You couldn't even lay beside me in our own bed . . . but you can sure find enough women to lay by that aren't carrying your baby. Susie Maynard for one!"

So this was the way a man made an out for himself! There was no semblance of guilt in him and his eyes pled for understanding. When I remained unyielding, he had the hurt look of a three-year-old when his own mother has failed him.

"Do you know of another man who would not have taken advantage of Susie under the circumstances?" he finally asked.

"Having gone so far, I think you showed remarkable self-control, Alex," I said coldly. "It's just that I can't understand how you would allow these situations to develop!" He sat like one stunned while I continued to gather all of his personal belongings and move them into the next room.

October 19, 1914

It was a strange life we lived, while I marked time instead of my calendar. Alex and I were being extremely polite to each other, each careful not to refer to anything unpleasant. Neither of us able to forget for a moment that I had moved Alex's things to the other bedroom and that I locked the door between us every night. Once Alex said to me, "But you can't be, honey, I swear it!"

"If I'm not, I'll make sure that I won't be until I'm certain!" I flared back.

"In any case you don't need to lock your door against me," he said carelessly. "I'd be the last person in the world to crowd in where I'm not wanted. There are too many places where I could find a welcome!"

After he had gone I stood for a long while, mulling this over. I knew that he had spoken the truth.

Thus it came almost as a welcome relief when I received an urgent call from Papa's sister, Aunt Nancy, to come to her. Uncle Jim was dying.

Lola and I were met at the train depot with a spring wagon. We arrived at the house to find friends and relatives crowded around, for the end was near. Aunt Nancy, exhausted by her long vigil, sat beside the bed holding Uncle Jim's hand, but at sight of us she motioned Grandma Wesley to take her place, tiptoed from the room and ushered us to the back bedroom across the hall.

"This is awful children," she choked. Her eyes had blue shadows under them and were red with loss of sleep and weeping. "The fever has been raging so. When I called you, it was taking five men to hold him in bed. He kept screaming at the top of his voice, 'I'll never kill a nigger. A nigger never dies!' You could have heard him a quarter mile away, over and over."

"What made him say that?" I asked, seeing that it lightened her burden to share it.

"Unless he was old enough to remember the time they lynched the four Negro boys that they said had raped the Lawson girl. He was just ten, but he probably saw it all. They dragged the bodies through the country behind horses, then strung 'em up in the oaks in front of the big house and shot 'em full of holes. It was a terrible thing for a child to witness, and I guess he never forgot it."

Lola sat on the side of the bed holding Aunt Nancy's hand.

I said, "As soon as I get the baby down, we'll go to see him. Do you think he'll know us?"

"It's hard to say, He can't eat any more. His throats swelled nearly shut and we have to give him water with a medicine dropper. Spinal meningitis is an awful thing. I know he can't last much longer and he seems to be paralyzed now, but I do believe he knows what's going on."

This did seem to be true, for as I leaned above him and gazed into the great blue eyes, now so bloodshot and blurred with pain, I was sure that I saw a flicker of recognition. The tongue was swollen till the end of it protruded beyond his teeth. If only he did not have to remain conscious through this horrible ending.

October 21, 1914

Lola went home just after the funeral, but I stayed on. Just why, I couldn't say of course. I felt that I was some comfort and help here, but that was not all. It was Alex. Our life together now was just an empty void.

So Aunt Nancy, her daughter Ruth, and I . . . they to forget their grief, and I to put aside my own nagging problems . . . threw ourselves wholeheartedly into constructing the "parlor" that Uncle Jim had planned for them before his death.

It was while hanging the wallpaper that the knowledge came that I was not going to have another baby. Alex had been right. Poor Alex. I so wanted to run to him that moment and tell him. But I could not go until the parlor was finished. I had promised.

October 30, 1914

At the end of the next week I was back in Paragould. Alex hadn't known I was coming. I wanted to surprise him, but I was the one who got the surprise, for the house was a shambles.

Even my room, which I had left in perfect order, was a wreck. I went through the house opening doors and windows. There was a case of beer in the back bedroom, or had been. Empty beer bottles were scattered all over. I had never in my life known Alex to take a drink of beer.

In the kitchen I found a basket of rotting vegetables and the sour gnats swarming above a box of fruit that was beginning to decay. These things were from the farm, and Mrs. Thomas would have been so glad to get them. Why hadn't he given them to her, rather than let them sit there and ruin? I opened the screen and drove out the sour gnats, changed into old clothes, and started cleaning with a vengeance.

Alex didn't come home at noon, of course. What was there to come home to? So I went to the grocery after I had rested. In the afternoon I baked a rich chocolate cream pie and had supper ready on time.

Alex looked a little startled and uncertain when he saw me, but when he looked into my eyes, he opened his arms and gathered me close. He was trembling all over, and so was I.

"My God, Flossie, I believe you're glad to see me!" he said brokenly, kissing me again and again.

"Well, Alex, you see . . . I'm not . . . well . . . there isn't going to be another baby," I sobbed.

"But, honey, I told you the whole time! It was just the long strain of nursin' the baby and the sewin', and I guess worryin' like you did didn't help things any."

"Can you ever forgive me?" I said.

And then he laughed until he was overcome with weakness. "You! Will you ever forgive me, she says! Well, I'll try, O Lady," and he caught me close again.

Long after Alex was asleep, I lay staring into the velvety darkness, remembering how the flames had leaped and curled around the big amber-colored hairpin I had swept from beneath my bed and thrown in the fire. This, I knew, was my fault. I had known that Kitty lay in wait for Alex. Yet I had closed my door and locked it against him. I had gone away and stayed away for nearly three weeks.

But here, in my own bed! Still, this time, it will not be my scathing tongue to bring the coldness between Alex and me again. He stirred in his sleep and his arm tightened around me. My hungry body sank gratefully against him and I slept.

Chapter 12

November 16, 1914

Alex woke me this morning, yodeling and snatching curtains and blinds from the windows like one gone mad. I opened my eyes to find him standing straight up in bed, bouncing me up and down, casting one curtain from him and leaping for another. He snatched a picture from the wall above my bed, tossed it on top of the curtains, hopped off the bed, seized a chair and turned it upside down and fitted it into another.

"What do you think you're doing!" I was alarmed.

"Moving back to the country, remember? My year in town was up yesterday, so's I resigned and arranged for Onnie to come get us today."

"Alex, I . . . ."

"Now don't start anythin'! That's the reason I didn't tell you last night. I wanted to be sure I got a night's sleep. I kept my promise. It was just for one year, and now it's your turn." He danced joyously from one foot to the other while he put a fire in the stove and continued to sort and pack things while I hurriedly got breakfast.

Milking . . . for Alex had said more than once that he never meant to milk, and churning, and washing, and ironing, and scrubbing, and gardening, and canning, and chickens, and . . . ."

"Where are we going to live?" I ventured fearfully.

"At Englewood."

And so, when we reached the farm at last, Onnie set the baby bed in the porch and drove straight out to the old log house and stored the remainder of our belongings. It had all been arranged! I had supposed, or perhaps only hoped, that we would settle in one of the tenant cottages.

Not so. We were settled in the big house and apparently it was for life. We occupied Belle's and Mattie's old room, setting the baby bed in the corner where Belle's once stood.

December 19, 1914

Middle of December came and went and we were still at Englewood. Mattie was now a little less cordial. Onnie and Ann came less often. Ma made no least difference now in Lester and Reecie, even demanding that he divide his pretties with her. This always set him in such a rage that he in turn demanded to be taken home. I got the feeling that the others thought we, who had the least right, had crowded into a soft berth with the old folks, leaving the others to shift as best they could. They'd stayed with Pa and helped make what was there. If they were going to take someone in with them, why not one of the faithful. Alex and I had jumped around like a grasshopper on a hot griddle! Mattie finally put it into words, that we were the ones they "killed the fatted calf" for.

Alex evaded the issue when I broached the subject to him. Ma said she had enough of her own to think about without trying to lay plans for somebody else, and Pa, I was finally convinced, took special pains to allow me no chance to open the subject with him.

One day when I pressed her, Ma said in that smooth, buttery tone I was learning to dread, "You're living, Flossie, easier than anybody I know of, with not a thought in your mind as to where it is all coming from. What have you got to worry about?"

"That's just it. I think very much about where it's all coming from . . . and many other things. I can't rest until I find out where we are to live."

Ma laughed softly. "I'm not ready to turn this house over to you yet," She arched her brow significantly. "But you are welcome to stay here . . . seein' that you've no place else to go." Ma was enjoying herself.

It was the first little dig that she had given me that I was "being kept." But I surmised that it wouldn't be the last. I pondered this for a long while, for I was just beginning to catch on to Ma's funny little ways. Gradually it was dawning on me that, as time went on, I would become no more than an unpaid servant in this household, subject to

Ma's every whim. She liked laying out my task for the day, and seldom did I have time for the nice little things I liked to do. I missed having something to pick up and read when I sat down, or a bit of fancywork to do. It seemed to irritate Ma to know end for me to attempt to do either. Well, if I was to be a household drudge, then I would much better like being one in my own house!

December 23, 1914

One day, as I sat before the fire mending, Pa came in. He took Cerece on his knee and began a game of "Trot a Little Hoss to Banbury Cross," and I suddenly reached the end of my patience.

"Pa, I can't get a word out of Ma or Alex as to where we are going to live. Maybe you'll be kind enough to tell me."

"Now, Flossie, you must have guessed. That all got settled whilst you was in Paragould." His eyes twinkled and his voice purred. "This is a big old house fer jist Annie and me. We find it pleasant ta have you and Alex and the baby with us here. We been dull and lonesome with all of 'em married and gone. They's no call fer you ta move anywhere. Alex is needed here. Annie needs help with this big house. Doin' his farmin' from here will save buyin' a lot of new quipment fer Alex, and he'd have to make debts, seeing he's got nothin' to go on. Him bein' here leaves me free ta ride the farms and look out after my business a leetle better."

"I can't believe it's the thing to do," I said, hardening my heart against Pa's plea of loneliness. He stopped trotting the baby and that still listening look came into his eyes.

"There's not another girl in the land but would think she'd landed on a featherbed. Not one of the others would but jump at the chance."

"Then let one of the others that could be happy here have the chance at it . . . if you really want someone in the house with you."

"So you don't want to live here with us?" He seemed unable to credit his ears.

"Only if we divided the house, giving us our own apartment and letting us plan and cook and live separately. I'm willing to make out with two rooms. I've been used to that. But I want to feel that they are my rooms, furnished with my things, and that I'm queen there."

He looked dazed, "Divide the house when there is only four of us and the baby? You mean you can't stand it ta cook and eat with us?"

I was suddenly quite sick at my stomach. How could I make Pa understand what I did mean?

"Pa, you might not understand, but would you consider giving up your own home and the privileges that go with it and living in a house with somebody else? Would Ma? It's the same way with me." I spoke more gently now. "And that's what makes it bad. Ma has her little ways and I have mine. I realize this is her home, and so I smother all my own preferences in order not to make a nuisance of myself in her home. But I'm not doing things as I would do them . . . and I'm not happy. It's different with you men. You're out all day and back in to a good meal, a clean house, and a rest. But Ma and I are shut up in four walls together all day long."

"She says you haven't had the first cross word. She says yore willin' and capable and that she has got cleanin' and things done that she'd been behind with fer months with you here to help her."

"Even so, Pa, it's cleaning, and it's being done her way. I'm having to forget now how I would do anything, for you haven't lived with Ma all these years not to know that there is only one way, and that's hers."

These last words had tumbled out in a breathless heap and I was appalled at myself. Pa sat there scowling into the fire. But I could not stop now and hurried miserably on.

"Besides, our ways are not your ways. I work all day long, looking forward to the two or three hours before bedtime in the evening. This is leisure time in my world, time to do the things that I really want to do. But with you and Ma there isn't any evening. It's just to have supper, hurry through the dishes, and get off to bed."

His shoulders drooped and then twitched impatiently inside his expensive corduroys. Suddenly Pa laughed, but there was no sound of mirth in the room.

"We'll see how bad you want to move, young lady! I only got one empty house right now," his eyes glinted with satisfaction, "the two room shanty that I keep fer transients. It sets in the wide open on the south bank of the crick right back of the church house. You're free ta move in it when the notion takes you!" He set down the baby and stamped out of the room.

When Alex came in, I told him about it, and he laughed hysterically. "Lord save us, Flossie. Wait till you get a look at that house and I think, twixt the two evils, you'll choose this one."

I had been somewhat dashed, There was a sixteen-by-twenty-foot front room and a ten-by-twenty shed room. A back step, a front step, the ceiling and floors were of good matched boards. But the walls were rough and unpainted, as was the outside.

"Something will have to be done," I said weakly.

"There's plenty of lumber stored in the big shed to do anythin' we'd want, far as that goes, and plenty of time before the plowin' starts to get it done. But gosh dang, think of all that work. Then it'll be to sort through and unpack enough stuff to furnish it, and then begin worryin' about grocery bills and stove wood and firewood again. Flossie, you are the out doin'est woman a man ever tried to live with! There at the big house we don't have a worry on our minds. All we'll ever get out of it is a livin' anyway. We could get a sight better livin' there without the worry of figurin' on ways and means."

"A front porch here, a back gallery, a smokehouse," I mused absently. "And a yard and garden fenced, of course. Thank goodness there's a crib and henhouse, and the mule lot is fenced in, that's something."

January 22, 1915

I had sent a plea to Papa and he sent me fifty dollars. With this I bought paint and wallpaper and set to work, turning the balance over to Alex for whatever he needed for his part of the job. Nobody came next to or near us during our days of travail. No one ever alluded to it or offered to help with it. Again we were in disgrace, and it had all been my doing.

At first I was more than a little anxious, but when at last Alex caught the spirit of the venture, it was as much fun as making a playhouse had been as a child. And truly it looked but little larger than a playhouse. Alex really put his mind on what he was doing and when the smokehouse became a reality, it was the pride of my life. It was floored halfway back with a set of sturdy steps leading down into the unfloored area. One end was kept stacked with wood for the heater, the other end with wood for the cookstove. But this was our reserve and never to be touched except in bad weather. The floored space was fitted with shelves and used to store canned goods, fruit and vegetables.

There was a huge oak at the east end of the front porch. A great box elder stood just inside the lot and cast its thick shadow on the west end of the porch, so that there was only an hour or two just in the afternoon that the sun could get to us in the summer. Alex rived every paling for the fences and fitted them into long twisted strands of wire. When at last he was through, he dug up the old reliable family formula for whitewash and went over every inch of the house, chicken house and fence, even whitewashing the shade trees halfway up their bodies.

Ann's manner had been more cordial ever since I explained to her what I had done with the money I borrowed from Papa.

"Well, we did wonder where the money to do these things came from. We thought you lit on some plan we hadn't learned about yet to get it out of Pa. We find it hard to get extra money for anything this time of year. We save our list till a time of big sales and get right in there with it then, or we don't get it. Once that money's in the bank they just don't seem to be no way of gettin' it out. But there for a while he seemed to've softened up a lot toward you and Alex."

"But not to the extent of letting us have any *money!*" I laughed, delighted at being on friendly terms with Ann again.

"Don't ever let on I told you," Ann's eyes were dancing now, "but one day I heard Pa tell Onnie that Alex had married a pore gal with millionaire ideas. I don't know what he thinks Onnie got when he married me!"

I sighed. "Ann, we're all as God made us, I guess, but I can't help wanting things bright and gay. It's no pleasure to spend your life working on a house that looks no better after you've killed yourself at it!"

"Ain't it so! You can get your milk and butter at our house till you get a cow," she offered.

"We're going to get a cow as soon as Alex can talk Pa into letting him have the *money*," I said.

"You'll pay 10 percent on the loan. I hope you're not forgetting that."

"Well, I hope we're not going to have to go on begging milk and butter till a crop is made. Alex argues that it's all right that we never have any money. He says when it's safe in the bank it's the same as him and Onnie saving it, since it will eventually come to them anyway. But you can't do without milk and butter just so a few more dollars can get added to the bank account."

"Oh, Alex and Onnie give me the cramps! They've just heard Pa say that about money till they think its law and gospel. I'd be willing to take a little less later on if we could have something more to go on now than what it takes to keep soul and body together."

I picked up a bucket and dish and went home with Ann for milk and butter.

January 25, 1915

We had invited Ma and Pa to come see us when we moved from their house, but they didn't. Strange to say, neither did Sherman and Mattie, though we always had fun with them when we chanced to meet.

When I mentioned it to Alex, he laughed grimly. "They wouldn't dare come to see us, long as Pa's got his back up. Pa might think they was sidin' against him."

January 30, 1915

For three days it had been snowing intermittently. The foundation had been laid for it by a big freezing rain, which later turned to sleet. Then a high wind and fine rice snow and, finally, hour after hour, the swirling, whispering swish of the biggest flakes I ever saw. Alex had got us nicely snugged in for the freeze and for three days I had enjoyed the coziness, but tonight I was restless. There was a big moon rising in the east and I couldn't bear it.

"Alex, I want to go for a walk somewhere!" I said tensely after supper.

"Go somewhere, my appetite! Flossie, there's drifts out there crotch deep and a body can't tell whether to step high or step low."

But I was looking out of the window and my mind was lost to all reason in the vision before me. Every tree and shrub was encased in a sheath of clear, sparkling ice that caught and multiplied the dancing moonbeams.

"You're out all day, going from one place to another, seeing things and having fun," I flared. "I'm shut in here in this little house like a squirrel in a cage. Oh Alex, please, I'll put on your boots and big coat and cap and mittens."

"Where would you go?" he asked curiously.

"I want to go to the bridge. I just want to see the snow and ice and the moon on the willows." I was already scrambling into his things.

"Only if you go by and make Ann go with you. I don't want you down on the creek alone."

Ann thought I was crazy and declared, "I wouldn't get up out of my warm bed for the sight of any snow that ever fell," getting up and fumbling her way into her things as she raged.

In some places the road had been swept clear of snow right down to the ice, and then in others we were floundering in drifts above our knees. There was still enough wind to buffet us about. It was coming in gusts, and no sooner would I brace my body against it than there was no wind and I would all but fall on my face, only to be caught unaware and lifted almost off the ground. The little church looked like it might be a half mile away, squatted back in the drifts beneath the ice-laden trees. The long windows of the schoolhouse caught and threw back the rays from the moon.

When we reached the bridge I leaned over to catch the dim light that gleamed from the east window of our little house, where such a short while ago I had stood and wished that I might be here on the bridge. It was high here and we could look out over all Englewood.

The big house was dark, for of course Pa and Ma had gone to bed, but smoke still spiraled from the chimney. From the other cottages smoke curled and pale lights flickered.

The stream itself seemed transfigured. Frozen over completely, it was further glorified by the blanket of feathery snow that hardly drifted at all inside those deep banks. The willow wands, covered with ice and frost crystals, were beautiful beyond imagining. The whole scene took on the magic unreality I had known as a child, when I was permitted to look my fill through the stereoscope at a series of Views of the North, with which we often entertained guests.

"I well know that Corrine Scoggins is fixin' to have another baby!" said Ann.

I shrugged impatiently. Who could think about Corrine Scoggins and her doings at such a moment?

"Ann, look how the ice piled up there at the waterfall! The little club footed thing she just had can't be more than seven months old . . . can it?"

"About that I guess, but I tell you she's gone again. I thought at first she was just taking a while to get her shape back, but she's on the bulge again or my name ain't Ann."

I could have stood for an hour in my tracks, lost to all else in this hushed bright stillness. The wild gusts of wind from the north snatched and tore at me like the eager hands of a boisterous lover. I turned my back and laughed rapturously as I tucked my chin tight against my neck lest those cold fingers slip inside my collar and find their way to my pulsing bosom.

"And for the third time I tell you, I'm going home," scolded Ann, and she whirled and started running toward the house. I took one last look at the frozen wonderland before me, and dashed after her.

"Thanks for coming with me, anyway," I called, as I turned toward home.

In pure exuberance of animal spirits, I picked the biggest snowdrift in sight and with a quick run plunged into it, glorying in the delightful creak and crunch of it as my body found its depth. Laughing joyously, I rolled over and over, then sat up and looked about me. Etched on an oak limb between me and the moon sat two small owls, staring solemnly down at me.

February 5, 1915

Pa had at last let Alex have the money for his cow and he had gone straight to Cline's Dairy and selected a fine-bred heifer from the Jersey herd. I loved her from the minute I saw Alex driving her before him down the road. She had a rich cream-colored coat with black nose and eyes, and the black brush of her tail barely cleared the ground as she stepped lightly and proudly along.

I ran and opened the gate and then got back out of the way when I saw she was afraid of me. "Alex," I breathed rapturously, "what a little beauty she is. How much did you have to pay?"

"Fifty dollars!" he said belligerently.

"And who's running us into debt now?" I could not keep from saying it, for he had reproached me more than once for making the loan from Papa.

"At least we can eat what I made a debt on," he said shortly. "We're going to have to feed and take care of a cow, so she might as well be a good one."

Looking forward to this day, Alex had sowed a rye patch as soon as he finished the fencing. It was barely ready for grazing, but he turned the heifer in on it. She lowed, looked from one to the other of us, straightened her tail to the wind and ran right round the enclosure and back to us.

"Mr. Cline said she's due around July or August, so as soon as she begins to feel settled for you to begin to rub her bag and talk to her and gentle her down so that when the calf comes and you have to milk her, she won't be afraid of you."

"But Alex, I don't know how to milk. Anyway, Onnie milks for Ann."

"You won't learn any younger! What Onnie and Ann do is between them, Flossie, but milking is the one thing I don't intend to do." He cast a last appraising glance over his purchase and turned to the house.

February 22, 1915

"But I don't see how I can stand that thing in the house, Alex!" I was on the verge of tears, but Alex continued, unperturbed, marking the eggs he had so carefully selected and counted, "Anyway, what are you marking the eggs for?"

"Please note that I mark only one side of the egg," he said, in that irritating *I am teaching a little child* manner he sometimes assumed with me. "The eggs must be turned each day, marked side up one day, plain side up the next. 201 . . . 202 . . . ."

"But I'm telling you the smoke and flame from that lamp will all but asphyxiate us, to say nothing of that awful stench when they start hatching."

"Keep your shirt on O Lady. I'm not fixin' to trust 250 eggs in this incubator anywhere except right beside my bed! You can watch it in the daytime but who knows what will happen at night? The incubator is going to set right where it is so I can turn over and squint at it at any hour of the night." He frowned and mumbled, "These danged kerosene lamps are the very devil to keep regulated, anyhow."

"But as the weather warms up . . . ."

"You can have every door and window in the house open but that one, Flossie, and I'm warning you, that one stays tight down for three weeks."

It was much worse than being shut in with a broody hen. I had been a softie to give in so easily, but I had the back side of the bed and slept with my nose to the wall.

March 8, 1915

Alex's interest in creating a home took a most astounding turn in regard to the yard. He plowed it up entirely, laid out flower beds and embedded boards in the earth to edge them off, then filled them with stable manure, pulverized and well worked in.

He set my beloved hyacinth bulbs and he surprised me with a dozen fine gladioli bulbs which he had seen advertised on the back of Farm & Fireside.

"That's for your birthday." He laughed, a little shamefacedly. "I was out a whole dollar for them, but so long as I saw it bloomed and you couldn't eat it, I knew you would be proud of it."

"They multiply too, Alex!" I was overjoyed.

"Well, you got four colors, yellow and wine and orchid and flame. Ought to be pretty enough for you."

"They will be, and for that you get my best kiss!"

"Hey, leave off, will you. I got no time to go back indoors at this hour of the day," and he turned me about and made as if to kick me soundly.

I planted the glads in the long bed against the west fence, a row of dwarf nasturtiums next, and edged the bed with sweet alyssum. On each side of the walk to the front gate, I set giant zinnias, and the walk to the back gate with marigolds. Along the back fence I planted cosmos, phlox, and a great bed of portulaca.

April 2, 1915

Never, as long as I lived, was I to forget the terrible hot and fetid stench that came from that incubator at the time of hatching. Though I opened every door and window except the one I had been forbidden to touch, the air was never sweet enough to breathe. Alex had unearthed an old square brooder with a vile-smelling kerosene lamp from the store house. He covered the bottom with white dry sand and as the chicks dried off they were moved to it.

"Now, I've hatched you off a nice flock of biddies," Alex said with satisfaction, "and from now on they are yours! Less than two dozen eggs failed to hatch. That's what it means to look after a thing right."

"But, Alex . . . ."

"But me no buts!" he glared at me.

"Are you raising them for market?" I asked meekly.

"Market, my appetite! I've never had all the fried chicken I wanted in my whole put-together. You're raisin' these, Miz Walker, so's we can have fried chicken on tap this summer anytime we want it, day or night!"

April 9, 1915

But though I did my best to look after them, there would sometimes be as high as a dozen trampled to death in the mornings. "You don't keep your brooder warm enough, or they wouldn't pile up like that," Alex fretted. But when I insisted that he regulate the lamp himself and they still died, I ventured my opinion that the brooder was too crowded. He dug up the old book that had come with it and found that it was a one hundred capacity. Then he brought large cardboard boxes from the store and lanterns and we divided them up and presently all remaining chicks were flourishing and fine.

April 16, 1915

I couldn't sleep because of biddies' incessant stirring and peeping, and the awful hot fetid odor that filled the room. Just about the time I was getting settled, Alex opened the brooder for another excited peek.

It was a relief to me when I heard Onnie step up on the porch and knock. "Get yore pore self together, Flossie. Corrine has overlay her baby and Hank come after Ann ta go set with 'em. Ann says she ain't fixin' ta go up there by her lone sef and fer me to come tell you she said it."

"Is the baby dead?"

"As a doornail," he nodded. He sat with his back to me and I slowly dressed. Ann met us on the road, took the lantern from him, and we hurried through the chill spring night, the news making its way around the bottomlands.

Hank Scoggins himself let us in at the door, his red hair looking as if it had just been milked, and his shallow blue eyes bloodshot and wildly restless. He motioned us in and offered chairs in a tense silence. He jerked at his untidy forelock and nervously licked his loose, dry lips. The atmosphere of the room chilled the very marrow of my bones.

Corrine, big and dark and stolid, stood regarding us suspiciously, her face set and her breathing heavy. At her shoulder stood the redheaded and obstreperous Becky, scarcely seeming to breathe, her pale blue eyes shifting unblinkingly from Ann to me and back again.

I shivered in a sudden terror and asked, "How in the world did it happen, Corrine?"

"I woke with my breast a hurtin', hit was in such a strut, and I thought to put the baby to hit fer ease, and hit war a lyin' as ye see hit now, stone dead."

Hank had stood as though awaiting his cue and now cut in, "Natcherly she called me, and when I seed fer shore that hit ain't a breathin', I went and called you'ns."

"Do you want us to lay it out?" asked Ann. Corrine nodded dumbly. "Well, Hank, you better get a fire in the cookstove and put on some water to heat. Corrine, you get together whatever you want it dressed in and we'll look after it." Ann had taken over.

Corrine went into the other room and returned with a clean shirt and diaper. She handed me a slip made from a flour sack and a little new dress of cheap material, made by her own inexpert fingers. She still breathed heavily. Her lips, always thick, seemed swollen, and they were compressed as though she struggled with emotions that might overcome her at any moment. I was suddenly overcome with pity for her and laid an arm across her shoulder. "It's over and done now, and can't be helped, Corrine. Try to think it was for the best. It would have had to go through life a cripple. Try not to grieve for it too much."

"Right shore thar's nothin' I can do?" asked Hank, nervously washing his hands in the air.

"Not a thing, so you might as well try to get a little rest," said Ann. "You'll have to get out in the morning and find a coffin and make some arrangements for the funeral." Ann gave him a slight push toward the other room. He turned and gave her a startled glance, then shuffled on out.

"I felt like if he didn't get on out I'd have to scream," Ann whispered to me. "He makes me nervous as a cat."

Once in the kitchen with the door shut we cleared the table and moved it near the stove. We folded a quilt four-double for a pad and laid the baby out on it. We leaned above it and made our plans in whispers.

"She still didn't get me a washrag or towel. I guess I'll hunt till I find one," said Ann, and dropped to her knees and started rummaging in the cabinet drawers. Finding nothing she opened the bottom doors, then gasped and sat back on her heels. With her forefinger pressed against her lips for silence, she motioned me to her. I tiptoed across and bent above her inquiringly. Deliberately she reached in and set two big tin coffee pots, badly smoked, on the floor in front of me and removed the lids. Then nodded and pointed at the contents significantly. For some unaccountable reason I was suddenly all over gooseflesh, though the sodden mess in both pots had no meaning for me. I looked back at Ann in puzzled wonder. "Remedies," she hissed. "Cotton root tea in one, cedar ball tea in the other."

"Remedies for what?"

"To bring her round. I told you in February that I bet she was up the stump again, and I bet she ain't six weeks short of her time right now. You don't see nothin', Flossie. Sometimes I think you're a plum gump. I bet you didn't even notice she's so wrapped and bound right now to keep from showing, she can't hardly breathe."

So that was the secret of Corrine's heavy breathing.

"And that's why nobody's doing any crying," whispered Ann. "They all know what's going on round here." She carefully replaced the pots and shut the cabinet doors. She eased the door into the front room open and found a washrag and towel in the wash stand.

When she returned I leaned over and whispered, "Ann, that Hank makes me think of some kind of animal. I think it's a *coyote*." I whispered the awful word fiercely.

Ann frowned. "Don't know as I ever saw a coyote," she said matter-of-factly.

"Well, neither did I, but I know he looks just like one." We looked straight into each other's eyes, then threw our arms around each other and laughed in hysterical silence.

We removed the bandage Corrine had tied under the little chin. The little body, though cold, was still soft and pliant to the touch.

"What makes its face so dark?" I asked, peering at it in the dim light from the smoky lamp.

"Because it smothered to death, I reckon." She soaped the washrag generously. "Besides, you know how dark Corrine is. Did I ever tell you that her mother was a full-blood Indian squaw?"

"No. But Ann," I persisted, "does it look to you like the baby's face is all mottled?"

She looked closer. "It is, for a fact. There's something you do to bring the color back to a corpse, if I can think what it is. Oh, yes, you wring a cloth out of strong soda water."

When the baby was ready she hunted up a clean flour sack, dipped it in a strong soda solution and pressed it gently down over the little face. We remade the bed with a sheet made from flour sacks that Corrine had given us, laid the baby out and covered it.

"Where'd they get so many flour sacks?" I whispered,

"That many young'ns eat a heap of bread," Ann nodded wisely.

We went back and cleaned up the kitchen and brewed a pot of coffee. Ann opened a can of peaches from the shelf. Winter was over, but there was still need of a fire early mornings and late in the evenings.

Ann stood in the north window looking across the orchard and I heard her laugh. "God save us all, Flossie, I'll bet they've had many an eye full here in this window. You can stand here and look right through my kitchen into the bedroom beyond. There's Onnie in his drawer tail right now, putting a fire in the fireplace. Many is the time I've took a bath right in front of that fire, never thinking to draw a shade on this side of the house." She giggled. "Anyway, if Onnie's up its five o'clock and this will soon be over."

"Let's see if the soda cloth helped it any," I suggested.

We went to the other room and Ann removed the cloth. Her eyes flew wide with horror. I gasped and pressed my hand tight to my mouth to still the cry that would have come tearing out of me. On the right side of the tiny nose was the print of a heavy thumb; on the left side, the print of a forefinger and spread along the rounded cheek were the other three fingers of a large hand. The face was no longer mottled. The skin was waxen, and the fingerprints stood out in clear red relief. With trembling hand Ann replaced the cloth and covered the little body just as we heard the door slowly creak open and turned to see Hank walking toward us from the other room.

"I thought I best had get right on up," he said. We stood speechless, feeling that we were the guilty ones. "I just happen to have some new pine boards that I got to make some kitchen shelves for Corrine, so I thought I'd get a bite a breakfast and set ta work and build it a little coffin."

Ann stood still and said nothing and I could not have spoken had my life depended on it.

Hank shifted his weight uneasily and continued, "I been layin' in thar plannin' what's best ta do. Money's skeerce, so I kin make the coffin mysef. They's some cotton battin' here som'eres that I kin use fer paddin' and line it with that little new blanket that ain't been used."

"Well, whatever you think best," said Ann, "and I guess we had best go now and get breakfast. Onnie's already put a fire in the stove. When will you bury the baby? Some of us will try to get back."

"Likely this afternoon, down to Palestine where Sofie's buried. I shore ta God thank you fer what you done."

"We'll tell the boys to be ready this afternoon," Ann managed, as we made our way hurriedly toward the door.

But at eleven o'clock Ann called me. "No never mind about the funeral, Flossie. They went right by themselves, the whole wagon full of 'em. Had all four of them young'ns and the coffin in the back on the hay. Becky and Corrine were in the spring seat, and old Hank sitting up front in a chair. They acted like they were in a plum swivet to get off."

"Ann," I said weakly.

"Don't Ann me, and don't tell me nothing on this phone.

I'm just telling you what I saw."

The next day Corrine left Main Shore. They said to visit her Ma's sister in Ohio.

Chapter 13

June 3, 1915

Lassie Howell, wife of the new tenant over in the field, was standing at my door saying, "And the minute I looked at her, Miz Flossie, I says, 'Worm colic, my eye!' Any man would have knowed what was ta matter and you can't tell me that Hank Scoggins lived with that Becky till the fullness of her time and didn't know it. I says to Hank, I says, 'You git a far in that stove and some water ta heat and quick about it.' And once he'd done it, I sent him ta Miz Ann's ta phone up the doctor . . . she was that bad off. When he got back, it took all him and me both could do to handle her. A hour later I caught a seven-pound boy and shoved it under his nose and I says, 'Thar's the worm you was so almighty consarned about,' and he hung his old head like a sheep-killin' dawg! Miz Ann is with 'em now and she said tell you she'd stay till you got thar."

"Well, don't worry any more about it, Lassie. Go get Gabe his breakfast and take over the house and children so that he can get to his work. Ann and I will do whatever is necessary."

"Anyways, that girl is human, and we can't let her want fer attaintion because she had the misfartune to be borned to Hank Scoggins."

Becky lay pale, watchful, and defiant, her little redheaded baby swathed in an old blanket beside her.

"Whose baby is it, Becky? Maybe Hank could see to it that he married you and gave it a name."

"That thars one thang I ain't never gonna tell nobody," she said flatly.

"Did Corrine know about it before she left?" asked Ann.

"Yes."

Ann had stopped sweeping to catch the answer and now she resumed.

"Then why didn't she stay to see you through it?" I asked.

"I don't know."

"You might as well save your breath, Flossie," said Ann impatiently. "She's took the studs and you couldn't get a right answer out of her if you took the day for it. I dressed a chicken in there, but I got to get back to the house. I'll take Cerece, if you want me to, and you keep the fire going under that chicken and make her some good strong broth. She won't need solid food for a day or two."

"Where's Hank?"

"He took the young'ns and went to the field."

After Ann had gone, I turned back to Becky. "What does Hank think about it, Becky?"

"I don't know." And that was her final answer to all questions.

June 4, 1915

Miss Pert's calf was several weeks old and the pride of Cerece's life. I had named the dainty little highbred thing Princess, but I also called it Calfie, with the result that Cerece, now talking quite well, called it Pincess Faffie.

What a desperate time I had trying to learn to milk. I had tried every way in the world to get Alex to take over, but he stubbornly held his ground.

One evening I called Selma, well knowing that she had a way with animals. "Selma, please, what can I do with this cow? She kicks so that she's got me afraid to go near her. I just dread milking time from one day to the next."

"Tie her head up, just leaving her enough rope to reach her feed box, Flossie. Then stick yore head tight into her flank and milk fast. She can't kick you then. If that don't work, lay a good heavy stick under her when you go to milk and when she goes to kick just hit her a crack on the shin bone. She'll learn soon to keep that foot on the ground."

And finally I won out.

June 5, 1915

The night of the box supper at the church everybody came from far and near. It was the custom to have one each summer to create a feeling of fellowship and to raise funds for the Sunday school literature or new song books.

I resurrected an old rose-colored satin dress from the depths of my trunk and couldn't help but remember that it had once been a favorite of Will's. The yoke and high-boned collar were of embroidered net, piped in rose. Bands of alternate satin and net made up the fancy sleeves. The skirt was a shocking mistake, except for the brief season that it was in fashion, being one of the sleek stovepipe models. Oh well, I'd be sitting all evening, and at least the blouse was becoming.

I aired and pressed the dress as I cooked. I found a small round hatbox, packed it with my food treasures, covered it with thickly pleated white crepe paper and made a bright red satin rosette to top the lid.

"What have you got in this box?" asked Alex as he dressed.

"You'd better buy it and see." But at the auction he bought Alma's box.

I almost choked with pleasure when I saw that Pa was bidding mine up to three dollars.

"I saw Alex hand it to Ed" . . . he laughed when he brought it to me . . . "and I jist made up my mind to find out the kind a box you'd pack. Guess I've bought a box, one time or other, packed by ever' other woman in this community."

He was in one of his rare good moods and looked extremely handsome in his Sunday black. If only I didn't muff my chance. I wanted so to use this God-given opportunity to set myself right in Pa's eyes. Alex must sometimes feel himself an outcast in his own family because of their resentment toward me.

"I hope you won't be too disappointed." I smiled, and when I raised my eyes to his, I was surprised to find him regarding me with an expression of frank approval.

Then he suddenly frowned. "I see you been pullin' Alex's leg agin." He was clearing his throat in that terrifying way he had. "You didn't need a new dress fer this shindig, Flossie," and he scowled mightily at the lustrous rose satin, which shimmered and glowed in the mellow lamplight.

"But this is not a new dress. It's four or five years old. I wouldn't have dared wear it on account of the skirt, except that I knew I'd be sitting down all evening. You'd die laughing at this skirt Pa." I hurried on anxiously. "It makes me look as though I'd been melted and poured in!"

His face cleared at once. "Well now, I made sure it was brand new, not seein' you wear it before. But I will say this, it makes you look powerful becomin' . . . powerful becomin'."

I laughed delightedly in sheer relief and felt myself flushing with pleasure. "You look powerful becomin' yourself tonight, Pa," I shyly assured him and was surprised to see his face light up. For the first time I felt proud to claim this unpredictable man as related to me by marriage. As my eye traveled over those present I could see no other man whom I'd have been willing to accept in his place.

He had opened the box and was sniffing the sandwich he had just unwrapped, finding it both small and unfamiliar, I had no doubt.

"Chicken salad," I said, in answer to his questioning look.

"You'd much better've kept that hen ta lay fer ye," he said shortly.

"You mean you don't like it?" I asked innocently, seeing the gratified look on his face as he bit into it.

"I like it all right. What's them crunchy bits in it?"

"Celery."

"Might highfalutin food fer people startin' out in debt as you and Alex are doin'."

"We don't make a habit of it. This was for special, you know." I was not going to let his carping get under my skin. He worked his way methodically through the deviled eggs, pimento cheese sandwiches, a big banana and presently was beginning a thick slice of my Lady Baltimore cake.

"You know, you got a nice touch with victuals," he said, while seriously waving the slice of cake at me. "Come ta think of it, I guess yore a right smart gurl, all in all. Makin' a home out a what you had to start on ain't easy. But I guess you done a right good job on it, from all reports."

I laughed. "Alex can tell you I didn't do it all alone." And suddenly I was overcome with the desire to have done with this sparring with Alex's people. To have all as it should be between us. I leaned toward him and asked earnestly, "Why don't you come to see us sometime?" Then my eyes strayed across the room as though drawn by a magnet and a chill ran down my spine as I met Ma's eyes in a long, venomous stare. Ma was looking at me as though she hated me. I shuddered and turned away from that deadly, unblinking gaze.

". . . and try some way to get some life and spirits into the community," Pa was saying. "I want you and Alex to see if you can't attend more regular. Do whatever you've a mind to do that will have a notion of tyin' us all more close together. Looks to me like we are all gettin' mighty sefish . . . mighty sefish!"

But the spirit that pervaded the community was of no concern to me right now. What I was worried about was the spirit that prevailed in this family. If we as a family could not draw closer together, what hope was there of establishing a feeling of brotherly love in the community? Pa sensed the change in me, gave me a puzzled frown, told me he had enjoyed the feast and moved on into the crowd.

June 13, 1915

Late Sunday evening, after a quick go at the night work, we dressed and went for a stroll. This was an unusual thing for us to do, but it was such a delightful evening. We had meant to end up at Onnie's and Ann's, but when we reached their gate we looked up the road and could see them, now almost to the big house, Onnie pulling Lester behind him in his little wagon. By common consent we continued to the big house. It was the first time I had been back since we moved. Ma was holding court under one of the big oaks. The boys flung themselves about in the long tender grass and were immediately tackled by their boisterous offspring.

Pa finished pumping the mule trough full of water, took his accustomed chair, leaned it back against the oak tree, and let out a long sigh.

"Well, I just don't know sometimes," said Pa wearily, and I noticed that the soft pudgy hand with which he stroked his forehead was none too steady.

"What now?" asked Mattie.

"I've come to believe that I'm a sick man," he said sadly, "and I might as well face it. I been shyin' round it fer two years past."

"Have you seen a doctor?" I asked, noting his sickly color for the first time.

"Nor do I aim to," he shook his head with conviction.

"Why don't you go over to Hot Springs and take a course of the baths? Maybe you just need a good boiling out," I suggested. "I heard Roy Bennett say today that his mother was like a new woman since she got back, and she's been ailing for a long time."

"It takes money to take a course of baths at Hot Springs, Flossie," said Pa, as though I hadn't known it.

"It takes money to get buried too . . . and that's not as much fun, either," I said shortly, and he flashed me a quick look.

"You ort to tell me that I am jist run-down and need a leetle mite of sassafras tea ta thin my blood!"

"Why?"

"Because what I don't spend while I'm a livin', goes to the rest of you when I'm dead. You ort ta try to see that I don't run through what I've saved before I go."

I was stunned . . . and angered. "Can't you think of anything except in terms of money? If that's the kind of thoughts you go around having, no wonder you're sick."

"I happen to know how that money got in the bank," he said undeterred. "Layin' awake nights, plannin' and schemin' and not always bein' too squeamish on the way I come by it. But I didn't pile it up there to leave with no doctors."

"But you made it yourself, and nobody's got a better right to spend it than you have," I contended.

"Money jist don't mean a thing in this world ta you, does it, Flossie?" he asked curiously.

I had the strange feeling that there was no one else present, just Pa and me, and so I answered him honestly. "Money means nothing to me except what I can buy with it. If I can buy pleasant surroundings, health or happiness, comfort or peace of mind with the little that comes my way, I will make the exchange with no regrets. And I'm sure of one thing: we'd rather have you than any money you could leave us, so go to Hot Springs and see if you don't come back feeling a little more cheerful, Pa."

"You don't need to ask me what I think about you going," Ma cut in, her voice as smooth as soft butter. "Just ask Flossie. She can always tell you what's best to do." Pa's gray eyes had been fixed on mine with a listening look, but he shrugged impatiently now and turned to stare at Ma with sudden irritation.

"Don't be a fool, Annie, 'cause it's yore gift! Pack our things tamarree. We're going to Hot Springs fer a month."

June 20, 1915

When the cat's away, the mice will play. So the first Sunday Ma and Pa were away, the boys piled the big farm wagon's bed full of hay, covered it with quilts, and stowed the children there. They settled the three spring seats into place. Arlien and Selma, Onnie and Ann, Alex and I went fishing. But Mattie and Sherman drew the line on an all-day spree, and they remained behind to "cast a shadder on the place" and look after things.

The boys contrived a camp stove, and the food supply was adequate in case we didn't catch any fish. But it was a fine sunny day, and the fish were leaping out of the water to catch the flies. Selma caught seven big perch and a catfish on her hook. So the meat and potatoes went begging, but the crisp fresh lettuce, onions and radishes, the corn dodgers and hot coffee disappeared in unbelievable quantities for such a small crowd.

Arlien gave us all a delightful qualm as we were eating dinner by remarking that they would be just about taking up Sunday school now. Onnie clapped a hand over his eyes and groaned, "Somebody's sure to meet Pa at the train and tell him all about our back slidin' from grace the minute his back was turned."

The boys grunted luxuriously as they tumbled about on the grassy bank and played with the children while we repacked for the trip home. "Why can't we storm Belle and Silas while we're this close?" asked Selma. "I've never been to see 'em since they've been married, and this is the best chance I'll have at it."

Belle and Silas took in our disheveled appearance and the fishing poles and pots and pans at a glance, and Belle burst into a laugh. She was wearing a blue chambray dress that matched her eyes, and presently she left the room and returned with a five-layer cake. The sight of it brought mock groans from the rest of us, but the boys managed to dispose of it with second and third helpings.

"How've you been gettin' along, Silas?" asked Alex.

"Well, I finally got the crop in, by the hardest trying," Silas said, but his face suddenly clouded with worry. "It's that new mule. He's young and he's skittish and he acts like he's afraid of me but I wouldn't trust him for a minute."

"Uh oh! Don't never let a mule get the down on you," said Onnie.

Silas flushed with some embarrassment. "From the first day I worked him, I've had the feeling he's going to catch me in the stable with him one of these days and kick the eternal daylights out of me. I try not to take my eye off him one minute."

"You could easy cure his monkeyshines with a little black snake," said Alex.

"I wouldn't dare try that," Silas shook his head with some spirit. "He's not a mule that would stand there and take it. He'd rear up and paw me into the ground."

June 24, 1915

We got a letter from Pa:

> We got two rooms in easy walking distance of the baths. Yesterday Annie and me took a long stroll into the woods and picked us a mess of wild sallet. It made

us homesick. Take good care of the garden. Look after the store and the stock.

Pa.
P.S.
The baths is awful hard on me just now, but the old timers say it is like that at first.

The next day I packed a box and sent it to them. Two big loaves of homemade bread, a pan of sugar rolls, a dozen eggs in a carton, a tin of butter, and a jar of jelly.

June 28, 1915

Monday morning I tied sunbonnets on myself and Cerece, Alex set us on Jude's back and led the mule up to the big house. There we pulled the English pea vines, past bearing, and planted more snap beans and squash, and set some late tomatoes. We stuck the pole beans and Alex plowed out the garden while I hoed.

July 1, 1915

Later in the week I left Cerece with Ann, and Alex and I went blackberry picking. Around the back field fences we went, breathing in the sweet pungent fragrance of the woods in the early morning, the tiny globules of dew outlining the intricate patterns of myriad cobwebs along the way. Only the first berries were ripe, so the buckets didn't fill as rapidly as we hoped, and all at once I found that I was too tired to go on.

Alex frowned in dissatisfaction and finished filling my bucket from his own. "I took the morning off to get you started with your berry picking, and I'm not fixin' to go back in with a bucket half full. You take these and go on up the lane there to Bill Nolly's and get you a drink and blow a little and maybe you can make it home. I know where's there's a fine early patch and I'll be in when my bucket is full." He squinted at the sun and started east through the woods.

I entered the Nolly dooryard with some misgiving. There was hardly room to walk for the numerous progeny of all ages and half a dozen skinny hounds. Bill Nolly's wife sat in a low cane-bottom chair, a five-year-old held firmly between her knees, and while it screamed and fought, she resolutely washed its dirty face and then set about the business of combing and braiding its tangled hair.

On the doorstep sat two who had already been through the torture, and they grinned shyly at me through lashes still wet with tears. "Good morning," I said hesitantly, faint with the first hot sun and the long walk. "May I have a glass to get a drink of water?"

Mrs. Nolly placed the first two fingers, slightly parted, against her lips and spat a long stream of amber juice into the dooryard. "Callie, you fetch Miz Flossie a cup. They ain't been a glass on this hill since Clint were a baby."

I took the tin cup to a pump in the side yard and, standing with my back to the rest, washed it thoroughly and then pumped a fresh drink.

"Amber, fetch Miz Flossie a cheer, she looks fitten ta drap," she said as I returned. "Ye'd best come in and set by the looks of ye. Hot a planty out thar this mornin' . . . fer them that's not use't to it."

"My, what a family you do have, Mrs. Nolly! How do you manage?"

"I get to where I don't know what to do sometimes with jist one. Well, Lennie and Tennie and Joe and Clint's all big enough now to roust out a thar ever' mornin' and git the house cleaned up and outside chores done whilst I git breakfast, then them and their Pa scoots fer the fields, and I try to git over the heads of this bunch a little'ns and then git dinner afore they all gits back agin. Sometimes I make it. Tommy's over a year now, which is the longest I been without another started since I married. If I could jist know that I wouldn't have ta have no more." She sighed deeply, then said sharply, "Sary Ann, I'd as lief slap ye as ta look at ye this mornin'. Now hold that head still whilst I plait this fuzz hir, or I'm a liables ta do it!" Her thin face had a driven, desperate look.

"How do you remember all their names?"

Mrs. Nolly laughed grimly. "Sometimes when I'm that upset I calls haif a dozen names and git mysef plum kivered up with young'ns afore I finally gits the one I want. Even gits Bill and Reller mixed up in it sometimes, and us with not a young'n named fer us."

"How do you spell your name?" I asked curiously.

"Pruellen, fetch me that ball of strang off'n the kitchen shef. I'm a goin' ta braid 'bout a yard of hit into Sary Ann's har this time and see if'n hit'll stay up till marnin' one time."

"R-e-l-l-e-r, Reller. Full name is Cindy Reller, but they calls me Reller fer short. Lennie and Tennie's twins you know and soon thirteen. They's a big hep, and the first I had since I bin child bearin'." Her voice was suddenly bleak. "I do well know me one thang. Was the men ta haif ta have ever' other child, no family would have more'n three, fer it come his turn a second time, he'd shore call hit off."

July 12, 1915

What a glorious day. The sky a deep blue with puffs of white clouds sailing lazily over all day long, and the air was so fine it seemed to lift me up and bear me along as I went about my tasks.

Pa and Ma were back home. Pa was really better and full of tales of his many new experiences. Also, for a wonder, he seemed satisfied with the way things had gone during his absence.

"Here I was, thinkin' maybe I was of some 'portance and that this place couldn't get 'long without me, then I git back and find things done and the records and figures on it all kept straight jist as if I'd been here."

The boys visibly swelled with pride under this unexpected praise, but Mattie said sharply "They ain't no cause fer you ta lay yersef in the grave with worryin' over yore affairs, Uncle Henry. Not a one of us but could be saddled with some of the 'sponsibility and be glad ta do it, anytime you feel it gettin' too heavy."

"I don't need you to remind me, Mattie, that I'm gettin' old and with one foot already in the grave," Pa said petulantly. "Don't you go jumpin' on me!"

Mattie snapped back. "Fifty-five ain't old and I wasn't referrin' ta yore age. You could git jist as sick if you wudn't twenty, and it has been knowed ta happen, and sick people don't need to be loaded down till they can't get back on their feet agin. You get home from takin' a month's treatment and don't even give yoresef time to get yore breath, but jist shoulder the whole thing right off agin, ridin' ta Paragould, ridin' the farms, ridin' ta the bottoms. End ta end of this two thousand acres you been already. They ain't a foot of it got away whilst you was gone, and you coulda took our word fer it that all the crops was up and growin'."

"Stop this fussin'," said Ma. "I took him off away from you aggravatin' young'ns to get him well, and not home a week till the fat's in the far again."

"Aunt Annie, they's a difference in a fuss and a argament," explained Mattie patiently, "though we ain't never been able to make you see it. I wasn't fussin' at Uncle Henry, and he well knows it, whether you do or not."

Pa grinned as Mattie snatched her sunbonnet from the grass and flounced out of the gate.

July 16, 1915

The garden had failed at our place just as Pa had predicted. After a few days of thunder showers the creek had washed over the banks and half the garden lay under water for three days. When the rain ceased, the sun grew hotter by the minute. The plants spindled, turned yellow, and the life went out of them. But it was a terrible drain on my strength to pull Cerece in her little wagon the half mile to the big house, keep the garden hoed out and replanted as needed, gather my vegetables, then trudge the half mile back in the blazing sun. It would have helped some if I could have paused and prepared my vegetables under the cool shade of the big catalpa tree at the back gate, resting and chatting with Ma and Mattie before taking the walk back, but Ma made it plain that she had no time for me or my baby. I had stopped for a minute on my first trip through after Ma's return. But she had said sharply, "I hope yore not figgerin' on leaving Reecie here fer me to look after. Let them as has babies tend 'em as I did mine, is what I say."

I had been hurt and baffled by her manner, for Lester was nearly always with her, yet she would not have my child near her for two hours now and then while I hoed the garden. She seemed to harbor a spite toward me now. The first time it had shown openly in her face was the night I had leaned eagerly toward Pa at the box supper. The next time it had been under the oaks when Pa had heeded my suggestion to take a course of baths at the springs.

The fact that Pa usually strolled up to the garden, chatted with me, played with the baby, or now and then took the hoe and urged me to rest a spell, couldn't be helping it any. I was coming to see that she hated everything he took an interest in, outside herself.

Pa liked me now. I reveled in this fact and was comforted by it. Even so, he seldom missed a chance to give me a dig about my millionaire ideas. Me, the daughter of a day laborer who had made a living all his life and hadn't saved a dime. Each time he did it, retorts like an overturned hive of bees swarmed thickly in my mind. But because of his illness, I would not let them pass my lips until he had once more regained his high color and his voice had lost the petulant tone of the physically ill. But all the while I promised myself that if ever he did get well again, I would give him a good clear picture of some of my own views on life.

Money! Money! Money! The very thought of it sometimes made me sick.

July 21, 1915

One late morning I had just pinned the first boiling of clothes on the line, bathed Cerece, put her down for her nap and returned to the tubs, when Ma came bounding onto the front porch. Never had she been in the little house since we occupied it, and she took no notice of it now.

"Sssssh!" I pled for silence. "I just got the baby down. Is something wrong?"

"Don't shush me!" she snapped, refusing to lower her voice. "Something is certainly wrong. Reecie might as well get her eyes open, she's going with me. I'm keeping Lester and her while you and Ann go to Spilling Brook and puts out a wash fer Belle."

"But I've got my own washing started," I protested.

"Which has nothin' whatsoever to do with the case," she snapped. "That new mule kicked Silas at last and he's out a his head. Henry's gone over to see about him. Belle was sick and didn't get ta wash last week. She's phoned his mother and sister, and she wants things cleaned up before they get there." She snatched up the sleeping baby and made for the door. "I got no time to stand here arguin' with you," she glared. "Get yoresef together and get over there as fast as you can git. Ann will be waitin' fer you."

She was gone, and Cerece's wild screams faded out in the distance.

"It's not that I mind washing for Belle," I told Ann as we took the shortcut through the woods to Spilling Brook, "even stopping in the middle of my own to do it. It's just the hateful high-handed way Ma came in telling me what I had to do . . . and her snatching Cerece out of a sound sleep and making off with her like that."

"She's a heifer, if ever one lived. Far as that goes, why couldn't Mrs. Campbell and that precious Charline wash after they get here? There won't be another thing they can do to help, so they'll just set and nurse their hands right on, I reckon."

"Ma said Silas was delirious."

"Well he might be. That mule kicked him in the groin and his penis is swoll up like your wrist. Had to make a bridge of tape across his thighs to prop it on and still he screamed with the awful weight and pain of it. No doubt he's ruined fer life, but when Pa called back a while ago he said he'd finally dropped off to sleep after a hypodermic."

Belle's great blue eyes were swollen and red with weeping. She had a fire under a pot of water and the tubs filled for rinsing. Pa had got Tom Wiggins to take over at the bedside. Hoops from the wagon had been erected above Silas and a canopy of sheets fashioned to hide him, for he could not bear the weight of his clothing or the sheet.

"This is Ma's doin's, I know," said Belle sadly. "This is everbodys busy time and I wouldn't have had you leave yore work to do mine fer nothin'. We could've managed somehow."

"We wanted to come, Belle," I hastily assured her, knowing how sensitive she was, "and with all the water drawn we won't be long about it."

"Such a pretty day. They'll dry fast as they're hung and we'll probably have time to iron 'em up before we go back this afternoon," said Ann.

Pa, impatient as always, would not wait after dinner when he learned that Ann and I were going to stay and do the ironing. So, after the hard day, we had to walk back through the woods. But it was pleasant in the late afternoon, for the woods seemed full of delightful smells. The wild grapes were in bloom and there was the rich sweet fragrance of sun-ripened berries mingled with leaf mold and sweet fern.

When I reached home I looked longingly at the bed, took a deep breath, put a fire in the stove, grabbed a bucket and dashed out to milk Miss Pert, who stood lowing at the gate. While I was milking, Alex rode in on Jude, Cerece in his lap. I could tell by looking at Alex that he had had a hard day too, so I fixed a quick supper and we ate almost in silence.

July 23, 1915

After Alex had shown me the best patches, I had planned to pick my own berries, but as the summer heat increased I found that I could not go on with it. Besides which, and in spite of all precautions, the baby and I were half crazy with redbug bites. If just to pick the berries had been all, but then I had to come right in and put a fire in the stove and stand over the heat canning them. Lush ripe blackberries won't keep waiting.

Alex went to town with Pa one morning and left the Woody children picking berries for me. I was ready for a long hot afternoon, for he was bringing me three dozen new quart jars. It would take longer, but I had the sugar and had planned to make some jam with the berries. I didn't have a recipe so I went to the phone and gave two long rings.

When Ma answered, I asked, "Ma, what proportions do you use in making jam?"

"What?"

"How much sugar to how many berries do you use to make jam?"

I heard another receiver leave the hook.

"Well," her too-bright laughter tinkled mockingly over the wire, "you just go ahead and test out different mixes till you find the right one, then you'll know how you come by it."

"Annie, I'd be ashamed of mysef on the face of this here earth!" Selma's voice was brittle with anger. "What was it you wanted to know, Flossie?"

"The recipe for making blackberry jam."

"Wash your berries clean and mash them. Use measure for measure of sugar. It cooks off quick so and is rich and good."

I heard Ma's receiver hang up with a bang, "How many blackberries you got?"

"The Woody children picked six gallons, but I'm only going to use two of them for jam. Thank you, Selma. I better run."

I went back to the kitchen, but my mind was occupied with Ma. She behaved as though I had done her a personal disservice that was hard to forgive. If I had, it had been without intention. She had seemed to like me at first. Now all touch with her was gone and there remained only this feeling of stark antagonism. Some afternoon, I would take the time to dress and go up there for no other reason than to talk this thing out with her. How glad I was that I hadn't settled down in her house. That would have been much worse than this. But I didn't like living in this manner, and if I could figure out anything to do to get it straightened out with her I intended to do it.

July 26, 1915

There were signs of untoward activity in the beehive that Alex had set in the east corner of the front yard. He had set it there out of pure pride, since it was a section taken from the body of a huge oak tree, bees intact in the home they had made for themselves in the hollow. The knothole entrance to the hive was worn slick and smooth. It hadn't been easy to do.

"There's just no tellin' how many swarms of bees have come out of that old tree," he said proudly when Onnie helped him deposit it on the framework. This morning he had run back to tell me to listen for them, for they were likely to swarm at any time, as the workers were busy killing the drones and carrying them outside.

"I've got the new hive lined up here and I'm leavin' you this big tin lid and iron spoon on the front step. The minute you hear them swarm, run out under them and start beatin' for dear life. They'll settle, then call Ann and she'll yell me out. I'm helpin' Onnie in the east field this mornin'."

Alex had built a long trough under the pump at the west end of the front porch. He had braced a strong frame out from the end of the porch and nailed an old horse blanket tightly over it, making a good stout awning to protect the trough from the hot sun at midday, which was the only time the sun ever reached the little porch. I had just settled my milk and butter crocks, let the old water runoff and was pumping fresh cold water into the trough when it happened.

With an excited roar the bees came pouring from the hive in a rush and spiraled upward. I grabbed the lid and spoon and dashed out the front gate, beating frantically and keeping pace with them, for they traveled slowly. Out by the church they went, and then circled back. Stumbling and beating, I kept under them and suddenly they began to settle on the tip of an oak limb and there before my very eyes they formed themselves into a great brown pulsing ball of life. I ran to the phone and told Ann to call Alex, and went back to my post, standing ready to make a fearful clatter again if they showed any signs of leaving.

Alex came galloping over on Jude and left her to crop the grass while he seized the new hive and settled it on a stump near the bees. He began tapping the top of it lightly with his knife and gradually the swarm disintegrated and swarmed down over and around him, at last finding their way into and settling down in their new home.

I watched these proceedings safely from the end of the porch. "What does the tapping do?" I asked when I opened the front gate for him as he carried the hive to the back.

"It drowns out the queen. When they no longer hear her, they take to the louder vibration and settle under it."

"Why didn't you ever get any of your old bees from Pa?"

"Pa wouldn't let me have 'em." He grinned a bit sheepishly. "Said I made them hives from his timber and hived 'em on his time, so's they belonged to him."

"Papa would have insisted on his boys taking the bees, if they had done the work, and would have been sure to divide them up if they hadn't."

"Which is probably one reason your Pa's got nothin' and mine has."
He was actually taking pride in Pa's miserly little ways!

July 28, 1915

It was a mellow summer day and Ann and I were canning peaches together in Ann's big kitchen.

"And I says to her, I says, Corrine, where's your baby? And she says, Ann, you know my baby died, and I says, I mean the new baby, Corrine, the one you had after you left here, and she denied she'd ever had another one. But she went with me to the orchard to get peaches and when we started back she stopped stock still and I looked back and there she was, tryin' to hold the nipple of her breast and stop the flow, but the milk was drippin' off the bottom of her middy blouse. I reckon stoopin' and bendin' had started it up. I says, I thought you said you didn't have a new baby, Corrine, and she had the gall to tell me her milk never did dry up after that one died. She was lyin' and she knew that I knew she was lyin', but what could I do?"

"Nothing. But Ann, I could cry for those poor orphans . . . if it would do any good."

"I could cry too, but how can anybody help them if they can't find out anything? After all, they are right here at my door. I feel like that case needs looking into, but who's to do it? There is sure something fishy going on. Hank was plowing the south field, and all afternoon Corrine would go out and hang on the field fence and they'd talk and talk, then he'd plow another round and they'd have another session."

"Have you told anyone what we saw?"

"Nobody but Onnie, but I believe Pa got wind of it. Else, why would him and Mr. Skaggs have gone up there this morning?"

"I hope and pray we don't get wound up in it," I said fervently. "I'd as soon stick my head in a den of rattlers as to tie into Hank Scoggins."

July 29, 1915

The next morning I was singing as I washed the breakfast dishes when I heard a heavy step on the front porch. I stepped to the partition door to see who it was, and my heart leaped into my throat and hit the bottom of my stomach with a demoralizing lurch. The sound of its beating filled my ears as I looked into the bleary bloodshot eyes of Hank Scoggins. He was badly in need of a shave and the greasy red flame of his hair hung in slack spikes as though it had been fresh milked. Without the least hesitancy, he opened my screen door and came in.

"I want to use yore phone, Miz Flossie," he said shortly. I tried to speak but no words came, so I motioned with my hand. He turned his back and rang central at the box beside the door.

I returned to my dishpan. Why had he passed by Ann's and come on here to use the phone? Why had he waited till he knew Alex was gone? I strained my ears to hear. He was calling the stock yards. Could they take a bunch of cattle if he drove them right in? He rang central again, then the receiver went back on the hook and all was still. I stood it as long as I could and ventured back to the partition door. He was seated in one of the big cane rockers. His eyes circled the room wildly for a moment, and then came to rest on me.

"Line's busy," he mumbled, sucking at the end of his long red mustache.

With quick resolution, I walked swiftly past him and rang for Ann and took the receiver from the hook.

"Ann?"

"Yes."

"You bring that pattern and come right on over. If you hurry we'll have time to cut those things out before dinner and get to sewing it quicker this afternoon."

"What pattern?" asked Ann blankly.

"No, he's not here," I said in desperation. "Tell Onnie he ran to the store to get me some soap, but he ought to be back this living minute, but you come right on."

"Flossie, have you gone crazy?"

"Yes . . . that is . . . no. Just Hank Scoggins. He stopped here to use the phone. So don't bother to change your clothes." I hung up, trembling in every cell of my body.

"She thinks she has to get a bath and change clothes," I chattered senselessly, "just to run over here midmorning and cut out a few garments." I was talking against the horror rising within me as Hank continued to stare vacantly at me as he rose from his chair and advanced.

I stepped onto the porch.

He again reached the phone and rang the bell. He gave a number and waited.

I leaned limply against a post and watched for Ann. She was coming over the fields on a dead run.

"Guess I'll have to give it up," said Hank. "A little early fer 'em to be down, I reckon."

Then he came into the porch slowly, his mind busy with his own thoughts. He walked to the end of the porch and pulled a leaf from the oak tree and folded it carefully in his nervous fingers. "I reckon I might as well go," he mumbled, "and thank ye, Miz Flossie."

"You . . . you're welcome . . . Hank," I gulped. Ann was in plain sight and hearing now, and so had slowed her pace to a rapid stride.

Hank ambled thoughtfully out to the gate. They met at the corner of the rye patch.

"Hi ya, Hank," she said.

"Tolable. All well yore way, I reckon?"

"All well, but everybody with too much to do right now," said Ann.

But once inside she sat on Alex's little trunk under the phone, panting for breath. "The minute you said Hank I dropped everything and flew. What he could have done to you and the baby here alone!" She wiped the beads of perspiration from her brow with a trembling hand. "Whatever did he say to you? What excuse did he give for coming here? I never saw a man look more desperate."

"*He* looked desperate! Heavenly days, Ann! I've never felt more desperate in my *life*! I'd felt awful things running through his mind when he just opened the door and walked in and said he wanted to use the phone. Why didn't he stop and use yours, first off? I've a notion to tell Pa exactly what we think. I don't see how I can stand much more of this."

"I'm sure Pa already knows. That's probably what's the matter with Hank. The old man's trying to get him off the place. But Hank's got a crop in the making, you know, and he may make trouble about that."

"Hasn't he been on the place ten years and no trouble? I've heard Pa say he's one of the best sharecroppers on the plantation."

"But Hank's changed since Sofie died. Corrine's the spittin' image of her Ma, and looks to me like Hank's got Sofie and Corrine and Becky mixed up in his own mind. Can Pa let them stay on there, with first one and then the other of them girls having a baby for Hank, on and on? If that's what's going on, and what else is a body to think?"

My mind was busy with speculation, but I couldn't shy away from the awful thing Ann was putting into words for the first time.

An hour later I watched the deacons of the church and a few of the older men of the community as they assembled at the church. Another hour gone by and I held my breath when they emerged. All took their way home, except a delegation of three that went at once to the home of Hank Scoggins.

July 30, 1915

Next day the house that had so long housed Hank and his brood stood empty. Late the evening before, Hank had driven his few head of cattle into town. The children must have packed everything that they could find room for on the big farm wagon and stopped by for Hank in town and all gone on to wherever they had decided to go. Things were a mess, with odds and ends wildly scattered over the house and yard. The two old coffee pots containing the cotton roots and cedar balls were gone.

No one seemed to know where they had come from in the first place. No one knew where they'd gone. But Pa took over the crop and the few hogs Hank left, and everybody heaved a sigh of relief that Hank Scoggins was no longer a member of our community.

Chapter 14

July 31, 1915

The church league baseball season waxed and waned, but by the third week of the games the ice cream parties would have to be abandoned. Through it all I had been careful to avoid Ma because her unpredictable tongue had come to seem like an asp, coiled to strike at my approach.

The last evening we served ice cream, her attention had focused on me as I came in. I had not a whole pair of stockings to my name, so I wore my canvas sneakers, an old white linen skirt and a blouse I had made from four bandanas I found at the store. Cerece sat in the front of her little "go buggy" as Alex called it, the bucket of ice cream, the cake and the dishes stowed in the back. I was late, but knew I would be there in time to help with the ice cream, and I didn't care much for the game, anyway. But I was snatched out of my relaxed and happy mood by Ma's sharp tones.

"Flossie, what do you mean by coming out where all these men can see you without any stockings?"

"I haven't any stockings."

"Then why didn't you stay home?"

"Because, I wanted to come to the ice cream party!"

Everyone seemed ill at ease for a moment, and then the buzz of talk was resumed. When the ice cream which I had brought was ready to serve, Ma was the first to sample it.

"Gracious, Mattie, where's your swill pail? I don't know who made this ice cream, but it's certainly not fit to eat!" She shook her head and made a terrible face and shuddered.

Selma calmly ladled a soup bowl full and passed it to Onnie. "The boys is not so particular, Annie. Just watch them lap it up and call fer more." As this proved to be the case, the ice cream party went straight on without a break.

As long as Ma kept her dislike for me in the family, I had not been unduly worried. But to have her come out openly with it disturbed and distressed me. My joy in the occasion was over, and I was glad when it was announced that the games would go on, but the ice cream parties would be discontinued. Alex could play right on, but I need not come again.

August 2, 1915

Monday I took my mending basket in the back of the little wagon and walked over to spend the afternoon with Ann.

"Now don't this seem funny? First time this summer that I've gone any place to actually sit and visit. Ann, what makes you so pale, are you sick?"

She nodded miserably. "And due to be sicker before I'm done with it!"

"You mean?"

"I mean! If I'd just to be sick a few weeks like most women. But no, I go on and on with it . . . for the full nine months."

"Well, I've heard you say you didn't want to raise Lester by himself, and I don't know how else you'd get him a little brother or sister."

"I did say that, but I wasn't actual meanin' to do anythin' about it." She grinned. "Though I think it's too late to save him, he's done ruint. He thinks he has to ride the farms with his Granpa now, with a pencil behind his ear and a notebook in his pocket. Sets something down every time the old man does, and a solemn job he makes of it."

"He won't learn anything bad from his Granpa."

"Which is just the half of it. Got so he don't know which is home. Half his clothes are up there and he just goes to bed whichever place night finds him."

"That ought to suit you all right with what you've got ahead."

"Yes, I'll be lyin' on a pallet with my head hanging off the porch the rest of the summer, puking like a sick cat." She sighed dolefully. "You and the old lady patched up your business yet?"

"No."

"I thought not, way she acted at the ice cream party."

"Ann, do you have any idea what it could be?"

"Only thing I can think of is that you used her sugar and eggs and popcorn to make the treat for your chivaree that night."

"Oh, but it couldn't be that. She's been lovely to me some since then."

"Well, it's the only thing I've heard mentioned. I heard her tell Belle that if her and Silas had gone to her kitchen and used her eggs and sugar, they could've had a nice treat for their friends too, instead of the boxes of stick candy they passed around."

"Well, I can soon remedy that . . . if you think that might be it. But I feel sure that it's something else. I thought she liked me a bit and I was beginning to get downright fond of her. Then the minute Pa gets so he treats me like a human being, she turns on me. It was always Pa that kept me worried."

"Say, that could be it!" Ann exclaimed with conviction. "Everybody knows how mean jealous she can be. I bet that's it."

Going home I made up my mind. If it was the sugar and eggs, then I'd make up that same amount of candy, pack it in a big tin candy box I had there and take it to her. Then, if she didn't change her manner, I meant to have a showdown with her.

August 5, 1915

As I neared the big house late Thursday afternoon, I saw that Pa, Sherman, Onnie, and Alex had gathered in the back porch for a cool drink and a moment of rest before the last go-round. I was grateful for that, for I was more than a little nervous.

"I brought you something you like!" I sang out, seizing the bull by the horns as I rounded the corner. I took the tin from the wagon and passed it over to Pa. "Remember when I used Ma's sugar and eggs to make the treat for the chivaree? I'd forgotten all about it, so since I thought of it, I came to bring back what I borrowed."

"Whooooeee!" said Pa, removing the lid and sniffing with appreciation. He selected a flakey white puff and bit into it, his gray eyes glistening. "My, my, Annie, have some! I want you to find out how she makes it, so's you can cook us up a batch of it once in a while." He held the box toward her.

"Keep it all fer yoresef, Henry. You're the one she made it fer," she said sweetly, and she turned and gazed out across the north field.

Pa winked knowingly at me. "Well, that sure leaves me with a nice bait of it now," he said happily, "and I sure thank you fer it, Flossie." He turned and carried the box safely inside with him. It was all I could do to keep from laughing at the disappointment on the faces of the three drooling boys left standing with open mouths.

"Well, I reckon, we might as well get on back to work," said Sherman, and they left.

Somehow I didn't have the courage to tackle Ma at this minute. I looked at her and the blood beat like a muffled drum in my throat, so I picked up the wagon tongue and pulled the baby on out to the garden.

August 9, 1915

But I couldn't forget about it. The next Monday when I went to the garden and saw Ma propped back, taking the breeze in her usual place in the back gallery, I went resolutely up to the back door.

"How's your back, Ma? Alex said you slipped at the front door when you got in from church yesterday."

"My back is all right!" she snapped, and turned her gaze to the north.

In desperation I blurted, "Ma, why don't you like me anymore?"

She pretended to be astonished. "Who said I didn't like you?" Her voice was sugary now.

"I'd much rather you'd say it, than treat me as you have been. I am a member of the family, even if it is just by marriage, and I'd like to be treated as such."

Silence.

"I feel that some time or other I must have done something that you didn't like. If you'll say what it was, I stand ready to do what I can to clear it up."

"You and me is gettin' along, Flossie, exactly as I want to get along with you!"

It was hard to believe that such harsh words could be spoken in so soft a tone.

"But this isn't the way families are supposed to get along, Ma!" Then I brought my voice back down to conversational level. "It isn't Christian, even if we were only neighbors. You don't seize on every chance that offers to try to make any of the tenants feel bad. Why should you set yourself to do this to me? I have even lost sleep worrying over it."

A shrill of tinkling laughter spilled upon the air. Ma was enjoying herself. She had me exactly where she wanted me. Begging at her doorstep. "I wouldn't worry too much about it if I was you, Flossie, seein' there's nothin' at all you can do about it," she said sweetly.

A sudden rush of hot blood surged into my throat, but I swallowed and met her taunting gaze unwaveringly. "I came to have an understanding with you, Ma. I have it, and I can now go on my way. If ever there is another moment's worrying done about the relationship that exists between us, you'll be the one to do it!"

Ma's good time was over and the front legs of her chair came down on the porch with a sudden thump.

"Remember this too. If ever there is another move made toward friendliness, it will be you making it," I added.

August 14, 1915

It was mid-August and the Saturday before Big Meeting. Alex and I went to Paragould, carrying a coop of the cockerels, now almost too big for frying. This was the only means we had of raising money to buy the few things we needed, and to pay the preacher.

We were fortunate to get in on the August clearance sale at Pendleton's. Alex bought a pair of white pants and white buckskin shoes. "I just can't go through the meeting in wool pants!" he declared.

I was happy with two new dresses, a striped dimity and a rose printed voile, made princess with a little cutaway jacket completely outlined with a row of oblong pearl buttons. The weight of the pretty buttons caused the sheer material to cling to my body in a very flattering fashion.

While in town we drove out and had dinner with Lola. "How have you stood it through this awful heat?" she asked.

"It's even worse in town," Alex assured her. "It's too hot to quarrel, I know, but the August sales and no money has got Flossie in a fit mood to fight a crosscut saw."

"She doesn't look that mad, Alex."

"I'm not mad, Lola, but crops are laid by and the timber job is going full tilt and not a penny do we see! I was just after Alex to attend State Normal and apply for the Eight Mile School. It wouldn't interfere with his farming and at least we would have the sixty-five dollars a month income we could depend on."

Alex grinned, twitching his eyebrows quizzically. "Six times sixty-five, that's over four hundred a year extra. We could use it all right," he conceded.

"Which is positively the first encouraging word I've heard on the subject," I said, much surprised.

"Time you drool over a pair of white gabardine britches and take a pair of white ducks instead, and everything else cut after the same pattern, a feller's bound to think a little about money. If only I could get it some way without teaching."

August 19, 1915

It was sweet going to church in the evenings. I had always put Cerece to bed early, and I usually remained at home until she was fast asleep, coming back at the end of the sermon to see about her, then returning for the end of the service. The singing of the hymns never failed to lift my spirit, and Alex found such joy in taking the high notes that his clarion zeal often brought a smile to my lips.

One thing troubled me greatly . . . Ma. She set great store by these revivals. She would settle herself not to miss one word of the message of love so lavishly showered on us from the soul-saving spirit that animated Brother Sherrill at these times. Always then would come the moment of overflow, and Ma would rise with a joyous shout, leaving her fan and pocketbook on her chair or with the sister next to her and, lifting her arms and voice in a paean of praise, she would shout her way up and down the aisles. "I don't fight it," I once heard her say, "I just listen and wait, and when God wants to shout me, I just let him shout me!"

It was my habit to enter during a song, and I usually found a seat in the center aisle near the front. One night I entered during the last song before the text was taken. Brother Sherrill chose this period for brief testimonials. Different members of the congregation rose and offered their remarks, and asked for prayers for themselves and their loved ones. To do this had never once occurred to me.

"There sits in this audience tonight a young woman who has not yet spoken one word publicly for her Lord and Master, Jesus Christ. Miz Flossie."

I gulped audibly at the sound of my name. "I baptized your father and mother at Old Macedonia. I come out here and find you married into a good Christian family. What have you to say for your Savior? What have you to say for yourself?"

My heart turned over. Was this *my* meeting too? Frightened, I rose to my feet and steadied my trembling hands by holding tightly to the back of the seat in front of me.

"Brother Sherrill, I'm sure that I've done little or nothing to set myself apart as one of the Lord's devoted disciples. The light that burns in me must be something like the light that was in our lamp this morning. Last night when we started to bed we found that we were out of matches. Rather than have Alex go to Onnie's at that hour, we decided to turn the light down and leave it burning until morning so that we could have a light to start the fire for breakfast. But when Alex got up this morning, he said he'd have to go to Onnie's for matches, for the light had gone out. Then while he was dressing he crossed the room and looked over into the fireplace and the coals were glowing, very low, but steadily. My light must be like that, not visible. Yet, if anyone took the trouble to look into my heart, I feel that they would be able to see that the light, though low, is burning." I resumed my seat, trembling and shaken.

"Amen! Thank God! Her light is burning, not high, but steady. Thank God for that. Are there any others who want to speak a word for Jesus?" He hesitated and when there was no further response he said, "Then rise and let us sing together:"

> *Come, Thou fount of every Blessing,*
> *Tune my heart to sing Thy grace,*

"Everybody sing!"

> *Streams of mercy, never ceasing*
> *Call for songs of loudest praise.*

This was my own song of happiness, but I found I could not sing it in this troubled hour, for as I opened my mouth to join the others, my eye fell on Ma, and all joy was stilled within me.

Brother Sherrill took his text and, as he warmed to his subject, he strode back and forth, gesticulating wildly and straining in his speech until the veins in his neck and temples swelled and quivered as though filled to bursting with a surging tide of rich purple wine. At last he reached up and with a dexterous twist of the wrist untied his four-in-hand tie and tossed it carelessly behind him, never missing so much as a syllable of the message that now poured from him. Next he unbuttoned his celluloid collar and flung it after the tie. Higher and higher, sounded his plea, as he shucked off his black alpaca coat and added it to the heap. Then he unfastened the metal gadgets that held his detachable celluloid cuffs at anchor, and rolled up his sleeves and went after the devil and all of his dastardly works with a power and strength that could never have been housed in that frail and failing body. The power of the spirit had lent him the strength of ten men.

"Who will join their strength to mine?" he screamed hoarsely, "Who among you is to take up the work when I must lay it down? I look out over this goodly number gathered here tonight and my heart bleeds for the Master's work, as yet scarcely begun. The harvest is ripe, the gleaners are few, and not one soul under the sound of my voice tonight has as yet dedicated his life to the Master's work. Oh, my friends, my beloved flock! Gird your loins for the battle of all time, for evil is abroad in the land. Stand shoulder to shoulder with me while I am yet with you. Stand shoulder to shoulder with each other, when I am no more. Be vigilant, be watchful, and root the evil from your community by first rooting him from your own hearts. Who will come to the Mourner's Bench and confess his sins and line up on the Lord's side tonight?"

"Now, while we join in singing 'Just As I Am Without One Plea,' while I stand here with arms out held to receive you, I admonish you, I plead with you, come to Jesus now! Come into the fold, come in from the deserts of sin and cast yourself on a merciful God and drink of the waters of life freely. The blood was shed for you. Won't you come?"

The congregation rose as one and the words of the old revival hymn rang out:

> *Just as I am, without one plea,*
> *But that Thy blood was shed for me,*
> *And that Thou bidst me come to Thee,*
> *O, Lamb of God, I come! I come!*

Half a dozen penitents went forward, gave their hands and knelt at the Mourner's Bench. Sister Sherrill ran an experienced eye over the sinners, decided on an old man who seemed under deep conviction, and knelt beside him to aid him in whatever way seemed best.

The congregation sang on and on, and when no more sinners offered themselves, the preacher and a few other workers joined Sister Sherrill in her efforts. There were pleas and prayers and exhortations, world without end, mingled with the prayerful hymns. Several of the older women, unable longer to withstand the rising emotional tide, now bounced and waltzed up and down the aisles, feet seeming scarcely to contact the floor, shouting praises to His holy name. Hands raised high above their heads, their words were strangely distinguishable above the swelling tide of song.

Ma sat always in the same place, to the right of Brother Sherrill, and never did she take her eyes from his face as he preached. I could not keep my eyes from straying to her now and then as the excitement waxed higher, wondering if she would dare to get up before me and shout and sing of the wonderful gift of God's love, with me knowing what she harbored in her heart toward me. Each time my eyes sought her, I found her gazing at me in baffled displeasure. Once she seemed on the point of rising, but when my eyes opened wide in horrified disbelief, she subsided.

August 20, 1915

The next morning Brother and Sister Sherrill came strolling leisurely toward my house, Brother Sherrill carefully holding over her a huge rusty black umbrella as protection from the blazing sun. I had meant to invite them over during the meeting, but I had not invited them for today, knowing that they were to spend last night and today at Ma's. When they reached the porch and I had greeted them, Brother Sherrill let down his umbrella and handed it to me, together with a brown paper bag. I looked inside it to find a mess of green beans strung and snapped for the pot.

"Sister Annie sent you these, child. I picked them for her this morning and she strung and snapped them for you with her own hands."

And I could have told him, I dug the ground and planted the seeds and kept them hoed with my own hands.

"And I might as well tell you first as last that I had a purpose in coming here today. There is a stone lying in the path of you and Sister Annie and it lies in my province to remove the stone away."

"Well, make yourselves comfortable and excuse me for a minute till I get the beans on to cook. I'll be right back." When I returned, Brother Sherrill moved forward to the edge of his chair. He had once been a sturdy man, but he was now hurrying on toward seventy and the years had taken a heavy toll.

"Flossie," his eyes were deep wells of sorrow as he spoke, "I loved your father and mother before you. Will you let an old man who knows only to love you for their sake, advise you in a matter that has come to my attention and which lies like a heavy weight on my heart?"

"I am sure that any advice you might offer would be in a kindly spirit," I said quietly.

"Thank you, daughter," He cleared his throat nervously and made the plunge. "Sister Annie tells me that she can't enjoy her religion this meeting because of you." He fixed his eyes sadly upon me.

"Because of me?" I asked faintly.

"Yes. It came out when I asked her why I had not heard her shouting during some of the rousing meetings we have been enjoying. When the Holy Ghost brings conviction to the hearts of sinners and they become penitents at the throne of mercy, it has ever been her habit to shout God's praises. Not once in all the years that I have shepherded this flock has she failed so to do. She says she can't shout this year, because when she starts to get to her feet she finds you sitting there staring her down."

"Oh Brother Sherrill! Then I'll sit in the back of the room, where she can't even see me."

He shook his head mournfully. "That's not the right thing to do, Flossie." Then his voice became stern. "The thing for you to do is to make your peace with your husband's mother."

The hot blood surged into my throat and my nerves tightened, but I said nothing.

"Get at the root of the trouble that lies between you, for I read between the lines of what she was saying that there is trouble! Annie is a sweet good woman and her voice was bitter for the first time since I've known her, when she said you had no right to set yourself up in judgment on her and her religion."

My thoughts darted desperately here and there like frightened birds. Should I tell him the truth? No! Ma was a cherished and beloved member of his flock. He probably wouldn't believe my story, but in any case I was a member of this family now and it would give me no joy to expose Ma's failings to another, especially one who now had complete confidence in her.

"Brother Sherrill," I managed to smile at last, "I appreciate the effort you have made to bring peace where peace is not." I laughed nervously. "But I honestly believe there is nothing that you can do about this unhappy state of affairs. It seems to be a thing that only time can take care of."

"But, Flossie, it's for your own sake I ask it! Make your peace with her and you will grow in grace and be a happier woman. This I promise."

"And I can only promise you that I will sit in the back of the church so that Ma will not even know that I am there. Then she can shout, if she finds it in her heart to do so."

It was not a happy day. Alex didn't come in at noon, and Brother Sherrill let the dinner get cold while he lifted his voice in a long and ardent prayer that my cold heart might be softened under his ministry. That I might humble my haughty spirit and so find peace with the mother of the man whom I loved and had chosen from all others. I simply couldn't eat after that, and sat miserably mincing at the food and politely passing things to both hungry guests . . . and thinking my own long thoughts.

That night I slipped in and sat near the back on the same side of the church that Ma was on. I felt that she had not known when I entered. Cerece had not gone to sleep as usual, and so I had brought her along. As the sermon got under way, the baby drowsed and slept on my bosom. When the hymns of invitation began, I slipped out and took Cerece home and put her to bed. If only I had not gone back.

Pleas were going out to the sinners, fears were instilled, and admonitions piled high, prayers and supplications offered. The crucified Christ was held up to those who still hesitated.

"He died that ye might live! Greater love hath no man, than that he give his life for another. All that He asks is that you put your faith and trust in Him and follow in the way that leads to glory." The Mourner's Bench filled and the penitents came through with shining faces and joy knew no bounds. When all joined in singing "I Feel Like Traveling On," I saw Ma bearing down upon me, her face transfigured, her arms upheld and her pretty little hands shaking as with a palsy. She had not seen me as yet and I tried to turn away from her approach, but too late. Her eyes had found me and she advanced with the purposeful zeal of a fanatic.

"I feel like traveling on, don't you, Flossie?" she screamed in a white frenzy, and reached forth her right hand and brought it down across my cheek with a blow that staggered me. I sank my teeth into my lip and lowered my eyes and prayed diligently for control, for strength and for guidance. Ma hesitated uncertainly for a moment, and then proceeded on her way, no longer rejoicing. Her voice had the sound of a broken tin whistle and died out completely, leaving her to make her way dazedly back to her seat in beaten silence. Alex, in the choir, was singing at the top of his voice and had seen nothing.

When we were getting off to bed, he leaned forward and asked, "What in tucket is the matter with your face?"

"That's where Ma slapped me while she was shouting tonight," I replied, turning away.

"Lord, I've seen her shout till she fell out cold. I can't understand what's quietened her down so. She's always shouted herself into a kind of trance and I've had to look out for her then, for Pa wouldn't touch her with a ten foot pole!" He paused in the act of undressing and sat gazing before him. "I think Pa really has a fear of her when she's under the power."

"Ma can always seem to get more than her share of the Holy Ghost, all right." He had forgotten about my face. I blew out the light and eased into bed.

August 21, 1915

"I do hate to go into town the last day of the meetin'," said Alex, "but Pa's about completely sold out in the store and he wants me to go to the wholesale house with him. Nearly every man in the country's got to go to town today, but all of us have paid the preacher all we can, so's you women will have to do the last honors, I reckon."

"I don't think I'll go today, Alex," I said, sending up a kite to see which way the wind blew.

"Why, certainly you'll go! Ann's been too sick to go mornings and there'll be a lot that won't go because it's Saturday, but you being right in the church door have surely got no cause to stay at home, especially with me not even going to be here to cook for."

I took my usual place in the center aisle. Alex had been right. There were not half a dozen men present. It was mostly women and children. Brother Sherrill was weary. He no longer exhorted sinners. These had been baptized and gathered into the fold. His concern was with another matter. He took his text from Ruth one, sixteen and seventeen, and as he read my heart stood still.

> *And Ruth said; entreat me not to leave thee or to return from following after thee; for whither thou goest, I will go, and where thou lodgest, I will lodge; Thy people shall be my people and thy God my God.*

In deeply sorrowful and beseeching tones he preached to a "mother-in-law and a daughter-in-law here present, who claim to be disciples of the Blessed Lord and who sit this day in the House of God, lost in the morass of misunderstanding, neither saying nor doing ought to right the wrong. This dear mother-in-law patiently awaits a change in heart from this proud daughter-in-law. This dear daughter-in-law sits in false and stiff necked pride, refusing to take the first little step which would be all that was required to establish amicable relations between the two again. I feel that my mission among you has failed," he said in sorrowful tones, "if I go forth from this tabernacle without having done all that lies within my power to bring about a righting of whatever wrong exists."

He pointed out the beautiful love that existed between Ruth and Naomi. Finally, with tears streaming down his cheeks, he held supplicating hands toward me and begged me to follow in Ruth's footsteps. To render to this older woman the respect and the reparations that were her due, and the love and loyalty that her many fine qualities merited.

I had dared to steal one surreptitious glance at the complacent face of Ma. A slow anger kindled in me. To think that Ma, by her calculated complaints, her cool and deliberate posing as a martyr, had precipitated this unpleasant crisis. That she had maliciously brought about this public accusation so as to force me to admit my fault and humbly ask her forgiveness.

"And now, my child, will you step forward and give some explanation of your unnatural behavior? How can you sit there, thus stubborn and unmoved in the face of my pleas, while this good woman sits here, her tender heart yearning for a word of kindness from you? There are few here this morning that are not in some way related to this family. It is a family matter and I have spoken to more than one member of this family about it. All are agreed that a misunderstanding *does* exist. I am here to establish understanding.

"Flossie, speak!" As he spoke a purpose was born within me, and when he ceased, I rose to my feet and went straight to the pulpit.

"It will take a little time to clear this up, so Brother Sherrill, you had better take a seat while I do it. If it is complete understanding that you are bound to have, I now welcome it. It is a thing that has given me a lot of trouble. It is a thing that I have tried to clear up, but which has remained unchanged, in spite of my efforts. But only two or three weeks ago Ma set me right in the matter of our relationship. The misunderstanding which remains is between the rest of you. Ma and I have at last come to understand each other perfectly."

"I forgive you, Flossie. That's all that's necessary," chirped Ma. I glanced impatiently at her, and then turned back to Brother Sherrill.

"With all my heart I wish you had taken my word for it when I told you it was not a thing that you could handle. And I'm equally sure that Ma placed that burden there in an effort to explain away a situation which had gotten out of hand for her."

Ma was sitting on the edge of her seat, nervously tapping the floor with the toe of her shoe. I turned to her.

"Ma, didn't I come to you some time ago and try to find out what it was that you held in your heart against me?"

"Now hush, Flossie, I forgive you." Her tone dripped honey.

"Isn't it true that you have refused to come to my house for a visit, or to welcome me into your home since we moved to ourselves?"

"Yes, Flossie, but yore getting excited. Please, jist sit down, darlin'." Her voice was anxious now.

"Isn't it true that the mess of snap beans, which I planted and tended with my own hands, and which Brother Sherrill picked and you snapped and sent me, is the first, last, and only neighborly gesture you have made toward me in all these months?"

She patted the air between us with a placating hand. "Jist don't excite yoresef like this, Flossie. I fergive you."

"Didn't I come to your back door and ask for an explanation? Didn't I tell you that I felt that I must have unknowingly done something to distress you very much, and that if you would tell me wherein lay my fault, I would be only too glad to make amends?"

"Yes, Flossie, but let's jist let the whole thang drop right where it is, honey."

"We will not let the matter drop till it is clear to all, Ma, since it was you who brought about this public hearing. We're going through with it till everybody here understands it all as clearly as you and I do. Didn't I say that I thought it wasn't Christian to live as we were living . . . that I was a member of the family now and would like to be treated as such?"

"Yes." Her voice was no more than a whisper.

"And what did you say?" I asked, but her tongue clove to the roof of her mouth and she could not answer me. I knew a momentary flash of pity, but the tide of my anger bore me ruthlessly on. "Didn't you say that we were getting along exactly as you liked and meant to get along with me?"

"Yes." Ma's face was pale now, her voice pleading and scarcely audible. "Please don't talk any more, Flossie. I fergive you everthin'."

"You forgive *me*? Forgive me *what*!" I turned to Brother Sherrill. "The facts are before you," I said. Still trembling with anger I resumed my seat. Brother Sherrill stood before us, his head lowered for a moment in deep thought.

"Sister Annie," he said at last, and his voice was stern, "are you completely honest when you say that you desire that peace shall be established between you and this child?"

Ma nodded humbly.

"This seems not to have been the case a month ago," he said dryly. Then his tone softened. "Will you publicly proclaim this fact by giving Flossie the hand of Christian fellowship?"

"I will."

Brother Sherrill came and stood beside me. "Daughter, are you sincere in saying that you desire peace and amity between yourself and your mother-in-law?"

"I did once earnestly desire it," I said honestly, "but I cannot now feel that it greatly matters."

"To him that overcometh, Flossie," he admonished gently. "Can you give Sister Annie your hand in Christian fellowship?"

"I can give her my hand in this, and it will have to do, that I will meet her halfway in any overtures made toward friendship and that I will not knowingly do anything to antagonize her."

"Are you willing to accept that pledge, Sister Annie?"

"I am."

"Then thank God for that much." He said this fervently, eased his hand under my elbow and guided me over to where Ma still sat.

Ma rose and held out her hand. I laid mine in it hopefully, but the clasp had no more friendliness in it than the touch of a dead fish's tail.

"Won't you go home with me fer dinner, Flossie?" Ma spoke to me in dulcet tones that all might hear, but the look in her eyes as they met mine bit into me like a deadly acid.

"Some other time," I murmured, strangely at a loss, "but not today, Ma." I could not bring myself to thank her and return the compliment by asking her to spend the day with me, as was the custom at Main Shore.

Brother Sherrill had done what he could, but things were as they had been between Ma and me . . . or worse.

Chapter 15

September 1, 1915

August had gone out with a rush of overpowering heat. Even so, the men were deep in the timber, for the sale of lumber to the various mills of Paragould would last them through the coming harvesttime. The women were drying fruit and making grape jelly and fighting endlessly to keep themselves, their families, and their homes fresh and clean in the face of so much dust and heat.

One evening late I was in the front yard watering flowers when Reller came by, driving a flock of dispirited-looking geese before her.

"Evenin', Miz Flossie," she called.

"Good evening, Reller. I rested at your house when I was hot and tired, now you rest at mine. The blood's all but popping out of your face. Where have you been, on a wild goose chase?"

She laughed a little and gave the geese an urgent scare toward home and turned in at the gate. "I'm obliged to ye fer that invite," she declared, taking off her sunbonnet and fanning her face with it as she took the chair offered. I went inside, fixed a pitcher of ice water, and returned with two glasses.

"Lawd no, real honest ta God ice! How I been cravin' ta cool my tongue with a piece of that bewdiful hard water this livelong summer."

After she finished the ice water, I went inside. If it was ice she wanted, I'd oblige her. I filled the glass with crushed ice, lemon juice, and sugar. The eyes she raised to mine were full of gratitude.

"I heard little Tommy died, Reller," I said softly.

She nodded miserably. "A God's blessin' fer him that he went on, I reckon, though it shore tore the heart right out a me. He chawed one of them wicks out'n that fancy fly killer Bill brung home. He was that cute a doin' it, and I stood thar a laffin' fit to die at the funny face he made whilst he chawed it, never oncet guessin' what it was he had in his mouth. Though I guess"—she sighed—"if the truth was knowed, Tommy is about the luckiest one of my chillen, to be well out of it."

"You certainly have had your share of children, Reller."

"Bill ain't found it out yet, Miz Flossie, but I've had my last un." A wild light shone fleetingly in her tortured eyes. "If'n I haf to leave Bill Nolly and go out in this wuld alone, Miz Flossie, I've had my last young'n fer Bill Nolly. Married fouteen year and here I am wit thuteen chillen, not countin' leetle Tommy that died. It's as fer as I'm goin' on wit it."

"I never did know exactly how many you had." I hardly knew how to cope with the confidence she was reposing in me.

"Two sets a twins, you know, Lennie and Tennie, which is now headin' on fouteen, and Thelmer and Elmer, which is nigh ten. Clever and Stacy, which is nine and eight and was in the yard the day you was thar."

I found myself without words.

"Come round the week I married and I ain't seen a thing since. Now Tommy's died is the fust time I ain't been pushin' one away fom the titty to make room fer the next un to grab it, and I git my fust full night's rest in fouteen year. If it ain't already happened, I made up my mind that this is one year that pore Reller ain't gonna git caught." She looked at me closely. "You lookin' putty peaked yo'sef. I reckon you ain't in fer it agin?"

"I think I'm just run-down. I've been working beyond my strength all summer. If only I had somebody to do the ironing for me. Swinging a hot iron in this heat seems to hurt me worse than anything."

"I'll do it fer you, and glad ta. Tunin' ova a new leaf, mysef. I'm sick and tard of livin' as I been, never a takin' foot outside my own dooryard. I coulda sent the chillen afta them geese this evenin', but I come a pupose ta git out a spell. Startin' tamorree, I'll come one day a week fer fity cents and my dinner and help you with anythin' you wants done. How does that strike you?"

It struck me as being pretty fine, and so it was arranged.

October 15, 1915

The weeks of a beautiful harvest came and went in autumn's flame and gold, but I saw no money.

"Are you still in debt to Pa?" I asked, well knowing that Alex would resent the question.

"I don't know," he said coolly.

"You haven't had an accounting yet?"

"No."

"Will you have one?"

"I don't know."

"But, Alex, that's no way to do business. How will we ever know?"

"Pa keeps the accounts, Flossie. Him and me will tend to the business."

"You mean your year's work in the crops and through the timber in this awful heat is a thing that you don't intend to stand up and have an accounting of?"

"We've lived. We owed Pa quite a lot, and I did get the fifty dollars back from him to pay what you borrowed from your Papa." He shrugged impatiently. "We'll go back into the timber next week and run till bad roads stop us."

"You'd rather do that than teach?"

"Flossie, I told you I don't intend to teach again."

"But that day at Lola's . . . ."

"I must've been out of my mind, so just shut up about it."

"And besides, I don't like forever feeling obligated to Pa," I said.

Alex laughed shortly. "You'll never see it, but I'll tell you once more that Pa says that if we get our hands on the money, we'll spend it. If he gets his hands on it, it goes for improvements or into the bank and since it's to come to us children in the end, it's the same as if we was saving it now."

"But we're under his thumb, Alex. We're not planning our lives nor living them. We're marching under orders every minute and doing only what Pa wants done. You're nothing but another pair of hands and feet for Pa."

Alex looked coldly at me, but my emotions carried me on against my better judgment.

"Look what a rage he pitched last week when Onnie and Ann and us decided to make a change and have salmon croquets and raisin cream pie for dinner. He said that poor people couldn't afford such store-bought foods in the middle of the week. We can't even decide what we'll eat without him having his lordly say about it."

"Don't pay him any mind in little things like that, Flossie. He gets a big satisfaction out of it and it don't hurt nobody."

"And I suppose I mustn't pay it any mind when I know it was his doing that not one day did I get to go to the county fair, either. You're not tied in, so it matters not to you. Ride on with the rest of them, free as a breeze. But, Alex, you always said we'd have such fun every year at the fair and I haven't been yet."

"Don't keep hatchin' up things to rake me over the coals about, Flossie. I'm gettin' about enough of it now."

"I'm getting about enough of some things too, if you want to know it. There was plenty of room in the surrey for me and the baby the two days they drove down for you, but I wasn't asked to go. You didn't even let me know you were going till they stopped at the gate for you." I turned on him desperately. "Alex, please. If you're going to keep on renting, then let's rent from somebody else. At least we had none of this pettiness to contend with at Big Lake."

His mouth hung open in blank astonishment.

"That would be a pretty come-off. To rent a farm where I happened to get a school was one thing. To just up and leave him for no reason except to take a farm with somebody else would be a thing he'd never forgive. He'd disinherit me as sure as my name's Alexander Walker."

"Then you're no better than any other buzzard," I flared angrily. "Just sitting up here waiting for the old man to die, so you can fly down and pick his bones!"

"Flossie!" Alex's voice was cold with anger, and I stood appalled at myself. How could I stand there and say those awful things to him? I could have wept at my own perversity. Without another word, Alex left the house and the yard. Well, I hoped I felt better, now that I'd got to tell him at last exactly how I felt about things. I hoped I would . . . but I didn't.

November 3, 1915

The long pleasant days of Indian summer passed uneventfully, and the season swept into winter with hardly a warning. Six inches of snow had fallen, when the boys came in with the first quail and squirrels. Lester was staying with the old folks, and though I knew how Ann hated getting out in it, I prevailed on her to come on over, for the boys had set their hearts on a hot tamale feast.

To the pot of wild meat I added half a fresh pork shoulder, with the fat carefully trimmed away, and cooked all, till it fell away from the bone, then set it aside to cool. Onnie and Alex had selected the thin inside shucks and had them in a boiling bath to soften and sterilize. I had the seasonings all lined up and most of the meat ground when Ann arrived.

"Come on in and help me put a stop to this war talk. Everybody's getting all excited about what goes on in Europe, like they haven't always had a war brewing."

"Like we don't have enough of our own to worry about without borrowing trouble from across the water," she sided right in with me, throwing her wrap on the bed. "I'm takin' my artics off in here, Flossie. They'll freeze to the floor outside."

"It was when the council at Potsdam decided to make war on Russia . . . ," began Onnie.

"I trimmed all the fat off that pork before I boiled it, Ann. I knew it would make the tamales too rich," I said determinedly.

"It's Britain intervening that looks so serious to me, trying to help out little old Belgium, sending aid to France," said Alex.

"Ann, if you'll grind the rest of this meat, I'll take what's ready and season it."

Alex and Onnie were spreading the hot clean shucks with a layer of the cornmeal mush, which had been cooked to a creamy consistency in the rich broth. I made the meat into finger rolls and placed it on the mush, and the boys rolled and tied the tamales in shape.

"Did Reller tell either one of you girls that she's fixin' to leave Bill?" asked Onnie.

"She didn't actually say she was going to leave him. She said she wasn't going to have another baby for him, even if she had to go out in the world alone," I said, remembering.

"We met him while we was out huntin' today and he was really in a fizz. He says Reller's had these withholdin' spells before, but never like this. He says she don't know nothin' else to do when she takes a notion against havin' another baby. But he says he knows one thing . . . there's no danger of her leaving him as long as there's another one comin' on, and that if he has to do it to hold her, he's intendin' to put another calf in her stall, as he calls it, or his name ain't Billy Nolly." Onnie snickered.

"That ought to hold her, all right," Alex said carelessly, and I wanted to hit him with my doubled fist. Poor little Reller . . . the last time she had ironed for me, she had looked almost like a crazy thing.

I was remembering what Reller had told me: "Bill's attar me agin, Miz Flossie. Night and day he pesters me. But God's my witness, if I have to spend eternity in hell, I ain't havin' another young'n fer Bill." An involuntary shiver ran over me.

"Possum trottin' over your grave?" kidded Ann.

"We'll call it a possum," I said grimly.

"All I got to say is," said Ann, pouring the seasoned broth over the pot of tamales and setting them on the back of the stove to simmer, "a bunch of you good men of the community ought to get together and take Bill Nolly to the choppin' block."

November 15, 1915

It was almost three o'clock in the morning when I sat up straight in bed with the feeling that the phone had been ringing for an hour. It was the alarm ring, five shorts.

Alex's feet hit the floor before I had time to shake him and he had the receiver down. "My God, Onnie! My God in heaven!"

The receiver dropped from his nerveless fingers, and then he made a mad scramble for his clothing. "It's Pa's house! Burnin' to the ground!" He shook now as with a violent chill. "Willie was up with the baby and saw the light. If she hadn't called the old folks, the house would've burned down on 'em."

"You'd better ride Jude." I was holding each next garment for him and trying to help him think.

"No. I'm taking straight across the fields. It's quickest."

"I can't get there quick with the baby."

"Don't you dare haul her out in this cold, or you either. You'd just be in the way. You stay right here till I get back." I shoved his earmuffs on him, and he snatched his cap and ran.

My outing flannel nightgown billowed out in the wind as I shut the door after him. I ran to the north kitchen window and looked. Above the treetops a pillar of black smoke rose into the heavens.

I stood spellbound as the angry flames licked and flickered through the black mass and broke it up, only to have it form again, over and over. Shivering, I crept back into bed, trying to picture the scene that must be being enacted there at this moment. It was less than a half mile to the big house across the fields, and a faint light danced weirdly over the furniture in the room. I thought first of the smokehouse and its generous store of good food. The season's first butchering, the new honey, the canned and dried fruits and vegetables, the great crocks of new lard.

I heard the wind tearing through the dry leaves on the oak tree outside the house and knew how it must be carrying those wicked flames through every crook and cranny of the grand old house, wiping it out as though it had never been. And then I thought about the featherbeds.

There were still seven, not counting the one Ma and Pa slept on. The beautiful handmade quilts. Years of time and painstaking effort had gone into the making of them. Ma's cherished phonograph with its morning glory horn, the organ, the treasured "lambrequin," and the family album. The handwoven bedspread too, an heirloom that she could not decide who should have at her death. The company dishes and the white bone-handled knives and forks, and the silver spoons.

"Of course Sherman and Mattie wants us to stay with them, and Onnie and Ann's beggin' us to stay with them, and I well know you and

Alexander's wantin' us to stay with you," Ma said feverishly, "so it's not like we ain't got plenty of places we can stay while we're gettin' the new house built." She nibbled daintily at the piece of chicken I had urged her to take. She heaved a mighty sigh when I said nothing in the opening before adding, "It's hard to say yet jist what we will do."

It was the first time Pa had been inside the little house he had so grudgingly turned over to us. It was the day after the fire, and they were having dinner with us, having spent the remainder of the night with Mattie and breakfast with Onnie and Ann. There had been no insurance, and I'd been at a loss to understand Ma's evident enjoyment of the stir-up. Had she been tired of her responsibility for the big house? For not once had I heard her bewailing the fact that this, that, or the other was forever gone. She wasn't looking backward. Her eyes were on the future. This was my chance, perhaps, to reestablish myself in her good graces, but I had a small heart for such an undertaking.

"Here me and Annie's been worryin' ourselves out of mind because you and Alex was off down here in this little unfinished shanty, and I vow you got the warmest and most comp'table house on the plantation. That weather strippin' at all the doors and winders, and the woolen carpet on the floor. Our own house was never as warm as this on such a cold day, Annie." Pa reached over and took another pork chop, and Ma settled her gaze absently on the east window.

"Have you seen their smokehouse, Annie?" asked Pa, pursuing his own line of thought. Ma shook her head. "Then when you've finished I want you to look at it. They ain't missed a trick on that deal."

"It was all Alex's idea," I said proudly. Pa smiled as any father might have done at the cleverness of a favorite child.

And the battle inside me went on. If only I had an extra bedroom, I might urge them to stay with me. But I felt a choking sensation at the thought of being penned in the same room with Ma, day and night, over a period of weeks.

"Ann and I will make your clothes, Ma," I hurriedly offered, remembering with shame the time she appeared willing and anxious to have me abide beneath her roof. "Get your materials and patterns together and we'll get right into it." Ma looked at me with level eyes, and I turned lamely to Pa.

"What kind of house do you plan to build?" I asked.

"I'd as lief have one exactly like this." He grinned. "It would be plenty big enough fer me and Annie."

"Nobody asked me, of course," said Ma sweetly, "but the house won't be like this. There's got to be a spare room, fer one thing. We do have the preacher now and then, besides other company. But you go ahead, Henry, get Flossie to help you plan it. No doubt she can tell you what would suit me better than I could tell you myself."

That buttery voice, how I had come to dread it, worse even than Pa's rasping clearing of his throat when displeased.

"Too bad you didn't carry insurance, Pa. It would have built the new house without digging into your savings."

"I always thought people didn't have a far what was careful enough." He grinned sheepishly.

"Well, you all were careful, weren't you? How do you think it started?"

"You can be careful as yore a mind to be, but it won't save yore home nor yore life either if you got a enemy like Hank Scoggins runnin' wild," said Ma.

"Annie, yore not to say that again! How many times I got to tell you?" Pa's voice was cold with fury.

"He thinks Henry was to blame fer him havin' to leave the country, so he made it back to see what dirt he could do," Ma said defiantly. Her lips straightened to a thin line, and her eyes met Pa's angry glare without wavering.

"Then I'll say now what it's been on my mind to say before, Annie. Did you stay with the oil heaters when you lit 'em in front of yore fruit shelves last night? I warned you time and again that the one on the south side had a bad burner, and if you didn't stay with it till it got adjusted, anythin' could happen."

"Are you sayin' that I deliberately set far to the house, Henry?"

"I'm saying that if that stove wasn't properly adjusted, it could have exploded and set the place on far, Annie. Which makes jist as much sense as sayin' that Hank Scoggins set the house a far."

"And as between Hank Scoggins's meanness and my carelessness, you'd rather lay it at my door than his?" Ma was enjoying herself now. Pa gave her one disgusted glare and then ignored her completely.

"Willie was ringin' the phone off the wall, fust I knew." He turned back to me. "If she hadn't been up and seen it, I guess the roof would've fell in on me and Annie and burned us to a crisp." Ma's eyes lighted with excitement at his words, and for a moment she seemed to forget her grievance.

"Henry shoved me out a bed and rolled the quilts, pillars, and blankets into the featherbed and ran out the front door with 'em. He spread 'em out in the snow across the road. I felt around fer my shoes and stockin's and grabbed my clothes off the chair and Henry run back and grabbed Lester up, snatched his britches off the head of the bed, and out he went into the snow agin. Such a cracklin' as went on . . . and the smoke! It was already thick enough in the house to choke a body to death. Henry said he wouldn't've dared open one of the doors into the back of the house fer fear of bein' swallered up in flames."

Pa took it up. "Of course you can always think of what you should've done aftawads. I could've broke out a winder into the palor and saved the few thing's small 'nough to be drug out through it. But most of the pieces in thar was too big and heavy fer one to handle, and nobody was thar to hep me yet. So we just stood in our tracks and watched it bun to the groun'."

"Never saw a far eat wood so fast." Ma seemed to be gloating over the memory of it. "There we stood, our feet haif froze from the run through the snow, and blankets wrapped round us fer all the world like Indians. We just stood and stomped feathers while everthin' we had went up in smoke, and Lester showed us how loud he could cry."

It was at last decided that Ma and Pa should occupy the extra bedroom at Mattie's so that Pa could be near the store and handy to the job of clearing the debris for the laying of the foundation of the new house.

November 29, 1915

For two weeks straight we sewed, constantly together. Ann and I drifted from one subject to another, discussing first and last about everything either of us ever heard of.

"Dern Ma, anyhow," fretted Ann. I glanced up, a bit startled. "These buttonholes," she mourned. "Nothin'll do her but plenty of buttonholes. She wouldn't have a hook and eye on a garment of hers to save our souls."

"I'm on my hundred and oneth"—I grinned—"and they don't seem to get any prettier as I go along."

"Mine look like first cousins to hog-eyes. It looks to me like she could at least make her own buttonholes. She's not doing anything else all day long." Ann's eyes snapped. "Thing of it is, she's got both of us right where she wants us, subject to her orders. I actual believe that Ma is having the time of her life, dashing here and yon, telling everybody what and when and how."

"Well, I say let her enjoy it while it lasts. Another day or two and we'll be out from under. How long did you and Onnie know each other before you married?" I was ready for a change of subject.

"We kept company about six months. Neither of us could see anybody else from the first, but I thought his Ma would surely to God bust a gut. She said then it was on account of him being so young, but she wouldn't have wanted one of her boys to marry, Flossie, if he'd waited till he was forty."

"Maybe you're right." I sighed, finding some small comfort in the fact that Ma hadn't been too pleased with Ann either. "I don't think I was ever in love with anybody but Alex after we met, Ann, though I stayed mad enough at him to wring his neck half the time."

"I reckon about the worst pill you ever had to swallow was Lizzie," Ann said carelessly.

My heart tightened, but I said nothing.

"You did know about Lizzie Bell, didn't you?" She was suddenly anxious.

I laughed outright. "She's one of the first things I did know about."

Ann visibly relaxed.

"You remember the night Alex brought me out before we married? Ma met us at the front door with the light held over her head and she asked Alex which one it was, and when he told her, she was really sweet to me and urged me to come right on in. But while she was putting supper on the table, she said that if it had been Lizzie Bell, she wouldn't have let her set foot in that house. She sounded like she meant it."

"She meant it, all right. But the thing of it is, why did she make Lizzie bring the baby and set it in her lap to hold right through Granpap's funeral? Beat anything that I ever saw. Lizzie was clean back in the crowd. Naturally she wanted to see Alex and his wife and his baby, but she never would have come up in the crowd. But no, Ma couldn't leave well enough alone. Sent for her to bring the baby there, and did Alex ever leave there like a streak!"

My heart stopped beating, and I now literally could not speak. Ann sewed and talked on, unaware of the havoc wrought by her words.

"I knowed the reason you and Alex didn't join the family at the graveside, and so did everybody else, but who could blame you? I think Ma did it just to humiliate you. I tell you, Annie Walker can do things that'll cook you to the bone."

Suddenly I was faint and dizzy from nausea.

Ann sighed and continued, "Alex could've got off a lot lighter than he did if he'd dragged other boys in on it, or if her Uncle Aaron had kept out of it. You're bound to remember all that talk about *a piece of timber at Big Lake.* I must say I never heard it called that before."

"Oh yes, I remember Uncle Aaron well." I was surprised at how far away my voice sounded.

"I told Onnie that there wasn't no way in the world for Alex to keep that from you, but Alex swore us never to let out a peep about it. He fair run us crazy on the subject there for a while."

She reached into my lap for a spool of thread, and her eyes met mine. She gasped, "Why, Flossie, you're white as a sheet. Is something the matter?"

"I think we're sticking to this sewing too close, so anxious to get through with it. It did me just like this the summer I sewed for Mrs. Thomas and Lily. Did you know Lizzie?"

"In a way I did. We went to the same school together. I don't think she was a bad girl, but she sure was a fool about Alex. I got a school picture of her here somewhere." She pushed her sewing aside and rummaged through a box of pictures in the dresser drawer.

Alex hadn't taken advantage of Susie Maynard the night he spent with her. I believed that he'd told me the truth about that. But was it only because he had learned a bitter lesson the hard way?

Ann dropped the picture in my lap. At the sight of the peaked little face and the big mournful eyes under a wide-brimmed hat, I suddenly hated Alex. I had never somehow been able to hold Kitty Crandall against Alex. Perhaps because I knew he could never hurt Kitty. But this poor little defenseless thing! I cast the picture carelessly aside and resumed making buttonholes, but when Ann left the room a minute, I snatched it up and tucked it into the front of my dress.

At supper I couldn't eat, so I fed Cerece, bathed her, and put her to bed. Alex settled to look over his farm magazine, and I deliberately laid Lizzie's picture, faceup, on the page beneath his eyes. For a moment he sat stunned and then flipped the picture from the magazine as though it had been a stinging scorpion.

"She found out in spite of all," he said, as though to himself. He then asked fiercely, "Who told you?"

"Ann, but she didn't know she told me. She asked me if I knew about Lizzie Bell and I told her yes, thinking I did, and as we talked on she said the thing she couldn't understand was why Ma acted as she did about the baby at Granpap's funeral. I remembered a lot of things then. She went on to say that Uncle Aaron was the one that brought you to accounts, and I remembered then the two hundred dollars he was asking for the timber at Big Lake. I suppose you got the money from Pa to pay him?"

He nodded miserably.

"Which explains a lot of things I could never understand . . . like why I couldn't get any money out of you to get ready for my baby. Is there anything you want to say?"

He shook his head and sat staring before him. My throat swelled tight, and the burning needles of pain shot up behind each ear. Surely I wasn't going to cry . . . not after all this time.

"Alex, I've got to get away. I've got to get where I can think."

"Can't you just forget you heard it? We've been getting along all right."

"Could you forget it if you just now heard that I'd had a baby by an old lover while engaged to be married to you?"

"I had hoped you'd never hear it," he said simply. "But because of one foolish act, I didn't intend to spend my whole life tied to a girl I didn't love. You're the only girl I ever wanted to marry, remember?"

"And I sometimes wonder why!"

"Just forget it, please. It's all over and done with and a lot of water has flowed under the bridge since then."

"Any happiness I have ever had with you, Alex, seems now to have been nothing more than a fool's paradise."

"Better to live in a fool's paradise, than a wise woman's misery," he said quickly. "When did you feel the best . . . after you heard it or before?"

I went to my trunk and knelt before it. With feverish hands, I began to unpack it and sort the things for a trip. "All I want is to get as far away from you as I possibly can," I wailed. "I'm going to Little Rock. If I can, I'll get a job. Everything out here is too hateful to bear, and you are the damn hate-fullest of all!"

I was sobbing now, awful tearing sobs that wrenched me horribly.

When I could get my breath, I went on. "Every time things smooth out and I begin to relax over one thing, something else pops up. I could take my own bare hands this minute and tear you limb from limb!"

Chapter 16

December 3, 1915

The thriving city of Little Rock was already bedecked for the Christmas season. One morning soon after my arrival I noted in the paper that Lang's was advertising for sales girls. There would be five or six weeks work if I could get on. I really needed a new winter coat.

I wasn't getting anywhere with what Alex had been pleased to call my "long-distance thinking." All day long my rebel thoughts trailed Alex about Englewood, did the special cleaning I had planned, decorated the little house for our first real Christmas together. It was too disgusting.

December 10, 1915

Working in women's ready-to-wear was fun, since I was so fond of pretty clothes. The twelve dollars a week was all mine, for Mama and Papa would not want it to be otherwise. My first week's pay went down on a brown broadcloth dressmaker's model coat, with rich brown velvet collar and cuffs.

As the days passed, I became weary unto death of the surging noisy crowds . . . the snatching, grabbing and unending effort to please. Each evening I returned home worn out. Once I asked Mama and Papa please not to mind if I scowled from then till bedtime, that my smile muscles were completely ragged.

Mama kept Cerece, did the shopping, baked a fruitcake, decorated her freshly cleaned house and got ready for the big day.

December 25, 1915

As of old we had the Christmas tree after breakfast on Christmas morning, Papa calling the gifts and Cerece proudly delivering them.

But through it all, I was seeing Alex and hearing his last words to me. "And remember this, when you get to where you can think, you are the only girl I ever would've married." Then he had grinned and added, in all honesty, "And I wouldn't have married you if I could have got you off my mind any other way."

I had asked, "Did you send for me because you felt yourself slipping into this other thing?"

"I sent for you because you stood between me and anybody else I ever tried to love! I never told another girl that I loved her. I never told another girl that I would ever marry her. With you around it maybe wasn't hard to go straight, but after you quit me there wasn't a thing to stop me from doing anything I wanted . . . but the girl . . . and they didn't always even try. State of mind I was in, I guess we're lucky I haven't got a string of young'ns from here back to the day you gave me the gate."

I guess we are lucky? Yes . . . we . . . for Alex's loneliness enveloped me like a cloak. I knew that no special thing would be done this day to brighten things in the way that seemed to mean so much to him. The tree and the pageant at the church, if they had it this year, would be the only break in the everyday routine.

I had sent him a box of imported linen handkerchiefs, knowing his inherent weakness for fine materials. It and the greeting card made up the sum total of any word I had sent him, except the one card telling him that I had gone to work at Lang's. I had nothing at all from him, except a card saying that he hoped I would have news for him "before too long." *Before too long!* The words were like a band of ice around my heart, and the delicious foods I ate were dust and ashes on my tongue.

My attention wandered unbelievably while Papa held forth at length on the European situation. A war was in the making that would leave a scar on the nations of the earth that would be a long time healing. Let them fight, thought I wearily, if that's what they want to do.

Papa was proud as a peacock of his job, but a little shamefaced too. The letter of commendation which he got from the "Big Boss" at Christmas had also contained a ten dollar gold piece. Moreover, an eighteen-pound turkey had added still more to his appreciation of the good fortune that had given him this coveted position.

"And another five dollar raise, Flossie, not on the month, but on the week. It looks like I must be giving satisfaction, doesn't it?" He was anxious for my approval.

"What about the union?" I asked, turning the thorn in his flesh.

"I've come to see that all the bosses would have to do to break up the unions, would be to give every man jack a big enough pay envelope to enable him to feed and clothe his family decently, and pay them out a home the year before he dies! This is the first time since I married your mother that I've found myself in a position to take care of her in the way that a good woman deserves, and by God, I'm not going to muff it!"

My ears cringed at the sound of Papa taking God's name in vain. This had never happened in all the years that I had known him and I looked at him. Yes, he was changing, but I honestly believed it was for the better.

"It wasn't easy to drop your work in the union, was it?"

"No, and I'm in absolute sympathy with the boys that are still in there fighting for all they are worth. Situated as they are, I still would have so little to lose, that I don't doubt I would give my all, even if it meant the fiddling little job. But I've got a chance where I am now, and that's all any man ever wants. We make a regular saving now, and it begins to look like we will have a little something for our old age."

But, of course, Mama and Papa would be old someday! Such a thought had never occurred to me before.

December 26, 1915

On Sunday morning I woke early, and not wanting to be the first to stir on Papa's only day to lie late in bed, I remained quite still, looking around me. There sat my trunk and my traveling bag. Toys and diapers lay here and there. If I were not here, this room would be in spotless order. Mama and Papa would sleep until ready to get up, would have a leisurely breakfast, look over the paper, dress and go to church or to the park, and maybe go to a restaurant for supper in the evening and on to the Majestic for a good show. Mama had written that their Sundays were often spent that way. They couldn't live their own lives with me in the home. Everything they did had to be planned after considering the baby and me. Not only was I not any happier or nearer to feeling settled than when I left home, I now saw clearly that it was an imposition to stay on with them when I had a husband and a home of my own. I slipped quietly out of bed, lit the gas log, pulled on my robe and started a letter to Alex.

> Dear Alex:
>
> I am ready to come home. I am writing to tell Lola to leave her key in the lower box and a bed fixed for us. That is so I can leave here in the daytime and Papa will not have to be up all hours getting me to the train.
>
> Did you think of me on Christmas Eve? It was our Anniversary, remember? Married three years, and I wonder what another year will bring to us! It will be better if we do not try to discuss the reason for my absence. In thinking back over it I find a good many things that we do not discuss, so we will add this to them. This will not be hard for you. You seem to find it easier to skip things that are unpleasant. It is I who must always probe into a sore spot to try to find out what caused it. But I will try never to start digging into this and dragging it in as a dog does a bone that has been long buried.

I stopped writing. Perhaps Alex wouldn't be interested in all this. In fact, I was sure of it. I sighed and tore the letter to bits and told him simply which train to meet on New Year's night and signed my name.

January 1, 1916

It was eleven o'clock when I stepped off the train at Paragould and turned the drowsy baby, heavy as a lump of lead, over to Alex. He took her eagerly and covered her with kisses, then grinned uncertainly at me.

"Well, let's go, we can drive by the station in the morning and get your trunk. I stopped by Lola's and she says we're going to sleep there tonight. I put Old Bess in the barn there. I thought we could better walk the three blocks than for me to be disturbing the neighbors at this hour."

"I don't mind the walk at all. I'm tired to death of sitting."

Cerece was sound asleep long before we reached Lola's, and we slipped her wraps and shoes off and eased her into bed just as she was. Alex said I looked like a stranger in the new coat and hat. We were both timid and shy of each other, but once in bed he was like a starving man, loving me with a fierceness and passion that was frightening, holding me as if he would never let me go. Long after he slept, I stared with dry, unblinking eyes into the darkness, too stunned and bitter for tears.

January 2, 1916

The following morning I huddled under the lap robe all the way home, my brain paralyzed with the thought that I might not be checking my calendar for nine long months to come. It wasn't that I minded another baby so much. It was that Alex patterned his behavior after Bill Nolly. Feeling that I might be planning to leave him, he had deliberately tried to "put another calf in my stall." His eyes refused to meet mine.

He held Cerece between his knees. She prattled endlessly of her visit with Papa and Mama Mounce, sang her doll to sleep, and finally settled down for a nap herself.

I was astonished when we reached Englewood to find the little new house completed and resplendent in a new coat of gloss white. The oak trees, whose branches had been so badly burned, had been trimmed back to within a few feet of the great trunks.

"The cottage has four rooms and a tiny reception hall. The rooms on the south are bedrooms, the one on the north is for a sitting room, and a kitchen and dining room combined," Alex said.

"He certainly made a quick job of it."

"Oh, Pa has ways and means," he chuckled. "I bet he got more work donated on that house. A poor man could have burned out and got his next house however he could, but everybody flocked to offer

Pa whatever help they could. They've been settled four days now, new furniture and all. Want to stop?"

It would probably be harder to stop the longer I put it off, but I couldn't bear it just now. "Some other time."

"I got Ann to go over and clean things up for me. I don't see how I managed to get things in such a mess there by myself. And I laid in some groceries. We can start right off under our own power. Mattie's baby was born the twentieth. Want to stop and see it?"

"Some other time. Boy or girl?"

"Girl . . . and she only weighed six pounds. They named her Alva."

January 29, 1916

Alex and I were always on guard. On the surface all was studied. Polite consideration, one for another, but never were we completely relaxed or at ease with each other. He was very aware that I was not, as yet, having him another child, but he was doing everything within his power to remedy that. The ice that encased my heart had not melted. I was simply living each day as I came to it, doing all that was expected of me and more, until I fell asleep each night in a state of mental and physical exhaustion.

February 12, 1916

I had finally summoned courage to go to the big house with Alex, only now it was only a little house. Pridefully, Ma had invited me in to see the wonderful new things. She stepped lightly about, watching to see what effect all of this splendor was having on me. I doubted if she had ever been so proud of the big house.

The living room, or "settin' room" as Pa called it, boasted a handsome red plush sofa. There was a long "liberry table" and reading lamp with an opalescent shade, a tan Axminster rug with huge red roses in the centerpiece and border, and two comfortable rockers. A tall, oblong mirror hung above the mantle, a low mantle clock below it, and standing like sentinels on each side of the clock, a pair of thin blue vases splashed with red roses.

There was a pretty bedroom suite of black walnut, a soft Axminster rug of blue and tan, the inevitable washstand with its wash bowl and pitcher and, on a newspaper beside it, the customary slop jar. Ma didn't show us the back bedroom, which was a spare for company, but hurried me on to the kitchen. Here the floor was covered with a linoleum into the corners, cream background with blue, red, and black tiles. The "eatin' table" was one of the new models, round and set on a great pedestal, with six solid oak matching chairs placed meticulously around it. All of the windows had crisp white curtains. Altogether, it was a very nicely arranged little house for just two people, and I said so.

"Yes, a feller can't rightly 'preciate a good thing till he gits one burnt out fom under 'im." Pa sighed. "A man's home is his haven, the only place on earth where he can rightly come to rest in soul and body."

"You just gave it a good name," I said, for lack of anything else to speak of. "Haven . . . New Haven." To my surprise he smiled approvingly.

"You have a good idee, now and then," he conceded, his eyes twinkling, "but I bet even you couldn't hatch up a name fer the place yore livin' in."

"Why, that was named long ago." I laughed, enjoying his humor. "I named it the Rye Patch. That being the only thing that seems to grow there that anything can eat!" He grinned back at me.

But this bit of byplay had not escaped Ma's watchful eyes and she darted to the cabinet, snatched out a cloth reeking with furniture polish, brushed me aside, and started polishing the chair beside which I had been standing, and upon which I had inadvertently laid a hand.

"It'll take me a good thirty minutes to clean up after this round," she said in that buttery tone. "Look," she exclaimed as we reentered the sitting room, "the whole print of Reecie's hand on my liberry table."

March 10, 1916

At breakfast I told Alex that I was three weeks past due and that I was sure I was going to have another child for him. He sat staring at me for a moment with a smile on his face. Finally he said, "I thought you had missed your time."

March 14, 1916

Personal relationships might not be so satisfactory, but the scent of the woods was just as sweet as the water in Rushing Creek and just as clear. Ann and I had a daily rendezvous at the swimming hole every day after the water warmed. Along about four o'clock, I would see her waddling down across the school grove, and I would call Cerece and join her. Sometimes Lester would be with her, more often not. It was good to sit on the boulder with the sweet clear water laughing and whispering over my shoulders. The tips of the willow wands, thick and spreading now like trailing skirts, dipped into the water, and then shook themselves free from the crystal drops with every passing breeze.

I worried about Ann because she had developed such a swelling in her hands and feet. She was nearing the fullness of her time and was filled with dread. Ann with her dread, me with my sorrow, for my pregnancy was just that, deep and abiding, and I could take no pleasure in it. We did not often speak of our woes. Only once did Ann tell me what was really in her heart.

"I wish I could know that I'd be lying in my coffin this time tomorrow!"

"Ann, is it that bad?"

"I feel like something is wrong. I haven't been right the whole time through." Then she changed the subject. "Things have sure come to a sad pass between Bill and Reller, haven't they?"

"Good heavens yes! Ann, it plain scares me lately when Reller gets started on the subject. Has Onnie seen Bill lately?"

"Yes, and he's fit to be tied. He told Onnie she hadn't been to bed with him for months."

"Since Tommy died, I think."

"He told Onnie that she swears she'll never let him at her again. How long will a man like Bill Nolly put up with that?"

How long will any man put up with it?

"She told me why she had taken that stand. It's because Bill threatens her that if ever he gets a chance at her again that Henry Emerson Walker will have one more little cotton picker on the way. Now, Ann, who can blame Reller? She told me the other day that, so help her God, that was one thing that was never going to happen again. With things at such a pitch as that between them, anything at all can happen down there, anytime!"

March 25, 1916

Two weeks ago, Alex attended a stock sale and bought a superannuated Poland China sow. She was of mountainous proportions, and instinctively I drew Cerece back out of her path.

Alex laughed. "No danger of her hurtin' anybody," he scoffed. "She's really too old for breeding purposes, but I got her cheap. Thought if I'd get her bred to Jim's new stock animal and could get even a couple of good gilts out of her, I'd come out a lot cheaper on thoroughbreds than any other way I could manage it. She's fine stuff, out of the Hastings pens." He penned her, poured the corn to her, and three days' later took her over to Jim's. Today he brought her back and turned her into the woodlot.

April 28, 1916

When Ann went into her labor, things were bad from the start. Onnie called me to stay with her and he went for Mrs. Snyder, the best midwife to be had. The doctor was already on his way.

"The best place for Ann is in the Paragould hospital," said Dr. Benson. "This is not going to be a normal birth, and Ann won't be safe in our hands." Ann went into another convulsion and Mrs. Snyder again put a wooden spoon between her teeth to keep her from chewing her tongue to pieces.

Onnie rushed to the barn and began hitching up the big farm wagon. They put a spring and mattress in the bed of the wagon and Alex drove while Onnie sat beside the now unconscious Ann.

The baby was a girl, but it was an instrument delivery and she didn't survive, and Ann was badly injured. They named the baby girl Stella, and beautiful she looked. Ann made a slow recovery, due largely to the accumulation of poison in her kidneys, which had been the cause of the swelling in her feet and hands the last few weeks.

June 11, 1916

When Ann had finally come home after two weeks in the hospital, she remained pale and listless, too spent to take any interest in anything. Her condition did not break until they had been home a full month. Then, for the first time, she seemed to slowly be getting back to herself, though she was still very weak.

June 16, 1916

The time came when I could no longer ignore the stir of life within me, and I knew that I must make some preparations for the baby that was coming. I was determined not to wait, and then feel like I was in a panic, as I had done with Cerece.

"Now don't go buy up a lot of stuff you don't need," said Alex. I had known he would say that when I mentioned it to him. "Get whatever you got to have on the store account."

"I need shoes too."

"Pa's got shoes!"

But when I got there, Pa was cross as two sticks. Grudgingly he took from the shelves the materials I asked to see. I wanted five yards from the pink and five from the blue bolt of outing flannel to make receiving blankets and little quilts for the basket. Then I asked for twenty yards of white to make up into diapers.

"What can you posbly use twenty yards of anythin' fer?" he snapped. I told him and he snorted savagely.

"What about shoes?" I said.

"Fer yoresef?"

"Yes."

"I got shoes," he said, and began searching through his stock.

The smallest thing he found was a size six in heavy gunmetal leather, with tiny unbound eyelets and round metal-tipped strings for laces. My size was four and a half. "They're much too large."

"Try 'em on. They'll do."

"There's no need to try them on . . . they're too large. Besides, if they fit me exactly, they still wouldn't do. What I want is a dress shoe for church. I can wear my old sneakers for every day."

"You could make out with these," he said shortly.

"If to make out is what I've got to do, I'll make out with the shabby ones I've got. As long as we'll have to pay for them, I don't want to buy something I could never use."

"Them shoes ought to look good to a gal that's got no shoes."

"Those don't look good to me and I'm not taking them!"

"Beggars can't be choosers, young lady!" he blazed at me.

"If I'm a beggar, it's you that has made me one!" I flared back. "I've worked harder since I've been in this family than I ever worked before in my life, and I've a lot less to show for it!"

His laugh sent a shiver down my spine. "It must undoubtedly be a big disappointment to you," he was using a falsetto tone and mincing his words, "to think you married the son of a rich old farmer, expectin' ta take a life of ease, and find out that he ain't such a easy mark afta all, and that you still have to earn yore bread by the sweat of yore brow. Least thing goes not ta suit you, off to Paragould you go, or ta Little Rock, wherever yore Ma and Pa happens to be hangin' their hats at the moment. Ain't got the guts to face through on livin' with a man. A squeamish, screamin' little white-bellied termagant, if ever I saw one!" The shoes were shoved back onto the shelf with vicious strength along with the bolts of material, and the cut yardage.

So that was it!

"So! My trip to Little Rock is lyin' heavy on your stomach and you just decided to puke it up, eh? Well, there's a thing or two that's setting pretty heavy on my stomach. Like Lizzie Bell's baby, which I just learned about just before I left, and like Alex's baby that I'm carrying now, with or without consent, it matters not to him, nor to you!"

In the wild anger that possessed me, I had crowded in behind the narrow counter and had him penned into a corner.

"Besides, who do you think you're talking to, Henry Emerson Walker? Maybe it's not possible for you to think less of me than you already do, so I might as well let you know a few thoughts that I have about you, while we're on the subject. Like charging us 10 percent on every penny we borrow, on every item charged to our store account, when we could get the same bill of goods at smaller cost for a 4 percent carrying charge at any store in Paragould. You're not doing me any favor to let me trade at your drizzly little store!"

He held up an admonishing hand and made as if to speak, his face livid with anger, but it would have taken more than that to stop me.

"You think it's smart, making two bins out of one shipment of coffee, selling to Onnie and Ann for twenty cents a pound, and the same to me at forty cents a pound, because you heard me say that Mama gave forty cents a pound for the coffee she used. It was a skunking, dishonest trick and I'm glad to have the chance to tell you of it to your teeth. It's through no choice of mine that I am a beggar at the hands of such a mean, contemptible man as you are. And if it ever came down to it and I did have to beg, you're the last person in the world I'd expect to get it from without paying for it somehow or other, three ways from taw!"

He was now leaning back against the shelf of yard goods with my angry face shoved close to his. Standing thus on my tiptoes, my eyes were now on a level with his which were beginning to flicker and dance as if at some obscure joke. Pa's anger seemed strangely to have passed.

He pushed a heavy box out of his way, circled the counter at the other end, went to the door, and stood waiting quietly for me to precede him. Once outside and the door locked, however, he pushed on past me at a rapid pace.

Alex was hitching Sadie to the buggy when we reached the lot, and suddenly I made up my mind to go into Paragould with him. Full of the strong purpose, I hurried forward and planted myself directly in front of Pa.

"I'm going to Paragould for those shoes," I said quietly. "Do you want to let me have the money for them, or shall I open an account at Pendleton's? Yours is not the only store where we can get credit." He cleared his throat with a threatening rasp and made as if to pass me without a word. I eased over in front of him, keeping my voice down. "You may not give me the money for the shoes, but you've got to be man enough to refuse it! Just tell me . . . YES or NO!"

"How much did you want?" Quite casually he reached into his pocket and brought forth the worn leather pouch with the snap fastener as though he had been handing me whatever I wanted from it all my life.

"Three fifty for a pair of shoes, and a dollar for a pair of stockings."

He thumbed through the bills, passing up the fives, and counted off four one-dollar bills into my hand, then searched in his pocket till he found fifty cents in loose change, not one penny more than I asked for. He then retraced his steps to hold the gate open for us to drive through. Suddenly my spirits soared and I began to sing merrily:

Mary had a little lamb,
A little lamb, A little lamb
Mary had a little lamb

At that moment we came even with Pa and I leaned over and sang,

BAAAAAAAAAAAAAAAA!
Its fleece was white as snow!

Pa turned his back quickly, and I looked back to see his shoulders shaking and the red creeping up the back of his neck and ears.

"You mustn't do Pa like that!" said Alex furiously.

"Then Pa mustn't do me like that first!" I said.

"What did he do to you?"

"He called me a beggar. He said I thought I'd married into a soft life and that I should take what I could get because beggars can't be choosers."

"But I thought I saw him give you some money. You mean he give you money after you all had such a tilt as that?"

"He gave it, all right, after I held his feet to the fire till they blistered."

"I guess he thinks I lied. Ma asked me if you were goin' to town with me and I said you wasn't. She said she'd hope not, that in her day women had more modesty than to go in public in the shape you're in."

I hadn't thought I was showing to hurt yet, but I knew Alex was ashamed to have me along with him, and the hot blood surged into my throat. I cried out, "I can't see why all the honor and reverence for motherhood has to come *after* the suffering and the sacrifice are over! When a woman could really appreciate a little consideration is right while she's going through the mill. That's when it's hard to bear. One little word of understanding would do her more good in the thick of the battle than all the to-do that's made about it years later."

Alex raised his hat, let it fall over his eyes, and gave the horse a gentle slap with the lines. "Giddyup, Sadie." he clucked softly.

July 10, 1916

I was gathering some peaches from the trees on the Scoggins old place. It was still the Scoggins old place to us and always would be, in spite of the fact that it was now occupied by the Payton family, clean throughout and with bright flowers growing in the dooryard.

I stopped by Ann's on my way back.

"I still say those are the best peaches on earth." She took one and sank her teeth into it, but stopped without really taking a bite, for Onnie was coming toward us across the field, yelling something at the top of his voice. He kept repeating it as he came and it finally registered.

"Reller has killed Bill Nolly!"

"Lord God!" gasped Ann, and sank to the steps, still too weak to withstand much of a shock.

"Now, Ann, don't go to pieces. We knew something was bound to happen there," I said. Onnie came panting up and helped me to get Ann back in and settled on her bed.

I considered going down there, but under a broiling hot sun I knew I wasn't equal to it.

Later in the afternoon, Alex came for me. "Constable Tally can't do a thing with Reller," he declared, helping me into the buggy. "He's called the police to come out from Paragould. Reller bit Tally's hand and fought him like a wildcat before I got there, but soon as she saw me she started hollerin' for Miz Flossie."

"Do they know what happened?"

"No. That is, they don't know how it happened. It's plain enough what happened. Reller shot Bill through the heart with that old pistol of his. Not satisfied with that, she castrated him! But she won't tell Tally why nor how. So's he don't know whether to take her in for murder or insanity, or what to do with the body, or what to do with them young'ns. My God, Flossie, I never saw such a bunch of half-fed, half-clothed humanity in one pile in my life!"

That's all Reller has been seeing for years, I wanted to say.

In the room with Reller sat old man Tally, his chair tilted against the wall, his gun in hand.

"You jist as well'st ta git out," Reller said scornfully to him as I entered, "fer I ain't openin' my mouth, even ta Miz Flossie, till you do."

"I'll be in the next room if you need me," he mumbled to me as he passed. I closed the door and approached the bed on which Reller sat.

Seating myself beside her, I placed an arm around her shoulders. "Reller, honey, why did you do it?" I asked.

"Don't feel sorry fer me, Miz Flossie, in the proudest day of my life!" she exulted. "Nigh fifteen years I had of this, fifteen long lean years, and all I got to show fer it is thuteen young'ns, sides little Tommy in his grave. What chanct has any of these chillen got?" Her eyes were wild now.

I sat silently regarding her, and waiting. What was there to say?

"I done it a purpose!" Her backbone stiffened and her shoulders straightened proudly under my arm. "I knowed when Bill routed 'em all out to the field this mornin', young and old, that this was the showdown, but I never let on. I loaded the gun and put hit in the front of my dress and sharpened the old butcher knife. All the time he was a comin' acrost the field I was a gettin' ready fer 'im. He was like a mad bull when he charged me and I saw he had no reason in 'im. He had a rope ta tie me up. The gun got hung and I like not've made it in time, but I got him afore he got me. Then I run fer the knife and cut him clean, just as I meant to do."

"But why, Reller? If you had shot him he could never do you any more harm."

"Which was only haif a what was a worryin' me, Miz Flossie. You see, Bill was a good hard workin' man, except fer that one thing. I wanted him shed of it, fer if he went on like that he'd likely be sent straight ta hell . . . ta burn with it. I didn't want that fer Bill, so I saved the devil the trouble and burnt the bad part of Bill with a far I built with my own hands. Now he's clean and can go straight on ta glory!" She paused, triumphant.

"But what in the world is to become of all these little ones?"

Her face took on a look of cunning, and she lowered her voice, to really confide in me at last. "Really, it was mostly fer the chillen that I done it. This wern't no popped up job I done. I been layin' my plans a long time, knowin' the showdown was bound to come. It don't matter none what happens to me. If they hang me, it'll soon be over. If they send me to the 'sylum, it'll be the easiest life I ever knowed. But they'll be better things fer the chillen now. I already made arrangements with Miz Porter to take Lennie, and with Miz Langley to take Tennie. Both them women works at Pendleton's, and they tole me in the summer they'd take the girls and clothe and feed 'em and send 'em ta school fer their help with the housework and little'ns, but Bill wouldn't never've let 'em go, and he tole me so. Now they can go."

"But there are still all those little ones," I prompted.

"Well, they's the orphnage fer the litttle'uns, you know." Triumph shone in the pale eyes and victory stained the hollow cheeks. In that moment Reller looked as pure and beautiful as an angel. "Don't you know they'll put them little'ns in a orphnage? And may they never haif ta pick cotton agin as long as they live. They'll have clean beds, with real sheets and pillercases, and they'll have decent clothes and better vittels than they've ever had. My young'ns is a goin' ta have their chanct at last, and some of 'em may get took out fer adoption in good homes, even."

"Then you're not sorry you did it?"

"I done what I done a purpose, Miz Flossie, and I'm glad I done it. Bill's on his way to glory. The kids'll have their chanct, and Reller won't never haif ta have another baby as long as she lives. It's the best thing that ever hapened to this family, though maybe it shouldn't a had to come about jist like it did."

They took Reller to Paragould. She had bathed and donned a gray calico Mother Hubbard, starched and ironed for this occasion, no doubt, and a stiffly starched apron and slat bonnet made of snowy bleached flour sacks. She marched straight out to the constable's buggy, her head held high and a light not of this world on her shining countenance.

I heard later that they had committed her to the State Asylum at Little Rock and my heart grew sick.

Then I forced myself to think of the asylum as I remembered it on a tour I once made with friends. The clean little rooms each inmate occupied alone, and the fresh beds and neat clothing. There is the big sewing room, where the women with mind enough, gathered to sew and mend the personal and hospital clothing and linens, under supervision. They were having a merry time of it the day I saw them. And the big recreation hall where Saturday night concerts and dances were held, the men and women patients being allowed to mingle on these occasions. I remembered too the great vats of dried apples and navy beans and beef stew that were cooking in the clean airy kitchen that day.

Then I remembered how Reller had lived, half-clothed and half-fed, picking cotton and having a baby nearly every year. I knew that, if she had no regrets for what she had done, the asylum could well be for Reller what Webster says it is: a refuge, a shelter, a retreat.

Chapter 17

July 17, 1916

Alex snapped, "I'm *not* goin' to milk! For the fiftieth time this summer, I repeat it!"

"It's getting to where it hurts me to milk," I insisted stubbornly. "Bending over doesn't come easy any more, it cuts my breath off."

"Then I'll make you a lower stool."

"It's the mosquitoes too. They eat me alive. If they do carry malaria, there's nothing can save me from it this year!"

"You can leave off milkin' till I get in, if you want, and I'll mind the mosquitoes off you, but I won't milk."

I closed my lips tight against the rising torrent and the moment's anger passed. Finally I said quietly, "Well, make the new stool as soon as you find time."

July 24, 1916

The day the Big Meeting started I had my first chill. It was a sweltering day and Alex was really alarmed when he came in to find me huddled under every quilt and blanket on the place, and still chattering like mad. When the chill passed, the fever mounted. When the fever passed, I found the little body within me quaking and trembling, and my nerves were stretched to the breaking point before the ague of the unborn subsided. Dr. Benson came, but he refused to give me the regulation treatment for fear of bringing on a miscarriage.

I was unable to go to church at all. Still I must do my work and stagger forth to milk, night and morning.

Since I must endure the malaria, I made up my mind to make a clean sweep of it and endure all else without complaint. Right now it was easier than fighting. Each time resentment or rebellion rose in me, I quickly buried them deep within, so that they could find no expression even in my face.

But under this rigorous discipline, life was dust and ashes on my tongue, and I wished with all my heart that I might die once Alex's baby was born. I would never be missed, I thought bitterly, for the meeting came and went and no one came near me. The crowds gathered, morning and night, and I could hear them singing and preaching and shouting their praises to God. Not even Brother or Sister Sherrill came to see me. *No one.* Once more I was an outcast, due this time, no doubt, to my long stay in Little Rock.

The bitterest pill of all came when Ann told me that Ma had laughed and said that she didn't see how Alex could be sure the baby was his, that Flossie was having it mighty soon after she got back off of a long trip, that she was wearing new clothes when she came home and Alex hadn't had any money to give her when she left.

Well, let them foregather in their little House of God, as they called it, and sing and shout till they fell on their faces! If that was religion, then the less I had of it, the better pleased I'd be.

A sickness filled my mind as well as my body, and as my fever mounted one evening, I dreamed I saw the people of Englewood, putting on their masks of piety before entering the church to sing and shout, then taking them off again as they came out, all worship ended, their faces evil with the desire to rend and tear each other. As they all turned toward me and I perceived their willful intent to torture me, I awoke with a start and fell forward on my face weeping. Surely God had turned His face from me, or caused His light not to shine upon me.

August 3, 1916

I had sent Alex to the store for the material Pa had cut for me, but he refused to let me have it.

Alex told me, "He said you could use the things Ann made up for her baby that she couldn't use. No use makin' more baby outfits."

Having no argument to offer, I dully accepted the things that Ann could pass down to me, as they were of no use to her.

August 20, 1916

This blessed Sunday I felt better than I had for weeks. I baked a chicken for dinner. I even baked a cake. Alex seemed to take on new life with this apparent change for the better. He made a quick run around with the evening chores, helped me with the milking, and then suggested that we walk over to see Ma and Pa. The fact that Alex had one time asked that I go with him had softened my mood as it had not been softened for weeks. It was sweet, walking along the country road as the sun sank toward the west. Maybe it was just that I stayed too close indoors. I must take to getting out more, if only to walk the creek bank.

The great oaks, that had been cropped close after the fire, had put out in a manner past belief in one brief rainy summer. When we turned in at the gate, we found Ma holding court under the trees, as of old. She held Mattie's delicate little Alva on her lap, and her eyes danced maliciously as Lester flung himself about in a rage of impotent jealousy. Sherman had not come in from milking. Onnie and Ann had settled themselves on the thick grass and Pa looked more than pleased to see us.

"Well, well, come on in! A most uncommon sight to see the three of you comin' in at the gate, you might as well jine the confrence."

"And what might the question under discussion be?" I asked lightly, thinking that I should do my part to help break the ice. Not only that, but I was conscious of a deep and abiding desire to be included in a group, any group, so sick and tired was I of myself. I sank to the grass beside Ann and the baby.

Pa cleared his throat loudly. "Question before the house is: Would I be justified in buyin' mysef a automobile?" He quickly slid his eyes around the circle to enjoy the effect.

"Poker Bill just flew by in one, so it's raised Uncle Henry's anxiety," giggled Mattie. "He thinks if Poker Bill, who is only a logger, can own a automobile, why can't he, the man what gives Poker Bill his job, have one too!"

"That ain't so!" Pa denied, but not ill-naturedly. "I been thinkin' about buyin' a car long afore Poker Bill thought of it. It jist seems such a awful lump sum ta take out of the bank at one time. You sure seldom get the chance ta put it in thar in sich hunks!" He looked directly at me and asked, "Would you do it?"

I laughed. "You surely wouldn't ask my advice about *money*, Pa, knowing as you do that if it was something that would round out my happiness . . . and I had the money . . . I would make the exchange with no regrets!"

Pa rested his elbows on his knees and leaned toward me. "Ever try *makin'* and *savin'* a few hunderd dollas?"

I shook my head solemnly.

"The fust thousand is the hardest," he assured me, a note of sarcasm in his tone. Then he nodded emphatically and sighed. "Yes, quite a chore, that fust thousand. But a car would make a smart deal of difrence in my life. If anybody in the wuld needs a car, it's the farmer. Look at the time he wastes goin' to and fom!"

"A car wouldn't last a year on such roads as we got," said Alex, being practical.

"What do you think about it, Ma?" I asked, seeing that she had said nothing.

"It seems not to matter what I think," she snapped. "It's yore opinion Henry seems to want."

"That's easy ta understand." Mattie laughed. "He asks Flossie because he knows she'd be fer you and Uncle Henry both havin' whatever's ta be had that'll make things easier and better fer you!"

I silently blessed Mattie's kind heart.

"Only thing is this," Pa said, "if I don't spend money fer a car, there'll be jist that much more left in the bank fer you chilren when I'm dead and gone." He looked around the circle, stirred uneasily, and then closed his eyes for a moment as though utterly weary.

I had seen very little of him lately and noted with concern that an ashy pallor replaced the once high color. There were blue pouches under his eyes, and the fine shock of hair was thinning perceptibly. Suddenly my heart held no rancor toward him.

"Let the rest of us get ours like you got yours!" I said impulsively. "You gave your boys all the schooling they would take, which was a lot more than you had, so they've got a better chance to make it than you had, even if you don't leave them a penny. The money in the bank is yours, nobody has a better right to it, so if you want an automobile, buy it!"

He felt his Adam's apple, sat quite still for a moment, then plunged, "You boys get here early in the mornin'. I want you both with me when I look at cars. Lookin' round a leetle mite won't hurt anythin', but I ain't sayin' yet that I'll buy one."

The boys did not betray by so much as the flicker of an eyelash their inward elation.

As we sat talking, the moon climbed high in the heavens. Pa, for once in his life, sat long past his bedtime, seemingly reluctant to let pass this first time the family had been together in many long months. At last we rose to go, all barriers down, laughing and teasing each other in the old familiar manner.

Sherman and Mattie dropped off at their cottage. When we reached the bridge, I paused to drink in the beauty of the moon-drenched, willow-studded stream, and to catch the fluted notes of a mockingbird on an overhanging limb of a cottonwood tree, showering the air with bright bubbles of sound.

My heart lifted as I recalled the winter scene when all this beauty was sheathed in snow and ice, when I had laughed and tucked my head to escape the seeking icy fingers of the north wind. Where was the wind tonight? I raised my face and waited a moment, expectant, then felt a soft caress, light as a butterfly's wing, against my cheek. Ah, so the wind was in a gentle mood tonight, pensive and tender as a lover.

"Goodnight!" I called back to Onnie and Ann, who were strolling on toward home. Their voices were muted and soft in the moonlight. A cowbell tinkled in the lane as Old Rose licked herself again and again. Alex swung Cerece up astride his neck and turned down the cattle path at the end of the bridge.

"Better watch out when you start down that bank, Flossie. It's a little steep for you," he called back.

Perhaps much of the suffering I had endured was needless. Maybe I made a lot of my own misery! I was sure that I had not shown a very friendly spirit toward anyone since my return from Little Rock. The others probably figured that if I liked Little Rock and the people there so much better than I did Main Shore and the people here, then I should have remained there. I could no longer hold myself blameless for the loneliness that at times enveloped me.

September 2, 1916

"But why can't Onnie drive for them this time."

"No reason at all, except that they want me," said Alex complacently, spreading the lather with a lavish brush. "Maybe it's because I'm the oldest!"

"Pa could learn to drive his own Chivvy, as he calls it. I hope you're not going to have to wet-nurse him and the car both from here on out!"

"Pa tried it Thursday, didn't I tell you?" Alex gave a careful stroke or two with his razor, then went on. "Sittin' there under the wheel, big as Fido, after spendin' a solid half hour watchin' me do nothin' but shift gears and work foot pedals, same way the salesman showed me how. He done pretty well till he looked up and saw Pride Owens comin' in his big farm wagon, his mules fair cuttin' a shine. Pa lost his head. He said afterwards that he couldn't feel there was room for the wagon and car both on that road, so's he headed for the ditch. Thought he was settin' his foot on the brake, but he had it on the gas and cleared the ditch with a bound and took a panel out of Johnny's fence!" He bent double, laughing at the memory.

"Was the car damaged?"

"We was shook up considerable, but just a few scratches on the car."

"Thing of it was he had to pay Pride to unhitch his team and pull the Chivvy back on the road. Pride'll never get through raggin' him about it. But I guess that put an end to Pa's drivin'. He hasn't wanted to take the wheel since."

"It wouldn't be quite so bad if I ever got to go!" I blurted. "But every one of you are so plagued ashamed that somebody will see I'm going to have a baby that you can't bear to look at me or have anyone else see me! If you're just going to drive around the rent farms, what would it hurt for me to go along just once?" I hated myself for pleading for this privilege, but I did so want to be included in some of the laughter and gay times the others were having.

Alex frowned with displeasure and whetted his razor on the strop. "How many times I got to tell you that Ma says you're not to ride in that car till after the baby comes? She says it's the vibration. They's somethin' about the vibration that would be sure to bring on a mishap."

"Is that why she doesn't take Cerece?" I said hotly. "Lester is taken hither and yon, but Cerece is not allowed to get inside that car. And the other day when she so much as laid a hand on it, Ma got out and wiped and polished and fussed for five minutes!"

Alex said nothing.

"All right, Alex, all of you go right on and *ride*. It means nothing to you that your own wife and child are no better than outcasts!"

If only I could have kept the words from coming. Since nothing was to be changed, my own position would have been less galling if Alex had not known of my discomfiture. But for a moment he looked troubled. It was perfectly evident that, in the excitement of the new car, he had never given the matter a thought.

I relented. "I don't mean that I'm not glad they have the car, Alex. I am. And I'm glad to see you get to go with them and have fun. Only it's got to where you're gone every minute that you're not asleep or at work or at the table. You leave as soon as chores are done on Saturday mornings and there's no need for me to look for you till I see you coming."

"Can I help it if Ma has set her foot down that you're not goin'?" He was using that tone of exaggerated patience that I found so maddening.

"It wouldn't be so bad if she'd be honest in stating her reason for not having me along. It's that she finds an out by saying that it's out of consideration for *me* that makes me want to fight!"

This must not go on. I fled through the back door and sought refuge in the corncrib, sobbing and disgusted, till I heard the door slam and peeked out to see him leaving.

September 30, 1916

All through the rest of September Alex had continued to go without ceasing. Not willing again to subject myself to humiliation and defeat, I did not mention the matter again. They went to visit friends and relations in the hill country west of Paragould, and to visit Aunt Roena in Miller County. Then to clean the graves at Brown's Chapel. Sometimes, as on the occasion of my open rebellion, just to ride the tenant farms.

The chills no longer came so often, or so heavy, but they were still not entirely broken. Sometimes, even on a chill day, I would manage to drag through and prepare Alex's dinner, only to have him call and say he was eating up there, as Pa wanted him to run them into town in the car for lemons, for ice, for anything at all that would give them an excuse for a quick run in the car.

Ma was very gay these days, keeping her shoes polished and her few best things ready to go at a moment's notice. "I used to feel that people passin,' me in their fine cars didn't speak jist because they was feelin' so biggity"—she laughed one day—"but, la, it ain't that. It's jist that yore goin' so fast you don't realize who 'tis yore passin' till they're by! Oft times I get past, and now I thinks to myself, why, Annie Walker that was so-and-so you jist passed, and you didn't even speak. But it's certainly not because I'm feelin' no ways uppity, it's just that the car rides so fast."

October 3, 1916

I sat in the porch with my mending one afternoon and saw Pa coming around from the creek with his back up. It was a golden autumn day, but he didn't know it.

"Makes me so 'tarnal mad!" he said, catching sight of me. "Thar I got ten acres of the finest eatin' peas in the country, planted a purpose so's nobody on the land would have to be short a peas this winter, but can I get anybody ta pick 'em? Not one soul! I'll even not get my seed back out'n 'em." I waited while he mopped his face with a fine cambrio handkerchief.

"Won't you come in and let me fix you a glass of ice water?"

"Ice water, my eye! I'm not lookin' fer ice water, Flossie, I'm lookin' fer somebody ta pick my peas! I'm going down ta Woody's now, then crost ta Howell's. I jist want to find out if even one of my tenants is not so well off but what he don't expect to have to eat no dried peas this winter! Onnie and Sherman put in their own peas, so's they don't need none of mine. The Paytons, it seems, don't pick nobody's peas on the haives. And that Glasgow has got to be the tarnashionist insolent sharecropper I eva had to deal with. Once his crop's done, he takes no more orders fom me, cuss his highhanded soul, but goes sweetly on his own plague-taked way, irregardless!"

"I'm not able to pick peas on the halves," I said, "but if they are going to waste, I'll certainly try to get out there and save enough of them for our own use this winter."

"You'll do nothin' of the kind!" he bellowed. "If ya can't pick 'em on the shares, then stay out of my pea patch!" And he stamped off down the road.

But for once I paid no heed to Pa's rantings, and as time and opportunity and my own frail strength permitted, I picked and shelled peas and sunned them each day in flour sacks. When I came to put them away I had about three pecks, clean and white and perfectly cured.

October 7, 1916

Last week, Ma and Pa and Alex had left by daylight on Saturday morning. They had not returned until after midnight Sunday. I'd had a very bad time of it. The stock had to be fed and watered, the chickens too, and the cow milked twice daily, and Cerece looked after. I'd had a chill too, the first in a good while, but somehow it had to be gotten through. So it was with a heavy heart that I watched Alex making preparations to leave.

The first frosts had touched the countryside with colors varied and brilliant, and this struck me with a new wonder as I stood in the porch staring wistfully after Alex's departing figure and thanking God that I had but a little ways more to go. Alex turned once and looked back, waving and calling to Cerece, then hurrying on in his prissy little stride. I sighed and returned to the dishes.

I was still not quite through in the kitchen when I heard the car coming. It stopped with the grand swish and sputter Alex liked to give it after making a dashing turn and heading back the way it had come. Alex hopped out and ran into the house, leaving the engine running.

"Decided I'd best come back and get my coat," he said excitedly, "seein' there's no tellin' when we'll get back. This sweater might not be enough when night comes on. Pa says we're goin' clean beyond Louder's Ridge this time. He's not been through that country since he was a boy!" Alex was in high good humor. He has the soul of a butterfly, Lola had once said, don't try to change him. There are already too many solemn, blue-nosed people in the world as it is. Well, I was pretty solemn and blue-nosed *myself* these days, but at least Alex still knew how to be happy, if left alone.

I would not have gone where I could be seen, but Cerece had darted out after Alex and they were trying to make her come back inside. Lester stood proudly behind Ma and Pa, who were both crowded into the front seat with Alex, for Onnie and Ann occupied the back seat. There was no light of joy in Ann's face however, so I knew that she felt she was there on sufferance. I caught Cerece up in my arms and the car started off with a rush.

Ma looked back and yelled in her most dulcet tones, "You'd better come go 'long!" And her taunting laughter tinkled on the air.

I swallowed quickly, but knew a momentary satisfaction when Alex's hand faltered on the wheel as he glanced anxiously back at me, then turned and yanked the car back into the road and sped on his way.

"Ride! Ride straight to hell!" I cried hoarsely, but they were too far away to hear me, and I was thankful for it. It would only have given Ma a chance to tell the people wherever they went what a vile temper Alex's wife had. That she was afraid to drive up to my gate and ask me to come go along because she was sure to get insulted. I was getting better acquainted with Ma all the while.

But this was Indian summer, the sweetest part of the year, and I brushed my mind clear of Walkers as I would have brushed the cobwebs from a room, and settled myself to enjoy the things at hand. I picked up my new copy of Comfort and read the continued story and another short one, then turned to the fancywork section. There before me was a picture of a beautiful nightgown yoke in a wild rose design and complete instructions. It was in filet. I resurrected a ball of number forty white crochet thread and a hook and started it, checking the rows off with a pencil as I proceeded. My heart eased as the work took form under my hand.

October 14, 1916

Saturday dawned with a soft autumnal haze over everything and Alex had gone again. I thought how glorious it must be to go spinning along the highroad with no feeling of responsibility, forgetting all cares, while savoring the beauty of nature and the pleasures of travel. And suddenly, as I fed Alex's mules and tethered the cow, a surge of nauseating hatred swept over me. I hated Alex with loathing and bitterness. I hated Ma and Pa for taking him from me at such a time. Most of all I hated myself for hating them. Then the chill, which I had every right to expect to escape by now, came on, and I hated with a devastating thoroughness whatever the god-blasted cause might be that had given me malaria. I hoped and prayed that whatever it was might in time be isolated and the last vestige of it wiped from the face of the earth. The chill passed and I tossed for weary hours with the burning fever.

But something was wrong with Cerece. Always she romped and played all day long, as busy with her small affairs as I with mine. Today she hung about my knees and fretted and whined. I felt her little face and knew she was running a temperature. Under questioning it was not hard to find out what the trouble was, so I laid down my pleasant task for one far from pleasant. I knew immediate help was indicated and prepared to give her an enema. This she fought with all the power that was in her sturdy little body, and by the time the ordeal was over I was completely exhausted. Most of the day both of us spent in bed, except for the time I had to be up doing the necessary.

Elimination again established, Cerece was playing about the yard in her usual happy fashion. I must have dozed for I was startled from my slumber by Cerece's wild screams. I staggered to my feet and through to the front yard. She had poked a stick into the beehive! The bees swarmed angrily out over her as I snatched her up in my arms and ran for the house, fighting them off as best I could. Once inside I slammed the screen shut, but two or three dozen bees had followed us in. I set her down and, in my wild efforts to kill them, grabbed a slipper and slapped wherever I found a bee, to Cerece's added amazement and suffering. Hands, arms and faces, we were covered with stings over every exposed part of our bodies. I was a demoralized wreck as I prepared half a pound of baking soda by wetting it thoroughly, and settled myself to the task of plastering the wounds with it.

"I didn't mean to hit you, darling," I soothed, noting the print of the slipper sole across her round little cheek. "I was only trying to kill the bees. Why did you poke a stick in the hive?"

"I . . . I thist wanted to see 'em fly big!" she sobbed.

"Well, you did," I said grimly. "They really flew big."

I gave her a glass of cold milk and a cookie and at last rocked her to sleep. I tucked her into her bed and fell exhausted into mine. As the stinging subsided, I fell into the deep sleep of exhaustion.

I heard pigs' squealing as in a dream, the wuff-wuffing of the angry sow and the terrified screams of Cerece. Still half asleep I ran, barefoot and in my nightgown, through the back door and gate and into the woodlot. Since the pigs arrived the big Poland China sow had been down on her back, but when Cerece had grabbed one of her pigs she had raised her great body and caught Cerece to the ground under one front leg and now she was making horrible sounds as her slavering jaws opened and struck at her bright head. I seemed to be years covering the few more yards to her. Cerece, screaming and struggling, still held the pig which was squealing with all its might. I seized her by her gown tail, released the pig, dragged her clear and fainted dead away.

When I came to, the sow was settling with her litter around her, and Cerece was hovering over me, whimpering and touching my face with endearing fingers, the blood running in a steady trickle down her left cheek. I forced myself up, and galvanized into action at the sight. The soft curls were now a mess of slimy slobbering's, there was a short gash in the crown of her head and the cartilage of her left ear was laid open.

The only reason she hadn't been killed was because the sow's teeth were decayed and missing from age.

Wearily I dragged myself up and led her into the house. Again I heated water on a burner and settled to the task of taking care of my little daughter, who by this time looked like no child of mine.

"Why did you go out there alone Cerece? Time and again Papa and I both have told you not to."

"But you never let me hold the tute li'l piggiewee. I would thist hold him for a minnit," she explained through her tears. This time when I put her to bed I meant for her to stay there. To impress this on her I went outside and brought back in a little switch and showed it to her.

"Miss Pert's lowing at the gate and I've got to go milk, but if you get out of that bed one more time today, I'm going to pepper you good with this switch, do you hear me?"

"Yes'em," she whispered.

Usually when I went to milk I was able to take the curse off the dreaded task by contemplating the beautiful sunset, this being my favorite hour of the day. But God's most magnificent handiwork was utterly lost on me that evening. Heaven held no solace, earth no joy for me as I fixed the feed and let Pert in. What had become of the short cotton rope that I tied her with? Always I draped it around the post and now it was gone. Angrily I yanked the stool from its nail as Pert started eating, and settled myself and began washing her udder. The mosquitoes swarmed around her as the bees had swarmed around Cerece. She lashed frantically with her tail and snatched nervously at her feed, looking wildly around at me as if for help. But I was in no mood for soothing her, being choked on my own spleen. If only I could keep from giving way to the tide of bitterness that was rising within me. Oh, God, don't let me cry! Only a little way to go, such a little way, and then I could rest. Then I would be out from under this awful, unwelcome weight that was pulling the very life out of me. Yes, I understood Reller. I could see why she would reach the point of saying that if she spent eternity in hell she would never have another baby.

I was milking furiously, buoyed up by an unnatural strength. I had pulled on the old faded corduroy robe over my gown, but in spite of the thickness of it the mosquitoes rose and settled on me like a stinging horde from hell, their stings maddening as I twitched my shoulders in a frenzied effort to dislodge them. The bucket was almost full when a huge horsefly lit under Pert's belly with a bite like a bee sting. She lifted her foot with one mighty kick, upsetting the bucket. On the down stroke she caught the pail handle in her cloven hoof, after which she went completely wild. She wheeled and knocked me flat and leapt across me, her sharp hoof pinching the fleshy part of my upper arm to the ground and bursting the flesh in an angry wound. Madly she kicked and plunged about the lot in an effort to free herself of the bucket, now no more than a crumpled mass of bright tin. Frantic with pain and fright, I scrambled to my feet and stumbled toward the house like a drunken thing.

Cerece, attracted by the commotion, had come to see, but at my approach, remembering the switch, she turned and fled back to her bed. I circled the house and went to the pump at the end of the front porch, turned the long bell sleeve of the robe back over my shoulder and looked in a cold bitter frenzy at the stream of bright blood trickling down my arm and dripping from my fingertips. I clamped my jaws tightly against the pain and with my uninjured hand I manned the pump.

"What in the world?" asked a quiet voice behind me, and I wheeled to find Alex standing stock still at the gate regarding me in a sort of mild wonder. When he saw my tortured bee-stung face, he started forward, "My God, Flossie, what has happened to you?"

"You!" I choked. *"You* stand there, cool as a summer breeze and ask *me* what has happened, as though it mattered one small damn to *you!"*

He came toward me, hands outstretched, but I retreated. "Don't you *dare* lay a hand on me! I've come this far through this without your help. I don't ask it now. But I want you to know that at this moment I hate you, Alex, as no other man on this earth has ever been hated!"

His face blanched and I gloried in the sight of it. I wanted to hurt him.

"I asked you what was the matter," he repeated sternly, "but if you want to go on frothing at the mouth like a blasted idiot instead of answering my question, I don't know of anything that's to stop you. But you'd better let me do something for that arm now and unload the rest of it later!"

"Let my arm alone!" I snarled. "Why should you care how much blood I shed? I'm not interfering with your plans. You're getting to go when and where you please and stay till your own precious fancy turns your head toward home!"

I swept past him and into the house for gauze, antiseptic, healing oil and tape. He followed me in. I fixed a pan of water and started sponging the wound, having caught sight of my swollen soda-smeared face in the mirror which fairly frightened me.

"Now, tell me what's the matter," he said, striving for control. When I said nothing, he snorted, "Besides being in the shape you're in, you look and act just like a crazy woman."

"But I'm *not* crazy, Alex, not now! I have just come to my senses within the hour, but I had to be knocked into Kingdom Come and stepped on by a cow before I could wake up. Beginning now there'll be some changes made in this house or there won't be roof or door left on it!"

"Or you'll go back to Little Rock?" he maliciously taunted. "You're in fine shape for going to Little Rock. I know they'll be proud to see you!" His anger now matched my own.

"Yes, you saw to *that*, didn't you!" The wrath that had threatened to strangle me flamed to a white heat as I daubed the wound with a wedge of saturated gauze. The harsh antiseptic didn't even sting as I advanced one slow step toward him, my voice now scarcely more than a whisper. "Well, for your information, Alexander Walker, your little game worked! This baby tied me to you, just as you meant for it to. When I came back from Little Rock I came because I loved you and I was willing to start over in spite of all that had gone before. You think you've had to bear all that's been borne between us, don't you? Well, I have borne the *last* and *all* of some things that I intend to bear. But I'm not leaving you . . . now or ever. Here under heaven, with only God for witness, I renew my vows to you, Alex: I am yours now and forever, *till death do us part!*"

I laughed wildly, and the laughter ended in a choking sob as the unwanted tears streamed down my face. "Never again will I leave you, hear it! And if ever you leave me, when you get back you will find me and your precious babies exactly where you left us, waiting for you.

What's more, I'll see to it that you are brought back, wherever you go, for there is a law. But it won't be on *Walker* soil that I'm left, for we're getting ready to move, *starting today!*"

"You said you'd come back to the country and never say town again."

"And I'm not going back on what I said. In the country, *YES!* At Englewood under Pa's notionate thumb and Ma's jeers, *NO!* We're moving as soon as you can make arrangements. I'll be obligated to them no longer, for they both think I'm indebted to them for a roof over my head. Never again, I promise you, will I try to please either of them. Never again will I look to them for anything. I have a husband, a man who was really going to make money, remember? And he'd better get to making some! If you are a man, now is your opportunity to prove it. I'm giving you your chance to take our affairs into your own hands and give them your full attention!"

"Flossie, please, I . . . ."

"You shut up and listen till I'm through!" My voice threatened to get out of bounds again, but with all the power at my command. I brought it back to a whisper again, because of Cerece. "I couldn't get money from you to get ready for the first baby because Pa was holding your feet to the fire on Lizzie's prior claims. I can't get money to buy me one decent thing to be seen in, now that I've outgrown every dress I have, because Pa says it will soon be over and I can wear the things I outgrew. And me now where there's positively *nothing* I can wear . . . but my nightgowns . . . and this old robe that I had when we married! *You* are going to teach school, Alex, and it matters not to me whether you like it or not. Get lined up for State Normal and file your application!"

"But, Flossie . . . ."

"Moreover, you're going to borrow money and make a down payment on a farm of your own. Or, if you expect to rent the rest of your life, then get out and rent from a white man that keeps a record and makes an accounting of returns at market time. Also, from this day forward, we're charging not one thin dime's worth of whatever at Pa's little store. I don't care to see any more money added to the bank account while I go without the things any pregnant woman needs in her diet, and without clothes, and without anything only what Pa says

I can have. You are through roosting on a limb, waiting for Pa to die so you can inherit. Oh, the *contempt* I feel for you this minute, Alex, can even *God* ever forgive it!"

I had finished bandaging my arm and looked up to find Alex, pale and undone, standing helplessly by. He could not have been more astonished than I, as the full import of all that I had been saying sank into my mind. The words had come of their own volition. I could not have stopped them had I tried. For one moment we stood gazing belligerently and miserably at each other, then he drew his handkerchief from his pocket, stepped forward, and gently wiped my mottled face.

"Get into bed, Flossie. I'll look after things," he said quietly.

I had my say at last. I was sure that Alex had heard and that he would remember every word of it. Having disgorged this vast accumulation of bitterness, I knew the first real peace that had come to my spirit in months. Relieved and relaxed, I settled against the pillows and permitted Alex to tuck the spread around me.

As in a dream I heard him speaking to Cerece. He had to dig her out from under the covers at the strangeness of our behavior. I prayed to God that she was too small ever to remember. Through half-closed eyes I watched with satisfaction as he took her in his arms as a father should, soothed her with soft words and kisses, and applied unguents to her hurts and stings after he had examined them and heard her story of the day's misadventures. How pleasant it was to lie here, feeling that Alex was with us, in deed and in truth. That he would fetch and carry while I rested, that I need not stir again that night. The sound was like music when I realized that he even remembered to fill the wood box and tea kettle. He put a fire in the stove and heated the pot of chicken, bringing me a cup of the rich broth.

When all was done and Cerece at last settled for the night, he blew out the light, but he did not come to bed. Quietly he let himself out the front door, thinking I slept, but I lay drowsily watching him through the front window as he seated himself on the steps, his hands hanging loosely between his knees. He shook his head impatiently, then, held his face to the sweet Indian summer air. He smoothed his hair, clasped his hands at the back of his neck, and bowed his head long in silent thought.

Chapter 18

October 16, 1916

Breakfast over, Alex saddled Jude and came in and dressed. "I'll be back in time to do the night work," he said, and kissed Cerece goodbye. He didn't say where he was going and I didn't ask. I was interested that he turned west, which would take him to town or wherever he was going without being seen by any of the family. We hadn't tried to talk, but there seemed to be no feeling of strain any more. I now felt I'd said all that I had to say, all that I would ever have to say on the subject.

An hour later, Sissy Moody stepped up on the porch and knocked, "Mister Alex sent me to do chores fer you," she began, shyly smoothing her fresh gingham. "He said . . . name of God, Miz Flossie, what's the matter with yore face?"

My face? Oh, bee stings, Sissy. Cerece poked a stick in the hive yesterday and things happened." I grinned.

"Looks really bad!" She shook her head sadly. "Mister Alex said you wasn't well and I was ta come ever' day fom eight ta two, clean up after the breakfast when I get through milkin', then stay after dinner till everthin's put away and leave plenty cooked fer supper."

I was at a loss for a moment, then I asked her to come in and showed her the work I wanted done. Sissy was seventeen, small for her age, but quick to learn and anxious to please. I was now free as a bird. What was I to do with these glorious golden days?

I had always been so busy. I remembered the crochet I had started and took it to the hammock and settled down, while Cerece started a brand new playhouse underneath the oak tree.

The Indian Runner ducks that I had raised in the spring were full-feathered now and truly beautiful. Their feathers, gleaming white and shining as though they had been lacquered, lay sleek to their bodies, but when they ruffled them luxuriously as they yabbled and splashed where the water pooled from a leak at the corner of the milk trough, I could see that they deepened to the pale gold of rich cream next to the skin. They ran at will through the day, usually finding their way down to the creek, but when night came on they always returned to the gate and quacked until someone let them in. I got up and let them outside. They shuffled their feathers down tight to their bodies, and stood about quacking uncertainly for a moment. Then the drake, the curled feathers of his tail marking him from the others and glistening in the sunlight, seemed to reach a decision and started briskly off to the east, the others falling in behind him without another sound.

With mind and heart purged of all resentment, it was sweet and restful to sit here and look quietly about, or to concentrate at long intervals while I counted stitches and fashioned the tiny windows and blocks that made up the design.

Cerece loved the woods and the water as I did. I took her to the boulder under the fall, for I realized that the cold would strike us now at any time. But even after the heavy frost it would be fun to gather possum grapes and persimmons, hazel nuts and pawpaw apples.

Thinking and planning thus, I was able to keep my mind from dwelling too long on the approaching ordeal. I sighed. I wished I had one pretty dress and that I could be with people once more . . . any people! There had been so much activity the year before, baseball and croquet and ice cream parties. I wondered if Ma was any better pleased now that the community gave every indication of me being dead as a doornail. But she wasn't at home long enough at any one time to know that this was true. And love feasts! Nobody seemed to have them anymore, or even all day singings.

What was life but a gracious gift? And I wanted to enjoy mine. But what we had been doing would never pass for living with me. A verse from the "Rubaiyat" came to mind and I repeated it softly:

FEATHERS IN A HIGH WIND

Ah Love! Could you and I with Him conspire
To grasp this sorry scheme of things entire,
Would not we shatter it to bits—and then,
Remold it nearer to the heart's desire!

I had done it! I had taken the whole fabric of our lives and torn it to shreds and thrown it at Alex's feet. It could never be pieced together again, for the things that had gone to make it up were in the discard pile forever.

What was it I wanted most of anything else in the world? A decent home, a quiet and a peaceful home, a chance to order my life after my own desires, to make my decisions in the face of whatever necessity, so long as they were my decisions. I wanted a chance to invite my soul now and then. Did I have a soul? What else was this strange stirring within that seemed ever to be groping and reaching for something, but never quite finding? The something, what was it? Was it God, or something that I could not even name?

I had felt it the plainest the night I had gone to the bridge during the big snow, the plainest it had come to me since I was a little child. When I could not sense it at all, I was lost. I had been lost now for months. When it was present with me, I seemed to be all with nature. Without its will-o'-the-wisp light to lure me on, I labored through life without purpose, without hope.

I had moved out of "my little house." The knowledge of this truth I hugged to my breast. My body of necessity must come and go until another roof for it was provided. But the thing that was myself hovered now, homeless and forlorn, looking doubtfully ahead, ardently seeking.

Alex came home at five thirty, and stabled and watered Jude. I sat quietly until he entered and tossed several packages into my lap. "I got Mrs. Porter to make the selections. I think you'll find them all right," he said, and took Cerece on his lap.

For once he had remembered to bring her the candy she had never ceased to expect. He shared it with her and with me as he watched me eagerly unwrapping bundles.

Into my lap fell a cloud of pearl-gray silk, printed with a spidery green vine and small intertwined purple and yellow flowers. There were two of the white mercerized broadcloth uniforms I had wanted earlier in the summer, with reversible fronts and finished with fine tucks and smooth pearl buttons. The sleeves were long, the cuffs button-trimmed. In another package I found a pair of white kid slippers, slightly soiled, a pair of silk stockings and a bottle of white shoe polish.

"Summer clearance," said Alex, "but they ought to be all right for as long as you'll need 'em."

"All right!" I breathed. "Alex, they're perfect!"

Since I had gotten them at last, how much heartache could have been saved if I'd had them sooner. But I pushed this thought from me, glad to let my life begin anew with this moment.

"Mrs. Porter said, there where the pleats are put into the silk dress, they are fastened with snaps, you just unsnap them as you need more room."

"I guess I'll have to unsnap every pleat in it," I said ruefully.

"Maybe I hadn't mentioned it, but Aunt Roena is comin' Saturday. They're havin' the love feasts under the elms at John and Martha's. If the weather holds, Lucius said he's takin' his croquet set over and John says him and the boys have got the court scraped and rolled."

So that was why Alex had bought the things. Everybody would have thought it strange if I didn't come to Aunt Roena's love feast.

"It's downright uncanny, Alex. I was wishing so hard while you were gone that I had a pretty dress and a chance to go someplace and be with people. Except to go to Ann's, and the time you took me to Reller, and the walk we took that Sunday evening, I haven't been off the place this summer."

Alex looked at me, incredulous at first, and then the truth of what I had said sank home. "Yep, that's right," he said, on a long sigh. "I guess the summer hasn't been much fun for you." Then he jumped to his feet. "Run along, Cerece, Papa's got to milk and do up his chores."

Papa's got to milk?

I went inside to bathe and try on my new things. Which should I put on first, I wondered? I let down my hair and brushed it vigorously. The swelling from the bee stings had subsided somewhat, and there was only one of the ugly fever blisters visible on my lip. Carefully I applied a little rouge, glad to see that my skin had cleared a little, and smoothed the powder on. I fluffed my hair and arranged it in rolls and puffs on the crown. But I had only been playing a game with myself. There was no question which dress it would be. I sighed ecstatically as the soft cool weight of the silk settled over me. I took one long delighted look in the mirror and, on an impulse, ran to show Alex.

"How do you like my new things?" I asked happily, turning myself before him. But he milked stolidly on.

"How in tucket do you stand to milk in these hide-raisin' mosquitoes? No wonder half Main Shore's havin' chills and fever this fall!"

"Look Alex, I've got it on. How do you like it?" I urged.

"Oh, why I . . ." He turned and looked at me and I saw him flinch, for he saw nothing except the unsightly bulge in my figure. His eyes dropped to my feet.

"Your shoes feel all right?" he asked in a strained voice.

"Yes . . . yes, they feel all right," I answered, and I dropped dejectedly behind him as he started to the house with the milk pail.

October 21, 1916

When the day of the love feast arrived, Alex brought the buggy down and took me in style and comfort. Not the latest style, of course, for Pa and Ma held the center of attention as Onnie dashed in and brought the car to a standstill with a grand flourish. Lester was standing up behind Pa and Ma, and in the back seat sat Sherman and Mattie and Ann.

Belle and Silas were there, Silas even paler than usual, if possible, and quieter. He and Sylvester were both in white linen suits and at the end of the day were just as spotless as on arrival.

I loved Aunt Roena. She was all of the merry, helpful, good-natured things that Pa was on the few occasions I had seen him without his dignity. Her face lighted at the sight of me and she came forward and kissed me heartily on both cheeks right before the whole crowd. My momentary nervousness left me.

"Anybody want to play checkers on my coattail?" cried Bula, as she flew past on her way to the kitchen. Alex had taken my basket and placed it with the others on the long work table. "Anything I can do?" I asked, going at once to the center of activities.

"Lawdy mercy, yes!" Selma laughed, shoving a great pan of chicken pie at me. "Corral them young'ns of mine and yores and fill 'em up on this pie while it's still warm. Maybe when we get to the table we'll have some chance at it ourselves!" I got dishes and spoons from the safe, filled them with the rich pie, and went to find Maudell and Cerece.

"I put the ironing board across the wood box there fer you ta sit on," Bula told me when I returned. "You need ta git off yore feet from the looks of you, and back there the rest of us won't be falling over you." She dusted sugar into a huge bowl of rich cream she was whipping. I seated the children, one on each side of me, and fed them alternate bites from the same spoon.

"I hoped you'd make it today, Flossie," called Willie, slicing cake at a great rate. "I wanted to come see you all summer. But with one thing and another, I never did make it, not even when the meetin' was on. It looked like I run from mornin' to night, and then missed part of it."

"It was that hayin' got me!" mourned Selma, tossing a salad. Went right to the field and worked like a man every time it was dry enough. Never had so much rain on fresh-cut hay, kept us turnin' and dryin' and still we lost a plenty a fine hay. Then it was the timber. Arlien's set his heart on buildin' a decent house one of these days. Last year he bought the bricks and stored 'em. This year he's gettin' out lumber ta season. Maybe we'll make it, time we're both dead with old age!"

"You're doing better than the rest of us, and you well know it," said Jenny, mixing lemonade and tasting it with a fine zeal, "and the rest of us want a decent home, same as you do."

At that moment I looked up and saw Susie Maynard dancing in at the back door in a cloud of pale green voile. At the sight of me she paused uncertainly. She giggled, then burst out, "I'd rather be on the outside looking in, than on the inside looking out." You could have heard a pin drop.

"You are!" I said crisply.

"Are what?" asked Susie unthinking.

"On the outside looking in." I gave Cerece a spoonful, then said, "I like it best on the inside looking out, so both of us should be happy." I went on feeding the children. Susie turned and fled without another word. When I looked up I saw Selma smiling at me with a knowing pride. The interrupted chatter was merrily resumed.

"Looks like a shame to cut this purty ham," said Mattie, "but that's the way it's got to be." She took two great platters from her box and began to slice the ham, it patterned with a crisscross, rubbed with brown sugar and red pepper and studded with cloves of spice and baked a juicy golden brown.

When all were gathered for the feast, Aunt Roena herself pronounced the blessing, moving us all to the verge of tears by her touching words. These feasts were never spread anywhere but on the grassy ground. The long cloths were covered with good things to eat and with stacks of plates, silver, glasses, cups, and napkins. Each found a likely looking spot and settled, or took a plate and went foraging about until it was filled with all good things to his notion. Lucius and Alex were prowling at the end of the meal.

"I just want to make sure I didn't miss anythin'." Alex laughed.

Lucius shouted, "Eureka, I have found it! Maud, nobody makes a chocolate pie as black and sweet and smooth as yores. Be a good gal and cut me a hunk I can't run and jump over."

"What pretty speeches Lucius can make, when he wants something." Maud laughed, as she pulled the pie toward her. While she was cutting it, Lucius stood above me and, just as I lifted a bite of angel food cake mounded high with whipped cream to my mouth, he laid his hand on my head and with a quick downward shove, plunged my face, nose deep, into the sweet goo. He yelled for everybody to look and I held my face so they could see before wiping it clean, which I did with the fine Sunday handkerchief I snatched from his pocket.

As Lucius knelt beside me and reached his hand for the pie, he said, "Lord, I wish I could eat this all at one bite," and opened his mouth to try it. I was sitting on an upturned cedar bucket and he was still kneeling beside me. On an impulse I reached out both hands, one on the back of his head, the other under the hand that held the pie, and snapped them together.

Pa sat directly across from Lucius and had just raised a glass of lemonade to his lips. At the sight of Lucius's chocolate-covered and surprised countenance, Pa burst into laughter, sputtering lemonade far and wide. When he could get his breath, he said, "Lucius, son, you sho'ly don't know Flossie like I've got reason to, er you wouldn't've stated anythin' with 'er. She'd be in thar at the finish if it took 'er a yeah ta do it!"

I had a good chance to study Alex as the games progressed, since I could do nothing but sit and look on. The only thing I joined in on was the target shoot and surprised myself more than anyone else when I knocked the can off the post seven times in succession. Each was allowed to shoot only till he missed. When I returned to my seat I could see Alex, but not the person to whom he was talking. He had his hands thrust, palms outward, in his back pockets, his head a little forward with that "nobody in this whole wide world but the two of us" air. An engaging grin flickered across his face and I looked frantically round for Susie. But Susie was deep in a game of croquet and, as I looked back, Arlien stepped from behind the bush that had hidden him from view and gave Alex a resounding slap on the back and both of them bent double in a gale of laughter.

I was suddenly ashamed. When would I learn that this "intimate" look and attitude was Alex's natural manner? Alex was like no one else present and my foolish heart told me that. Even knowing beforehand what I now knew only too well, I still would have fallen in love with Alex and married him, whenever he gave the word.

October 23, 1916

Onnie was doing the driving for Pa these days, but the new had worn off the car and they were not so often on the road. The expense of this constant travel may have had much to do with it, for Pa could not long engage in anything without computing the cost in dollars and cents.

Alex made several mysterious trips into town, going always by the west road. He offered no explanation and I asked for none. It was enough for me to see that he had his mind on his own business and was looking after it in his own way. He was now doing things that he himself had decided to do, not just something Pa had told him to do.

He had always liked the red corduroy robe I had when we married, and one evening he came in from town, bringing the material for another and a pattern, and even a length of heavy satin ribbon for the sash. With this I found a pair of leather-soled red felt bedroom slippers. Another time he brought the material for nightgowns, a fine grade of lustrous sateen in blue and pink and plain white.

October 25, 1916

The harvest had been bountiful. I could hardly glance toward the big road that I had not seen wagonloads of corn and hay trundling toward Paragould, and lately great snowy banks of cotton for the gins. Fall gardens were thriving, mostly parsnips, collards, shallots, carrots, lettuce, and turnips. The sweet potatoes had been dug and taken to the kilns for curing, the sorghum cane was cut and ground and the juice cooked off into thick red molasses. The new orchard had done pretty well and the apples were being hauled to market, made into cider, sauces and jellies, spiced, pickled and dried.

Alex was doing a lot of figuring and writing at night. He wrote a long letter, addressed, sealed it and stuck it, address to his body, in his hip pocket. When the fall returns were in, he said nothing about his standing with Pa. I asked nothing. He paid no more attention to me than it had been his habit to do, but at least he was there. He was never ill-tempered or morose, only thoughtful, and he attended to his own chores and milked in the evenings.

But because he could not bear to look at me or touch me when I was heavy with child, I made up my mind that I would never bear another for him, so help me God. Just how this magic feat was to be accomplished I had only one notion. Dr. Sewell would have to tell me what to do. Alex didn't like sick people and he hated to be around when I was ailing. With pregnancy there were too many unpredictable complaints popping up at the most inconvenient moments. Alex and his butterfly's soul! Well, clumsy-footed elephants couldn't flit with the butterflies, so I must be careful not to get heavy and clumsy ever again.

If only I could have the baby and get through with it! The long drag didn't seem near as long as did these past few weeks. Then the chills, which I had thought were over, returned. Alex brought chill tonic from town. When he asked me to make out a list for groceries and other supplies, I rejoiced in the knowledge that he was adding nothing to our store account.

I knew I was fast approaching my sojourn into the Valley of the Shadow, and I was suddenly so heartsick and soul-weary that it simply did not matter. I knew now what Ann had meant when she said that it would be a relief if she knew that the same hour tomorrow would find her laid out in her coffin.

November 15, 1916

Five days before, Alex had looked at me and told me not to wait till the last minute to call Mama. She was packed and ready when I called Tuesday. Alex was there waiting when she arrived at the train depot Wednesday morning. And the tedious days wore on.

November 18, 1916

The heavy frosts had come. Sissy had piled and burned the blackened and ugly flower stalks. Another short stretch of unseasonably warm weather arrived and the nights seemed endless. I often wakened after a brief sleep to lay awake for hours, staring into the darkness. The rhythmic, heavy breathing of the others disturbed and distressed me, so taut were my nerves, and I sometimes fled before it. Cautiously I would sit up and slip my feet into the new slippers and my arms into the heavy warm robe and quietly let myself out the front screen. I had carefully oiled the hinges so that I made no sound in my restless comings and goings.

It was a clear starry night with a beautiful quarter moon and the wind was again my lover, the only lover I had now. I lifted my face and bared my throat to the soft caress. The moon's magic spread a splendid glory all around. I walked back and forth across the yard until weary, then sat on the steps, and listened . . . and watched . . . something was there, important to me, but just beyond my knowledge. I felt it each time I was alone in the night. I had felt it even when I was a little child. I had strained toward the starry heavens. I had tried to hear and see things hidden beyond that veil, but I had never succeeded. I tried now. Nothing happened, nothing ever did. I sighed and relaxed and returned to the muted night sounds about me.

There was now no need to go inside. New strength and vigor had come to me from some unseen source, and I was suddenly wider awake and more alert than I had been for months. I arose, let myself through the gate and took the cattle path to the bridge. As I stepped softly along I felt so light and airy, like a cloud floating. Not heavy. Not clumsy.

At the bridge I paused, not wanting to go beyond it. What was it I had sought? Was it happiness? I could not feel it. What then had I hoped to find, here at the bridge, peace? A kind of peace had been harboring in my mind. The fact that I knew Alex was working on some change for us had quelled the rebellion that so recently soured my soul.

Was it God I had been seeking? Who was God? God was spirit. Yes, that must be it. And God was love. Love and a spirit were in me, therefore God was in me. No, this could not be. God was far off, somewhere. Was God in the wind? Was the wind His messenger? Was it for this reason that the wind had ever and always the power to thrill me so? Was it God's message of love on the wind to me that comforted me? Was that what made me want to laugh and cry for joy because I felt myself to be fondly loved and cherished?

Considering what lay before me, I thought perhaps I should pray. But for almost a year now I had not prayed, though never had I stood in such need of help and guidance as through this past year. I sighed. If I lived beyond this, I promised myself that I would search until I found the true and living God. Until I had such proof of His presence and His love that I could never doubt it again. Not the God of the Little Churches, who threw one into a frenzied fever of praise at revival time, then left one high and dry and unblest till another revival rolled round.

No, what I sought was power to be free and unhampered in spirit, a power that would fill my heart with rejoicing because I could see and know that I was on the upward way. This forever standing still, stomping up and down in the same tracks, eternally marking time, this was not the religion I sought. To me this was only sham and pretense, things people fabricated, rituals they observed, because they knew not God. Why pretend that you were growing in wisdom and grace, when you knew you were muddling along with no least idea as to how to reach the heights?

No. I would never again pretend. In this moment the God whom I had revered as a child vanished from my consciousness completely. I would have to go far beyond this for any help that I would ever know. The stars didn't seem so far away. Perhaps God was not as far away as He seemed. I groped for words.

"Father, whom I someday hope to find, strengthen me for what lies ahead. Let something, it matters not what, melt the bands that press so tightly round my heart and set my spirit free. Teach me to love this child and the father of this child, and hold me in the safe protection of Thy everlasting love. Amen."

For one shining moment I was absolved of all sense of blame or of suffering. For one glorious and peaceful moment I was free as I had longed to be. I clasped my hands tightly to my breast so as not to let escape this newfound solace and began to make my way back to the house.

Suddenly my labor was upon me. I remained in the yard. No need to wake the others. The doctor would only tell them to "walk me" for hours. I could do that myself.

The grass looked like pure gold in the mellow light, the ducks, making white patterns against the gold, gleamed glistening white as dream birds, their heads tucked under their wings.

How keen my senses were! Everything registered on my consciousness with electrifying poignancy. I bit my lip to still the cry that rose as I fell to my knees with pain, and a melancholy wind touched me with tender fingers. And then the onslaughts of pain became terrifying and, with Christ, I would have cried out, *If it be Thy will, let this cup pass from me!* But I knew this could avail me naught, so I thanked God that the hour of my deliverance was at hand, and went inside to wake Mama and Alex. Alex called Dr. Sewell, and then took Cerece to Ann on his way to get Mrs. Snyder.

"Don't you dare leave here, Doctor, till she's safely out from under the chloroform?" It was Mama talking. No sooner did I catch the words than the great wheel on which I was spinning carried me swiftly beyond hearing.

When I swung back around, Dr. Sewell was bending over me. "Flossie, I'm going now."

I struggled to answer him, but the merciless wheel swung out and around, then back again.

"Flossie!" he spoke sharply now. "You're awake. Tell me something to let me know it!"

It was a command. With all my strength I shoved my feet against the ground to stop the big wheel's turning and stammered, "I . . . I . . . I hear the ducks!" How thick and dry my tongue was, and my foot slipped and the wheel spun relentlessly round and round and round. It stopped at last and I slid off at the sound of a baby crying, at the feel of Alex fumbling at my breast, at the twinge of pain as a strong little tongue cupped a tender nipple.

"Let this boy suck!" Alex spoke boisterously, as he gave me a gentle shake. Then his voice softened. "O Lady, we got us a boy!"

O Lady, now! I smiled grimly, thinking of the long weary months during which he had not once called me that. I heard the ducks yabbling and splashing at the pool under the milk trough. I heard Mama, coming and going on hurrying feet.

"What time is it?" I asked wonderingly.

"Six o'clock. You sure held our feet to the fire with one full day of it! I marked it down in the book. Born on November 18, 1916, weight 9 pounds. All but the boy's name."

I had held *their* feet to the fire. Suddenly I laughed in wild foolish hysteria, before finding relief in a moment of tears. Then I sank at once into exhausted slumber, the baby, which I had not yet seen, still tugging hungrily at my breast.

November 25, 1916

Ma came to see me after the baby came and that while Mama was still with me. She had been very gay and friendly, bustling in and making as much to-do over me and the baby as if we'd been her beloved and cherished own. Her astonishment when she learned the baby's name delighted me. When Alex had asked me what to name the baby, I had said wearily, "I named the girl . . . this is your boy, name him to suit yourself," little guessing what the name would be, "Jewell, I name him Jewell. I always have liked that name!" That was bad enough in my mind, having always considered Jewell to be a girl's name. But when Mama had come to the front with her suggestion, I had hid my face away and started mumbling things against the pillow. "I want to add Blessing to that name," she had said resolutely. "I never got to name one of my own, and I always wanted a daughter named Hope and a son named Blessing!" Mama had been so wonderfully sweet and good to me, how could I refuse her. So Jewell Blessing Walker he became, and as soon as I could hold pencil to paper, I marked it down in the bible. Then I wrote this news to Papa and would have given three straight meals in a row could I have seen his reaction to it. But when his reply came, he said simply, "I'm sure the baby is a jewel, and I hope and pray he lives to be a blessing."

"Who in the name of all that's right and jist give 'im such a handle as that?" gasped Ma.

"His Papa named him Jewell, and his Grandmother Mounce named him Blessing," I said, enjoying myself hugely.

"Well, I never!" she said faintly.

"I don't know about a boy," I said, "I never had a son before, and I'm afraid I'll be a little short on wisdom. A girl I would know how to talk to, but how does a mother talk to a son, when it's time to tell him the necessary facts of life?"

Ma smoothed the lavender gingham over her smooth high bosom complacently. "If he's like his own Papa, he'll never ask you a single question about . . . you know." She flickered her eyebrows significantly. "I never had to speak a word to Alexander on such a subject in my whole life."

I stared, seeing many things for the first time. No wonder poor Alex got so far off the straightaway now and then. He'd been given no compass to steer by. I dropped the matter, realizing that Ma could not know that I would want my son to ask questions, that my only concern was in not being able to give the right answers at the right time.

Chapter 19

November 28, 1916

My heart lifted at the sound of Alex yodeling in a high rapture, and I looked from my window to see him bounding toward home, hitting the high spots, an open letter waving in his hand. For days he had managed to make it to the mailbox around eleven o'clock, the box being situated across from Onnie's on the high road.

"I didn't want to tell you till I was for sure," he panted, "but I was too late for State Normal this year, so's I thought about the round I took as a railway mail clerk and put in for extra during the holiday rush. I got it! I'm off on the eighth of next month."

"Alex, will we live in town again?" My heart leaped in hopeful suspense.

"I don't rightly know yet," he said, shaking his head doubtfully.

"I thought I'd try this job as extra. Might not be able to stand it, you know. If I see I can, I can try for a straight run. But the job itself wasn't why I wanted it."

"Then why?"

"Because I'd rather break with Pa on an outside job than to take another farm while I'm livin' here, when he thinks I ought to be glad to stick by him and live however."

"Oh."

"Comes spring I know I'll get the itch to plow. I've been away from the farm in the spring before and it ain't a thing I enjoy."

He paused, and then hurried on. "I hadn't meant to tell you this, but I'm going to have to leave and I'd rather you heard it from me than to try to piece it together after I'm gone. I've got a line out for the old Thompson place."

The picture of it flashed in my mind: the house in need of paint and the window panes missing and front porch sagging. Identical with the big house of Pa's that had burned, even to the same pattern of iron fence, only it was now red with rust.

"Maud inherited the home place. But Maud married William Esswein, and he took her and his derricks and went to the Texas oil fields. Then after Uncle John died, Aunt Roena married old man Seales and went with him to his farm in Miller County, so's that left the place for renters, and one unholy mess they made of it. Aunt Roena never expects to live there again, so naturally she don't want to pay out Seales' money on it. Maud's busy payin' out a place of her own in Texas, so she never spares the money and the place is a wreck."

It was indeed. "Alex, the fences are bad. Santos even turns his horses into the orchard and they've mangled some of the finest fruit trees. It would take real money to get that place in shape to be lived in."

"But I've got a plan, Flossie. That's what I'm tryin' to tell you. I told Maud that I would take the place over and put in a new porch, new window panes, paint it and fix the fences for the first year's rent. I think she rents the farm to Santos for about four hundred a year. I told her if at the end of the year I saw I couldn't pay for it, I would turn it back to her in a lot better shape than I found it. But if I saw my way clear to payin' it out, then let the four hundred count as down payment and we'd take it up from there. I ought to be able to handle that with all ease."

Again the picture of the house rose before me: the glass front door, broken end nailed over with odd boards, bundles of paper and rags stuffed in broken window panes, black, frost bitten weed stalks standing shoulder high in the front yard. "But the money to do all this, Alex?"

"That's what I'm going out to make right now," he explained. I glowed with pride for Alex in the way that I had longed to do.

"Think of all the stuff we have stored that Mama left with us," I exulted. "We'll be able to furnish the downstairs completely." The happy tears were running down my cheeks. Alex reached over and shook me roughly by the shoulder.

"Stop it, now," he spoke gruffly. "Here I juggle my brains till I'm crazy tryin' to get things the way you want, and then you go wailin' like a banshee the minute I get it lined up. How's a feller to know...."

"But it *is* what I want. Oh, Alex. I'm so proud and happy this living minute I could dance for joy!"

December 8, 1916

Neither of us were surprised at the way the family took it. Alex went calmly on with the butchering and laying in of sufficient supplies to do me, even sneaking beneath the bed one evening a box that he said held the gifts for the Christmas tree.

But Onnie finally spoke his mind when he came to take Alex to the station. "Never in my whole life saw farmers act the way you two do. Though it jist might be that only one of you is a farmer!" It sounded so like Pa that I wanted to laugh.

"But we just never see a penny, Onnie! If I knew Alex was trying with all his might and mind and this was the best he could do, I could make up my mind to do it. But when we could as well have a good job and live in comfort or in town, or pay out our own farm and work no harder than he's working now, why should we spend the best years of our lives no better off than the poorest tenant farmer? Pa can get all the renters he needs. Alex will get nearly a hundred dollars a month, plus expenses, and that will go a long ways toward what we want to do."

"Well, ever' feller to his notion. Like the old gal when she kissed the cow. But me? I wouldn't stay penned in no railway coach, day in, day out, for nobody's little hundred dollars a month!"

Mattie told me it was really bad when Alex stopped to tell the old folks bye. "And there stood Alex, treadin' up and down like an old turkey gobbler, explainin' to Pa how he hadn't really expected to get the job, but now that he had it he saw no reason why he shouldn't take it, as he would rather do that than teach school. And come spring, he didn't doubt but what he'd be right behind the plow again. Ma had the same look she gets on her at a funeral," Mattie declared. "Pa never once took his eyes off the far. Finally Alex took the bit in his teeth and offered his hand to both of 'em, and said he hoped he'd find Pa feelin' better when he got back, and Pa said he didn't expect to be feeling no better, no matter who got back from where."

December 18, 1916

    I felt that I had a lot of thinking to do, once Alex was gone, but I hardly knew where to begin with it. My whole life would have to be reconstructed, but I was not yet strong enough to do more than look after the baby and my own needs. Alex left the two dollars a week for me to pay Sissy, and she continued to come as usual. Indeed she practically lived with me, not because I was afraid to be alone, but because she was learning to crochet and embroider and found it pleasanter being here than in her own crowded home. The mules had been turned in the big lot at Pa's, but I kept the cows and chickens, since Sissy was there to look after them.

    I blessed Mama with every breath I drew for the three little packages she had left me. Used according to directions, she had assured me I need never conceive again, except by my own wish and desire. I hugged the knowledge to me as the greatest boon of my future existence. No longer would motherhood be thrust upon me during one of Alex's unpredictable moods. I could now relax, secure in the knowledge that if ever I bore another child it would be of my own wanting. And that only after I had smoothed some of the rough edges off of life and hewed and molded it to a pattern more to my liking.

    My mood softened toward Alex each time I remembered him with his boy. He had seemed to shrink from handling Cerece when she was so small. For this reason I had dreaded the first few months of the new baby's life. But his son's little wrinkled face and skinny body were not repugnant to him. From the first day he hung solicitously over the basket, making soothing clucking noises in his throat, feeling the tiny feet anxiously to make sure that they were warm, even taking a certain pride in clumsily mastering the art of changing a diaper.

    But that little boy was not growing. In fact, he looked smaller and skinnier than the day he arrived. Occasionally I would hear him stir and grunt and would hurry to his basket to look upon him in wonderment. Was this really my baby? There was no bitterness now, but an ever-present yearning to get to know this little stranger better.

    With Alex away, I had to think hard to remember the things that had caused trouble between us. Only his fine qualities shone forth in such splendor that all else faded into insignificance. Alex did not speak swear words or obscenities. I had never heard him take God's name in vain . . . an unforgivable thing. Alex didn't drink alcohol or use tobacco in any form. Not once had Alex ever deliberately raised a row with me. He was lighthearted and gay, except when I kicked up so much dust he couldn't be. I must try hard to become once more the girl that Alex had fallen in love with, instead of the "blinger" and "termagant" that Pa declared I had become.

December 26, 1916

Were we never to be at home and together for our anniversary and Christmas? Last year I had dashed off to Little Rock, leaving Alex alone and frustrated. This year Alex was gone. I tried to believe that next Christmas we would be settled in our own home and have a decent Christmas together for once.

Sissy and Cerece found a tree a few days before Christmas and decorated it. I sang carols with them, and wrapped gifts. I told Cerece we're putting them under the tree for Christmas morning. She handled the packages each day, but made no effort to open them until the right time, and then her joy knew no bounds.

January 9, 1917

But always my troubled mind returned to the baby. He scarcely stirred when I bathed him. His breath came in little wispy gasps and the blue veins made a faint tracery over his temples and nose. His eyes, neither open nor closed, and the listless hands more than anything else resembled bird claws. When Sissy came I sent her for Mrs. Snyder.

After breakfast Cerece was busy beside the stove with her new doll and the tin tea set. I heard the baby stirring and returned to the basket. His skin had taken on a mottled purplish pallor. Was he dying? I pressed a hand over my mouth to still the rising cry and fled through the kitchen and smokehouse. Out through the mule lot I went and fell at last to my knees on the frozen ground behind the corncrib. The floodgates opened and a rain of tears washed down my face as my own petty, worthless soul stood naked and ashamed before me.

Hoarse sobs tore at my throat and words, raw with agony, burst from my lips. "Dear God, forgive me! Don't let my baby die, dear Lord, without giving me the chance to prove I love him. I don't deserve him. I'm selfish and mean, but, O God, if he dies I'll always believe that I killed him with my own hands!" I sat back on my heels and leaned my head forward till it touched my bended knees and wept until I collapsed in an abandonment of grief. How could I have been so blind, so wrapped up in my own petty sufferings that I gave such little thought to the small life so quietly fading out in my very arms?

My baby would not die. This assurance was suddenly mine. There being no further reason for weeping, I rose with a firm resolve and returned to the house. I knew nothing to do until Mrs. Snyder got there, so I warmed a blanket, turned the covers back and took the little one into my arms. I tucked the fuzzy little skeleton's head close under my chin and settled in the big reed rocker and sang Jewell Blessing his first lullaby:

> *Hush, be still as any mouse*
> *There's a baby in our house,*
> *Not a dolly, not a toy,*
> *Just a laughing, crying boy.*
>
> *Rockabye baby, up in the tree top,*
> *When the wind blows, the cradle will rock,*
> *When the bough breaks, the cradle will fall,*
> *Down will come rockabye baby and all.*
>
> *He's a handsome fellow too*
> *With his eyes so bright and blue,*
> *Cheeks so smooth and rosy lips,*
> *Dainty hands and finger tips.*

As I sang, I envisioned my baby as laughing, as having smooth rounded cheeks and fat little dimpled hands. He had to live.

FEATHERS IN A HIGH WIND

Mrs. Snyder came in hurriedly, her small wrinkled face further puckered with concern. "Hives," she announced positively. "Bold hives, Flossie, and we got to get 'em broke out on him or he's a dead baby."

"Do you know how to break them out?"

"I sure do. But young mothers nowadays turn up their noses at the old remedies, call it just being fogey. They want up-to-date doctors and store-bought medicines." She eyed me speculatively.

"I sent for you, didn't I?"

"So you did, and you could as well of got Doc Benson on the phone. Well, let's get to work, there's no time to lose. Get me a big onion and the sulfur box, Flossie. Sissy, you go underneath the house where the ground ain't froze and scoop me up a little pan of dirt." She spoke as one with authority, and Sissy and I hastened to obey while she put the baby, now apparently in a coma, back into his basket.

She scooped the heart out of the onion and filled the cavity with sulfur. Then she mixed a heavy mud out of the earth and plastered the onion with a thick coat of it, wrapping it then in a double thickness of porous brown paper, which she soaked well with water. Then she pulled out a bed of coals into the ash box of the stove, covered them over with ashes and laid the onion on it, covering that over with a thick layer of ashes, then more hot coals and more ashes. Then she closed the box lid down with a decisive clatter.

"Now," she said belligerently, and her eyes fixed me with a hypnotic stare, "bring me the white from the hen droppings under your roost. Nothing but the white, and at least a tablespoon full of it." I swallowed uncertainly, but could not withstand that level stare. I reached for a thin paring knife and a cup and set out for the henhouse. When I returned she examined the contents of the cup, seemed satisfied, poured boiling water to half fill the cup, placed a saucer over it and left it to steep.

"This is all going to come out all right, I think." She said this as if to herself, then called me over for further instructions. "Bring me a small empty quinine bottle, a bottle of turpentine, a strip of paper, a spoon and a match."

When the things were assembled, she took the baby on her lap. "Get me a razor," she commanded, not looking at me. Alex had taken his razor, but I remembered the big hollow-handled one that Granpap had given him, and brought it to her.

She dipped the paper in turpentine, struck a match to it, and dropped it burning into the bottle. Then she turned the baby on his stomach, swished his clothing high, caught the tender flesh between his shoulder blades twixt finger and thumb, slit the skin with the razor, and pressed the smoking bottle down over the wound. Jewell Blessing cried and my heart bled. Grimly she removed the bottle, took the spoon and caught several drops of the blood that the suction from the bottle had brought to the surface. Then she turned him on his back and pressed the bowl of the spoon against the trembling little tongue and let his own life's blood trickle down his throat, She wiped the last vestige of blood off on his tongue before she was satisfied. He looked like a little dead baby except that he stirred and moaned occasionally. Mrs. Snyder silently laid him in my lap and went to the kitchen. She returned with some of the hot hen-white tea, slightly sweetened, and fed this to him as long as he would swallow.

While he had a brief rest, banked round with bags of hot salt in addition to the hot water bottle, I fixed a quick lunch and we ate. By that time the onion was baked to her liking and she took the wrappings from it and dumped the soft mass into a straining cloth and squeezed every last drop of juice from it. Again she strained the juice, sweetened it slightly, and fed the baby all he would eat of it as hot as he could bear it.

She had called the operation with the razor "scarifying." And she did it but the one time, but continued to alternate the two brews fifteen minutes apart until four o'clock in the afternoon. Then the hives popped out and Mrs. Snyder stood triumphant. He looked like he had a heavy case of red measles.

"If he gets the least bit chilled, they'll go back in," she warned me. "Keep him warm if you have to keep him in bed with you. It won't hurt you to get wet down good once in yore life! Sissy, you be sure to stay here tonight and keep the fire going. It could easy enough be the end of him if he gets a setback."

I tried to find words to thank her, much to her embarrassment.

"There's yet something I haven't told you, Flossie. Your little baby is purely starvin' to death. Your milk is no good. Has your cow got good milk?"

I nodded yes.

"Then put him on it. The very idea . . . lettin' a baby starve to death in a land of plenty!"

January 11, 1917

Alex had told me to open the letter from Maud when it came, then send it on to him. I had, and now lived in the blessed assurance that the deal would be closed, and that Alex and I would at last be embarked on the great adventure of securing a home for ourselves.

Out of his first check he sent me money to go to Little Rock. It came by the time I had the strength to travel. The old weakness was there, not in the painful way it had been after Cerece's birth, but enough to preclude activity of any kind.

When Onnie came to take me to the station, I suggested stopping by to tell Ma and Pa bye, but he vetoed it. "Pa's got the mulligrubs and you'd think Ma had busted her gall bladder, everthin' she says is that bitter. Seein' that you're bound to go, I'm tellin' you you'd feel a heap better to jist go on than to try to make anythin' right with them whilst Alex is gone."

Pa was in the woodlot when we passed, walking toward the house with his head down, his hands clasped behind him. He looked up when he heard us and I waved a hand at him, but he stood stubbornly in his tracks, not recognizing the gesture by any outward sign.

Onnie dropped me at Lola's, taking my trunk on to the train depot and checking it through on my ticket, which he left with me on his way back out. I wanted to leave on the ten thirty so I'd get there in the daytime, otherwise someone would have to meet me at night in Little Rock.

January 12, 1917

When Papa got in from work that first evening and took one look at Jewell Blessing, he put his hat back on and went right out again.

He returned with a standard brand of condensed milk, half a dozen bottles and nipples, read the formula on the can and set to work. He rigged up Mama's preserving kettle as a sterilizer and prepared a night's supply of the formula. Papa was in charge. He waited up for the ten o'clock feeding, and took much satisfaction in the way the baby applied himself to seeing how quickly he could empty a bottle.

Then Papa pinned a lap pad around the baby's little bottom and took him right into bed with him. I had brought the baby bed and we set it up for Cerece. Mama slept on the davenport with me.

"You haven't got enough pep to feed a sick kitten," Papa declared, "so quit trying to fool this boy. Get yourself some good sound sleep while you're here, and see if you can't go back looking a little less like your own shadow."

January 25, 1917

Mama took me in hand with as much determination as Papa had taken over the baby. Every dainty and nourishing thing she could contrive was prepared to tempt my appetite. I began to feel nourished. She bought a good hair tonic and massaged it into my scalp and brushed my hair each day until it shone. She had taken great pride in my hair when I was a child. It seemed right and good to sit for long sessions with the brush, my head against her knee. She bought creams and rouge and powder, and reminded me to use them. In two weeks after she established her routine I began to show results. I perked up like a flower that has taken too much hot sun, then stands upright and looks fresh again after a cooling shower.

Mama put me to walking too, as she had after Cerece came. At first only round one block, then around two and at last I was walking three blocks and into the park.

January 30, 1917

Being in Little Rock with settled plans for my own future seemed entirely different from being there not knowing what was to become of my home, myself, or my baby.

I enjoyed that visit, especially when I was strong enough for the trip to J. W. Hamlin & Son, It was a breathtaking experience to watch thirty Negroes whip thirty barrels into a finished product by machinery, after being used to seeing them made step by step by hand.

I paused beside a hogshead and peeped over. Papa caught me under the elbows. "Steady now!" and he swung me clear of the floor, high in the air, and deposited me down inside the great barrel. I could remember the time when I couldn't even jump high enough to see over the top of one. Now it came only about as high as my waist. I ducked to my knees and began to squeal as of old, "Papa, don't leave me! Don't leave me, Papa!" He leaned over and placed his hands beneath my elbows and laughingly swung me out beside him once more.

I loved the smell of the hot staves and the rain of wood chips from the chamfering knives. Papa further delighted me by taking the crozier from one of the Negroes and running the roman numerals around the staves with such speed that I still found it hard to believe. When the barrels were finished, they were knocked down, and the staves, in numerical order, were packed, bound and nailed securely at each end by nicked strips of hickory bark which had been soaked long in water, so that they were pliable and easy to manipulate as a piece of cloth. The heads of the barrels were numbered and shipped with the bundles. When they reached their destination, they would be reassembled and ready for use.

February 2, 1917

With all my heart I wished that Alex could be happy living in town. It would be wonderful to be buying a home there instead of at Englewood. If he only could bring himself to like being a railway mail clerk. I had little hope of this however, for he had written that arrangements with Maud had been completed and that Santos had been given notice to move. He would be coming for me soon so that we could make needed improvements before time to put in a spring crop.

February 9, 1917

When Alex came for me, he was overjoyed at the change in me and the baby. "We'll get home with $165 actual cash in hand," he exulted.

This seemed a small fortune to me, so long had it been since I'd seen any money. He'd bought presents for me in Memphis, two pairs of "farmerettes," soft blue-and-white striped cheviot overalls, with bibs and suspenders. The trousers were pleated full to a wide waistband and gathered into tight fitting ankle bands. Two pretty chambray shirts and a sunhat with red percale lining and ties completed his purchases.

"I couldn't tell by your letters whether you were thinking about me or not," I said. "You kept writing about everything under the sun but us...."

"Well, I was sure you wanted to hear about everything under the sun, but I wasn't sure you wanted to hear any more about me." He grinned. "Plans for this move and this little job were the first things we've been able to really talk about in a good while now."

I considered this . . . it was true.

"Comes dark and I get you to myself, I expect you'll find out I been thinking about you quite a bit."

My heart stood still, and then resumed a steady, undisturbed beating. I had brought with me the three little packages Mama had left with me after Jewell Blessing was born.

Alex sighed. "I wrote Pa and told him he'd have to look out for another renter. I didn't get any answer from him."

"Are you sorry you are doing this?" I wheeled on him, tying the sun hat on as a finishing touch and inviting inspection.

"No, not for us I'm not sorry, only for Pa. Gosh, you look sweet! That's just the outfit you need for paintin' the house and helpin' build fences and porches. I bought them things with an eye to encourage you to do the sort of work they're supposed to fit you for!"

We laughed, and suddenly I was in Alex's arms in the way I had longed to be. He pulled me down beside him on the davenport. Softly he kissed a muted circle around my face, lingering long each time his lips met mine.

"Alex, you are so sweet!"

"I'm so starved, you mean!" He grinned.

Was that all it amounted to? Just that he was hungry for me at the moment, and when his hunger was appeased, all would again be as it had been?

"Tell me what kind of things happen on a railway mail clerk's run." I settled myself in his lap, my head against his shoulder.

Alex's voice and manner were hesitant. "I didn't mind being cooped in the coach as much as I'd thought I would. We kept movin'. The job wasn't too bad. Bob Hutchinson worked with me and he was fun. Sometimes the stops were excitin'. It was when I got to the end of my run both ways that I was hard hit, lonesome and blue. Made me understand a lot better how a road man drifts into doin' the sort of things most of them do."

"What things?" My throat tightened.

"Oh, drinkin' and women . . . mostly women. There's nothin' like a woman in your arms to make you forget how lonesome you've been."

"Alex, you didn't . . . ?" I swung round and set my feet flat on the floor, my eyes glued to his rueful countenance.

"I came so dang near to it that I get pale thinkin' about it, and I've thought about it quite a lot." He brushed nervous fingers lightly across his mouth. I waited anxiously. "The run was from Memphis to New Orleans, see? Well, the hotels where the railroad men hang out seemed to be favorites for women that were lonesome too. Not all of them were white women, either. The one I had trouble with wasn't."

My heart turned a flip and hit the bottom of my stomach with what might well have been an audible splash.

"She was Hutch's woman. She called herself Li'l Lonesome Gal, and I never heard him call her anythin' else."

He ran his fingers jerkily through his hair, and seemed to forget me for a moment. I kept still, wanting to hear the worst, even while I shrank in horror from it.

"Hutch hadn't made the run with me that day. She'd got to know me, for I came in with him every night. She looked disappointed when I told her he wasn't on. I turned and went up to my room. I don't know how she managed it, but before I got my things put away she was there with me. I hadn't heard a sound. She was just there. When I turned, she put her arms around me. All she said was, "Are you lonesome, honey? Then come on, let's be lonesome together."

"You know how long it had been with me, Flossie. She was pretty. She smelled clean, and fresh. She had big soft black eyes, and the whitest teeth. Her skin had the rich look of brown velvet. She put her hand over my mouth when she thought I was going to refuse her, and the palm was as pink and fragrant as a rose. Her bosom was full and high, and she was tall enough that I could have leaned over and rested my face against it. God knows I wanted to!" He shuddered, "How I ever got her arms from around me I'll never know. Then next thing I knew I was tearing down the street like mad, without my hat."

"What then?" I breathed. He went on as in a dream.

"Never had I put in such a night. I walked till after three o'clock in the morning, with the north wind blowin' a gale. Every step I took against the wind was as though I was walkin' against her, her thighs pressin' me back as I tried to go forward." He sighed.

"Then did you go back to your room?"

"I didn't dare, for fear I might find her in my bed. Hutch said that was the way she got him, just curled up in his bed and waited for him! I got a room in another part of town. I hadn't eaten any supper. I finally dozed off to sleep about daybreak. I'll take me no steady road job, Flossie. It's no place for a family man, unless he's where he can get back to home through the week. But I don't feel half as cocky as I did. I mean about fellas that sleep with a black girl, seein' that I wanted to all that night and almost did."

The role of Mother-confessor was again mine to play. But he had not yielded to temptation. I took what comfort I could from that.

After we'd gone to bed he kept drawing long breaths against my face, my hair, my breast. "You smell wonderful."

"Why, Alex, you make me feel as cherished as a bride. But you can thank Mama for how sweet I am. She has really been working me over."

His muscles tensed suddenly and a small groan escaped him.

"What now?" I murmured.

"Oh Flossie, I couldn't have stood it if you'd been like I was afraid you'd be, all freezy and standoffish like you been for so long."

Like I'd been for so long! Here it was at last. I was the one who had made all the trouble. I was wholly to blame . . . I . . . Eve.

"Tell me that you love me and that you're glad I'm back," he pleaded.

"You say it first, Alex. You haven't said it yet." I steeled myself against his blandishments. The minute I yielded all the way he would have me where he wanted me, and it would then be the same old round.

"I'm practically eatin' you alive. Can't you be satisfied with that?"

"You're practically eating me alive because you're so hungry and I smell so good. These are the things you've told me, Alex. And you must not be too anxious to hear me say I love you, or you wouldn't mind saying it first." I waited, but he would not say it.

"Well," I tried to laugh, "If it's of no more importance than that, for heaven's sake let's try to get a little sleep. Tomorrow's a hard day."

Alex lay back on his pillow regarding me as if I had been a stranger. I smiled calmly at him and turned off the light.

Chapter 20

February 23, 1917

Two weeks sped by with such a rush of work as I could never have imagined. Mr. Santos, the strange foreign-looking man who had for three years rented Maud's place, found another place for himself and had moved by the time we returned. The money that had seemed a monumental sum to us had been deposited in the bank to tide us through the crop. Charge accounts had been opened at the lumber mill and at Pendleton's for things we needed to make the improvements, with a 4 percent carrying charge instead of the 10 percent we had been paying.

But the inside of that house! My spirits hit a new low, until I had the big idea of writing Papa for another fifty-dollar loan, without even consulting Alex. As soon as the money came, I sat down with the mail-order catalog and ordered what I needed for interior decorating, bracing myself against Alex's displeasure when the things came. But instead of finding fault, he was interested and pleased with my purchases: a cool green matting for the guest room, gray and rose linoleum for the hall, blue with cream and black print linoleum for the kitchen. There were materials for couch covers, drapes, and curtains; paint for doing over the downstairs woodwork in gloss white; pretty wallpapers for all the rooms downstairs.

We piled Cerece into the wagon, leaving the baby asleep in his basket, and started gaily for the little log house in back of Pa's. Here we appropriated wooden sawhorses and scaffolding used in building the new little house. We were chattering happily when I heard Pa grunt. He was standing with his feet wide apart, arms crossed on his chest. He was regarding me with a baleful stare, and I remembered guiltily that I was to blame for Alex's leaving, for our moving, and for Pa's displeasure.

"Turned blinger right at last, I see!" he snorted.

"Pa, what is a blinger?" I asked innocently, trying Mattie's tactics.

"A blinger, Flossie," he spoke pityingly, "is a blinger, the wide wuld over. In pants or skuts, you manage ta keep right on bein' one."

His voice had the querulous tone of one long sick.

"Shad Morley's wife was a blinger . . . wore the pants, run the business." He threw out both hands, palms up, and shook his head for the very shame of it. "I been knowin' fer some time you'd took over yore husband's business, but this is the fust time I see you actual wearin' the pants!"

If Pa had been well, I would have taken great pleasure in giving him a run for his money, but there was no fun in badgering a sick man.

"Oh, the pants. Alex bought these for me while he was in Memphis. He wanted me to help him paint the house and didn't want my dress blowing over my head in the March winds."

"Oh. So yore husband *wants* you to wear the pants. Now I no longer misdoubt the old sayin' that it takes all kinds of people to make a wuld go round. For my own part, was I a young man choosin' a wife, I'd choose one that wore skuts and liked 'em, as well as likin' the home I could make fer huh . . . and stayin' in it."

"I think I am going to like the home Alex is making for me!" I flared.

"How you feelin' this mornin', Pa?" Alex asked softly, struggling to get by with some scaffolding to the wagon without Pa giving an inch.

"But leetle does it matter to you how I'm feelin', Alex," Pa spoke sharply. "I jist been admirin' yore manly-lookin' wife."

But Alex laughed in rare good humor. "It would take more'n a pair of farmerettes to make Flossie look manly, Pa." Alex stood smiling. Pa gave a tremendous snort and stomped off toward the house, his back up.

March 3, 1917

The old house was staunchly built of fine timbers. Alex ripped away the sagging porch and built a new one. He made the front steps wide and long, as I had asked. He put in new window lights all round and fitted new screens to the frames. Then he began painting.

He climbed the ladder and painted the house all around down to where I could reach it by standing on a scaffold. The south and back of the house eventually stood gleaming white, screens and window trim in black.

Inside I took on the rooms one at a time, starting with the west room. The wallpaper was in sunshine yellow, with lacy fern shadow patterns. Here I set up the bedroom furniture that had once been mine and Lola's. I polished the old wood till it shone softly. The long mirror set where it would catch and reflect the light from the south windows. I resurrected an old washstand set of bowl, pitcher, slop jar, and soap dish that had been Mama's before she had a bathroom built. The set had a fluted edge of delicate pink. Two of Mama's old rockers and a center table, which I used at the bedside, completed the room. With new green shades and crisp white curtains, the room looked cool and inviting.

March 10, 1917

At odd moments I would dash hither and yon on tours of inspection. Aunt Roena must have used the strip along the fence by the grape arbor for sticking down any slip or odd seeds that came to hand. Here I found a few clumps of garlic, a mint bed, and tufts of catnip. There were several bunches of blue grape hyacinth and a few lilies of the valley. There were patches of spice pinks. A big snowball bush budded and bloomed in the corner of the front yard while we still shivered from the chill in the early mornings. The great lilac bush beside the garden gate shook out its heavy purple panicles, loosing floods of heady fragrance on the sparkling air.

Between house and garden stood a huge blackgum tree. Beneath its dense shade Alex built a rough table and bench where I could drop down to rest or to prepare vegetables. He built a wash bench, staunch enough to withstand any load, beneath the big pin oak tree at the back.

The big catalpa tree inside the mule lot brought back happy memories of childhood when it leafed and bloomed. How many leaf skirts and hats had I made from the broad leaves, pinning them together with the sturdy stems, trimming them with the sickly sweet snapdragon-like blossoms. I had no time for this childish pastime now but instead wore clusters of the blossoms in my hair or stuck them in the band of my apron. I could hardly wait until the caterpillars started eating the leaves. I'd collect a few and go down to the creek and catch us a mess of those goggle-eyed perch.

March 17, 1917

Today I was papering the hall, and Ma decided to pay us her first call. Except for the day she had visited me before Mama went home, when the baby was born, making a pretty pretense of an intimate relationship, I had scarcely seen her.

Alex had Cerece with him in the mule lot, where he was pulling the dead weed stalks and collecting trash in a pile for burning. I was half through papering the hall, taking much joy as the gray and rose paper hid the ugly walls.

Reluctantly I put down the paste brush and prepared to visit with Ma. I ushered her into our own bedroom and asked her if she would like to see what we'd done to the house.

She held up a hand in protest. "Please, Flossie, I been seein' this house since before you was born and lived in one jist like it fer years and years, except that mine had another bedroom on the south so that I could use my front room fer a parlor."

I took her pretty starched sunbonnet and laid it carefully on the bed. I seated her near one of the north windows where she could look out on Alex and Cerece. Alex lit the trash pile presently, and the acrid smoke boiled up, like incense to my nostrils.

"Isn't this a heavenly day?" Surely this was a safe thing to say.

"Days like this mean bad weather is on the way."

"How are you, Ma?" Alex called to her, leaning over the fence and mopping his brow.

"I'm all right, Alexander, though I can't see why you should trouble to ask," she said, with a martyred air. Alex turned back to his task, giving no sign that he had heard her, and the satisfied smile that flickered over Ma's face was gone.

"Must be nice to be rich." She sighed presently. "South side of yore house shines like new money from down the road. Has Alex got paint fer all of it?"

"Yes. We've finished the back too, but he decided to stop and burn all the trash before we finish the front and north side."

"Going ta paper all the rooms, are you?"

"Just the downstairs rooms and the hall. We cleaned upstairs and stored the extra bed we had at Big Lake and a lot of the other odds and ends up there."

"We thought you must have bought this on a mighty sudden notion, till we heard *through others* that Alexander was workin' on the deal before ever he left here. Maybe he even already had closed it?"

"No, he still didn't know whether or not he could get the place when he left."

"But he *was* tryin' to get it?"

I didn't know what Alex had told them, if anything, but I could see no point now in evading the issue. "Yes. And we think we were lucky to be able to arrange about the payments in a way that we could handle and get started on a home of our own."

"Well, the news put Henry back in his bed. Not that that matters to either one of you. He just lay there with his face to the wall and wouldn't even eat. He said his own had turned against him. Though of course, both of us knew which one of you was back of the whole thing."

She looked at me archly, her eyes showing patience world-without-end and forbearance. Her voice flowed over me like warm honey. "Left to his own self, Alexander would never've thought of such a thing." She laughed softly.

I forced my voice to come quietly. "I didn't even know this place was for sale."

Heaven as my witness, I wished Alex had been able to get a place a thousand miles from Englewood, and I longed to say so.

"No more'n did we, or Henry would have bought it his own sef and saved Alex the trouble! After all, it's his own sister's place. He thought he had it understood with them that if Maud ever wanted to sell, he would take it off her hands."

"Pa really should see a doctor," I said, to change the subject. "It's only because he is sick that he takes things so to heart."

I saw she was laying for me on that one, so I said hastily, "Move nearer to the hall door if you will and I'll go on with my papering before the paste dries out." I went quickly into the hall, suddenly determined that I would not continue this verbal sparring with Ma when I had so many more interesting and worthwhile things to do. But she ignored my invitation to move nearer, though she continued to talk, even in softer tones, so that what she was saying scarcely carried beyond her own lips.

I could tell she was asking questions by the inflection, which made it necessary for me to hold my breath and concentrate in order to hear and make a reply. It wasn't hard to get the general trend: where was all the money coming from to pay back what we were bound to have borrowed to do all that we were doing?

I had fitted a length of freshly pasted paper at the top, carefully matching the pattern. I reached for the brush to give it a careful long downward stroke. She seemed to lack the nerve to repeat her last question. When I asked what she'd said, instead she said, "I say, Alexander must be expectin' to teach at Eight Mile School this year?"

"Yes."

"It's his gracious good luck that his Pa resigned from the school board last year or he'd never get it! He might not anyways, if Henry sees fit to put in his oar."

"Well, it won't greatly matter," I lied gallantly, for my steam was beginning to rise in spite of all my resolutions. "It's just that he thought it wouldn't sweat him quite as hard as going into the timber when crops are laid by. He'll have to do something with so many things to be paid."

"Did he think all this out by his own little sef, or did he have help on it?"

"I thought it all out and told him what to do!" I raged, weary of this petty game of words.

"Um-hum," she gloated. "Well, they's an old sayin', that a woman makes or breaks a man. I guess it's jist not his to say anymore what he will or won't do. Things seem to have gone beyond that point! But you couldn't have lied fast enough to make me believe that Alexander would ever willingly take a job that would pen him up in summer. I s'pose he'll come in at the end of each month and lay his check in yore lap, same as Shad Morely did with his blinger." She laughed, a jeering little sound that infuriated me. "She always met him at the door with her apron helt out when he come in off the timber job on Saturday night."

Hot blood surged into my throat. This was as bad as trying to milk Miss Pert in a swarm of mosquitoes. I wheeled to make a quick retort, missed my footing, and screamed as I stepped off into space. When I hit the floor flat on my shoulders, the house trembled, and Ma screamed.

"Alexander, yore wife! Run quick!" But Alex had heard the crash and screams and was halfway to the house.

"Are you hurt anywhere?" he demanded, pulling and tugging at me.

The breath had been knocked out of me. "Give me . . . a minute," I gasped.

He was running his hands over me and continued to lift and tug at me until I sat propped against him. "You're pale as a sheet. What happened?"

"I turned to answer Ma and missed my footing."

"I didn't want you to paper this danged house in the first place!"

This was the first I'd heard of that.

"I could have found a man to do it if you could have waited till fall. But NO! I told you when I was puttin' that scaffold up there it was a good place for you to break your neck." Then he blurted, "I got a good notion to set my foot down that you ain't goin' to hang even one more strip of paper!"

Ma's soft laughter tinkled mockingly. "Do you think that settin' yore little foot down would ever stop her?" she taunted.

"No!" he flared, and I had all I could do to keep from slapping him. "She is the headlongin'est woman in Greene County, bar none, once she's got the bit in her teeth."

"When ain't she had the bit in her teeth, Alexander?" Ma prodded softly. Alex continued to tug manfully at me. I permitted myself to be half lifted, half dragged to my bed. I tumbled in, my face to the wall. Alex grabbed a corner of the spread and drew it over my shoulders.

"Now lie there till I have time to get dinner, and let that danged paper alone."

"Where's yore baby, Alex? Flossie offered to show me the house but not the baby. You know I ain't seen him but once since he come into the world." Her voice bespoke a deep self-pity.

But my heart gave a little plunge of satisfaction to hear Alex say, "I don't know whose fault that could be but your own, Ma. He's in his basket in the kitchen and you're welcome to see him as often as you want."

I lay looking steadily at the wall, hardly breathing, till I heard her leave. Alex and Cerece returned to their trash piles. I returned to my paper hanging. If I had to fall and then pretend I was really hurt to stop her badgering me, then I was glad it had happened.

March 30, 1917

Another spell of bitter weather at the end of March and we had held our breaths for fear fruit and vegetables would be killed. It passed. High winds sailed in, took a last fling, and blew themselves out. Grass and spring flowers flourished at last, though we sometimes felt the need of a fire morning and evening. The fields had dried out from the spring thaw, and farming operations got under way. Alex was cutting stalks in the east field. When he came to the house for a drink, I took my courage in hand.

"Alex, I've hauled and stacked the bricks and marked off two big diamond flower beds in the front yard, but I can't handle that thick sod. Will you dig in and set the bricks and make up the beds? I've got a wheelbarrow load of stable manure beside each one."

His face tightened. "Me with a summer's work starin' me right between the eyes and before I can get well started she wants me to stop and make flower beds!" He was addressing his complaint to highest heaven.

"I'd do it myself if I could, but I just can't. That sod must be six inches deep, and the roots tied in so thick that all my weight on the shovel hardly makes a dent in it."

Alex staggered as though from a mortal blow and leaned against a post.

"Once the beds are made I'll take over." Then I added on a sudden inspiration, "I'll cut your stalks while you dig for me."

"You . . . cut stalks?" I nodded. He eyed me doubtfully. "When?"

"This living minute. Well, as soon as I change the baby and feed him." I could tell he was going to do it, and I flung my arms around him in rapture. "Alex, you're so sweet!"

"I'm a spineless worm, you mean. You're runnin' things with a high hand these days, O Lady. I'll go make a few more rounds. Yell when you're ready."

Jewell Blessing was ready and yelling at the top of his lungs. He was wet and hungry. I dashed into the kitchen and snatched him out of his basket and went into gales of happy laughter at the startled look on his face as he shut up and threw both hands wildly about in an effort to find something to hold on to. He'd been beating against the air with both hands and feet, his eyes shut tight while he screamed bloody murder. But there wasn't a single tear to be seen. He quickly emerged from the depths of his own misery and blinked at the light. I caught him up under my chin and hugged him in a high glee, spanking his wet bottom almost harder than I dared. It was astonishing how much rough treatment he could take in love's dear name. I took long plays with him now, and he liked roughhousing. The hours I spent tumbling him about, sometimes end over end, rolling him and tossing him, were hours of bliss for both of us. At four months he in no way resembled the infant that had been born to me. He was rounded out and healthy looking, as full of smiles and gurgles as if he'd started life with the best chance on earth.

"You're the funniest li'l feller in this whole wide world." I laughed, pinning a dry diaper in place. He had that still listening look in his eyes. "But just remember one little thing, buddy, you listen with your ears and not with your eyes, hear me? And with this dry bottom and your warm bottle, you'd better sleep like the dead until noon. The way you been bellowing is a shame and a disgrace to the crickets! We have stalks to cut! We have trash to rake and burn! And we have flower beds to be made! We're having everything we want this morning, even to a good baby, so just get ready to settle!"

Twenty minutes later I was on the stalk cutter, and Alex was headed for the flower beds, none too easy in his mind, now that he'd had time to think it over.

April 7, 1917

Alex ripped the boards from the big carved front door. When he had refinished the woodwork and set the new glass, I felt a keen excitement. I polished the glass till it shone, then carefully unrolled the transparent film of bright onionskin I had bought for it. The pattern was a strange mixture of prisms, squares, triangles, and circles, all in the rich deep colors of the stained glass windows in Paragould's First Methodist Church. The sun was starting to set as I smoothed the film, and the slanting rays of the sun shone through and cast a pool of dancing colors on the hall linoleum—yellow, purple, blue, gold, amethyst. I called Cerece, and she danced up and down in glee. She tried again and again to catch a handful of the lovely colors, but always when she opened her little fist they had flown.

Alex was proud that the hall was finished, for all his fussing. He even bragged that if we got in a jam for money I could hire out as a paperhanger and save the day.

April 14, 1917

We stopped work in the house long enough to put in a garden. When it was finished, Alex said, "Now that's yours, Flossie, from here on out. When it needs plowin' out, I'll do it, but that's all. Giddyup, Jude!" He slapped Jude's rump with a masterful hitch of the lines and followed her to the lot with quick, decisive steps.

We started keeping the ducks penned till midmorning after they started laying, and they kept up a tremendous fuss. But I was even more upset by the potter-racking of the guineas. I protested. Alex insisted. He'd been raised with guineas and danged if he meant to run a farm without 'em. I learned that their eggs were very choice and that the meat, though dark, was sweeter than chicken, with something of the flavor of wild duck. Alex almost had to be pinned out to dry when one of the guinea hens, who had hidden her nest, showed up with nineteen little ones scarcely bigger than the first joint of my thumb. They were agile and suspicious, and they kept always in the hen's shadow. Alex built a pen so she couldn't drag them around in the early morning dew. It was fun to watch them. The mother kept a keen eye out for hawks. If even a sparrow flew low over, casting a shadow on the grass, she let out a squawk, and each little one flattened itself to the ground, head extended, and lay as though dead until she clucked an all-clear signal. Alex had the big incubator going again. This time, thank heavens, I had prevailed on him to set it up in the smokehouse.

"We're going to have so many things creeping about underfoot we can't step," I protested. "What are you going to do with everything?"

"We're goin to eat all we can hold of it and sell the rest. I want to be able to have a piece of fried chicken every hour of the day if I want it, and eggs piled so high you can't have that for an excuse to not make me all the custard pie I can eat. I'm through with havin' such things only on a Sunday or when company comes, then endin' up with only one pizzlin' little slice for myself."

It became my settled habit to make three custard pies every other day and one or two big layer cakes each week. This baking came to be no more trouble to me than stirring up a mess of biscuits. And it was a source of amusement to me to watch Alex when a casual caller dropped in. He would invariably maneuver them toward the kitchen and feast them on pie or cake. This seemed to compensate him in some small way for some lack he needed to make up for in his boyhood.

"When it comes time to can, don't pay me any mind if I start gripin' about the amount of sugar you're usin'. Not a man in the countryside but lets out a howl about sugar while the cannin' goes on. Your job's to see that no fruits go to waste. Get plenty of stuff under seal to run us a year, and make sure you stay with me on it till I get you whatever you need for the job."

"I'll remember that," I warned.

April 21, 1917

It was after the first fried chicken dinner of the season that Alex looked around him as he left the dining room and made for the hammock. There he sprawled happily for his noon rest. "I declare to my soul, O Lady, it makes life a little more worth livin' when you can see what it is you're workin' for and enjoy it as you go along."

"Life's what you make it, so they say. But you've got to have something to make it out of. And if you can't find that something where you are, I'm strongly in favor of going where you can find it . . . and the sooner the better."

Alex looked lazily at me.

I rocked and thought back to what I had just said and sighed. "But even after you lay hands on something to make it out of, it looks like just making it is a full-time job. I'm weary to the bone."

I was thinking that now that I had the garden and chickens off my hands, it was time to go into the long hot weeks of canning.

"Well," said Alex, "a feller has to put in his time at somethin'. Might as well put it in tryin' to get what he wants. Otherwise he's like to put in more time cleanin' up messes he's made foolin' with somethin' he never actually wanted to do in the first place."

May 20, 1917

Alex was determined to have his own featherbed if he had to grow the feathers himself. But picking the ducks was a thing I really labored through, putting the snowy feathers and the down into clean feed sacks and hanging them on the rafters to cure. I had black-and-blue spots on my arms and thighs where the ducks nipped me, for I could not learn how to properly hold the plunging quacking things. How queer they looked, shriven of their only beauty, waddling morosely off to the pool after the plucking.

May 21, 1917

For the dining room, I had chosen oatmeal paper in a dusty rose, with a conventional border. I used a faded old Axminster rug that

Mama had left for the floor, turning the worn place into a back corner of the room. The old mahogany sideboard and serving table glowed softly in the new setting. I sighed as I polished vigorously at the cheap walnut chairs about the table. I could hide the table with a big cloth, but the chairs I could do nothing about, and I stood back and envisioned the high-backed handsome carved chairs that belonged with the sideboard as setting about my table in stately dignity. But my heart lifted as I hung the snowy curtains at the big double window in the north end of the room. In the south end, there was a single window and a glass-topped door leading into the long back porch.

The kitchen wall, which had been painted a dull gray, was now a glistening white. I made blue hairpin lace for the curtains and tiebacks. A great fireplace opened into the east wall, and I unpacked and polished Mama's old clock with the brass pendulum for the mantle and set it going. But I had nothing for each end of the mantle. Finally I laughed exultantly as I cleaned and covered with red enamel the tops from two fifty-pound lard cans. These could be used as serving trays, and they added a pleasing bit of color.

Today Alex had come in full of talk about an all-day singing next week. Was he going? No, he had far too much to do. Then I remembered. He had said the same thing about the box supper the week before, but at the last moment he had changed his mind and gone . . . after it was too late for me to do anything about it. He had said he wasn't going to the Association Meeting when it was held in Paragould in March too, but he had gone.

"Have you ever missed an all-day sing in your life, Alex?" I asked curiously.

"No, but there always has to be a first time, and I've got a notion this is going to be it." I smiled to myself, remembering the date and determining to be prepared for it this time.

"I want to have Lola and Phil out Sunday. We're having such good meals now, and we're not under quite as much strain as we were before we finished the house."

"You can ask them for this weekend. I'm goin' into town Saturday and could wait for them."

May 23, 1917

Washing was a task that was always hard for me. It wasn't only that I hated to do it, but the clothes never had that crisp, clean feel and look that some women knew how to impart, which didn't just mean that all the dirt had been washed out but that all suds had been rinsed out and the sun and wind had loved them dry. The sheets and work clothes were heavy and unwieldy to my hands, and I seemed never to be able to wring anything to where it wouldn't drip.

The Lancasters lived in the cottage across the road between our house and Pa's. Since an exchange had worked so well with Mrs. Thomas, I tried out sewing for washing on Cora Lancaster. To my surprise, she offered to do the washing for money, a thing I would never ask anybody again, charging me fifty cents a week and her dinner. Sometimes if Clayton was in the timber, she brought Tressie, who was eleven, to help her. If Clayton was in the fields, she left Tressie at home to fix her Pa his dinner.

"I wouldn't do this for another person I know," she told me earnestly, "but I like bein' in this purty house! 'Sides, it gives me money along to buy my quilt pieces. Comes fall I'll have a top ready. I'll take it in ta one of the merchants and give him a dollar or two for displayin' it and sell about fifteen dollars wuth of chances. Then he'll hold a drawin' and I git enough money all in one pile to git me or Tressie some clothes."

It was the same thing Burma had done. "I had a friend when I lived at Big Lake who used to do the same thing, Cora. She made such lovely quilt tops and always seemed to have a little money in her pocket. That's something I never have . . . money in my pocket."

Cora laughed. "With everthang a soul could want, what would a body want with money?" I felt suddenly ashamed. Compared to Cora I did indeed have everything.

When I talked with Selma, she was disgusted with me for managing somehow always to get out of doing my washing. "Is there a trick in it that you can't catch on to or jist that you hate to do it that bad?"

"It's a little of both I think, Selma. There's just so much of it in the summer and the weather so hot and the canning and all else. Cora has every line and the back fence full every week."

"That, I know, is not necessary! You got only one more to wash fer than I have and my wash is on the line and fergot about by nine o'clock. None of the rest of us have any sich wash as you do come summer. Neither do you have to keep yore best scarves done up and in use and white tablecloths and napkins fer ever' day. Comes the first of May and sich stuff as that is put away at my house till the big rush is over, unless I know company's comin' in time to get 'em out. An oilcloth goes on my table and oilcloth runners on the other furniture. You only got then to give 'em a quick wipe ever' day and use 'em right on. You're no better than the rest to do it, that I can see."

Never again did I bewail my big washing to anyone. Moreover, the next time Alex went to town I let him bring out an oilcloth for the breakfast table in the kitchen, as well as gay-printed runners for the dressers and washstand and tables. The dining table was seldom used except for the noon meal—and then just because of the heat in the kitchen.

May 26, 1917

I spent most of the day getting everything ready for Lola and Phil's visit. For the Saturday evening meal, I fixed fried chicken, squash casserole, and mashed potatoes with gravy. I would make fresh biscuits with honey and coffee for dessert.

Onnie, Arlien, and Alex had a good catch from their fishing trip to Spilling Brook on Friday, so I made most of my preparations for the Sunday meal as well. With the catch cleaned and well iced and fresh vegetables in, it would be a small matter to fry the fish, french-fry potatoes, and bake corn sticks. I would top the meal off with raisin cream pie and coffee.

Alex brought Phil and Lola out early Saturday evening. "Oh Flossie, your house is so sweet. You have such huge rooms and everything is so fresh!" Lola's praise was heartening to me.

"A house always seems so when it's freshly done over." I smiled happily.

"After a night in these big airy bedrooms, we'll feel like a couple of sardines packed in a can in our two-by-four," said Phil. "It reminds me of some of the hotel bedrooms I get on the road!"

"This house was built in the good old days. You can't even buy timbers like these now," said Alex proudly. "Had we been buildin' from the jump there wouldn't have been so much of the house, nor would it have been so nice."

"You'll have to get busy, Alex, and raise enough family to make use of all that upstairs."

"I'll have to get somebody else to mammy 'em, then. Flossie seems to think she's through," he said, half resentfully.

On that question, I was glad to keep still.

May 27, 1917

Sunday after we had demolished the fish dinner and the raisin cream pie, I got the pallet quilts from the hall closet and the sofa pillows and turned the babies over to Phil and Alex, sending them all to the shade under the great oaks on the front lawn, while Lola and I cleared the table.

By the time we got to the yard, the boys scarcely noticed our coming, so deep were they in a discussion of the latest developments on the various battlefronts. The war had occupied a small place in my thoughts heretofore, yet it seemed to me now that I had long been deliberately pushing the thought of it from me. The dread, now that I became fully conscious of it, seemed an old dread. It was as if it had always been with me.

I positively didn't want Alex to go to war. And Alex just as positively didn't want to go. On the other hand, Phil was on fire with the idea.

Lola sighed and threw up her hands helplessly. "Wherever you find Phil, there you find the European wars being fought all over again. Can't we have a little something else for a change?"

"There's one little feller they're goin' to have to get along without, unless they drag me in by force," said Alex. Phil looked at him with ill-concealed contempt. But Alex went on unperturbed. "War makes interesting history, but I never had any ambition to get in and fight me one, hand to hand."

"Alex, don't we have some early peaches in the orchard?" It was a ruse to change the subject, but it worked.

"You mean you don't even know what's on the place?" chirped Lola, taking her cue.

"If there's an early June peach on this farm, I'm going to have one," said Phil and was on his feet in a flash.

"Sure, I'd forgot. Aunt Roena ordered trees for this orchard at the same time and exactly like the ones Pa ordered for the Scoggings' farm," said Alex, "so of course we got ripe peaches."

And so the bad moment passed, and the rest of the day was spent in full enjoyment of their visit.

Chapter 21

June 1, 1917

Alex was one of the first to sow alfalfa at Main Shore. He had spread the seed in one of the upstairs rooms and inoculated it with great care, He was a proud and happy man when it came up to a good stand.

I rushed from house to garden to chickens to flowers in a long run, and paused to catch a whiff of heavenly bliss in the air one day and knew the grapes were blooming, Nothing had smelled so sweet since the spring lilacs faded.

Alex had raged when the marigolds bloomed. "They stink," he said resentfully, "worse than I ever thought a flower could stink."

I plucked a blossom and made him smell it. "It has a clean tangy fragrance," I argued, "and does not stink."

"Then it's the foliage! I hope you never plant the things again. I feel like pulling every one of them up by the roots."

Cerece trailed me all morning while her bathwater sunned. When I started to cook dinner, I stripped her and put her in the tub. She splashed and played happily till I heard Alex bring the mules in to feed, then I gave her a clean rub down and fresh clothing. I was so anxious for Alex to love her as he loved Buddy.

I had been promising Cerece a picnic, but still could find no time for it. When she got up from her nap, I packed her Easter basket with party sandwiches and cookies, tied on her little pink sunbonnet and sent her down to the orchard. How I longed to go with her, but there was no time. I stood at the gate and watched her bonnet bobbing happily along. She was singing tuneless ditties to the butterflies as she went. As I started back to the house I caught a June bug and went to the house for a string to tie to its long hind leg. I would surprise Cerece with it when she came back. I'd often tied them so as a child. But I'd forgotten how terrible they smelled. If my marigolds smelled half that rank to Alex, no wonder he wanted to yank them up by the roots. A pair of yellow butterflies caught my attention. They were doing a love dance with rhythmic grace, back and forth, kiss, back and forth kiss. They were making love! Well, what more lovely expression could love find than in two yellow butterflies kissing in midair on a drowsy summer afternoon?

June 5, 1917

We had become so submerged in the general upheaval that the specter of war had been relegated to the background of our thinking. Then Alex burst in on me one day, pale and shaken.

"We've got to register for the draft," he said through tight lips. "I knew it was coming to this the whole time. I could feel it."

"Well, surely you won't have to go now, Alex. By the time they get to farmers and the fathers of children, let us pray it will all be over."

He was dressing to make the trip in to register and gave his tie a vicious yank.

"I'll never volunteer. If they get me they've got to draft me. I don't care who hears me say it. I don't believe all the inhumane tales they're telling about the Germans. They're just tryin' to build our hate up to a fightin' pitch. I say the Germans are just like other people, under the thumb of their rulers, and would be glad of a chance to quit fightin' and stay home and mind their own business. We call ourselves civilized! Fight and kill, or get killed, and put a premium and a glory on it. We ain't no more civilized than the wildest heathens ever born, nor can we ever lay claim to being, till we've learned to settle things without fightin'. Who starts all these wars anyhow?"

He turned and glared wildly at me.

"Who profits by them?" I asked. "For God and for Country is all I ever hear that we fight for."

"For God and for Country, my appetite! We got a new one now, or hadn't you heard? The War to End Wars. The whole stinking business makes me retchin', pukin' sick."

FEATHERS IN A HIGH WIND

I went about my manifold duties under the shadow of impending disaster. Phil had been traveling for the wholesale company for some months, and Lola had been restless and too much alone. She called to say that she was taking the job as registration clerk.

"Alex is going in today with Onnie to register. They both got their notice in the mail. He's not happy about it. Tell me, Lola, does Phil still want to go?" I asked.

"Phil intends to go, Flossie. Nothing can change him or stop him now."

"How do you feel about it?"

"Exactly as you would feel in my place," she said, and then spoke cheerfully of other things. Lola had never been one to dwell on things that made her unhappy. She would lose herself in her work, trying not to think of something she could not change.

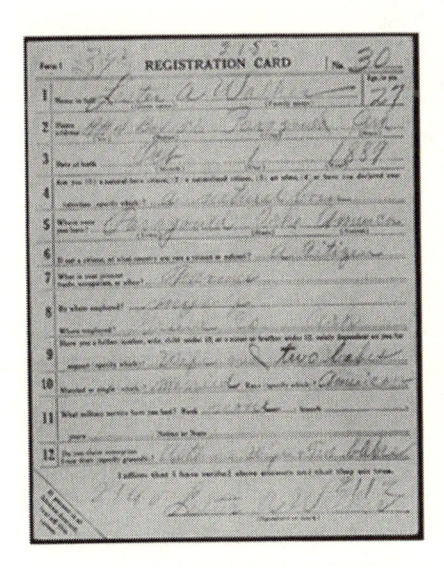

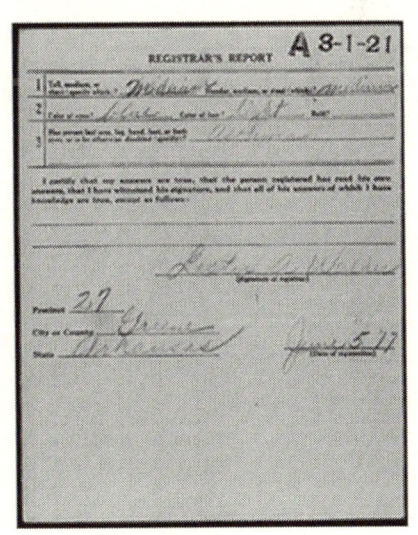

June 8, 1917

But by June over nine million had registered. When Alex read the figure he looked bleakly at me.

"Over nine million of 'em. All of 'em given a serial number like any other criminal, and none of 'em mean any more to the government now than a number. When they call your number, you go like sheep to the slaughter. Whatever else do mothers bear sons for, if not to make bigger and better armies?"

June 11, 1917

The canning came on with a big rush, and I held Alex's feet to the fire in the little matter of sugar and other supplies. By the greatest effort, I got what I needed, but usually after he had held back until I was ready to scream with frustration and the fruit and vegetables threatening to get too old.

But when he brought my new jars, I was beside myself with enthusiasm. I wouldn't have to fool with that canning contraption again. The jars were widemouthed self-sealing jars, and with them had come a mouthwatering book of instructions. Forthwith I went on a canning bender, getting under seal everything from corn on the cob and stewed tomatoes, to whole small spiced apples and stuffed cabbage.

I watched everything, snatching the produce when it was at its succulent best. Even Alex was jolted out of his seeming indifference by the sight of my pickling and preserving. Relishes of all kinds, tomato juice and grape juice as the season advanced, even pitted cherries and translucent gooseberries.

As I lined the jars up on the shelves I swelled with pride, so off looking for something else to put under seal I went.

June 17, 1917

I didn't go to Sunday school anymore and rarely to church. I was completely losing touch with the life of the community. I no longer wanted to go, but when I came face-to-face with it, I was troubled. Living in a community and not being a part of it wasn't right and I knew it.

Alex did nothing to encourage me to go, it's true. He always told me he wasn't going to go to love feasts, all day sings and fishing trips, but when the time came, and it was too late for me to do anything about it, he invariably dashed in from whatever he was doing and caught a ride to the scene of activity, leaving me alone with the babies and all else.

I was in the garden at work when the crowd began to go by. Suddenly my attention was caught by the slamming of a door, and Alex burst from the house and jumped into the surrey with Arlien and Selma. He had said he wasn't going, yet there he was, laughing and throwing kisses to me as the others waved.

As I stood lost in thought, my feelings weren't helped any by the sight of Susie Maynard sailing past, decked out in pale yellow organdy dress and a yellow organdy hat. Would Alex and Susie stand singing from the same book, as they sometimes had? No doubt.

It now appeared to me that Alex didn't want his wife and children along. That roughed me. Everybody would be there of course, everybody but me and my babies. I'd be at home where Alex had decided we belonged. I resolved then and there that on the next big occasion I wouldn't even ask Alex if he planned to go. I'd fix my dinner and hide it, have the children's clothes and mine ready to hop into, and when he started dressing, I would too. He could just hitch up and take us with him as a family man should . . . the very idea!

For one thing, I thought, turning my full attention to my thinking, Pa's mantle would one day fall on Alex's shoulders. Say what you would about Ma, one thing was certain. She did all that lay in her power to fill her place as Henry Walker's wife, leading light of the community. I'd do well to pattern that much of my life after her at least.

When the crowd came surging back by, I sat in the shade on the front lawn with my mending, the children playing on a pallet at my feet.

Selma called out, "I wish I'd had sense enough to stay home. I'm tired as a dog."

I knew that she must envy me my leisurely day. Not that it had been leisurely, for heaven's sake, but it must seem so from where she sat.

"You know, I'm worried sick about the way Pa acts," said Alex, sinking wearily to the grass at my feet. He had sung until his voice sounded thin.

"What's wrong with Pa now?"

"The same old thing, only more of it. He looks as fuzzed up as a broody hen, and you can see unpleasant things playing tag in his mind. I doubt he ever has a pleasant thought anymore."

I sighed. "What a pity, Alex. Do you suppose he could have some trouble on his mind that we don't know about?"

"I can't believe it. He's always been full of goodwill at a singing, giving everybody the glad hand and the good word all day long. Today he drooped like a chicken with the cholera, kept to his Amen Corner, looking neither to the left or the right."

I tried to recall when I had last seen Pa. "Did you know that I haven't seen Pa except in passing since the day we went after the scaffold at the old house? Alex, you know that's not right. Isn't there any way we can get us all together again?"

"I don't know how you'd go about it. Pa is going around with his stinger out all the time. I don't think he's riding the farms now. I keep seeing the tenants go in and out of there in a way they never did before."

"Did you mean all along to go to the sing today?" I asked abruptly.

He grinned a bit sheepishly.

"Was that what made you duck into the house and dress when you caught me out of it, so I wouldn't have time to dress or try to stop you?"

He cleared his throat, for all the world like Pa when he was displeased. "I just changed my mind. I've often heard that a wise man will do that sometimes, though a fool never does. I'll bet I was more surprised than anybody else to see me there."

He was trying to be funny now, so I let the matter rest.

July 6, 1917

The wheat threshing came and went like a whirlwind. I was caught up in it and at times felt as I did when I was going through the figures of the square dance, being tossed about from one to the other.

I had the big house now, so Ann and Mattie came to help me cook for the hands each day. This was a welcome change to me, and I thoroughly enjoyed every minute of the hustling days.

"Aunt Roena is having a love feast next week," said Mattie.

"Maud's coming from Texas," added Ann. Walter and his girls from Tennessee and Graham from Mississippi, and of course, Martha and John from St Francis, and with all the family that's here, it should be quite a gathering. The first time this much family's been together in seven years."

Alex hadn't told me and he must know it. They would have the love feast under the Elm trees.

Later when I asked Alex if he was going, he said he couldn't make it, he had to go to Brookland that day. But I knew he would go, though I refrained from making an issue of it at the moment. I made up my mind to come up with some way to let him know that I knew what he was doing. But I didn't want to raise a ruckus about it.

July 13, 1917

When the day of the love feast rolled round, though Alex went to Brookland as planned, he nevertheless ended up at the feast, making merry with the rest, but looking very ill at ease when he returned home.

"I'm having an ice cream party here for Aunt Roena tomorrow night," I told Alex, making no to-do over the fact that he'd tricked me again. "I'd think she and the children would like a chance to come for an evening's frolic in their old back yard."

July 14, 1917

The crowd began to gather the next evening as the sun went down. I'd borrowed all the lanterns around and hung them in the lower branches of the big blackgum tree. Alex had moved the wash bench up to hold the freezers of cream, and my work table, covered with a snowy cloth, held all kinds of homemade cakes. The children rolled and tumbled in the sweet grass, except for Sylvester, Belle's little boy. In a white linen suit he stood by Belle's knee, looking on, saying nothing, taking no part. Such a serious child.

We took Aunt Roena through the house and she shook her head at some of the changes we had made. "This light wallpaper, now, I'd never have thought I could have such light paper with all my young'ns to mess it up, but it does make the rooms seem big and airy." She paused at the foot of the stairs.

"No need climbing up there, Aunt Roena, we just use those rooms for plunder," said Alex.

When we got to the back step she made the long step down. When she was safely on the ground she turned on Alex. "You married a smart good girl, Alex. Do you love her?"

"Sure, or I wouldn't have married her," Alex said quickly.

"Then build her a decent step there. You'll have her longer and with less doctor bills. Dragging in and out of there's enough to pull her little insides out. Let me see you step up there?"

Alex seldom used the step on this side of the house, the lot being on the other side. He had to catch the post to pull up. "But that step's not my doings, Aunt Roena," he protested. "Santos put that block of wood there."

"Well, Santos was a poor renter and he had poor ways. Shadowlawn is yours now. You are a land owner, a home owner, with a family to cherish and care for. These are little things to you maybe, but not to the weaker vessel. When are you going to fix it?"

"When I get time." He grinned and started backing away.

She hauled him right back to her. "When are you going to fix it?" she repeated in level voice.

"First thing in the morning, I swear it. Now can I go?" he asked. Aunt Roena gave him a fond pat, linked her arm in mine and we joined the others.

Ma was being very pensive and quiet, a new role for her, always in the middle of things. This time she sat back and waited to be served like a guest. Pa, his chair tilted to its hind legs, sat morosely looking on, I started dishing up the ice cream, putting others to slicing cake and lining up dishes.

As Aunt Roena joined Pa, he said in a querulous voice, "Your children don't need you any more, Roena, nor do mine need me."

"Thank God for that!" said Aunt Roena fervently. "I'd hate to think my children had reached the age they have and still didn't have enough gumption to stand on their own feet and keep off mine. Nothing pleasures me more than to see mine doing well in their own right. I'll soon have Bula married off and I can spend the rest of my day's loving my grandchildren."

"Well, mine's been a awful disappointment ta me somehow, Roena. I feel like they got no use fer me whatsoever, now that they don't need me no more."

"Henry, maybe I shouldn't say this, but no child, even your own, is goin' to love you because he should do it. You got to make 'em feel welcome and happy when they come near you. Jumpin' on 'em with all four feet, like I been seein' you do this past year or two, ain't goin' to bring you what you're pinin' for, now nor ever."

Pa sighed. "Young people got no respect for their elders any more. Look how yores talks to you."

"As free as they talk to each other," snapped Aunt Roena, "which ain't no set back to me, Henry, but a pleasure. They ain't under any strain when I'm around. And if I get off the track, and we're all likely to do that time and again, my own young'ns is the first to tell me of it, God bless 'em, and that without malicious intent, and never do I take it so."

"Well, I don't want mine talkin' to me like that. It riles me plenty."

"Like it or not, they'll treat you as they get treated. You could get pleasure out of your children if you didn't stay drawed up in a knot inside like you do and your face lookin' like you'd et a green persimmon. Don't you ever laugh anymore?"

"I'm gettin' old, Roena, can't you realize it?"

"Sure, we're all gettin' older every day we live, but why let that spoil your whole life. But I don't think that's all. I think you're sick and too stubborn to see a doctor."

As we were getting into bed I told Alex, "I know what's the matter with Pa. He's lonesome, plain heartsick lonesome, and too stubborn to do anything about it. He wants his children around him, Alex.

I told him what I had overheard, shamelessly listening. "Isn't there anything we can do about it?"

"I don't know how we'd go about it. He didn't even step one foot inside our house today. He and Ma's not invited a soul to see them since they got the new house that I know of, only to take the preacher, when it comes their turn. Acts like he hates me and mine in his sight. Far as I can tell he feels the same way about Onnie and the rest."

"Maybe it's Ma that doesn't want anybody in. Ann says she stands with a polishing cloth in her hand when anybody goes in, wiping fingerprints as they go. For that reason I don't feel like I should go in there with the children, but surely you can go."

"Ma ain't got no call to act so about that spittin' little furniture. People have had furniture before her, and a few may have after she's gone. Don't know what gets into Ma sometimes. Well, I tried everything with Pa I know, nothing works. Ask him how he's feeling and he gets the idea you're wonderin' how much longer he can hold on and keep you from takin' over. Ask if he wants you to look after something, and he says he's looked after it long before your time and can still make out. It's a mess, and for my own part, I'm sick of trying."

I had a bright idea. "I tell you what, Alex. Offer to take Pa to the fair next week. Maybe he wants you to drive him places." I swallowed hard, hating to get that started again, but I was desperate. Something had to be done about Pa.

July 20, 1917

None were more surprised than I when, on returning from the fair, the car stopped in front of the house and Pa and Ma got out and came in with Alex. So that *had* been the right thing to do. I hurried to the kitchen, snatched a tray from the shelf, cracked some ice for the pitcher and filled it with sweetened grape juice, added glasses to the tray, and met them in the dining room.

"Come right in and set your selves down," I said gaily, pulling out chairs for them, trying not to appear flustered. "What a hot dusty day you all must have had at the fair."

Most of my summer flowers were gone, but I had filled a blue bowl with marigolds for the center of the table.

Pa's eyes were taking in everything. Ma was sitting patient and aloof. "Quite a tray you got there, Flossie. Ain't that made from a lard can lid?"

"Yes, it is."

He sipped his juice slowly, eyes listening intently, and then swallowed it in long cool draughts, smacking his lips in appreciation. The late afternoon sun slanted in across the sideboard and he got up for a closer look at my canned foods. He gave a long whistle. "If you'd been there with a passel of this stuff today, you'd a toted home all the blue ribbons. It shore shows out in them glass jars." He smoothed his stubby mustache and passed his glass for a refill.

"Yes, you should a went with us, Flossie," said Ma sweetly.

I would have been glad to go, but nobody had asked me. Alex had never taken me to the fair, and I was surprised to find that it no longer mattered to me. Perhaps you could only want a thing so long, then, if you didn't get it you switched your longing to something else.

"You never canned as much stuff as this in yore whole life, Annie." Pa turned to Ma.

Pride alone had caused me to make this display of my handiwork, and I felt suddenly ashamed, and so mad at Pa I could have choked him. Me trying so hard and him now saying the very thing that would set Ma against me forever.

"Pa's in such a flattering mood, he must be feeling better." I laughed nervously, trying to include Ma.

"Flatterin' to who?" she asked coldly. But Pa had turned to Alex, seemingly unaware of the havoc wrought.

"Now that we're in the house I'd like to go all over it," he said. "Don't you want to make the rounds with us, Annie?"

"I've seen this house enough times in my life, Henry, and lived in one jist like it, except that I did have an extry bedroom downstairs, so's I could have the front room fer a parlor," she added spitefully.

When Pa came back he stood looking at me, his eyes kind. "Yore a putty smart gurl, Flossie. Alex ought ta feel proud of you. And I reckon he does."

Alex gulped. I gulped.

This we had not hoped for, but Ma rose from the table and walked straight to the car in a stiff-legged silence. This visit had been no help at all with her.

July 27, 1917

Alex had got the habit of taking Cerece to school with him on Fridays. He always had her to break the ice for the others by opening the program that marked the last afternoon of school each week. He spent much time coaching her and she took a delight in pleasing him. I was astonished when he asked me to come for the program. I went.

Came time to begin the program and he called on Cerece for a recitation. A lump came in my throat, for without the slightest hesitation, she went to the rostrum, made her little bow, and sang in a high clear voice:

Sojer boy, Sojer boy, where are you going
So ferry proud in your red white and blue?
I go where my country and duty is calling
If you'll be a Sojer boy, then you may come too.

Everything was about the war now, I thought sadly. Even the school programs were planned around it, and *they* were beginning to siphon off the youth of the land, even the farm youth.

When the clapping continued, Cerece went back, bowed gravely and sang seriously:

I went down to the turkey pen
I dot down on by dnees
I like alaff myself adeff
To see the turkey steeze

This put everyone in a laughing mood, and the program went through in fine shape. Just before it was finished, there was a big stir at the back and Alex brought forward a newcomer.

"This is Mr. Brinson, children, parents, Flossie. I have a happy surprise for all of you. He has come to take our picture, so all pass quietly outside and wait for us."

So, this was why Alex wanted me to come to Eight Mile School. But Buddy acted like a wiggle worm, and Alex had to give him his watch to concentrate on before he would settle.

But my heart was singing. Alex had wanted me and both children in the picture with him.

Chapter 22

July 28, 1917

I woke up with the feeling that the phone had been ringing for hours. Alex scrambled up and flew to the kitchen and I followed.

"When did it start? You mean . . . Yes, I understand. I'm coming right on."

I'd gotten up and lit the lamp and Alex was hurrying into his clothes. "It's Silas. He's out of his mind. Belle called Pa and told us all to get there quick."

"What will you do?"

"Whatever we have to," he said grimly. "If we can't get him quiet, then we'll have to take him to the asylum in Little Rock."

"He hasn't seemed right to me since the mule kicked him," I mused.

"No, and teachin' that flock of young Hessians and trying to run a farm at the same time is enough to run a well man crazy . . . I ought to know."

After he'd gone I stood hesitating for a moment, then I called Ma. I could tell she'd been crying.

"He was reading his Bible, Flossie, preparing his Sunday school lesson like always. He got down to pray as usual, prayed for an hour, sung his sef hoarse and then started all over prayin' again. When Belle couldn't stand it any longer she slipped to the other room and called Henry. Belle said that Silas was getting ready to go over and tell Ned Grambling about Jesus. He didn't believe that Ned knew that Jesus died for him. I tell you, Flossie, there's just no telling . . . ." Ma's voice choked into a smothered sob.

"I can't think of a thing we can do now, Ma, so let's get back in bed and pray that it's not as bad as it sounds."

At least she had answered me decently for once.

Next morning they drove by on their way to Little Rock. Alex, wan and haggard, staggered in to change clothes.

"Don't go where the poor fellow can see you, Flossie. It'll just start him all over again and he's exhausted as it is. We got his feet tied together, and his hands, and Sherman on one side of him and Pa on the other in the back seat. There's no doing anything with him."

"Did you have a doctor?"

"Yes, but eyen a hypo hasn't downed him yet, though he's not quite as violent. Doctor says he thinks it's a temporary thing, but we'd better get him where they know how to judge and handle such cases."

I followed Alex into the porch, forgetting what he had said about not letting Silas see me. When he saw me he surged forward, his bloodshot eyes beseeching.

"Oh Flossie, I want to tell you about my blessed Savior. Oh, how I love His precious name. Oh, let me praise Him."

But Alex had shoved me roughly back indoors, with muttered imprecations. I leaned against the wall and wept for pity, chastened by the unearthly light that shone on a ravaged countenance, and the memory of a pair of bound hands extended pleadingly toward me.

August 25, 1917

It was about three weeks later that Pa announced, without preamble, that he and Ma were going to Hot Springs.

"The baths helped me once, maybe they will again," he said, and there was a sudden flurry of preparation. Poor stubborn Pa, he had not yet seen a doctor.

Alex drove them to the station on Tuesday morning. On Saturday Aunt Rhea called for them to come get Pa, put him to bed, and call a doctor. He had made it back to Paragould and was at her house. Ann called me and she and Mattie and I aired the little house and cooked dinner for all. I ran over the furniture with polish just before Ma came in, erasing the last fingerprint, and took Buddy in my arms.

Pa looked ghastly. "I just don't know what the matter was that I couldn't take the baths this time. Before when I took them I felt weak, but at least relaxed. This time every time I took one I went into a rigor and turned deathly sick to me stummick."

Without a word, Onnie walked resolutely to the phone and called Dr. Benson. Pa started to rage, but with every eye on him and every hand against him, thought better of it and submitted to being put to bed.

The doctor was a long time in the room before coming to the kitchen, where all but Ma awaited him. He looked grave as he wrote two prescriptions. "I might have helped Henry ten years ago, or even five," he said. "But there's nothing I can do now but try to make him comfortable while the thing runs its course. He's in the last stages of Bright's disease. I don't see how he has kept going."

To everyone's surprise, Pa was up and around in a few days, although he said his heart felt "mighty uncomftable" and was given to "having the flutters these days."

August 31, 1917

The harvest was in full swing. Alex came in one day and I saw he was troubled, eating hardly anything.

"What's wrong with you?" I asked.

"Pa's wrong with me, and something's mighty wrong with Pa. He has ordered me to cut and burn the new orchard."

"But he's been so proud of that orchard."

"So I told him, but he said he wouldn't be needin' an orchard where he's going."

Alex rocked his chair to its back legs and sat precariously teetering in the way I found so irritating, but I had not the heart to scold him now.

"I reminded him that he had called that orchard a perfect work. I said all I knew to say. He stuck with it. Wants that orchard cut and burned before he leaves here, the sooner the better."

"Are you going to do it?"

"I am not. But he was in no mood to hear it, so's I just put him off till I had more time, and I'll never have time for that."

October 26, 1917

We had butchered on the first cold, being low on meat. Alex had twenty hogs for market, with enough for our own meat and lard, and still the sows left for breeding, and six fine pigs for next year's meat supply.

We could no longer dodge the fact that there was a war on, even here at Shadowlawn. There was no transient labor coming in to harvest, and there were only two Negroes in the whole county, one a hotel porter and the other a bootblack in Paragould. I had been trying to pick cotton, but had been very little help at it while doing myself much harm.

"Things going to really bust here one of these days and the whole world's going to be in it, the way they keep sinkin' our ships," said Onnie, tying on an apron as he got ready to help Alex make sausage. "Not but one good thing this war's done, that I can see, and that's that it has got us all pulling together again. I like harvestin' as we're doing, drawing straws and goin' from field to field. We could do that every year and save ourselves labor costs if we would do it."

"Shut up about the war, will you! I never want to hear it mentioned again," snapped Alex, setting up the sausage mill.

Sherman came in with a number one washtub of meat ready for the grinder and slid it from his shoulder to the table. "I'm with you on that, Alex," he said. "Bible says, love one another. That's the way I been raised and the way I try to live. I'll take no part in large scale murder, and that's all I can make out of war, and they can lock me up someplace till I rot, but no man's blood is ever going to be on my hands. It's the devil's business and I want no part of it!"

"A lot you'll have to say about it when they get ready fer you, they'll jist come get you," said Onnie, gathering up a handful of meat and feeding it into the grinder as Alex turned.

"Pa's give us fair warnin'. Said a wholesaler told him that there'll be rationin' on in another month. It'll come first on tea and coffee, sugar and spices, rice and flour, so your blood be on your own hand if a month from now finds you without a supply of these things," said Alex.

"If only it would rain," said Onnie. "We need to get the oat field seeded. It'll soon be too late."

"Busy as we've been I'd like to know when we'd of sowed it, had the weather been ever so nice," said Sherman.

I went to the back porch for water and looked up to see billows of smoke coming from Pa's. "Pa's house is on fire again!" I screamed running back to the kitchen.

The boys threw everything down and began tearing off their aprons and wiping their hands as they ran. I couldn't leave the children, so stood watching from the back porch.

"It wasn't the house," Alex said. "It was the orchard."

He didn't have to tell me that Pa had found somebody to cut and burn it for him.

"Cool as a cucumber," said Alex, when I asked him how Pa had seemed. "Looked happier than I've seen him for many a day. He got Cleve Corley and his son to do it for thirty dollars. I'd have paid them a hundred not to, if it was money they wanted. When I got to Pa he told me he guessed I could see that he still had a few friends, and that he didn't have to depend on me for the few things he yet wanted done."

"Alex, Pa has lost his bearings. No man in his right mind would have done such a thing. Did the doctor tell you his mind would be affected by this illness?"

"Only that we might find him full of funny notions. This one ain't so funny to me."

December 24, 1917

Alex and I had both worked feverishly toward Christmas. Looking back over our brief married life it hurt to find that something had happened to every Christmas. This was the first time we'd got ourselves assembled and in our right minds in our own home. We both wanted it to be a time that we could long cherish and remember. Our first real

Christmas, and if the war kept up and Alex had to go, it might well be our last.

How good the house smelled. He had found a strange little cedar studded with bright blue berries for the Christmas tree. The hall and dining room were decorated with boughs of holly and pine. He had risked his neck for a bunch of mistletoe to hang under the swinging lamp in our bedroom. And it was there that we set up the tree, the weather being too bleak and cold for us to try to keep fires in the whole house.

I had baked a White Mountain coconut cake, my favorite, a hickory nut cake for Alex, and pumpkin and mince pies. We decorated the Christmas tree on Christmas Eve, letting the little ones help. This is no fool's paradise I'm living in now, I told myself. This is real happiness. What Papa would call "paradise boiled down."

We piled the packages that had come by mail, still unopened, beneath the tree together with our own gifts for each other, and then hung our stockings along the kitchen mantel.

December 25, 1917

The wished-for snow fell thick and fast during the night, and the next morning the air seemed to be filled with flying white feathers of snow flurries. Alex slipped out to the kitchen and made fires, sneaking back to bed until the children stirred. When Cerece sat up in bed and blinked he nudged me.

"Did Sandy Claws comed?" she asked.

"I'll go see," said Alex, and bounded out of bed. He came tearing back with a red and white celluloid flutter mill held aloft, looking back every step to see it whirl. Cerece squealed with delight. Buddy sat up in his bed, and Alex and I hustled them to the warm kitchen to watch them empty their stockings.

I'd got what I wanted in my stocking: the world's best rotary egg beater, and my favorite candy, fruit and nuts.

While I fixed breakfast and the children played, Alex warmed the bedroom and later we had the presents from under the tree.

"Wish we still lived in a pizzlin' little town, O Lady?" asked Alex, slipping into the maroon turtle necked sweater I'd got for him, "Or are you gettin' satisfied with being established in the country."

"Being established in the country is not bad"—I laughed—"or even trying to get established. It was marking time as a renter that I most objected to. If I've got to be poor folks all my life, then let me be poor folks in town. At least there's an end to the work hours and a free evening to look forward to."

"And if I got to be poor folks all my life, then let me hide in the country to be it. Not right out where everybody can look on whilst I suffer."

We were having a young blizzard, but Alex had worked like a trouper getting the stock housed against such a possibility. When he went to feed, Onnie called across through the snow and asked him to bring Cerece over to see what Santa had brought. To my surprise he bundled her up and took her. An ache, which had long been in my heart, had now subsided forever. Alex loved our little girl now as much as he loved his boy, and she repaid his small attentions with ardent adoration.

I was just tucking Buddy in for his nap when Alex returned. I made a sound to silence him and he stopped in his tracks. When I turned away from the baby's bed, he said, "Cerece stayed to play some with Lester. I'm standin' right under the mistletoe. Ain't you goin' to come and kiss me?"

I gave him a bear hug and he caught me roughly to him, kissing me in a high rapture. "Why, Alex, what do you mean?" I whispered. "I can't go back to bed now, and look what you're doing to me! I have . . . Alex, the goose . . . I need . . . ."

"Yeah, we both need," he chuckled, and gathered me into his arms and tossed me on the bed. "Merry Christmas, O Lady," he murmured, laying his top coat aside.

A moment later I whispered against his lips, "And a Merry Christmas to you, Sun."

And a Merry Christmas it was.

Chapter 23

January 3, 1918

Suddenly our little world lay stripped and dormant in the chill arms of winter. We had done all in our power to block the thought of the war and the consequences of it from our minds for Christmas holidays. But the weight of too much sorrow and responsibility kept our spirits from rising to the high point we would have expected, though we went through all of our small observances of the day and the children knew no lack. For my own part, I found that my mind was much too preoccupied with the business of living, human relations, and the problems that daily confronted me to be able to joyously let go of it all even for a few days. Alex seemed to share my preoccupation, doing all that he did because it was time to do these things, but showing no great enthusiasm with the doing at any time. He seemed relieved to be able to be up and doing again at the New Year and opened Eight Mile School again on schedule with an eagerness he'd never shown for that dreaded undertaking. Alex had girded his loins as for battle. Being shut indoors was not so hard on him in the winter as in summer, but he still didn't like it.

Miss Pert wasn't due to drop her calf until March, a month earlier this year. I had just turned her dry, so we were getting milk and butter from Ann.

"Thought I had it fixed so's we never have to be without milk and butter again," grumbled Alex, irked because of this added expense.

"For heaven's sake don't fuss," I begged. "I'm having the first real rest I've had in ages, and I need it for the summer that's ahead of me. It'll be six more glorious weeks before I have to start milking and churning again. It's heavenly. No chickens, no garden, no canning."

I had found two twenty dollar bills in his collar box while putting away his clean clothes. I knew he had the money and thought it would be a good time to put in for some fabric and patterns.

"Maybe I can get some sewing done. How about giving me ten dollars for materials?"

"Not ten cents. I'm fixing to try to save something this year if it takes the hide off. Bought them grade heifers in the fall and I want to get somebody to go in with me and buy a registered bull, time they're ready to be bred. I want to build up my range cattle to where they'll bring me in a nice round sum every year. I'm ashamed to put my mark on some of that stuff that belongs to me."

"Alex, I need ten dollars," I insisted.

"I want you to shut up about money. Been trying to get a bunch of these yokels to help me put up a fight for a hard road. Need one from Paragould to Lake City, and if they put it in, it will run by our farm. Think what it would save in wear and tear and time, but all some of 'em can see is the added taxes, not stopping to consider how it will up the value of their property."

"Alex, quit trying to sidetrack me. Do I get the money?"

"No, and I don't know how to say it any plainer."

After he had gone I tried to reason with myself, but it was no use. My heart swelled with rebellion. His sheds were full of whatever he needed in the way of farm machinery. He'd save something, even if it took the hide off, but whose hide was it? None of his own, that was certain.

Other women throughout the countryside were busy with plain and fancy sewing. It was the only time any of us had for it. There was more money in our household than most. But none of it was ever available to me. Didn't Alex see that I worked hard to help him make what we had? Then why couldn't I also be a partner in the spending?

January 19, 1918

When the next big snow fell, Alex came in in high spirits. He and the other boys had rigged up one of the big farm sleds for a sleigh ride, not bothering Pa to lend his precious sleigh for the occasion. Two long benches from the church had been set inside the high sideboards they'd nailed on, and the bottom of the sled covered with hay. We got into our heaviest wraps and heated bricks and covered our laps with heavy quilts. We piled the children in the hay and went from house to house picking up the ones that were going. Two teams of mules had been hooked to the sled to pull the load, all of them with strings of sleigh bells in their harness.

We tore around the country roads at a great rate, and down every side road, being the first to make tracks in the new snow. We sang until our throats were raw from the cold wind, waving and calling out to wistful faces pressed against the window panes of every house along the way. It was such a joyous experience that I wished the whole world could have shared it with us.

January 22, 1918

I had the shock of my life one evening when Alex came in and said he'd be danged if he didn't believe he was getting to where he liked to keep school. I flung out my hands and rolled my eyes heavenward. "And what hath wrought this great change, Sir Lancelot?" I asked.

"Why, some of them kids are intelligent. You'd be surprised. I never saw 'em buckle into their books like they're doing this winter. It gives me a lot better heart to teach."

"Maybe it's the other way round. You teach with a high heart, and it inspires them to study harder."

February 4, 1918

I looked at Alex speculatively. It had been a month since I'd found the two twenty dollar bills in his collar box. I'd said nothing to him about them, thinking he had set them aside for a certain purpose. Two weeks later, when I went to put his clean collars away the money was still there. I'd taken it and tucked it into my machine drawer. Now two more weeks had gone by, and the money remained uncalled for. I got out the mail order catalog and made out an order. I felt rich beyond the telling with forty dollars to spend. It was four times what I'd been willing to make out with.

February 10, 1918

My order came and I saved it till Alex came in to open it, then invited him to share that pleasure with me. "Where'd you get the money for all this?" he scowled. "You promised me you wouldn't borrow any more from your Papa."

"You mean you don't remember giving me forty dollars?" I opened my eyes wide in fake astonishment.

"I distinctly remember telling you more than once that you could not have ten dol . . . Hey . . . how much did you say?" he croaked, and I had to laugh.

"Forty dollars, Sun." I was enjoying myself hugely. "I want you to go through these packages with me and see if you could have gotten more for the money, or if you think I wasted any of it."

I could have shouted when I opened the first package and found it to be the warm robe I had ordered for Alex. For a moment he hung back, trying still to be angry, but I shoved him in front of the mirror and settled the comforting warmth of the robe around his shoulder tying the silk cord around his waist. The gray and burgundy stripe was vastly becoming, and he stood a long moment admiring himself. "No wonder you fell in love with me." He swaggered about, letting his hands stray over the soft thickness of the material. "You know, I been needin' one of these warm robes. About freeze my tail off making the fires these cold mornings."

"Then you're not mad at me?"

"To tell you the truth, I've never been so relieved. I've put in forty hours and wore out three pencils in the last few weeks tryin' to figure what could have become of that forty dollars. I'm glad it went for some good instead of being lost, which I'd finally decided was what had happened to it."

To my surprise he leaned over and kissed me, of his own free will and accord.

February 11, 1918

The Irish potatoes had been planted and the onions set in the dark of the moon in February. We culled the chickens, taking all to market except a hundred laying hens. Alex took part of the proceeds and bought two fine registered roosters from the Leggett pens, the other side of Paragould, and started saving eggs for the incubator.

February 20, 1918

Alex failed to come in from school and I had begun to feel uneasy when I heard a step in the porch. But it was Sherman, looking very grave. "Alex toll me to do the night work and fetch you. The old man's took his bed, I guess for the last time. I'll tote Buddy down for you, Flossie."

"But the children will worry Ma to death, putting their hands on things."

"Aunt Annie's not the one to be considered now. Uncle Henry's callin' for you and the babies. He wants us all with him now. I'm afraid Aunt Annie will have to bear up under the strain as best she can."

When we entered the room, Pa was tossing and turning. "Won't nobody go get Flossie and them babies?" he moaned. I pushed Cerece gently toward the bedside, still in her wraps. "Tell him you're here," I whispered.

But he saw me and motioned me to him. I took Buddy in my arms and knelt at the bedside. He laid his hand as in a blessing on Buddy's head and tears flooded his eyes. Then he took Cerece's little hand in his and I thought he was praying, his lips moving, but I could hear no words.

Presently he said, "Granpa's sick, leetle gurl, leetle boy," and I choked back the sob that rose in my throat.

Poor, lonely, stubborn old man. These little ones had hardly known they had a grandfather, yet I knew his loneliness need never have been. All of us would have loved him if he had let us. His eyes traveled around the circle. I had been the last to be sent for.

"All together now where ye belong, one more time. All but poor old Silas. Does Silas know I'm sick?"

"You jist got sick today, Pa," said Belle. "I'll write Silas about it tamorree, and he'll come if they'll let him."

"I been sick many the long day, Belle, and well you know it," Pa said sadly.

He'd had a hypodermic and little by little quieted down. One by one we tiptoed from the room and gathered in the kitchen to decide what to do. It was Mattie who settled matters.

She turned to Belle and said, "You and Ann get supper fer the boys. Flossie and me is going to take these young'ns across ta my house and feed and bed 'em down. We can get here in a matter a minutes if Uncle Henry wants any of us, and it's not to be thought of that we try to keep this many little uns satisfied and happy in sich close quarters."

February 25, 1918

I wondered if Alex would remember to turn the eggs and fill the lamp in the incubator, but this was no time to worry about that. In the next few days we did nothing but stand ready for action when Pa expressed his next wish. Word of his illness spread and kin came in from the hills and from the bottoms. Each turn for the worse was ground never recovered. Then he began fretting about making a will.

"Sedley Carter been trying to git me to make a will fer years, but I ain't done it. Get him out here quick. I want to get things settled so's I can git me some rest."

February 26, 1918

After the will was made, leaving Alex one dollar, a small farm each to the other children, and all else to Ma during her lifetime, Pa was even more restless than ever. In fitful doses that he drifted into from time to time, he murmured, and fussed and fumed until, bad roads and weather notwithstanding, there was naught to do but make another trip in and bring Sedley Carter back to do the job all over again.

This time Pa left Belle, she being considered the baby of the family, the home place, but Ma was to retain a lifetime dowry in it. It was his expressed hope that Belle would come back home, and Ma could live on there in the same house with her, and not be left alone in her old age. And this time Pa left Alex two thousand dollars to finish paying out his own farm in the clear, seeing that he had left everyone else provided for. For the first time in many days and nights, he rested.

February 28, 1918

Alex had suspended school, as Pa continued to grow worse, and then he closed it altogether. It was Alex who assumed responsibility for keeping the chart, faithfully setting down any changes and giving medicine on the minute.

Pa gradually came to believe that Alex was poisoning him. "The law can't touch Alex," he fretted, "but I can tell by the taste a that stuff he gives me that it's pure pizen. But Alex has got witnesses ta prove he closed school and watched at my bedside day and night. He's been given ta steppin' out a line fer some time now. I don't believe Onnie would be in on this scheme ta do away wit me. That's it. I want this here thang changed up. Onnie will give me my medercine fom now on."

Pa was being given hypodermics regularly. It was the only way he could get any rest, or Ma, for that matter, for she refused to lie down as long as he was conscious. Always a light sleeper, she seemed scarcely to doze now before she was on her feet again, her great mournful eyes ringed with violet circles.

She'd had the boys take out the rug in Pa's room and beat it. When they brought it back in, she had them lay it with the nap to the floor, thinking Pa too far gone to notice. But he did notice and went into a rage. "Turn that rug, so's I can enjoy its softness when I get up to the slop jar, and so's I can see its gay colors. I got it cause I liked it, and you, Annie, are tryin' ta save it fer yore sef after I'm gone."

She let the boys turn it right side up, but the first day he was partially unconscious she had them roll it and store it, putting a large gay scatter rug at the bedside.

"I can't stand all these people trackin' in on that pretty rug," she wept." Got foot wipers out there, but nobody seems to know what they're fer. Henry bought the things him and me liked, and I ain't aimin' fer 'em ta be ruined in this few days. I'm aimin' ta take good keer of 'em the longest day I live."

March 5, 1918

Having settled his earthly affairs, it seemed that Pa was now giving himself over to the business of dying. He thought and cared less and less about what went on around him, drifted in and out of consciousness with no show of petulance or resentment. He had stopped looking backward, indeed seemed scarcely aware of the present in his few lucid moments. He was finished with life on this earth, and on that last day it was evident that his attention was fixed on a Far Country where our earthly vision could not follow him.

In the last hour of life, he focused his eyes above the door, and the radiance that shone about him kept me in a state of puzzled wonder. How I wished that I might gaze upon the wonders he beheld, and I could not doubt the glory now visible to him when he murmured, "Eye hath not seen, nor ear heard . . ." just before he drew his last shuddering breath.

In that vision, all things of this earth had been wiped out completely. Even as we stood to marvel, the lines of care and resentment, so marked in Pa's countenance, were smoothed out as by the touch of a loving hand, and his face now bespoke an eloquent and ineffable peace.

Chapter 24

March 15, 1918

Winter had returned again and again, and there were days when the earth appeared reluctant to let him go. Then suddenly it seemed that the earth was growing young again as she turned her back to winter and gave herself over to the gentle wooing of spring. But through soft quickening nights the earth played hide and seek with the spring through uplands and lowlands. The keening of newts in the swamplands began at last, and the tremulous cry of the screech owls. The fulsome bulge of new buds appeared on slender twigs, and one day I saw the first violets in the wood lot. It was then that winter, finding the earth pregnant with life not of his giving, departed for good in high dudgeon. And the earth, happy in giving, laughed in great glee, the robins returned to the dooryard and the mocking bird to the oak tree, blue jays screamed, and at last the earth donned her dress of translucent green, the glorious gift of spring, and twittered and shuddered in ecstasy through the sweet lengthening days, a veritable minx, laughing in the bright sun in one moment and weeping in a mist of rain the next, changing, eager, expectant, altogether enchanting.

Alex was forehanded in all that he did toward his farming. It was as though he'd finally grown up and had a man's affairs on his mind every minute of the day. While he resumed school, he engaged Clayton to cut stalks and harrow the fields and clean the farm from the front fence to the woodland that skirted the back fields.

Everything we planted that spring seemed to come up double and grow for the joy of growing. Jim's red clover, which stretched for acres in his field across the road from us, was a daily delight to see. Just the mention of Alex's alfalfa, a fairly new crop with him, would start him swelling with pride.

April 15, 1918

When at last the school closed till crops were laid by, Alex and Clayton worked early and late. No hoe hands were to be had, Alex said, so I put in every spare minute hoeing cotton and corn.

But Alex still looked at me with unseeing eyes and was as grumpy as Old Scratch. I was still at his beck and call, and still planning to do something about that when I could decide just what to do. I couldn't seem to find a proper place for making a readjustment in our lives. I often felt badgered and put upon. Perhaps Alex could feel it, for in the next moment he would do something so sweet and unselfish that my heart forgave him utterly.

But I continued to study him, his actions and reactions, and I finally decided that this attitude on his part was his idea of expressing the dignity of responsibility that rested on him as a husband, a father, a farmer, a school teacher and a land owner.

Well, wasn't it necessary for a man to feel that he was *"in charge"* if he was to make a success of things? I wanted him to feel confident and courageous, but what was there *"confident and courageous"* in a man browbeating his wife, a wife who wanted only his happiness?

As his work piled up in the spring, his manner became almost insufferable, and there were moments when I longed to knock him flat and stomp on him.

And of course there was always Ma. He had to pass there going to and from school, so I came to dismiss a lot of his shortness with me as leftover irritability from a session with her, and I could understand and sympathize with that, surely.

May 17, 1918

A letter came from Mama. It was just one more rock cast into turbulent waters. She was beside herself with joy. She had heard from Marion. He was going to New York on business the first of June. They were leaving the two small children with a trained nurse, and Tamla, his wife, would make the trip with him. Mama wanted Lola and me to get there for his visit without fail.

It was unthinkable with so much to be done, that I should go to Little Rock. When I called Lola she told me she couldn't go either.

"It's not just my job that holds me. I had a telegram this morning asking for four men to enter Tulane University for special training in wireless. I've called Phil and he will be home next week to stand examination. Since it is I who must send him wherever he goes, I can stand better to send him to New Orleans, which is the first call I've had for men where I could feel that he'd be reasonably safe for a while. I just have to be here through this."

June 7, 1918

One day Onnie, pausing just long enough to roll a cigarette with trembling fingers, said, "By God, it would take one man full-time to wet nurse the tenants on this land." Onnie was often heard roaring, harried beyond endurance.

"If your Pa was present you wouldn't be takin' God's name in vain," Ma spoke sharply, "and certainly tending this place is a full-time job. What do you think yore Pa was puttin' his time in at all these years?"

"Never saw him wear a pair of overalls in my life. Never saw him do a day's work." Onnie glared at her. "All I ever seen him do was climb on a horse and ride all over creation, or loll about the store."

"But he was doin' what he called *'castin' his shadder'* on ever' job that was going on, Onnie, and keepin' his accounts. Try fillin' his shoes one year, then come to me and tell me yore Pa didn't work!"

But the summer of 1918 was like a nightmare at Englewood and Shadowlawn. All thought of the war had slipped from our minds. Pa's relentless *"shadder"* might well be hovering over us, for all struggled valiantly to carry through on his old plan of operation. Every foot of the land that he had loved so passionately had been seeded, as he would have wished.

Pa had always advocated a heavy cotton acreage. The boys, trying to go along as Pa would have had them do, increased the cotton allotments considerably, due to the war situation. But there was no longer anything that resembled routine. It was a mad rush on everything, and a catch as catch can on the loose ends . . . that showed up hourly.

Men appeared as from everywhere seeking counsel, seeking credit at the store, asking for a loan of hard cash for doctor's bills and medicine, wanting to borrow a mule to see them through the rush, asking for a cow to milk until theirs could come fresh because of a new baby, trying to arrange for a brood sow, or a couple of pigs for next winter's meat, or to be supplied with meat and lard to run them through the summer.

Accounts had to be kept on all transactions, and Onnie was forever forgetting to make a record of the deals he handled, and Alex was riding him mercilessly for his laxity in small matters.

June 10, 1918

Mama had written that she was disappointed that Lola and I would not be there for Marion's four days visit. Neither of us could go, though both of us longed to. Today I had a letter from Papa:

> Flossie,
> Well, this seems to match the outcome of the bad dream Mama has had from time to time since Marion left home. The dream that he has come home, but that she always hears him as at a distance and sees him as through a mist and wakes with the pain in her shoulder.
> She went about cleaning and singing after she got the telegram that he was coming. That last morning before he was set to arrive, she decided she should do up the living room curtains. When she went to hang them she didn't go for the stepladder, but set a footstool on a chair and climbed up. In reaching to adjust the curtain she stepped on the edge of the stool and it turned and threw her to the floor on her right shoulder. In landing she broke the shoulder and her collar bone.
> This was just two or three hours before Marion was due. When he got there Mama was in the hospital,

under narcotics, waiting for X-ray pictures. It was well into the next day before she was fixed up in a cast, and she still had to have drugs for the pain. She was practically in a state of shock the whole four days.

He could stay no longer because of a business appointment in New York. Now she cries a lot and says she knows she will never see him again.

All my Love,
Papa

Well, of all things! That Mama's bad dreams should have foretold this dreadful thing, and I had a feeling that she was right in believing that she would never see him again.

June 15, 1918

On Saturday morning Alex had caught up with odds and ends, cleaning the stables and mending a harness, ending by plowing the garden and a late patch of roasting ears in the field.

It was a happy day. There'd been a good rain the day before, washing the whole world clean. My flowers were coming into bloom. The grass was freshly cut, my curtains newly done and the house clean and shining. I was using my best linens just for the joy of it, knowing I must soon put them away for the summer. I sang as I sliced ripe red and yellow tomatoes in a glass dish:

> *Come, Thou fount of every blessing,*
> *Tune my heart to sing Thy Grace.*
> *Streams of mercy, never ceasing,*
> *Call for songs of loudest praise.*

I thought I would have time to bathe the children before noon, but when I took them into the back porch to see if their bath water was warm enough, I saw Alex coming in, leading Jude. "I wanna wide on

Jude's back!" squealed Cerece, and before I could prevent it she had broken from me and was running through the field gate to meet Alex.

But I was in time to catch Buddy and ran into the kitchen and hooked the screen, with him kicking and screaming to go. More than once he'd been snatched from under the mule's feet lately, not knowing to be afraid, and Alex had warned me to keep him with me when he was about the lot with the mule.

Buddy wasn't happy. Cerece had got to go with Papa and he hadn't. I scooped the scowling little rebel into my arms, making a noise like a choo-choo, and rushed with him to the front porch. Loving him extravagantly, I started telling him about the three little bears in an effort to divert his attention. He finally gave me his full and undivided attention, and when I'd finished the story, I started bouncing him on my knees. "He's his Papa's li'l man and his Mama's li'l feller and we don't want him to wide a mool today because the mool might step on him and queeze his li'l geezard out, then what would Papa do without his li'l man, and what would Mama do without her funny li'l feller?"

At last he was happy and laughing and threw his arms about my neck and solemnly kissed me on the end of the nose. Always, in these moments, Buddy kissed me on the end of the nose.

Then I heard a rush of steps in the back porch and went to the front door to look. Alex stood at the back hall door, waiting for me to open it. Cerece was huddled close in his arms and very still. I hurried to open the door, my heart in my mouth. As Alex passed me, white and shaken, I looked into Cerece's eyes, black, solemn and unblinking, staring up at me.

"Is she hurt?" I faltered, as Alex staggered forward and sat on the bottom step of the stairs.

As he lifted his face a single tear rolled down his cheek. The only other time I'd ever seen this happen, was when he folded Pa's hands after he'd breathed his last.

"You didn't hear all the commotion? Cerece was on Jude's back at the lot gate. I saw that big chicken snake and grabbed up a limb to kill it, and I scared Jude. She took off across the field with Cerece on her back. I yelled to her to hang on. She lay flat against Jude's back, hanging on to the manes, and Jude cleared the fence and raced on and clear around the pond with her belly to the ground. Cerece was sticking on like she'd been glued there. Never saw the beat. I finally cornered Jude and pried Cerece off her back. She was still holding on for dear life."

He hugged Cerece's soft little body close, letting his cheek come to rest on her bright head. The sight was like balm to my soul. Alex loved our little girl now as he'd always loved his boy.

Chapter 25

July 10, 1918

Alex was teaching summer school. Since he took his lunch I found myself free to plan my days more to my liking. I had baked pies and a cake and taken Cerece and Buddy on a picnic. After their naps, I pulled the two big reed rockers to the back porch and set my little sewing table between them. I put the children to play in the yard and sat finishing buttonholes in a Russian blouse for Buddy, when Alex came in from school. He gave a big sigh and dropped into the other chair.

Just for fun I brought a coconut meringue pie and set it before him, with a knife, a fork, and a small plate. Instead of cutting a piece of pie he went to the kitchen for a spoon and began gouging the big swirls of meringue out by the spoonful and rolling his eyes as he savored the flavor.

"Alex, you're not going to eat that whole pie, are you?" I couldn't believe it.

"Yep . . . and I'm eating the meringue first. I've always wanted to and now's as good a time as any to realize on it."

"You'll be sick, with all that sweet goo on an empty stomach, and don't start yelping for me to hold your head."

"Well, I've heard you say, after I used to go off and stay all day when you had one of your headaches, that you hoped to see me sick enough to die one of these times, so maybe this is the time." And he kept ladling in the coconut custard.

I suddenly felt wonderful for some reason, and then I knew that we had passed a new milestone in our personal relations, that we had come at last to the time where such a sore spot could be mentioned as a joke—and taken as a joke. It was a good reason to feel wonderful.

"Don't expect me to have any sympathy for you. You're bringing this one on all by yourself. Oh . . . I want to spend the day with Alma tomorrow. I have most of Buddy's nicest things and she'd be glad to have them for the new baby when it arrives. I went so little when he was small that he hardly wore his two best dresses, and the white wool cap and booties are like new."

Alex made no objection to that, so I continued with my plan.

"I thought I'd pack enough lunch for you and Cerece both in the morning and let you take her with you for the day. I can manage Buddy in the little wagon, and we'll be home by the time school is out."

Even that went over, so I sighed with contentment.

July 11, 1918

Alex wasn't feeling too well in the morning. He ate very little and refused his coffee. "Feel like my stomach would heave if I put that coffee in it," he said.

I looked closely at him. His eyes and lips looked puffed, and he lacked his usual high color.

"Too much pie," I said. "There were four eggs, a cup of sugar, three cups of milk and two tablespoons of butter in that pie, Alex, besides the rich crust and the coconut, and you drank almost a quart of rich milk with it. It's a wonder you're not really sick."

I felt like dancing as I started up the road to Alma's. Over half a mile to walk and pull that little wagon, but Buddy was all slicked up and being an angel, and I was wearing my new yellow and green sprigged brown voile. I had resurrected the old floppy leghorn and pinned a bunch of yellow daisies on the crown and sewed some brown grosgrain ribbons to tie it on with.

Visiting was something I rarely did. Having company, especially in summer, was something that rarely happened with any of us. I'd phoned Alma the day before, so she was expecting me. Both her children were in school, and we put Buddy in the fenced yard to play and had an old-fashioned gabfest while we fixed dinner.

"This is a real treat, Flossie. I'm so glad you came. We all stay so submerged through the summer months." She laughed. "I just wonder what Alex and Lucius think now about the two town girls they married? Sometimes I think there ought to be a law against it. Country boys and town girls getting married, I mean. There are just too many adjustments to be made."

Halfway through the meal, the phone rang. "It's Alex," Alma said. "He had to dismiss school and is at home, sick as a dog. Would you please come home and do something for him?"

"Let me talk to him," I said, taking the receiver from Alma. "Alex, it's hot as blue blazes out there right now. Can't you bring the buggy and get me?"

"Gosh no, Flossie. My head's splitting and I've been vomiting. Come on home now. I can't stand much more of this."

When I got home, Cerece had one of my best napkins in a bowl of water, trying to bathe his face and dripping water all over the place. I fixed a glass of cold saltwater, strong, and made him drink it.

"What's this for?"

"It will come back up before it's warm and wash your stomach out good, if it doesn't work the other way, and then we'll do something else."

But after he'd vomited a couple of times, he told me he wasn't going to take anything else and I needn't bring it to him.

"Then, if you're better off without me, I'm going to take the children and leave and you can do for yourself," I said. Then with Cerece counting one for the money for him, he finally got a couple of aspirin tablets down.

That night I gave him a liver pill and a bowl of chicken broth.

All next day, Alex lay around the house, having me call everybody on the line and tell them he wasn't able to teach. In the afternoon he finally felt better and came to sit on the porch with me.

July 20, 1918

I had suggested that we invite Mama and Papa to come to the farm in September. Papa would have his birthday on the twelfth, during his vacation, and it would be nice to have them with us. Alex thought so too.

"And the first time we have the time for it, Alex, I want us to get a set of dishes and some silver."

"Now, here, if you're using their visit for an excuse to work me for new dishes and silver, we can just call the whole thing off."

The mention of spending money, for anything I wanted, still drew Alex up in a knot.

"Well, it's not just for that," I said, imperturbably. "I've been intending to speak to you about it for some time, but we so seldom sit down together and talk about things. It's just that, since I'm going to get it anyway, I'd like to have it in time for their visit."

"You're making crazy talk and I can't hear you."

"I never ask for things you can't afford, Alex. I'm not asking for real china, or for sterling. Just a set of American-made stuff, so that it all matches, and any of the name brands of silver plate will do me fine."

"How much money do you think I've got to put in an order like that?"

"I have no way of knowing. I just know you're able to finance anything you take a fancy to, such as fishing tackle and a new hunting rifle. I think the things I ask for are just as important."

"Well, I don't, and I'm the one that handles the money," he said on a note of triumph.

"Which makes me awfully glad that my husband's credit is good at any store in Paragould, and that I can catch a ride in with Jim any day I choose."

"You wouldn't dare," said Alex. But I knew he wasn't too sure that I wouldn't.

"I overheard you tell Arlien that the profits on the timber job usually ran you around fifty dollars clear each week. Well, that much one week will twice over pay for what I want."

"You hear too much," he said, but he had the grace to blush.

July 27, 1918

Ma was pretending to keep store, but Mattie would rather have been left alone with it. Ma complicated matters so. She hadn't let the boys put in a garden for her. Moreover, she'd had every turkey, duck, guinea, and chicken on the farm gathered up and sold. It developed that she had always considered them a nuisance and no longer intended having them underfoot.

She said, "If my boys can't see to it that I have vegtables and fruit in season, and a hen to bake when I want it, and a couple a fryers a week, then I'll just do without."

Alex and Onnie took turns helping Ma with her wholesale buying or taking her to town to spend a weekend with Aunt Rhea. She liked her visits there, coming home with much talk of the conveniences of city life. Running water and bathrooms and kitchen sinks and drain boards.

"I've got to do some looking around. I've decided to buy me a little house in town. Belle wants to move to the big house, but she'll come in over my dead body, long as I'm in possession."

Silas was back at home, even quieter than before. It was decided that he should farm the place at Spilling Brook, rent free, until such time as some kind of an agreement could be worked out.

August 12, 1918

I had the surprise of my life one day when I answered a knock at the front door. A rough redheaded young man was standing there and said, "Yes'um. I've come to deliver and install the acetylene light plant."

"That must be a mistake," I said. "I don't know anything about a light plant."

He pulled a sheaf of papers from his pocket, drew out a contract, and handed it to me. It was signed with Alex's name and in his own writing. "You know the gent?" he asked.

"Oh yes, I know him, but I don't know about the light plant. Come in and have a glass of milk and some cookies while you wait. I can call Alex and have him here in twenty minutes."

"My name's Choate," he said, accepting cookies, "and I feel sure you are Mrs. Walker?" I nodded, and he added, "Will it be all right if I call my helpers in?"

"It will."

He strode to the front door and called out, "Hey, Counts, you and Roscoe come in and have some milk and cookies. We have to wait a little while."

August 14, 1918

Having these men in the house was an exciting adventure to me. I enjoyed cooking for them as much as they enjoyed the bountiful meals, but I could never get over Mr. Counts and Roscoe always just wanting a piece of pie and a couple of cups of coffee for breakfast. Mr. Choate occupied the guest room, making his bed and sweeping his room, the hall, and front porch each morning. Mr. Counts and Roscoe slept on the extra bed upstairs and kept their room just as clean.

But I never saw Alex so arrogant and cocky. He found fault with the meals. He ordered me about as though I were his servant. He hollered for me to bring him a wrench, a screwdriver, the hammer, or saw. To open the gate for him. To shut the gate after him.

As a matter of fact, now that I thought of it, this bossiness had been growing in Alex for some time, especially yelling at me when he was still a long way from the lot gate to "Open that gate!" so that when he did get there, he could drive straight through without having to get down and open it himself.

But of course it was no time to thresh this matter out with Alex. I was so happy over the installation of the light plant, for I learned I was to have a chandelier in every room, even the kitchen, with four lights, a gas iron, and a small gas table stove for quick cooking. But Alex was too high-handed to talk with me about it and cut me off short anytime I tried to express myself on the subject.

What in the world got into men that they had to take all the joy out of even the nice things they did for you?

So I hovered about, picking up such information as I could, like a beggar snatching at the crumbs that fell from the rich man's table. They were even wiring the chicken house for lights—or that is, laying the pipe for the gas to flow through. They sunk a tremendous big tank to hold the carbide solution.

Then Alex had a brilliant idea: he got hold of the headlight of a car from somewhere and hooked it up in the front corner of our bedroom. It was rigged in such a way that he could turn the light on the front yard and flood it with light if anyone rode up and hollered in the night, or to the side window to throw a light on the chicken yard or mule lot should there be a commotion there.

August 15, 1918

Busy at my tasks in the afternoon, I heard Alex yell my name, and I hurried to the door. "Look in my little dresser drawer and bring me that account book, the red one with a rubber band around it."

"Yes, my lord and master," I muttered angrily to myself as I rushed the book to him and returned to my kitchen, with no thanks for my pains.

August 16, 1918

I had baked a ham and a fat hen to feed these hungry men, and pies and cakes, an unbelievable array of them. The weather held good, and the men worked early and late. But the last day they were there, Alex had to make a quick trip over to Arlien's for something they needed, and the job was held up. Mr. Choate came into the house to wait, and I invited him to sit down. He did so, thoughtfully rolling himself a cigarette.

"You're ruining a mighty fine man," he said, deliberately.

My breath caught in my throat. "What do you mean?" I asked.

"Just what I said. How did Alex ever get started, ordering you around like a galley slave?"

"Honestly, this is something new with Alex, and he's been worse since you all have been here. I think he just wants you men to see that he's boss in his own household and I'm trying not to let it upset me."

"You'd better let it upset you and put a stop to it. A thing like that grows on a man and you can spend the rest of your life hopping to his orders, only to find that all your hopping doesn't please him. He doesn't want you to hop, you know. No man does. Listen, little lady, I'm leaving here tomorrow. I never saw you before and never expect to see you again. It so happens that I like Alex, a lot, and I don't want to see him ruined by a woman like you."

If he had slapped my face, I couldn't have been more surprised. "Tell me one place where I've failed in my duties to Alex! You've been in our home," I flared.

"Oh you've laid yourself out to do your duty to Alex, so flat out that you're now under his feet and he's using you as a doormat, as is only natural. Pick yourself up and brush the dust off and try to be more like the gal he fell in love with. I know damn well you were not like this when he married you. I've seen the sparks fly from your eyes when he's acting like Alexander the Great more than once since I've been here."

About that time I heard Alex's voice yelling, "Flossie!" I held my breath, and he yelled, "Open that gate!"

"I don't want to quarrel with Alex," I faltered. "He might have to go to that dreadful war and I'd never forgive myself." I was on my way to the door.

"All right, sister, go ahead and make yourself a big fat blister. Nobody's going to have to sit on it but you!"

Choate's words followed me as I dashed hurriedly out and opened the lot gate in time for the lordly Alex to drive through without having to hesitate. Thoughtfully, I closed and latched the gate and returned to the house, unthanked.

August 22, 1918

My Kentucky Wonder beans were ready for canning. The way the vines ran on the poles, set in squares, they looked like green Indian teepees standing in the garden, and the vines were hanging as thick with the long beans as fingers on my hand.

But in the morning, I woke with a splitting headache. Since Pa's death, Alex had been giving me a shot of morphine-atropine when the monthly cycle rolled round, which was all Dr. Benson had ever done for me at these times. One shot would see me through it, but there were no more little white tablets in the glass tube.

I told Alex I had planned to can beans, so he volunteered to pick them for me before he left for town on a business trip. He set two number two washtubs full of the green beauties in the back porch. It took me all day long to sterilize jars, keep up fires, and boil each boiler of quart jars three hours by the clock. Alex had made a slatted wooden rack for the wash boiler and another to fit a number two washtub. I set the jars of beans on the rack in the boiler and got them going on the stove, the tub of jars, with another tub turned over it, on the cookstove.

It was late, dusk had deepened, and a huge full moon was rising in the east. The heat was terrific, so with the last beans on, I put the children to bed and got into a tub of bathwater.

Then I dressed only in a pair of umbrella panties and a new polka-dotted bungalow apron, with an over-the-neck strap and wide ties at the back, and felt more like a human. I had just slipped my tired feet into a pair of old sneakers when I heard Alex yell for me to open the gate.

Alex drove in, not bothering to greet me. I latched the gate and thought I'd pump water for the mules while he unloaded his farm supplies. I was pumping away when he took the bridle off of Jack and the mule shook his head and started in a lope for the yard gate, hoping to find the hoop off the palings, for he could work the latch undone with his strong muscular lips.

Alex wheeled and came toward me. "How many times do I have to tell you to put the hoop on that gate when you go in or out?" he yelled, and he raised his good right hand and gave me two terrific slaps on my thinly clad bottom.

There was a sudden pause in the universe. I couldn't believe that Alex had struck me. But he had.

All at once I seemed to rise and fly through the air. It was as though I'd been catapulted from a springboard. I landed on Alex, and he staggered under my weight and crunched and covered his face in an effort to shield it from my flailing fists and scratching nails. I tore madly at his face and hands. I kicked him with both my feet. He was wearing an old shirt, and I ran my fingers into the collar of it and tore it off of him. All the while Alex kept backing until he backed up to the front of the barn. Then he slid to a squatting position, still covering his face, laughing as if at a royal good joke.

"Hey O Lady, I didn't aim to hurt you. I was just trying to have a little fun," he said.

"Do you think this is funny?" I asked and whipped back my apron skirt and the circular leg of my panties and showed him the two prints of his hand on my bare bottom, plain to be seen even in the moonlight.

"If you think it's funny, you go ahead and laugh. And while you're enjoying your little joke, I want to tell you some news: you've just lost the best little body servant and general all-round flunky that you'll ever have, Alexander Walker."

Alex had risen and made as if to pass me. "But, Flossie . . . ."

"You stand right where you are till I finish telling you this, Alex, for I never mean to mention it again. I have gone to your fields with a hoe or a cotton sack for my last time, if the grass takes the crop and the harvest rots in the field. Moreover, I'm cooking no meals for your field hands, granting you can find some."

"I tell you Flossie . . . ."

"You're not telling me anything this time, Alex . . . I'm telling you. You are always telling me to leave your business alone, and then putting as much on me as I can stagger under. Well, from now on, your business is truly yours and you can tend to it or let it go. I will handle my business, without interference or criticism from you, and I intend to plan for a little leisure time . . . no matter what's hanging fire at your end of the line."

"But Flossie, all I said was . . . . "

"You look back over the past year and I think even you will admit that I tried to keep things from reaching this point. Now that they have, you might as well know that I'm glad. I've been wondering what I was going to do about your arrogant hateful attitude toward me. Now I know. You should have known this would have to end somewhere. Well, this is the end. Your supper is ready and waiting, and your bathwater's warm in the back porch."

Suddenly all anger left me, and I laughed to find Jack still nuzzling at the yard gate. "Go back to your master, Jack. He needs something he can boss!"

I called out to Alex. "Jack's as disappointed as you are, Sun. The hoop was over the palings."

Alex had followed me midway the lot, and he stood there staring thoughtfully at me. When I reached the kitchen, I gazed wonderingly at the riddled old shirt in my hands. I hastily stuffed it into the corner of the linen drawer in the sideboard. I wanted to put it with my keepsakes. It was the sign and symbol of my declaration of independence.

September 5, 1918

I was a busy woman, going over the house from top to bottom, making the guest room especially fresh and inviting. Mama and Papa were coming to see us, and a song was on my lips from dawn to dusk, no matter how tired I was. Lola would get the first weekend of their visit off, and Alex would bring her out. Oh, it was a delightful prospect.

In her last letter, Mama had sent a number of snapshots, showing that she had full use of her arm again. One with her hand to her head; another with her back turned, showing that she could tie her apron on at last; and another holding a pan of chicken feed and scattering the grain to her hens. She said she thought it would do her good to visit with her other children, help her to forget what a dismal failure her visit with Marion had been. Her stay at Englewood, when Buddy was born, could not have been a pleasant one for her, and Papa had never been to see us.

Buddy was now nearly two, strong and robust, and slippery as an eel. No matter where I left him, even for just a moment, when I turned to get him he was no longer there. I hugged the wriggling little body to me fiercely before I let him go, suddenly remembering the time when I had thought he was dying.

Cerece had become Alex's shadow, and wherever the fire raged hottest, she could be found.

In the midst of preparations, the phone rang. It was a long distance call from Little Rock, and Papa's voice sounded very anxious. "We won't get to come, Flossie. Mama is mighty sick. A different kind of sickness to any we've ever had or seen. Even the doctors haven't decided what it is, but it's plenty bad and we just can't come."

"Oh Papa! The first vacation you've had in years and Mama just now over that awful accident."

"Try not to worry, Flossie. I'll get a bunch of postcards and drop you one every day or two."

"Is it contagious?"

"We don't know yet. So far I'm feeling about as usual."

September 13, 1918

About the time Mama and Papa would have been bringing their visit to a close, I received a letter from Mama, written in a wavering, uncertain hand:

> Flossie,
>
> I have been up some every day for four days, now, but I am unbelievably weak. The doctors say now that what I had was Spanish influenza, and it's spreading everywhere like wild fire. There's a rumor that German planes have scattered the germs all over the nation, for it seems to be in the very air we breathe, we don't have to be exposed to it to get it. Rosedale cemetery lies at the end of the block and funeral processions are almost continuous. I feel like some times that everybody is dying. When you begin to hear about it there, lay in a lot of supplies and keep close at home and maybe you won't get it.
>
> All my Love,
> Mama

And so it was that we came face-to-face with a new dread, seemingly as fraught with peril as Alex's possible call to the colors.

Chapter 26

September 17, 1918

Usually when harvesttime rolled round, prices went down until the buyers got the yield in their own hands. Not so this year. Prices were high and we knew they would go higher, but so were all other prices. None of us were prepared to hold over the cotton and grain for the spring market. We couldn't believe what we had to pay when we went in to buy.

I thought things were going rather well, in spite of all the hard work. One day Alex's mood was soft to the extent that he piled Cerece and Lester atop a load of cotton and gave them a ride into the gin, bringing them back with their faces happily smeared with ice cream and chocolate candy. I was gathering apples and grapes, and trying to get my fruit out and dried between whiles.

September 30, 1918

I was in a softened mood, baking Alex's birthday cake, and I thought it would be a friendly gesture on my part to invite Ma to have dinner with him. I called her on the phone. "Tomorrow is the first of October, Ma. Alex's birthday, remember? I wanted to ask . . . ."

"I certainly don't need you or anyone else to remind me when Alex's birthday rolls round, Flossie. After all, I borned that boy."

"Well, yes, of course. I just wanted to invite you to come have dinner with him."

"Not with the rest, eh? Jist with Alex?"

"With . . . with all the rest too," I floundered. "Will you come?"

"Well, I'll think about it. You can call me tomorrow and find out." And she hung up.

October 1, 1918

When Alex came in I told him I'd heard nothing from Ma, that perhaps she was waiting for him to invite her too, and finally prevailed on him to call her. I saw he was angry when he snatched up his hat and left, muttering something about Ma and her car. I didn't ask what, but they came back on foot, Ma puffing and appearing to be almost spent with the effort.

"Alex made me walk," she said, resentfully, "and me with a nice car just settin' there in the garage."

When we were seated she asked the blessing, which she did in her sweetest manner. When I passed the food to her, she spread her hands over her plate. "Not a thing fer me, Flossie. I waited until eleven and I hadn't heard a word from you, after tellin' you to call me, so I ate my lunch. I couldn't hold another bite."

"Then won't you have something to drink?" I asked, trying to pretend all was as it should be. I picked up the pitcher of lemonade, but she refused, saying she'd maybe drink a glass of buttermilk. I got a pitcher of fresh cold milk from the icebox and poured a glass full for her, but she didn't touch it.

At the end of the meal we sang a "Happy Birthday" for Alex and he cut his cake, but Ma refused it. If Alex felt the strain he didn't show it, but I was feeling it, just as Ma intended that I should. Why did I always have to play up to her lead like this? The woman had what it took to undo me completely.

Alex flung himself on the couch when he'd finished eating. "I've got to rest a while after that," he said, stretching luxuriously, and he left me with it.

Ma helped me clear the table, asking what I wanted done with the buttermilk somebody had left. I told her to pour it in the pan of chicken scraps. It was a little cool so I put sweaters and caps on the babies and put them outside for a run until I could get through in the kitchen.

When we settled down to washing the dishes at last, it came over me that Ma was simply vibrating with the strength of her feeling on some matter as yet obscure to me. But I had the feeling I would know what it was before we were through. Then, out of the blue, she said: "I'm not goin' on like this much longer, Flossie."

"Like what, Ma?"

"Like messin' with that fiddlin' little store, like bein' under them boys thumbs. Since Henry saw fit ta have them appointed executors, and never bein' able to decide anythin' fer myself. Havin' always ta smooth Onnie's and Alexander's feathers the right way when what I'd like to do, would be to turn them acrost my knee."

"I thought things were going smoothly for you, Ma, all things considered."

"With all of you keepin' on puttin' me off about a new car? With all of you sayin' I can't buy a little house and move ta town? Those are the only two things I've asked fer since Henry died, and do . . . ."

"Don't say *all of you*, Ma. It's none of my business whether you get a new car or not, nor whether you live in town or in the country."

"Then why do you keep makin' it yore business?" Her voice was rising.

"I haven't tried to make it my business," I denied hotly.

"But it's Alex that keeps holdin' down on me, and don't think I don't know by this time who stands behind all that Alex says and does. You have high and mighty ways fer somebody that never even had a featherbed to yore name when you come into this family."

God help me now, I prayed.

"You may never believe me, but as God is my witness I have not said or done one thing to try to hinder you from getting a new car, nor to keep you from buying a house and moving to town."

"And I tell you flatly, Flossie that I don't believe one word yore sayin'."

How could so much venom be evident in such soft dulcet tones? Then her voice rose excitedly again.

"You'll never know how I feel about you, young lady, until some girl steps in and takes *yore son* away from *you*. Well, hear this: I want a new car, and I'm goin' to have a new car, and I want a house in town, and I'm goin' to have a house in town and I'm goin' ta live in it."

Alex, scowling like a thundercloud, stumbled through the kitchen and out, slamming the screen door behind him with considerable force.

"Now, what's the matter with him?" asked Ma, and then her face went blank. "I fergot he was in there. What does he mean tearin' through here like that, scarin' a body plum to death? What did I say, Flossie? Tell me what it was that I was sayin'?"

"Don't worry about it, Ma. It doesn't matter what you were saying."

"For once you spoke the truth," she flung the tea towel down. "It truly don't matter to you one word I'm sayin'."

She stepped inside the dining room and picked up a package she'd had with her when she came in. "Here's three pairs of socks that I knitted fer Alex's birthday. He likes them to wear with his boots on cold days when he goes huntin', and so much else came up, I clean fergot ta give 'em to him."

She snatched up her bonnet and started for the door. I breathed deeply of the sweet autumn air as I followed her out.

"Isn't it a lovely day?" I asked, in one last effort to make the parting pleasant. "Come back again, anytime you feel like it."

A sly look came over Ma's face and she said softly, "I'm so full of buttermilk. I don't know when I've ever felt so full."

"You might be feeling full right now if you'd drunk any of it." I said, hurting in spite of myself.

"Well, it's like I always say, I have to know who handles milk before I can drink any of it." And with that parting shot she minced daintily on down the road.

October 5, 1918

Saturday Alex said that he was riding into town with Onnie and Ma. He had some business to attend to. Late in the afternoon I heard him yell for me to open the lot gate and I ran out, only to find him sitting there in Ma's car, alone. He sounded a series of honks on the horn and the children came running too. He drove in, with a wide grin, and while I was latching the gate a brand new car whizzed by and I caught a glimpse of Ma, smiling and waving triumphantly, and of Onnie at the wheel, tooting the horn like mad.

I followed to where Alex had parked the car under the catalpa tree.

"How do you like your new chariot, O Lady?" He bounced out and made a sweeping bow.

"You mean this is ours?" I could hardly breathe.

"It's ours. They didn't want to allow Ma but three hundred fifty dollars trade in value on it, and I told 'em it was worth a lot more than that to me." He suddenly sobered. "Ma *would* have a new car. She *would* have a house in town. She'd finally won Onnie over and they'd been in several times and had the business all lined up. Well, I can't go on with Ma gigging at me at every turn, especially after Onnie began to side with her on it. He said he just wanted some peace, and if that was what it took to get it, he was willing to sign on the dotted line and part with some of Pa's tidy little bank balance, so's that's what we did."

"Is Ma happy over it? I think that's the main thing we all want."

He nodded. "She's in seventh heaven."

"Well," I said, "as long as Pa lived he treated her like a child. I know she'll feel like a bird out of a cage, away from us all, with a weekly allowance, and a chance to flap her little wings and fly around a bit."

He sighed. "I wish I could feel that we'd done the right thing. I know Pa turned over in his grave this day."

The children were clambering over the seats in the car and begging for a ride. Alex opened the gate, then ushered me to my side of the car and seated me with a grand flourish.

"I've always wanted to ride in this car. I've only been in an automobile twice before, and never in this one."

Alex stood with his mouth open, Pa's listening look in his eyes. "You mean you've never been in this car?"

"Can you mention time or place?" I asked.

He stared blankly, shaking his head.

"Neither can I . . . and the only time I ever rode in the family surrey, until after you bought it and the mares from Ma, was the day we went to Granpap's funeral."

Alex shoved his hat low over his eyes and settled himself under the wheel. He seemed lost in thought as he drove slowly along to where the road turned toward Paragould, made an expert turn and then drove slowly back home.

This was *our* car now! The wonder of it filled me with such happiness that I spanked Cerece's round little bottom and she squealed for joy as I lifted her out. I felt so strong that I lifted the laughing Buddy to my shoulder and carried him to the house without feeling his weight. Ma was welcome to her new car. This one was plenty good for me.

With Ma happily settled in town, Belle would be free to move back to the old home place, her inheritance, at Englewood. Ma had forbidden this as long as she occupied the house, and I longed to remind her that I had felt the same way about living in somebody else's house with that somebody else. Even the suggestion that we build another bedroom and kitchen for Ma hadn't helped any. Pa thought he had provided for Belle, and for Ma to be taken care of, but Ma had no intention of letting anybody "take care" of her . . . yet.

What to do about Ma? What to do about Belle moving home? What to do about the store? These matters were all settled at last. The stock on hand at the store would be tallied up and divided among all households, Ma declaring that she didn't want to have her house messed up with all that clutter.

October 14, 1918

The revival was held late in the year because Brother Sherrill had been so busy with funerals for members of his scattered flock. I still couldn't find it in my heart to attend. Since it troubled me considerably, I put myself through the sweat of trying to figure out why. Was I concerned for my soul's welfare? For the good I might get by attending? For the stumbling block I might be in the path of another by not attending? Or . . . just for what the people of the community might think and say, most of them very church-minded when it came time for a revival?

I certainly wasn't troubled over the fact that Alex wanted me to go and I just wouldn't! Nothing short of fire, flood and death could keep him from going to the little church Pa had founded. His going was a duty he owed to Pa, if not to God, and he could sing just as high whether I was there or not. Was it because Ma was there, and I couldn't face up to looking on if God took a notion to "shout" her?

Perhaps my soul needed reviving, but I didn't feel that Brother Sherrill could do that little job for me, even when he was "under the power." The longer I put off going, the harder it was to go, and I ended by not going at all, though I did considerable praying.

Funny thing, just as Alex felt that our talk always had to get around to money, just so, my prayers always got around to me laying my most personal need at the foot of the throne of grace and asking God's help in working things out. We'd been wonderfully blessed, and I gave thanks. We had prospered, which all of our work could not have achieved without God's sunshine and rain and tempering of the winds. We had our home, though I realized its being in the clear was due solely to Pa's change of heart at the last minute. Now that the home was ours, we were working together to improve and take care of it. We had two beautiful healthy children. Perhaps that was what marriage meant, not the happiness of the two involved in it, but the progeny that sprang from the union. I sighed often in these days, knowing that the one thing I didn't have was Alex. We were living together, greatly blest, but there was, as yet, not a true marriage. I could but only work toward that happy day, and pray, and wait.

October 18, 1918

With the revival meeting over, I went on my way singing. What a joy the moonlight nights brought me. The moonlight softened my mood, mellowed my manner, and sweetened my speech. There was certain magic in the moonlight for me. If only I could get Alex to walk with me in the moonlight, the miracle I awaited might be wrought. But he would not. He was getting more like Pa. When the sun set it was time to go to bed. But one night, bathed and ready for bed, he had gone to the guest room across the hall. I waited . . . and waited . . . not a sound. Finally I said, "Alex, what in the world are you doing?"

"Finding out what it means to be a guest in my own home."

"You mean you've gone to bed in there?"

"Yep, and I'm here for the night, so don't wait up for me." He laughed, and I knew that he was enjoying his little joke. "It's just like being in another world, O Lady. You must try it sometime . . . it all looks so goldy, the moonlight through the trees, casting leaf shadows on these yellow walls. Hush, now, so's I can enjoy it. That's one reason I settled in here. You're worse than a duck and just never stop yabbling on a moonlight night."

"You'll never know how I hate you sometimes," I called back, but I was nearer to loving Alex than I'd been for a long while.

October 19, 1918

"Before I get into making gooseberry jam, Alex, I want you to take me in to see Lola." To my surprise, Alex had said that he would take me.

We stopped by Ma's little house and found the front doors and windows closed and the blinds drawn, but when we went around back Ma was there. "So many country people come and go on Saturdays," she said, with evident distaste. "I close up the front of the house to keep out the dust, and ta save mysef fom havin' a lot of comp'ny right when I might want to be doin' somethin' else."

The house was pretty and not a finger mark anywhere. The children were fascinated by the running water and had to have a drink three times before we could get away. When Alex offered to keep the babies while I had my visit with Lola, I was overjoyed, but Ma was visibly put out. "I been wantin' one of you boys ta come in and take me to the cemetery. I wanted to go in my new car, but I'm certainly not goin' to put these chilren in that car. So you can jist take me in yore car, Alex. Get the rake and the hoe out there and stow 'em. I know the graves need attention."

On their way out of town they left me at Lola's office. She had rented her house out, furnished, and had taken a two room apartment about a block from the courthouse.

She gave me the key. "If I'm to take the afternoon off to be with you, honey, I've got a pile of work to catch up on. You'll find things to fix in the icebox and cabinet. Rest and fix us a bite and I'll be on as soon as I can get away."

Lola was home by noon. After we ate, she washed her shining hair, bathed, got into a negligee and sat under the fan to dry.

Speaking of Phil and how she missed him she said, "I keep going like a house afire. I couldn't stand it if I didn't. I felt like I'd signed his death warrant when I fixed up his papers, but I hear so much about slackers, and I know Phil can never be called that. There I was, sending men every day with one and two children. At least Phil and I had no children. I felt like the heart was being drawn out of my body as his train pulled out, but he leaned out laughing and waving to the last like he was off on a lark."

Her breath caught on a sob. "I feel like that is the last time I'll ever see Phil on this earth."

"This is supposed to be the war to end wars," I reminded her. "But they'll probably hatch up another slogan for the next one by the time Buddy's old enough to go. Taking the cream of the male crop as often as they do and leaving only Four Fs to breed from, the nation's bound to grow weaker, though maybe not wiser."

"Let's don't be cynical, Flossie. We must have faith . . . ."

"Faith in what? Patriotism and religion? How those two 'causes' get tied into one during a war? For God and for Country, the patriots scream, and the cry has the sound of brass and of tinkling cymbals to me."

"Flossie!"

"Well, how many soldiers that spill their life's blood on a battle field know why they're fighting? The real truth about it, I mean? And how many want to fight? A few men like Phil, maybe, that have been successfully indoctrinated with hatred for the enemy, and some that are just eager for adventure. But when they are at the battlefront, who do they come up against? A bunch of raw young recruits on the enemy side, with no more idea of what it's about than ours have, and no more desire to kill. They'd all much rather be at home with their families than slogging it out in the trenches and spilling each other's blood and guts all over the place."

"Well, but religion, Flossie. Surely you're glad we have that to fall back on, the promise of glories to come to bide us through the trials in this Veil of Tears."

"Lola, I just wonder sometimes of late, if religion, as we know it, truly has any saving grace. We learn the tenets as laid down. We observe the rites and ceremonies. We go to church, most of us do, and try to hold to the line, but as long as we go out for mass killings, I wonder if we haven't missed the spirit of the thing? I just can't fit true followers of Christ into the framework of war to save my soul."

"But the good would be trodden down by the powers of evil, Flossie, if we didn't defend ourselves and the right."

"Even if we have to cross the ocean to defend it?" I asked. "Why don't those who make the wars go out and fight them? But they never do . . . the very idea . . . that a few leaders in every country can declare a war and send millions to their death!"

I pushed the hair back from my heated face. I had not known such thoughts were buzzing around in my mind. Suddenly I was ashamed. The first time I'd been with Lola in ages and here I was acting like a fanatic on a soap box. Anyway, did I really think as I'd been talking?

"Let's cool off." I grinned. "Who am I to question the whys and wherefores of our social disorder? But this I know: such religion as we have is not enough to save us from wars, and I do think that Christian people could work out their differences without bloodshed, if they tried. There are times when it seems to me the nations want to fight and hopefully await an *incident* that will justify it in their own eyes. I'll bet if the men that make wars had to bear these sons they wouldn't be so ready to offer them, a living sacrifice, on the altar of whatever cause."

"Well, for heaven's sake, let's hang on to such faith and religion as we do have until . . . ."

"Sometimes I get the feeling, Lola, that as long as we hang on to this religion we'll never find anything better, and I believe there is something much better for the human race. If not, in God's dear name, why bring sons into the world?"

"I give up. Let's go shopping and see a movie. This kind of talk leaves me feeling bogged to the gills in uncertainties."

For once I had some money in my pocket. Alex would never lower his dignity by taking our small surpluses to sell in town. But Jim had established himself with a nice list of customers and took produce to town twice a week. All summer I had been preparing offerings of such produce as I had in plenty, which I turned over to him on commission. The dollars and cents had finally added up to almost fifteen dollars, all mine to spend. What a glorious afternoon we had, much better than going to the picture show, which we couldn't find time for.

When Alex came by to pick me up, Lola and I had forgotten our serious discussion and were deep in plans for my sewing. I loaded my bundles into the car and climbed in. Lola kissed me through the window and stood waving as we drove away.

But I took home with me a feeling of sadness too, for Lola's grief over Phil's going, for the things that had come up and come out as we talked. Was that really the way I felt about . . . well . . . about things?

October 21, 1918

Tonight Alex rode in with a heavy scowl on his face and flung a big roll of bills on the table. "Blood money!" he sneered. "How many had to die before the rest of us could get a decent price for our crops? The farmer's a no good simp. That's the attitude of the buyers every year, for him expecting anything for his year's labor. This year all that is changed. Every buyer in Paragould is walking around with his arm around some old farmer's shoulder, talking sweet. Just trying to get his hands on what the farmer's got. The most sickening sight I ever saw in my life."

"Listen Alex, there have been plenty of lean years and there'll be plenty more. Can't you take your profits this one year and make yourself secure? You didn't start the war . . . ."

"No, but I'm liable to have to help finish it, and all I hope is that the ones that started it will have to eat bloody meat and drink blood for water from here on out."

I was dumbfounded, I tried to comfort Alex, but the tirade came in a flood until I ended it by saying, "Get ready for your supper," and started putting the meal on the table.

October 22, 1918

On that wonderful shopping spree, I'd bought a good bleaching cream and I secretly applied it daily to face, neck and arms. In my zeal to become beautiful I overdid it and my skin broke out in an irritating rash. I left off the treatment a few days, and then cautiously resumed it. All this while I was sewing for myself, and among the things I was making was a negligee as near like Lola's as I could contrive with yards and yards of fine white voile and shadow lace.

In the midst of all this, the top layer of my skin began to shed off. In a few more days my skin looked as fresh and tender as the day Alex first walked home with me. How clean and good I felt when I would wash my face. This was the day I'd been waiting for.

I made the house fresh and put the babies down for a nap. I took a leisurely bath, using the fragrant lavender crystals Lola had given me. Then I got out the tiny pot of rouge she had insisted I must have. I spread a tiny bit of the rosy cream over my cheeks, just under my eyes as she had shown me. Then I smoothed a bit of it on my lips and dusted my face with powder.

My spirits rose. I took my braids down and brushed my hair, which had just been washed the day before. I slipped the long princess slip on, then the elegant negligee. But it was too early for Alex. I'd have time for a little nap. I took off the negligee and slipped on the new dress. I spread my lovely dress carefully about me so that it wouldn't get crushed and lay there, resting and thinking, and went sound asleep.

The next thing I knew Alex called my name. I opened my eyes to find him staring down at me as though I'd been a spirit from another world. He tossed his book and papers to the foot of the bed and sat down beside me, reaching out his hand to touch my hair.

"Gosh O Lady, you look and smell like you used to," he said wonderingly, and buried his face in the hollow of my throat and drew a long ecstatic breath. "What's happened?"

I sat up on the side of the bed. "Now you've spoiled it all," I scolded. "You weren't supposed to come in until I had my hair done in puffs and was seated on the couch reading a magazine. I meant to impress you with your wife's grace and dignity. Instead you find me all sprawled out with my hair down and dead to the world." I sighed in mock resignation. "Well, all that for nothing . . . ain't fair."

Alex had sobered and was gazing steadily at me. "Why did you decide to do all this?" he asked.

Somewhere I remembered reading that when a child is old enough to ask an intelligent question, he is old enough for an intelligent answer. Well, so be it. I took a long breath and put out a feeler.

"Since I took your handmaiden away from you, Alex, I'm trying to give you something we can both enjoy better. I thought you might sometimes get lonesome for the gal you married."

His face clouded. "Why did you ever let her get away?" he asked coldly.

"Will you tell me how you expected to keep that girl through some of the places you took her? Some of that was enough to change anybody, Alex. Besides, it takes a little money, and that's something you've never offered me."

I swallowed hard. Explaining wasn't easy, and I regarded the toes of my new white slippers.

"You are now looking at about eight dollars' worth of refurbishing. If I had asked you for eight dollars for this purpose, would you have given it to me?"

"Probably not," he frowned. "Why does the talk always have to get around to money, Flossie?"

"Because Pa, it takes money to make the mare go," I said flippantly, and that didn't help things any.

"I honestly didn't notice how much you'd changed until I found you like this," he finally said. "Where's the kids?"

"I pulled Buddy's bed into the back porch so that he could catch the breeze, and had to let Miss Walker lie down on the guest room bed to get her down at all."

Alex had risen and I stood beside him, shaking my hair back on my shoulders. A breeze lifted my airy skirts and they billowed about me. Alex's eyes suddenly suffused with desire and he caught me roughly to him and kissed me again and again.

Wasn't this what I had hoped for? Then why was there no glad response in me? Alex, sensing my lack, released me and stepped back, both of us more than a little embarrassed.

"Well, I've got to change and ride the timber job before night. What kind of pie did you bake today?"

"Peach cobbler, and there's a pint of whipped cream for it in the icebox. Why did you start a timber job with the rent farms to see after, crops to get in, and your school going full blast? You've taken on too much."

And the moment I had planned for and built toward for so many days came to naught. I sat down on the couch and hated myself to pieces for not being able to seize on that moment when Alex might have become mine again.

And then I knew. There was still something lacking in Alex's feeling for me. A sudden desire on his part to possess me for a fleeting moment, and then go on as before, was not enough. I had no desire for half a loaf.

I thoughtfully unhooked the lovely dress and hung it and the slip on a rack. I put on a pair of umbrella panties and a fresh bungalow apron and my sneakers and went to water and feed the hens and gather my eggs. But as I hurried hither and yon, I kept trying to get it straight in my mind exactly what I did want in my life with Alex.

Then I remembered the sound of Mama and Papa at breakfast, the sound of soft smothered laughter from their bedroom, Papa's tender concern for Mama when the bad dreams came, his unfailing kiss when he left the house and again when he returned. Mama and Papa were together in a way that Alex and I had never been. Could I hope ever to have that kind of life?

I doubted it, remembering the things Alex had told me about his parents. He had never seen Pa kiss Ma in his life. He had never seen Ma so much as reach out and touch Pa for any reason. Not only that, but Alex didn't remember that his mother had ever kissed him, and certainly she had never encouraged him to kiss her!

In one of Papa's letters to Mama after he had gone to Little Rock, he had said, "I miss you more at breakfast than any other time. You could always send me off to work feeling like I could whip the world with both hands tied behind me."

When Alex had kissed me, I felt that his senses had been intrigued by the clean body, the powder and rouge and perfume, and the different dress. He was kissing those things, not really thinking of me. Well, it wasn't enough, so I must go on waiting. Time had done such wonders in our mixed-up lives. If only Alex didn't have to go to the war maybe a miracle would be wrought.

For something to do that would let my hands keep pace with my busy mind, I gathered up all the flower vases, washed them, and filled them with fresh flowers. When the children woke, I spread a cloth and gave them a tea party on the work table under the blackgum tree.

October 23, 1918

The next night Alex was late coming in. I bathed the children and got them down. After my own bath I put on my new pink batiste nightgown and the beautiful white negligee. I took some sofa pillows and sat on the front steps, my back against the square white pillar. As the golden moon flooded the scene with soft light, I seemed to be living in fairyland. I doubt if I'd have been surprised if Prince Charming, on a white charger, had come dashing up, snatched me to his manly chest and dashed away again.

Such thoughts for an old married woman to have . . . but what a perfect night for romance.

My thoughts went back to such evenings when I was a girl. Marion, with his guitar, and I used to walk down to Mable Hubbard's home. I recalled one evening that stood out from all others. We had found Wake Light and Quirta McDaniel there and had spent the whole evening singing, with Mable at the piano and her brother Arthur playing the violin. No such fine songs were written any more, at least I didn't hear them. Now it was, "How You Gonna Keep 'Em Down on the Farm" and "K-K-Katie."

Sitting there, I could hear in my mind the violin singing along with me, the piano, and the soft strum of the guitar:

> *To you, beautiful lady, I raise my eyes*
> *My heart, beautiful lady to your heart sighs . . . .*

I sang it all and was surprised to find that I remembered every word after all this time. I went on to sing "Love Me" and "The World Is Mine." I'd heard Alex come in and was dimly conscious of him eating his supper and getting his bath, but it would have taken more than that to break the spell I was under. My mind dug up another old favorite and I sang it:

> *Come out in the garden of roses, dear,*
> *And stand where the moonbeams fall.*
> *Sweet perfume arises like incense pure*
> *To one who is fairer than all.*

Then I sang the heartbreaking ballad called "Blue Belle," and there I was, back with the fear and the dread of the war:

> *Blue Belle, the dawn is breaking,*
> *I've come to say goodbye.*

I sat stunned with the possibility that Alex might one day soon be saying such words to me, when he came and dropped down beside me. He was fresh shaven, in pajamas and house slippers and the white terry cloth robe I'd bought him for summer. He leaned against me and sniffed. "You smell and sound mighty pretty tonight, O Lady."

"I'm feeling kind of pretty too, remembering the old songs Marion and I used to sing when we were kiting around in our young days. If you've never sung such songs in the moonlight with a gang of good friends, you've missed a lot."

"Well, I've missed a lot then. I never even heard such songs. You've never sung them before . . . not where I could hear them."

"That's because I've had a thing or two else on my mind, I think. Things are easing for me now with the babies out of my lap and the house fixed. There was another old one I liked: "In the Evening by the Moonlight," oh, and "My Sweet Irish Rose" and "The Trail of the Lonesome Pine"."

"Would you mind if I laid my head in your lap?"

Only then did I realize that I'd made no welcoming move toward Alex when he sat down beside me. "Do you need encouragement? Time was when you would have made room in my lap and settled yourself to your liking."

"Time was when I was certain enough of my standing with you to do that. I'm not so sure any more."

I held my breath. God grant that the path of understanding lay before us and Alex is ready to walk that path with me. "Tell me exactly what is on your mind, Alex."

"I'm facing up to the fact that you don't love me as you once did."

That couldn't have been easy for Alex to say. "When did you find that out?" I asked, not bothering to deny it.

"I've suspected it for months, and now I know it."

"Have I failed in my wifely duty at any point?"

"Oh duty be hanged! What's the fun of having your body when I need it, if you're not even there? And you know danged well what I mean. Shy as you was when we married, you yet had little ways of letting me know you was glad when I turned to you. Are you ever glad anymore? And don't bother to answer that one. I've found out the answer for myself too many times lately."

"I'm sorry, Alex, truly sorry. I hung on to that warm, tender, outgoing and outgiving love for you just as long as I could. I'm no good at pretending...."

"I'm not asking you to pretend, for gosh sake. I've had the real thing, so I could spot an imitation of it the minute you pulled one. No, I can't tie it down, but there's something...."

"Something missing? I feel it too, Alex."

Dear God, he was not an insensitive brute, concerned only with his carnal appetites.

"We seemed to have such a richness when we married, but it didn't take me long to discover that as soon as you were physically satisfied your need for me was over until the need arose again. That's a killing thing for a girl, as much in love as I was, to have to face. I'd thought our moments alone together would always be something to look forward to, and the memory something to be treasured forever after. I never thought our moments of union would become debased to the extent that they meant no more than the gratification of the moment's urge, and ... well, it makes me feel used, and any such handling kills whatever urge I may have had, and keeps me from responding as I long to do. This all came as clear as I'm saying it to you after you went so far as to strike me that night."

"But look what you did to me, and I never held it against you. I never sulked or took it out on you. I forgave it as soon as it happened."

A bell rang far back in my mind. *He forgave me,* for a thing he'd brought on by his own act, just as Ma had forgiven me that night in church for the situation she had created out of whole cloth!

"No, you didn't show an ugly spirit over that, Alex. But listen what you did do, you went out next day and rustled fourteen hoe hands and got the crop hoed out . . . ."

"Well, you didn't have to cook for them, I saw to that."

"I didn't have to cook for them because I would not. The thing I'm trying to get you to face up to, if you're really trying to find out why I'm like I'm 'not there' when you make love to me, is that I was doing as much of the field work as I could *because* I loved you and I *wanted* to help, and because you had told me you couldn't get any field hands, and you were treating me worse than you treated your livestock. Moreover, you would have let me go on doing your field work till I fell in my tracks, *if* I hadn't thrown it back in your lap myself, and after telling me that you would never want me in the field with you, that you would always look after your own part of the business and I could do the same. It's been hard for me to get all of this straight in my mind, to believe that it could be like that between us, but once I saw things as clearly as I'm telling them to you, I knew then that you didn't truly love me and that you were a selfish and unfeeling brute, or you couldn't have done these things to me."

He took my hand and pulled me to my feet, running the other hand worriedly through his hair. "You're always wanting to walk in the moonlight, let's walk. I want to get to the bottom of this business while we're at it."

We walked slowly along the flower bordered walk to the gate and the birds in the oak tree stirred and chirped sleepily. Alex still held my hand and tucked it snugly under his arm next to me. I had the feeling that I was walking along in the moonlight with a *lover*, of all things. Could it be? God grant it, my heart had been hungry for so long.

"Your hands are almost as soft as they used to be. Is it the new jar of cream I saw on the dresser?"

"That and less hard work. Hoeing doesn't make soft hands . . . or picking cotton."

"Well, I like you better as you are than as a field hand. You were sure stingy with your kisses before we married, but there was plenty of response in the feel of your hands in mine. Why *did you* always shy away from my kisses? I used to worry about that some."

"I guess Papa was the cause of that. He told me that I never had to watch a boy when I was out on a date, that all I had to do was to keep a watch on Flossie. Your kisses . . . *disturbed* me, and so *no kisses*. Does that make sense?"

"Want to go back? I got a kind of surprise for you." We turned back and when my eyes fell on our house I was stopped in my tracks by the sight. Alex had lit every burner in all the chandeliers. I was speechless for one fraught moment. I said, "Why, Alex, the house is *immense*, and how beautiful!"

"The rooms, being so big and airy, give it that look, yes, and all the lights on. It's a mighty heartening sight to me when I drive in tired at night and see our home, and know that you're in there with our two babies scrubbed and a good meal waiting. Doesn't the house, fixed as near as I could like you want it, prove anything to you? It took a lot of money and hard work . . . ."

"And, you breaking with Pa, when he was already a sick man. Alex, I'll never forget that." I was melting fast, but there was one more thing that must be said. "But you can't just *buy* a woman's love with *things*, Alex. That doesn't mean that I don't appreciate all that you've done. But the one thing I do suffer over is the fact that you never *say* you love me. You *never* mention the things I do that you like, only the things you *don't* like."

"Then, after you're out of the house and I think back on what's been said, I don't have anything for my heart to feed on. You don't want any make-believe responses from me, and I don't want any *forced* or *duty-bound* words of love and commendation from you. I just want you to say *something* by way of love and appreciation when you *do* feel it . . . no other time . . . and especially not when you're trying to get me in the mood for lay-around . . . at least not just at those times."

"By gosh and the devil . . . *so that's it*. Well, honey, I *do* love you. I think about you all along through the day. I lie awake missing you at night and you right there by my side. I've thought about you so much lately that . . . ."

"Oh Alex, I'm so happy I believe I'm going to cry," and I turned and hid my face against his chest.

"Bawl your little eyes out, O Lady. I never heard a sweeter sound. You haven't cried on my account since the cow kicked you over before Buddy was born. I've worked like a dog to prove my love for you, and I'm aiming for you to believe it, if I have to make a song out of it and sing it to you morning, noon and night."

We walked back to the house, *one*, at last. In the hall he kissed me and pushed me gently toward the guest room. "Make your preparations and wait for me in there, honey. I'll turn out the lights and be right with you.

The lovely gold-flooded room. As I fixed the bed I was suddenly all a tremble, as on my wedding night. I felt that I had already been married to Alex twice: by Brother Sherrill, and the time I renewed my vows until death us do part, before Buddy was born. And tonight I was getting married to Alex again . . . this time for keeps, for the third time is the charm . . . so they say.

Chapter 27

November 1, 1918

Indian summer came, and the world got lost in a soft blue haze, and I wondered how there could be war and pestilence in a world so luscious and ripe and beautiful. Alex yielded to my suggestion and we gave a tacky party and everybody came. Alex put on the big porch light, the house facing west, then lit the big flood light and turned it toward the north front window. The front and north yard were as bright as day, and there we played.

Sugar had been rationed for a long time, but I still had about fifteen pounds of our share of the sugar on hand when the store stock had been divided, so I baked a chocolate layer cake as a prize to be given to the tackiest couple, not thinking what a furor that would create.

Alma won the prize for the women, Johnny Raines for the men, and there was nothing to be done except to divide the cake and give each half of it. Then the talk started about sugar. This one and that one had not been able to get sugar, steal, beg, or borrow, to preserve their fruits. Most of their fruit was put up in plain juice and water and couldn't be eaten till it was sweetened and no sugar to sweeten it with, and no jams, marmalades, or jellies, much less layer cakes! And where did we get so much sugar that we could ladle it out on such an occasion?

Alex told them how it was that we had sugar. "But you're supposed to have declared it. I bet you kept buying your ration of sugar right on, like you didn't have a grain," said Arlien.

"I'll bet I did too," said Alex, coolly. "Just as you would have done if that little windfall had come to your hand. I can tell you something else I did too, and if any of you want to turn me in for it and call me a slacker, do it and be danged! When we threshed wheat, I took enough of the grain in and made my year's supply of flour, had it ground and sacked and stored it on a swinging shelf upstairs. A man's first duty is to his family. Well, I'll be among the next to be drafted into this war, and it will comfort me more than somewhat to know that my family has a year's supply of food to hold them together when I'm gone.

"Hey, everybody, this is a party, not a town meeting," said Onnie, and I could have hugged him.

So all piled out to the yard and we played London Bridge, Marching Round the Levee, Stink Base, Wolf Over the River, Farmer in the Dell, and, best of all, Charades. The little matter of extra sugar was forgotten. When it came time for refreshments everybody was panting for breath, laughing till the tears ran at the antics of this one and that one. "Haven't had so much fun since Ma hung her tit in the wringer," declared Johnny.

"We need to get together oftener," said Alex, thoughtfully winding his watch after they'd gone. "I think a round like that now and then is what we need. Otherwise we're likely to get hidebound with our own selfishness."

He picked up a stiff brush and began to brush his hair back in shape. He had plastered it tight to his skull and one of his front teeth blacked out. Suddenly he laughed. "That Alma, I didn't know she had it in her. I never saw anybody act more like a hussy. If she's a little younger, she'd make a first-rate flapper."

"That come-hither look she cast over her shoulder when she'd start walking off from you," I remembered. I placed my hand on my hip, swung around and fluttered my eyelids at Alex.

"You don't have to do that to get me to follow you around tonight, O Lady. That stock collar and buttoned shoes and walking skirt . . . I do believe that's the very clothes you were wearing the day I first walked home with you."

So he did remember.

He snatched Buddy up and tossed him high. "To bed with you young man. What do you mean staying up till it's all over? Your big sister fell by the wayside two hours ago."

I could hear him rocking Buddy to sleep while I got ready for bed. Only then did I realize how tired I was and dropped down on a stool and took my hair out of puffs and began to brush it for the night.

Alex put Buddy to bed and came back. "Why don't you go on to bed?" I asked.

He sat on the edge of the dresser, idly swinging his foot back and forth. Thought I'd stick around, just in case I'm needed." He grinned. "Besides, I've got a little news for you: I've decided that each of us is to have one week's timber money for clothes, and we'll call it our Christmas gift to each other. That will be fifty dollars apiece, and I might as well tell you that I've picked out the material and I'm having a suit tailored for myself. I always wanted one and this looks like my best chance to get it. And an extra pair of pants.

Clayton can look after things Saturday and we can have a day in town together. It'll probably take you a whole day to get a complete outfit. It's not like a man just going in and buying a suit. Maybe we'll get our picture taken again. The kids too."

I finished braiding my hair and laid the brush on the dresser. Alex had offered me *money*. I was speechless.

"I see that one got you"—he laughed—"so I guess I'll have to carry you to bed."

November 2, 1918

Flossie Deane Craig

November 8, 1918

    Alex had loaded the wagon with wood, apples, grapes and other produce to take to Ma. He opened the gate for himself, led the mules through, loaded it himself, and turned to wave goodbye as he climbed into the wagon, both children screeching for him to bring them candy from town.

    Alex had set a couple of tubs of apples in the back porch for me before he left. I hooked the apple peeler up to the back shelf, settled down on my kitchen stool and went to work, the children settled at their play beneath the blackgum tree.

    As the morning wore on I took great dishpans full of the juicy slices and spread them on the drying frames, pulling the mosquito netting well over to keep the flies at bay. Bees buzzed round me as I worked and settled in swarms on the growing heap of peelings and cores. Songs of happiness bubbled up and over:

> *Come, Thou fount of every blessing,*
> *Tune my heart to sing Thy grace*
> *Streams of mercy, never ceasing,*
> *Call for songs of loudest praise*

    "Remember, I love you more and more as the days go by," Alex had told me before he left the house that morning, and new life and new joy went with me all through the day. Now that we had reached this wonderful place, I was hard put to recall any of the old causes for doubt and resentment.

    More and more, I was molding my thoughts to rhyme, always hiding the verses away when they were finished. There was the one I'd written when I felt I'd failed to make a go of this marriage:

> *Have I been weighed, dear, in the scales,*
> *When I no thought was taking?*

And the one about the lover I could not find, though my husband held me in his arms. There was a poem taking shape in my mind now. I went in for pencil and paper, and as I worked and my thoughts shaped themselves into rhythm, I would add a line or two under the heading I'd written down. When I finished this was what I'd written:

<u>The Husband's Lament</u>	<u>The Wife's Reply</u>
Wherein have I failed?	*The tantalizing, gay*
Has my touch been too rough?	*Little thing that is me*
Do you think what I hold	*Must ever be wooed,*
In my arms is enough?	*Your neglect set her free.*
Where's the you that I held	*I am glad that you found her*
On our sweet wedding night	*The times you came wooing.*
Who smiled as she kissed me	*I'm sorry you lost her,*
With such shy delight?	*But that was your doing.*
Why yield me this flesh	*You may hold in your arms*
And withhold from my view	*This soft flesh till it perish*
The tantalizing, gay	*And never possess*
Little thing that is you?	*What you promised to cherish.*

At last it was finished, Alex's very thoughts and mine, and I tucked it away with the stack that kept growing.

Then I thought of Ann. She'd been on my mind for days. Her brother Jack, at the battlefront, had been killed in action. I'd had only a brief word with her on the phone, saying the little that I could by way of comfort when I heard about it. I called to see what she was doing. "I'm here right by my lone self. Onnie had to go to town this morning and he took Lester to visit Ma."

"I'm alone too, except for the children. Come spend the day with me and maybe it will help a little."

"I'll just do it, though I'll be a while getting there. It's over a mile to walk, you know."

It was good to have Ann with me again, but there was a new sadness about her.

"Earl's been shipped over too, Ann," I said.

"Well, let's hope you don't get the same news about your brother that I got about mine before this thing is over," she said, and then added fiercely, "I'm never going to let Lester join the navy when he grows up!"

I lit the gas stove for a quick lunch. "That hissing would drive me out of my mind," said Ann. "We've about decided on an electric plant, but we want to build us a good house first. The houses on all the rent farms, and that's what our house is, ain't much shakes. At least you and Alex had a substantial house to start with, even if it was run-down."

"Yes, but we couldn't have done what we have if Alex hadn't made up his mind to teach. It's something we can depend on, no matter if it isn't much."

"Well, of course Onnie ain't qualified to teach, but he couldn't bring himself to be cooped in four walls if he was. He said the other day he wouldn't do all that worrying with somebody else's brats for a thousand dollars a year, laid right in his hand."

"Everybody to his notion, like the gal when she kissed the cow," I said, placing slices of ham in the skillet. "For my own part I think it has been good for Alex. It has given him more time to think and plan, and I think he's housebroke at last, or at least resigned. He never lets out a peep about the confinement.

The phone rang and when I answered it, Alex's voice said, "Take it easy, O Lady, Phil's been shipped. He had only three days with Lola."

"How'd she take it, Alex?"

"She's right on the job, but she looks like a little ghost."

"Alex, this is awful."

"Well, while you're thinking about it just remember that Onnie and me will be caught in the next draft. Be making up your mind to that."

"Phil's been shipped," I said to Ann, and rebellion rose in me. "All over the land it's like that. One person turning to another and saying *Bob's been shipped, Dave's been shipped, John's been shipped, Carl's been shipped....*"

"And each one knowing the next news may be, *Missing in Action*, or *Killed in the Line of Duty*. I tell you, Flossie, sometimes I can't see beyond this war."

The long afternoon dragged to a close. My apples were finished and the mess cleaned up. The children were asleep, and Ann and I sat quietly rocking on the front porch when the boys got in. Onnie and Lester were in the buggy behind Alex in the wagon.

"Hold open the back door," Alex called out. "We're bringing you a surprise, Flossie."

Onnie helped Alex to roll a barrel into the kitchen. Then Alex went back to the wagon for a large heavy package. I stood wondering, still holding the screen open. Once inside Alex got the hatchet and he and Onnie started opening the barrel. Ann and I dived into the excelsior and came up with dishes.

"Oh Alex, I'd forgotten all about dishes." I laughed.

"Then you'd better start thinking about them fast. Where are you going to put that many? There's a hundred pieces there." He ripped the paper from a red felt lined walnut chest and displayed an array of silverware. "Service for eight, so let's hear no more about dishes and silver for a long time to come."

"But you said I couldn't . . . ."

"Never mind what I said." He grinned. "A wise man changes his mind . . . a fool never does."

After Ann and Onnie had gone home, I followed him to the porch when he went to wash for supper and kissed him! "Go along with you, I'm not fooled a bit. You're kissing your dishes and silver, you're not kissing me."

"So now we're even, then. The day you came in and found me in paint and powder and my new dress and kissed me like you hadn't for months, I told myself you were kissing the pretties you saw, not me."

"I was kissing you because you thought enough of yourself, and of me, to get your poor self together again," he said.

"Well, then, I'm kissing you now because you love me enough to get the dishes and silver for me, though you do hate to part with the money for such, as bad as Pa ever did! I tell you . . . ."

"You don't need to tell me anything, O Lady. I feel like I know you like a book now, without having to be told."

November 9, 1918

Johnny and Willie gave a party. What fun, all meeting together again just for a social evening. The men filled the great fireplace with oak logs and sat back until the flames died down, then they manned the corn poppers till great pans of the fluffy white grains were heaped up. In the kitchen the women made molasses candy to pour over the corn and molded it into balls of sticky goodness. Then they made more candy for the joy of pulling the platters of brown syrup, until it had cooled sufficiently, and it was a bright gold and ready to be whacked into the right lengths for eating. Everybody rejoiced over the bountiful harvest and the good prices. The men mentioned those who had been drafted for the service and those who had a chance of deferment.

"This is one time I'm glad I'm a family man, a school teacher, and a farmer," said Alex. "Never had anything to give me the go-rounds like the thought of being snatched up and sent across and ordered to shoot somebody. I believe if I came face-to-face with the enemy in the line of battle, I'd just stand there and let him do the bloody deed. I don't believe I could kill a man if I had to."

"I believe I could, if ever it reached that point," said Johnny thoughtfully, "which I hope it never does. God ferbid."

The women talked about food and fuel for the long winter months, and the possibility of certain foods being rationed, so that those in the front lines might have what they needed, and other unfortunates in the war torn countries wouldn't starve to death. And, as is usually inevitable when a bunch of women get together, the talk turned at last to the precarious business of childbearing.

Bula had big news for us: "Shirley Morley is going to have a baby at last. They've been married seven years and nothing to show fer it. Comes this war and they belatedly get one started, but not in time but what Aaron got caught in the draft. Now she's left to bear on through it alone. Can't teach, can't live right by herself, so it's back to her Ma's fer her and she's the scaredest little thing I've seen in my life."

"Well, seeing that I've already got two, I guess nobody can say I started this one in the hopes of savin' Lucius from the war."

Everybody turned in astonishment. "Alma, you don't say," I said.

"I do say."

"You mean you're . . . ?"

"I mean, I'm going to have a baby, Flossie."

"Oh I never would have planned one at a time like this," said Selma.

Alma smiled a bit sadly. "I wouldn't have planned one either, jist at this time in my life, Selma, but you know the old saying: Accidents do happen, even in the best of families."

Chapter 28

November 11, 1918

The day dawned clear and crisp, and we had no way of knowing that this day would be different to the days that had gone before and would come after. Arlien and Selma had materials assembled at last for the building of their new house, and Alex had gone to help with the laying of the foundation. I rendered lard and pickled pigs feet, for we had butchered the day before. Then I realized that I'd been hearing something unusual for several minutes.

I went to the back door and listened. Every factory and mill whistle and church bell in Paragould was ringing, and the siren screeching on the fire engine and the bell clanging. The din was borne to me on the wind as I stood on tiptoe trying to see the smoke. Then I heard Alex "yoo-hoooooing!" and looked up to see him stumbling toward me across the field that lay between our house and Arlien's.

"Meet me at the fence!" he yelled, making a megaphone of his hands. I closed the door behind me and ran through the lot to the board fence and climbed up to wait for him. He paused, gasping for breath, and yelled, "Go get me my new Panama hat!"

I stood, trying to think what he could mean. He had so longed for a good Panama hat, but they were so expensive. At last he'd gotten a really good one at an end-of-the-summer sale but had worn it only a few times till cool weather came. Now it hung upstairs in the storeroom.

"What for?" I called back.

"Because. I want to fill it full. You hear the bells and whistles? An armistice has been declared."

He was panting for breath as he climbed up the other side of the board fence and shook me by the shoulders. "Try to realize it, O Lady, the war is over! Onnie and me and Arlien and Johnny and Jim don't have to go!"

I threw both arms around him and kissed him half a dozen times, sobbing, "Oh thank God, Alex. Nothing lasts forever!" And we started laughing even while tears ran.

Alex told me later, "When we got back to Arlien's we were much too excited to work. Arlien walked with me back to the edge of the field, and he said the occasion demanded a celebration of some kind. But what could we do that would be like nothing we had ever done before? Then a drove of Old Man Skaggs geese came waddling by, mud-fat from a season's feeding in Arlien's late pea patch. We looked at each other, then as one, turned and whopped ourselves flat on an unsuspecting goose, pinning her to the ground. In a trice her head was off, and we were on our way with it to the house to get Selma to help us get it ready for the pot."

"So I came back for you and the children."

What a feast we had, and such happy chatter, and then we faced the fact that we had eaten a stolen goose! We decided that no one would be the wiser if we didn't tell it and went on our way rejoicing.

November 17, 1918

We went to church Sunday, wanting to offer thanks formally at God's house that the shedding of blood had been stopped. Arlien and Selma drove up about the time we did, and Selma and I took the children and went on in alone. Onnie and Johnny and Jim were standing together and called Arlien and Alex to them.

We learned later that somehow the dreadful secret had leaked out. They told Alex and Arlien that Old Man Skaggs—he was a stern-faced deacon and always sat in the Amen Corner—had learned of the theft of one of his fine geese.

"We thought he was too mad to talk to you all about it and there might be trouble, so we told him we'd see you. That we felt sure you'd want to pay for the goose. He said it would just cost you two bucks apiece, that you grabbed one of the finest of the flock."

And so Arlien and Alex forked over two dollars each, and they all went into church. When the plate was passed for the morning offering, Johnny, who was to have given the money to Mr. Skaggs, looked significantly at Arlien and Alex, and in addition to his own usual offering of a one-dollar bill, he waved four other ones at them and laid them ostentatiously in the collection plate. Not until then did Alex and Arlien know that the stolen goose was still a family secret and that the price of it would never reach Mr. Skaggs but would go instead toward helping to defray incidental church expenses.

And this was all to the good. How long since the boys had had such smiling faces? How long since they had played a practical joke on each other?

I looked over the crowd as the sermon got under way. Nobody had a drawn and anxious face, and my spirit was exalted. And suddenly I knew why I had not wanted to go to revival meeting. I could not bear to hear Christian people hymning God's praise in one breath, and in the next asking God to be on our side, to give us the means and the strength to conquer our enemies and return victorious, when the churches of our enemies were filled with still other Christians asking the same favors for their side.

My concept of God and His relationship to his own somehow excluded all thought of war and precluded the possibility of asking Him to take sides with us in our seasons of wholesale carnage. If Man must have War, then let him recognize it as man-conceived and man-nurtured and fight it out on that level without dragging God into it, or trying to. If God is the very spirit and essence of love, and if God's will is that we love each other, then what has God to do with war?

But Brother Sherrill saw it differently. God had answered our prayers and had given us a glorious victory. At least we hoped that the armistice would result in a complete cessation of hostilities, and we as a people were now free from the terrible fear of losing still more of our precious boys and young men.

But all I could see was that Man was stupid beyond all power to believe and that he had the makings of heaven at his fingertips, yet he managed to make for himself a hell, wherein, if one listened, there might always be heard weeping and wailing and the gnashing of teeth.

I wept as the rest wept that day, but my tears were shed because we could not learn the ways of peace, could not pattern our lives after the Christ we professed to love and to follow.

We hymned God's praise, but we did the devil's work.

November 19, 1918

I rode in to town with Jim so I could meet Lola. She wanted to buy something new to wear when Phil got home. When we went shopping, I bought a beautiful black suit and hat. When I got home and I tried it on for Alex, he didn't like the dress or the small black hat.

His face clouded over. "I'm goose pimples all over," he declared. "I feel like I'm sitting here looking at my own widow. Anyways take that black veil off that hat. If it just had an edging of crepe, now, that would be it, and don't ever let me see you wear it again."

He shivered visibly and got up and stalked out of the room.

My joy in the elegant suit and hat was gone. I folded them back in their tissue wrappings and set the boxes on the top shelf of the hall closet.

November 28, 1918

The boys had been hunting, and all had gathered in our big kitchen for a hot tamale feast. The big iron kettle was swung out on its crane in the fireplace, and into it went the game that had been killed, along with a hen and a pork loin.

The men all went to their different homes to do up the evening chores. I settled the children to play in the kitchen and took the women to the bedroom with me.

"How good it seems to get together for hot tamales. I do believe it's the first time we've made them since before Pa's house burned, Ann."

I settled my sewing basket on my lap and picked up my crochet. Selma snatched it out of my lap and set it on the wardrobe.

"Not this time you don't. She tells us all before we leave the kitchen to come sit down for an old-fashioned gabfest, then grabs that eternal lace and starts knitting!"

"I think Flossie's got what Ma calls the habit of industry"—Ann laughed—"and can't content herself unless she's busy with something."

"Well, I know how she feels," said Selma. "I was hooking a rug and could have got a right smart done on it while we sit and wait for that meat to cook and the boys to bring in the shucks."

But we didn't get much visiting done except by snatches. The children became so rowdy that we had to go to the kitchen and make syrup candy and popcorn to keep them happily occupied for the next hour or two.

"Oh, nobody ever told me what time the doctor finally got there and how Belle and the baby are doing," I said.

"The baby was a girl and she named her Lorene. Doc got there in plenty of time," said Ann, "but he looked like a booger. Said he hadn't shaved nor slept for three days and nights. It's that Spanish flu you keep hearing about. He says it's sweeping the country like wildfire, several cases above and below us, so I guess this will be our last get-together for a spell. He says we'd better den up and stay close, for it seems to be in the air, and not to go no place where there's a crowd if we can help it."

"So there it is," said Selma. "We no more'n slay one dragon till another raises its ugly head. I reckon the ones that didn't get killed in the war will die in this epidemic. Nine hundred of our boys was piled out like cordwood for mass burial before they could be shipped back home. That's what I heard."

"The last time we was in Paragould," said Ann, "Onnie cut his business short. Said all he could hear was another sad tale about the sick and the dying, and looks like it's taking people like Horace Whitsitt, that ain't ever been sick a day in their lives. Once it hits 'em, they're gone."

I'd heard some of those wild stories the day I went to town, but I was so engrossed with my shopping. I had heard no names mentioned of people I knew and none of our family or neighbors were ill. So I had pushed it to the back of my mind. "Mama had it, in Little Rock. She said it was awfully bad, and she's still real weak. Did Belle have a bad time?" I asked, still trying to change the subject. I didn't want to think about the epidemic.

Ann looked thoughtful. "Well, it's never easy but it wasn't so bad. She'll be up and around no time, and she's rejoicing over that."

"I've always said I could eat fifteen hot tamales at a sitting," declared Onnie, as we set two big platters of the delicious morsels on the table, and he leaned over to inhale the mouthwatering steam rising from them. "But I've never made it. However, the old saying is that if at first you don't succeed, try, try again . . . so here I go, boys!"

"Well, dive in, dirty face. I'll guarantee to eat one every time you do!" said Johnny. They ran their race, and neither won it.

"What do you honestly think about the flu epidemic, Alex?" I asked as we got off to bed.

"I think it's too bad to talk about. They say the taste and the smell of that sickness is enough to gag a mule. I feel like if I get it, it will be the end of me. I want to lay in some supplies and dig in for the winter. If it keeps getting worse, I won't open the school out here this year. They've closed the picture shows in town, and they're talking of closing the schools and churches."

December 14, 1918

Alex dressed in his best for a trip to town. I suggested that he let Jim get the things he wanted, pay him for his trouble, and stay at home. "Jim couldn't get me examined and take out some life insurance for me and that's what I'm going in for," he said. "I'm just wearing the new suit for the same reason a little boy whistles in the dark. It might be the only time I'll ever get to wear it."

This wasn't like Alex. "You're the healthiest person I ever knew in my life, Alex. Don't even think about not living to enjoy your pretty suit. You've never been sick but the one day after you ate all that pie since I've known you."

"Horace Whitsitt wasn't a sickly man either, nor Red Arnold, nor Dick Nelson. Look at the ones it's taking already? And the little weak scrawny ones, always ailing, seem to get over it and go on about as usual."

He was more serious than I'd ever seen him when he came in that evening, but he didn't tell me until we were settled in bed what was on his mind. "I went by Lola's office before I started back home. She was so happy. She had just got a letter from Phil and he was expecting to sail home on the next ship. While we were sitting there talking, a telegram came. He'd died and was buried at sea, along with a number of his shipmates. It was the Spanish flu. The epidemic seems to be everywhere. I told Lola I would bring you to her, but she begged me to get home and stay there, and to keep you here."

When I could speak again, I asked him what Lola would do.

"She said she would work right on. That there are now other things about as grim as death to be battled with in Paragould, with so many families left hungry and cold, young widows with young babies tugging at their empty breasts coming in there, and old folks whose only dependence was that boy that will never come home again."

"She called it the aftermath of war and she's trying to help them get identities established and compensation started. Oh, I forgot to tell you. She says that Jack left Ann ten thousand dollars insurance. That she's started unwinding the red tape and it will come through in time. She said it's about fifty-two dollars a month for twenty years. Since Jack is gone, it's good that he left that for Ann."

December 28, 1918

Christmas meant nothing. The pretty new clothes meant nothing. Dread had been our constant companion, it seemed forever, when we were expecting Alex to be called any day. Now fear was always with us. The Death we were then trying to shun walked far battlefields across an ocean we'd never seen. Now Death stalked the town and the countryside, breathing down our necks, and never a day passed that another and another weren't stricken down, so many of them never to rise again in the flesh. People sick all around us, and Lola and Ann in our own families bowed low in their grief. None right in our community, as yet, were ill, but well we knew that picture could change any minute.

To make things worse, my periodic headache laid me out on Christmas Eve. No tablets. I called Dr. Benson, and he told me, "If a headache is all you have, you're lucky. Grin and bear it. I'm not going to anyone these days unless they're having the flu or a baby," and the harried man hung up in my ear.

January 20, 1919

By order of the courts, schools didn't open in January. Churches and schools and theatres closed all over the land, and business was practically at a standstill. Nurses could not be had for any money. Nobody was fool enough to stick their heads into that plague.

Then the awful thing struck home. Lucius and Alma were the first to go down, and we knew that each family and community must care for its own. Alma stayed on her feet three days after Lucius was stricken. With a sick husband, she didn't give up until she woke the fifth morning and couldn't raise her head from her pillow.

Just after we heard that Alma was down, Arlien rode over on his fine mare and tied her to the hitching post. What we had been dreading had arrived. There were no smiles with our greetings—in fact, no greetings.

"We might as well face up to it, Alex. We've got to take turns stayin' up with the sick. The women can manage in the daytime, but the men need to take the night shifts. Besides keepin' fires night and day, the ones that are able need to go out and haul wood for the ones that fall sick. No man's supply of wood can outlast a siege like this, fires all over the house, day and night."

He hadn't bothered to wipe the mud from his shoes and sat with his feet dejectedly sprawled before him.

"Of course, it can hit any of us . . . anytime."

"How will we team up?" asked Alex, the light of dread in his face. "Maybe I sound like a danged coward, but I'd like to do my stint cuttin' and haulin' wood, or goin' for medicine when the doctor can't get around, tendin' the stock, even milkin'. There's enough chores that's got to be done, and I'll do 'em in order to leave them that knows somethin' about how to wait on the sick to do for the sick. Never even stayed around when Flossie was sick. I can't stand it to be around sick people, never could."

"Somebody's goin' to have to be around for you, young feller, when your turn comes. So you can just learn how to do somethin' to ease the other feller's sufferin' as you go along. You're no better than the rest. You go with me tonight. Onnie went with Jim last night, and Johnny can go with Skid tomorrow night. That way, until somebody else gets sick, each pair will have only every third night in the sick room."

"I'll go," I said.

"You'll do nothin' of the kind." Alex glared at me. "You've got these two babies and you're goin' to stay right here and take care of 'em. I'll go, Arlien."

By the time night began to close in, he had made up his mind to it.

"The flu is here with us now, and there's no place to run and hide. In case you think that the reason I didn't want to help sit with the sick, is that my rest would be broken, I'll tell you the truth of the matter. I'm afraid. I feel like if I get the flu, and how can I help but get it if I go and sit with it . . . that I'm a dead duck."

"That kind of fear is as bad as the disease, Alex. It's almost like you're licked before you start."

He stared at me for a long moment, then turned and left the house without another word.

January 21, 1919

The next morning, Alex looked like he'd been sick a week. At last, I prevailed on him to eat a bowl of hot cereal and drink his coffee. I urged him to go on to bed, said I would do up the chores when things warmed up a bit, but he sat staring before him, seeing I knew not what.

"Beats any sickness you ever heard of," he finally said. "Of all things, it fell to my lot to wait on Alma! I thought you'd just have to sit with the flu, but in God's name you've got to work with it, almost every minute. First the slop jar, then the basin to vomit in, and Alma so slaverin' limber sick that I had to hold her to puke or she'd a slid off the bed and onto the cold floor. Then I had to wrap her in a blanket and hold her on the slop jar ever so often, and between times the vessels had to be emptied and scalded, with her maybe callin' for both of them before I could get back with 'em.

Arlien with Lucius, me with Alma, and it went on like that all night long. I never thought I could stand it through till mornin'."

He laid his head on his arm on the table for several moments, and I could think of nothing to say that might help. Presently he sighed and got up. "I'll go on to bed and leave it with you. Be two nights before I'll have to go again."

He slept until well into the afternoon. Then he piled the long back porch full of wood, fed and watered the stock, even gathered the eggs and milked for me.

January 22, 1919

The next morning he was up on time. I knew by the clothes he was putting on that he was going somewhere, and when I asked, he said that he wanted to get started with some sheep. "The last time I was in town I ran across Old Man Norton, and he said he's gettin' too old to look after his. That he has a nice small flock and will make me a good price on 'em. I thought it might help if I go about my business as usual, as far as I can."

"I wish you wouldn't go, Alex. Even with your warm clothes on you could get chilled through, riding on horseback. Why expose yourself needlessly?"

"Well, I just can't stand it, sittin' here day in and day out waitin' for the flu to get me!" His face had such a desperate look that I let him go without another word.

Once he was out of the house, I felt the same restlessness that had overtaken him. When the sun warmed up, I bundled the children and put them outside to play and turned the house inside out. Sunning and airing and making everything sweet and fresh.

I had given the little ones half a dozen feathers each to toss on the wind, one at a time. The first reason I'd had to smile for days came when I heard their rollicking laughter and went to the dining room window to watch them chasing the feathers, which swirled and dipped and rose on the cross currents of the wind.

Something about the helpless way the feathers were buffeted hither and yon set me to thinking of the first years Alex and I were married. Without a home of our own, we were picked up and set down in first one place, then another, with no power to decide for ourselves . . . at the mercy of circumstance.

Young marrieds without a home of their own were just like feathers in a high wind. I laid my hand lovingly on my own windowsill. God bless this home. It was truly a haven in a time of storm.

I had told Alex how thankful I was that nothing lasts forever the day the glad tidings of the armistice went out, but that was after the danger had passed. Nothing lasts forever worked the same if you were speaking of love, contentment, and security, no matter how hard-won.

Ah, how short-lived ours had been and how long striven for. Well, the flu epidemic couldn't last forever either, and there was comfort in realizing that, but would we be together to thank God that it was so after all the dead were buried?

By two o'clock I had finished mopping and dusting and started bringing the bedding back in and making beds for the night. I didn't know Alex was back until I heard the children screeching a welcome and went to meet him. The children, thinking he'd been to town, clamored for candy. He'd stopped at a country store and bought a box of Cracker Jacks for each, and they went dancing ahead of us in high glee. I pretended to cry, trying to make a bit of fun where there was none, saying, "You brought them something and you didn't bring me anything, boo-hooooo!"

To my surprise, he took a box from the other pocket.

"You too itty-bitty to open it by yourself? Papa will have to find the prize for you."

He ran his fingers down through the sugarcoated popcorn and brought up a small bright tin beetle and began popping it for me as we walked slowly to the house. I laughed and held up my face for a kiss, but Alex turned his face away.

"No more kisses for a while, O Lady. Just get me to bed and get the basin and the slop jar ready and plenty of water hot. I had a hard chill at Norton's and called Dr. Benson from there. He'll get around to me as soon as he can."

He spoke quietly and took my arm and steered me gently toward the doorsteps. "Didn't the sun shine pretty today?"

He was just making conversation now.

"I thought I never saw it so bright."

January 26, 1919

I battled with the plague for two days alone, trying to keep the children away from Alex. Sherman came and milked twice daily, taking half the milk for his trouble, since Jim was no longer making his run. Onnie came to look after the stock night and morning. I fixed washtubs in the kitchen and between times washed every dirty garment on the place, down to the last rag, for rags we had to have through this mess.

When I felt my chill coming on the third day, I called Mama, and she was there the next day. Onnie picked her up from the train depot and brought her out.

Buddy was the next to get sick, and Onnie and Ann wrapped him in a blanket and took him home with them to nurse. The extra bed was brought down from upstairs and put in a corner of the room for me. When Cerece got sick, she was put in the bed with me, and Mama was running in circles. Onnie left Ann to nurse Buddy. He had taken Lester in to Ma, and he remained at our home to fetch and carry.

From Alex, to Cerece, to me, Mama went, day and night. She seldom lay down more than an hour or two on the couch. I was barely conscious as the doctor came and went.

Onnie burst through the front door and said, loud enough for Alex to hear, "Jim's hogs are in Alex's alfalfa! I'll have to get somebody to help me get them out!"

But Alex was out of bed like a flash. He staggered across the room like a drunken man, flung the north window high, and yelled across the road, "Jim! Come get your danged hogs out of my alfalfa!" and collapsed. While he had stood there yelling, the north wind sent his pajama shirt billowing out behind him, and him just sweating his fever off.

"Alex, have you lost your mind?" I gasped, trying to raise myself and falling back on the pillow.

"Gosh, I wasn't even awake when I got out of bed," he chattered.

Mama ran in and got him back into bed, where he immediately went into a hard chill. The sound of hogs squealing and woofing came to me as through a fog, then died out. Then Onnie came in to tell Alex that the hogs had been penned and for him to forget it.

But none of us would ever forget that.

January 27, 1919

Alex's temperature soared, and by the time Dr. Benson could get to him the next day, he was gasping for breath. Mama called Dr. Sewell to come out from town. He had been with me when both babies were born and with Mama when Lola and Jan came. She pleaded with him to come at once. He said he was between calls. The road was passable, so he asked for Dr. Benson to wait for him and he'd be there in a few minutes.

The consultation was held in the hall, but the examination went on right before my eyes, even to pushing that cruel needle between Alex's ribs on each side and drawing off the fluid from both lungs. I was not surprised when Mama whispered to me later that Alex, besides the flu, had developed pneumonia, in both lungs.

When Dr. Sewell started to leave, he came to my bed, took my hand, and said, "I'm going now, Flossie. I have left medicine. If Alex is not better by Wednesday, call me. There's no need to call me before then."

I was trying to read the truth in his eyes, afraid of what I saw there. "You mean there is nothing more you can do for Alex . . . until Wednesday?"

He nodded. "And there are so many that I can help, Flossie . . . I must give my services where there is still hope of recovery."

Was he telling me that Alex would not get well?

"Keep just as quiet as possible, Flossie, for the sake of your children."

He turned and spoke to Mama and was gone.

January 28, 1919

The change came Tuesday evening when Alex started calling for me and for Buddy. The doctor had ordered that no fire be kept in the room and a window be left up. Cerece had been moved to a cot in the dining room. Shortly after dark, Alex began calling for me.

"But, Alexander, she can't come to you, her temperature is 103," said Mama.

"I want . . . her . . . to . . . sit . . . by me!" he gasped. "I couldn't stand not to go to him. One of the big reed rockers was brought to Alex's bedside and Mama and Onnie got me into Alex's woolen socks and fleece-lined house shoes, my corduroy robe and his flannel one, and over all that his heavy overcoat and Mama's thick pink fascinator. A big double wool blanket was spread in the chair and, after I was seated, hot bricks were wrapped and set on a piece of tin to keep my feet warm. Hot stove caps were wrapped and put at my back on each side, with a hot water bottle in my lap to keep my hands warm.

"This is awful," Mama murmured. "Her temperature's 103 right now."

But Alex was hungrily reaching for my right hand and snugged it close under the cover with him while Mama brought a big warm comforter and tucked it all around me. Alex seemed relieved.

Sherman was sent for Ma and Lester. Onnie went for Buddy when Alex would not be put off. It had been snowing all day, and though Onnie had run in with Buddy from the road, the thick blanket that covered the baby was heavily sprinkled with snow. He knelt at the bedside and turned the blanket back only enough for Alex to see the wan little face of his son. But Alex reached for Buddy's hand, and I thought I could not bear the sad yearning look in his eyes.

A single tear spilled out and ran off Alex's cheek and made a wet splash on the pillowcase . . . funny, how these little things stand out in the mind at such moments. I knew he was telling Buddy goodbye for the last time.

"He's . . . his . . . Mama's . . . funny . . . li'l . . . feller." As he whispered the words on a long sigh, he laid his beloved son's hand in mine. I knew in that moment, as Alex looked pleadingly into my eyes, that he was begging forgiveness for what had happened the night of my return and that he was now bequeathing to me, in love, the child that had been begotten in such doubt and uncertainty.

Suddenly, Alex was overcome by weariness and closed his eyes. Onnie took Buddy back to Ann. Nobody could stay in that cold room except when needed, and so I sat alone through the long night with Alex. Now and then someone came with a cup of hot broth or tea and to bring hot bricks and stove caps and take away the cool ones. Then I could hear others begin to come in, and I knew that the word had gone out that Alex's life hung in the balance.

Both doctors had been called, but neither of them had come. Call them again tomorrow, they said. I tried not to think, only to hold myself together and be in readiness for whatever developed.

Alex opened his eyes and tried to smile. "We sick . . . ain't we . . . O Lady?" he whispered hoarsely.

"I'm not as sick as you are," I said. "Don't try to talk, Sun, until you can breathe better."

"Your . . . Sun . . . is . . . about . . . to set. You . . . know . . . that . . . don't you?"

Even as he spoke, death pinched the nostrils white and drew the lush lower lip to a thin line.

"I . . . knew it . . . would be . . . like this," he gasped.

"Are you afraid?"

"Not afraid. No. Just . . . that I . . . dread it . . . so. I'd rather . . . march straight . . . to the front . . . line trenches."

Remembering how he had dreaded the possibility of that, I could not speak for a moment. Then I said, "I wish I could go in your place, Alex."

"You think . . . you could . . . stand it . . . better . . . than me?"

"Nobody could stand it better than you, Alex."

"No use . . . honey.

"Maybe...."

"This... is the... end... of me. Is it still... snowing?"

"Yes, somebody said it's already two feet deep."

A long quivering sigh escaped his lips, and a deathly pallor overspread his face. "If only I... could see... the sun... come up... once more," he gasped, then strangled.

When I thought he slept and would have withdrawn my hand to rub the cramp from my arm, he tightened his grip. "I didn't get... the insurance... in time... to do any... good," he whispered.

"Don't concern yourself with such things, Alex. That's not important now."

It must have been eight o'clock that night when Ma came into the room. She took one look at Alex and then turned to me. "I reckon you all just goin' to sit here and let him die?"

Alex appeared to be unconscious, but his hand twitched in mine.

She called his name softly, but he did not answer.

"Ridiculous, not having any far in this room. I don't care what the doctors said. Besides, I don't think all the fresh air in the world can help Alex now... It's the livin' we've got to think about." And she walked over and shut the window down tight.

"I'm going to have a far put in here," she whispered as she passed me on her way out.

Sherman came in and made a fire. As the room warmed up, others came and went.

January 29, 1919

At five thirty Alex said again, though the words came in gasps, that he wished he could live just long enough to see the sun come up once more. Johnny came in and said that the wind was breaking the clouds up and he thought it would be clear by morning. "Never saw the stars look so big and so close," he said.

I prayed that Alex would see the sun rise on a world lying wrapped in a new blanket of snow.

A little later Alex opened his eyes and stared anxiously about and said, "Is the . . . carbide out? There's . . . another . . . tank."

"No, Alex, there's plenty of gas," said Onnie.

"Then why . . . don't you . . . light some . . . burners? It's dark . . . as pitch."

"The lights are burning, Alex," said Onnie.

"Then why . . . can't . . . I see . . . the light?" he gasped in terror.

I made a motion, and the men in the room shoved the bed Alex was on until his face was directly under the chandelier, but he still could not see the light.

"The . . . light," he gasped. "Oh God, let me . . . see the . . . light!"

I could bear no more, throwing aside the covers that held me. I sprang from my chair and ran from the room, closing the door behind me. I ran down the hall and jerked the back door open and ran the full length of the back porch, stuffing a handkerchief against my lips to still the screams that threatened to break through my aching throat.

I felt the cold snow sifting into the shoes that were too big for me and forced myself to take three long deep breaths, praying, "God, help me now."

When I was able to return to Alex's bedside, I stood beside him, numb with grief and helplessness, until the sun burst in sudden brilliance and flooded the world with light. In that very moment, Alex breathed his last. My strength forsook me, and I fell across his lifeless body.

Again I saw Alex leave the schoolhouse at Big Lake, lock the door, and drop the key into his pocket. "Alex!" I screamed. Without a backward glance, he set briskly off toward home. "Alex!" I ran forward, knowing that my only hope of catching him was to cut across the cotton field. "Alex!" I climbed to the top of the fence, dropped my bundle over, and cupped my hands and cried, "Alex! Alex!" Again and again I shouted, but Alex did not pause or look back. I jumped down inside the fence, picked up my bundle, and started running, across the soggy rows. The cotton stalks, tough and wickedly strong, whipped at my legs unmercifully as I sped along. I stopped to call again, "Alex!" Only to see Alex entering the deep woods. I stumbled forward, trying to say his name, but only a small whimper could squeeze past the terrible lump in my throat. Without knowing quite how it happened, I found that my feet had become embedded in the sticky mud and that I stood now rooted in my tracks.

Because he had such perfect sense of direction, Alex could take the shortcut home. I must manage somehow to pull myself out of this bog and go the long way around by the road . . . alone.

Epilogue

Ma's voice was sharp. "Let her alone, Miz Mounce! If it's God's will that they go together, then let God's will be done."

But Mama was tugging frantically at me. "Get away! Get away, I tell you! I work night and day to try to save your child and then you say, let mine die!"

With superhuman strength, Mama lifted me and carried me to my own bed. Poor Mama! I must let her know in some way that I was not dying. But I was under some kind of strange spell. It was as though my spirit wandered far from my body with no interest in it. I was still alive, but I could not get back inside. I could not speak to Mama, though I could hear every word she said, and I could feel her tender hands as she slipped the heavy garments away from me and got me tucked in.

She gave swift orders for Dr. Sewell to be called. "For Flossie, tell him . . . not for Alex! He won't come if you tell him it's for Alex."

No. Promise that you won't call till Wednesday, he said. Today is Wednesday. He had known that Alex would not be alive on this day.

But there was something I had to do!

Oh yes, to let Mama know that I was not dying. I struggled valiantly to form one single word of reassurance, but no muscle moved in my face, and no sound came. Mama's tears were falling on my face, and I felt her sobs shaking the bed, though she wept silently.

I must do something!

Making one frantic, prodigious effort, I succeeded at last in opening my eyes, but they immediately rolled back and set in my head. This was terrible . . . I must look more like death was upon me now, for Mama's sobs were no longer silent.

In a perfect agony of inactivity, I lay as if under some evil spell, fully conscious the whole time, until Dr. Sewell arrived and administered a hypodermic. Mercifully, I felt the old familiar languor stealing through me as the drug took effect.

I heard, as in a dream, Mama's fervent little prayer of thanksgiving when the lids of my eyes settled over my staring eyes and relieved me, for the time being, of any feeling for necessity of action. I drifted out on a swift tide of forgetfulness.

LESTER A. WALKER
1889 — 1919

More than a week had gone by. Alex was in his last long rest at Brown's Chapel. Papa had arrived, and Lola and Jan. All personal belongings were packed, for Buddy and Cerece and I were going to live in Little Rock. I would have my wish to live in town fulfilled, but at what cost? Our home, into which had flowed so much of the very life of our bodies, was to be dismantled and the furnishings sold to the highest bidder! And that before we had completed many of our plans, already in the making, for desirable improvements!

Those thoughts had a numbing and paralyzing effect on me. That I should, in one day, be able to wipe out all that it had taken years to assemble and coordinate! It was like a mad fantastic dream.

Without pleasure, I fastened the silken frogs on the new black suit. I ripped the jaunty white cockade from the small black hat. As protection from the cool wind outside, I tied the long black chiffon scarf over my hat and under my chin. I left the crisp white jabot in its little box, and the white gloves, instead wearing a pair of older black gloves. I glanced at the mirror, and a sudden horror came over me.

Alex was standing by, scowling at me. *"Why did you have to get black?"* I saw the long black scarf falling from my hat. *"I feel like I'm looking at my own widow!"*

I sighed, remembering many things. How often in times past, Alex had gone places without me. He was always doing it. Well, one last time Alex had gone on without me. This time I had been ready to go, and there seemed to be no reason why I should not have gone . . . but I had not been allowed to pass. A power stronger than my own will . . . even stronger than Alex's . . . had blocked the passage. I could not break through.

"We'll ride in the day coach," I told Papa, firmly. "We might as well keep counting pennies. I'm used to it."

I was glad that the ordeal of telling the others goodbye was over, that at last I was out of those haunted rooms at Shadowlawn.

Papa ordered pillows, and when at last the porter brought them, he adjusted my chair so that I could get some rest. Buddy was excited and refused to settle. Two traveling men were in the seat behind me. I heard Mama explain to them, with Cerece sitting quietly at her side, that the boy's father had just died. They jumped to their feet and took Buddy to the smoking car with them. The lights were turned down low in the car, and the voices of the people around me sank to low murmurs.

My thoughts turned as the wheels turned, clicked as the rails clicked, clanged as the bell clanged, shrieked with the screaming whistle. The whistle sounded a warning at the crossing.

I was now at the crossing. I thought of the day I had watched Cerece and Buddy as they chased feathers about on a windy afternoon. How it had reminded me of our lives being tossed about like feathers on a high wind.

Well, tomorrow I would be in Little Rock . . . but Alex would not be there . . . nor would he come for me . . . nor would I return to him . . . ever again.

Oh, Alex! I smothered a sob and buried my face hard into my pillow.

THE END

Made in the USA
Lexington, KY
24 March 2017